THE NEW INDIANS

THE NEW INDIANS

Stan Steiner

A DELTA BOOK

CONTENTS

ILLUSTRATIONS

The following are grouped after page 78:

Log and mud hut on the Assiniboin Reservation, Fort Peck, Montana
Sanitation facilities on the Bad River Reservation of the Wisconsin
    Chippewas
Three women oracles
Courtyard of Governor Abeita's house, Pueblo of Isleta, New Mexico
A child of Ponemah
A combination cafe, gas station, trading post and used furniture store
    on Maricopa tribal reservation in Arizona

The following are grouped after page 206:

A tourist "trading post"
A bookmobile on its regular stop
Abandoned church, Chippewa Reservation, Bad River, Wisconsin
A jail at Mission, South Dakota
A new-style community center in Gallup, New Mexico
John F. Kennedy Center, Sioux tribal headquarters in Devils Lake,
    North Dakota
Navajo tribal council building, Window Rock, Arizona
Suburban housing on the Turtle Mountain Reservation, North Dakota
New-style hogans
"Women Strike for Peace"
The New Indians
Canadian and United States Indian youth join hands
The Makah Indians hold a tribal dance in honor of the Fish-Ins

FOREWORD

Into the banquet hall opulent with the dignitaries of wealth and the indignities of power there strode a young Indian. He was a Sioux. He had been invited to feast his naïveté on how the political leaders of the civil-rights movement raise funds. And he was told to "go back to your people" and do likewise.

He listened politely to the resplendent oratory. To the Governor. To the Senators. To whosoever else was on the dais. And then he uttered not a war whoop but a yawn.

The last suppliance of the banquet was done and the last brandy drunk when the young Indian was introduced to the guest of honor, a distinguished Negro leader. They shook hands. Someone quipped that the young Indian was an advocate of Red Power. The phrase brought forth an uplifted eyebrow and a smile.

"Oh, no!" the guest of honor laughed. "We don't want Red Power. Besides, isn't that presumptuous of you Indians? What can you few do?"

"Red Power will win," the young Sioux replied. "We are no longer fighting for physical survival. We are fighting for ideological survival. Our ideas will overcome your ideas. We are going to cut the country's whole value system to shreds.

"It isn't important that there are only 500,000 of us Indians," he
went on. "What is important is that we have a superior way of life.
We Indians have a more human philosophy of life. We Indians will
show this country how to act human. Someday this country will revise
its constitution, its laws, in terms of human beings, instead of property. If Red Power is to be a power in this country it is because it is
ideological."

The gray-haired Negro leader was taken aback. His smile flickered
uncertainly. "You don't understand," he objected. "The Indians ought
to fight for equality, for their civil rights."

"We do," said the Sioux. "But that isn't the question. The question
is, What is the nature of life? It isn't what you eat, or whether you
eat, or who you vote for, or whether you vote, or not. What is the
ultimate value of a man's life? That is the question."

This was the voice of the new Indians.

If those who heard the unexpected after-dinner speech of the young
Sioux—Vine Deloria, Jr.—at the banquet did not quite believe their
ears they may be forgiven. His generation's voice is not often heard
in the councils of power. His advocacy of Red Power and tribal
nationalism was incomprehensible to those who were listening to him.

Yet, in the distant hills of the Indian reservations, there has arisen
a new generation of university-educated Indians. These young men
and women have given voice to a human morality and tribal philosophy of life that weds the ancient with the modern. And they cannot
be understood by harking to the echoes of old prejudices, false
images, and the ugh-ughing of Hollywood Indians who no longer
exist, if indeed, they ever did. The emergence of the new Indians demands that the country listen with new ears.

It had been thought by many that the Indian was the vanishing
American. He was thought to be culturally extinct. He was thought
to have unhappily vanished from the face of the land.

One hundred years ago a cadet at West Point—George Armstrong
Custer—wrote in a term paper for his ethics class: "The red man is
alone in his misery. We behold him now on the verge of extinction,
standing on his last foothold . . . and soon he will be talked of as a
noble race who once existed but have passed away."

Since those halcyon days of conquest the Indian has been hopefully, by eulogies of logical doomsdays, dispatched to his cultural obliteration by his would-be conquerors. His land was taken from him and his people were all but destroyed by ingenious genocides. He should have died. For the nation's peace of mind it was best that the ghost of the Indian be extinguished from the public consciousness. And this was done, until, in modern times, the reality of Indian life was cast beyond the pale of knowledgeable truth into romantic myth.

So sympathetic a friend of the Indian as the anthropologist Franz Boas observed, in 1911, that the proportion of people with Indian blood "is so insignificant that it may well be disregarded," for the Indian population had "vanished comparatively rapidly."

His dirgeful view was re-echoed by the chronicler of the West and Indian life Frank Linderman. In *The Passing American,* written in 1932, Linderman lamented that even the Indian had forgotten his Indianness: "The young Indians know next to nothing about their people . . . and now it is too late to learn."

And *his* dirgeful view was re-echoed more recently by the sociological journalist John Keats, who, in 1964, wrote in *Venture:* "But, who speaks for the Indian? Amazingly his cause is almost without rebels to support it."

These sorrowers assumed the inevitable defeat of the Indian, and the triumph of the white man. It was told in the last lines of Paul Radin's *The Story of the American Indian:* "The white man had triumphed . . . the Indians were crushed. Broken, disorganized, externally and internally they gave up the fight."

But near the end of World War II Radin began to wonder whether the triumph of the white man had been as complete and lasting as he had thought. Radin asked himself, "Can There Be an Indian Renaissance?" And under that questioning title, in 1944, he wrote a new last chapter to his book:

The last twenty years that have seen the break-up of European civilization, ushered in so hopefully and optimistically in the sixteenth century, have also witnessed the dawn of a new era. Cultural values that have been dominant for the last hundred years will have to be partly discarded. People and races whose course appeared to be run, and lost, only a generation ago hope to play a new role. . . . What role can we assume the future has in store for the American Indian? . . .

An Indian Renaissance is quite within the realm of the possible and attainable [Radin concluded], if it is not left in the hands of well-meaning whites and romantic and unrealistic government bureaus.

The old Indian had been defeated, but not vanquished. His way of thought had been submerged, not destroyed. In the aftermath of World War II, when the society of his conquerors had been so badly shaken up and disorganized, the old ways began to surface in modern forms.

A new harmony emerged out of the old.

When word that I was writing this book was whispered through the tall grass of the Sioux country of the Dakotas there were both laughter and anger. It was said that the wandering white man, known to some as the White Navajo, was writing a strange book. It was said that he was writing a book about the new Indians. Who were they?

One group of old Sioux men gathered to chew over what was meant by the "new Indians." "Hell with the new Indians!" spat an elder of the tribe. "There are no new Indians. There are only old Indians. Or dead ones."

The friend who told me of the impromptu seminar on the prairie told how a younger man argued that even Indians do change.

"It is so." The elder nodded in mock resignation. "There may be old Indians in a new way. And new Indians in an old way. But an Indian is always an Indian. Until he dies."

Laughter most likely echoed in the room. I was not there to hear it, but I can imagine it. To the Indian what this book reveals is not new. His reticence and self-effacing quiet, in the past, were not because he had nothing to say, but because he knew no one would listen to him. He is merely saying in public what for generations he said in private. Like the people of Africa and Asia the Indian has now broken the silence imposed upon him, by others and by himself.

In these pages the survival of the old Indian and the emergence of the new Indian are told in their own words. The story is theirs; and so is the book.

Hundreds of Indians and dozens of tribes cooperated in putting these thoughts on paper and this book together. Of these the National Congress of American Indians, "the United Nations of the Tribes," has been especially helpful—and most of all its young and brilliant director, Vine Deloria, Jr. So too was the National Indian Youth

Council, and particularly its founding director, Herbert Blatchford; its chairman, Mel Thom; and its president, Clyde Warrior. So too were the Robert Choate, Jr., Foundation, whose generosity aided in the initial stages of the wandering, known as research; and Mike Hodel of WBAI-FM, in New York, whose interest aided in the gathering of the formal interviews that were later broadcast.

There were hundreds, perhaps thousands, of Indian youths who in truth had written this book before a word was put to paper. It is their book most of all.

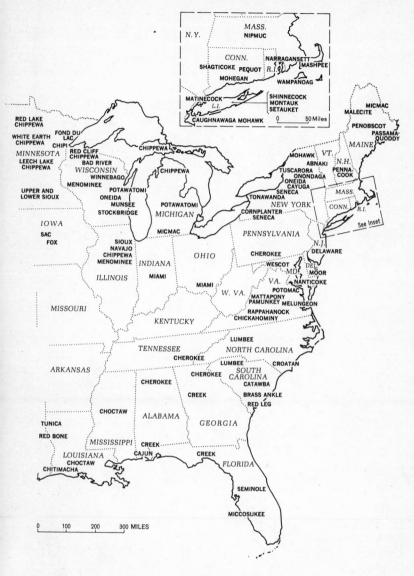

THE NEW INDIANS

There are drums beyond the Mountain,
Indian drums that you can't hear:
There are drums beyond the Mountain,
And they're getting loud and clear. . . .
PETER LA FARGE from "Drums"*

THE NEW INDIANS

1

THE CASE OF
THE DEERSLAYER

In the quiet of the courthouse square the dark-skinned men sat under the leafless trees of spring, waiting. With brooding and ominous eyes they scrutinized the town. Hundreds of Indians squatted there with old pistols in their belts, or they leaned on the aged trees, eying their pickup trucks, where they had hidden their rifles.

A hunter was on trial for killing a deer. The deerslayer was a Cherokee named John Chewie.

Out of the windows of the dim courtroom the handful of small-town officials who had gathered watched the crowd of Indians with growing disquiet. Laughing, someone said it was a scalping party. The whispered rumor spread: "I hear the Cherokees got guns!" It was not to be believed, for it was safer not to believe it; after all, this was not the set of a shoot-'em-up on television, nor could anyone imagine an Indian uprising of the Old West resurrected on the docile Main Street of Jay in uneventful Oklahoma. This was the United States of America, spring, 1966.

Was the ancient Cherokee war chant to re-echo beneath the Coca-Cola signs on the town square?

> *Hayi! Yu! Listen!*
> *Now, instantly, we have lifted the red war club.*

1

> *Quickly his soul shall be without motion.*
> *There under the earth, where the black war clubs shall be*
> *moving like ballsticks in a game,*
> *there his soul shall be,*
> *never to reappear.*
> *We cause it to be so.**

That morning, and the night before, the young men and the old men of the Cherokee villages had been coming out of the hills. Into the town they came, past the GET RIGHT WITH GOD sign on the roadway, the gas stations, the hot dog stands, and the neon-lit bars that were the outposts of civilization.

In twos and threes they came walking along the roadway, with their rifles in their fists, in pickup trucks hunched down to duck the night winds, in old cars that rattled along like farm wagons.

> *I am rising to seek the warpath,*
> *The earth and the sky beside me;*
> *I walk in the day and in the night,*
> *The star of the evening guides me.*

Jay, Oklahoma, is a little town, population 1,120. Not much more need be said of it. In eastern Oklahoma, deep in the wooded hills of the Ozarks near the Arkansas line, the town is surrounded by fields where game birds gather and rough stands of woods where the tracks of deer and possum are visible to the myopic eye, and mountain brooks. Hunters say the region is a paradise; perhaps it is. It is as well the county seat of Delaware County, a "depressed area," where the hills are crowded with full-blooded Indians.

Hostile in a way so ingrained that no one needs to say anything about it, the town is not off bounds to the Indians. But they rarely

---

* These religious chants, or sacred formulas, of the Cherokee are reprinted from *Sacred Formulas of the Cherokees* by James Mooney, 7th Annual Report of the Bureau of American Ethnology, Washington, D.C., 1891. Mooney wrote that he had translated them from writings, in the Cherokee language, by religious men of the tribe who had transcribed them "for their own use."

Cherokees believe it is sacrilegious for a non-Cherokee to publish, print, or use these sacred formulas. In deference to these fine, deeply religious people I therefore wish to explain that I have merely reprinted them from James Mooney, as he reprinted them from the writing of the Cherokees of the nineteenth century.

come into town, unless they have to. Except, of course, on Saturday nights. It was unheard of for so many to come. One could feel the tension.

The courthouse in the town square is a fortlike building of no particular architecture. It looks like any other county courthouse in rural Oklahoma.

In the corridors of the courthouse there was a residue of exhausted air. The judicial chambers opened upon rows of gnarled and initialed benches. The benches might have been mistaken for the pews of an ascetic church. The pedestal of the judge who sat in judgment on the boredom that passes for sin in a small town was like a pulpit. The jailhouse, an ugly structure of heavy stones, was visible from the courtroom; a reminder of the swift justice that was a tradition of the Old West. The prisoners, on the Ozark frontier, were mostly Indians. John Chewie had waited in this jailhouse.

And still they came, the silent Indians with their silent weapons. "When Cherokees go armed, they generally carry pistols. They may be of almost any type, from ancient .45 caliber 'hot legs,' to modern compact automatics," said a man in nearby Tahlequah. "Pistols tucked under the waistband of pants, in the deep back pocket of overalls, or in a coat pocket. Pistols in the glove compartments of cars, or behind the seat of a pickup. Rifles, too, are 'kept handy' in a nearby car or pickup."

"There were four hundred armed Cherokees in Jay ready to use them if that man was prosecuted," said the principal of a rural Delaware County school, Harold Wade, who was in town that day.

In a town of little more than one thousand, the sudden appearance of four hundred armed Indians was frightening. In any town if that many men, bearing loaded guns, were to appear at city hall to surround the town square, not demonstrating but sitting silently, with rifles and pistols cocked, there would be reason to fear. But in Jay these Indians could have occupied the town in hours.

Were it to happen in New York City's Harlem, whose Negro population is about equal to that of the American Indians, or in Los Angeles' Watts, as it almost did, the alarm would ring out, on the wire services, "Insurrection! Call out the National Guard! And the *Life* photographers!" But the armed Indians were met with

silence. Not with the National Guard; not even with the television
cameras. The newspapers, except for the local press, ignored the
threat of the armed uprising in the hills.

Was it incomprehensible to the townspeople that the stoic Indians,
the long-suffering and eternally enduring, the apostles of patience,
were so violently angry? The Indians were the town joke, as they
were the national joke. They were not to be taken too seriously.

"Lo, the Poor Indian," mocked the Tulsa *Tribune* in an editorial
of fatherly disapproval. And yet the newspaper at the oil capital was
somewhat apprehensive too. The reports of rifle-toting redskins
would have been easier to laugh off if it hadn't been for scare words
like "Red Power" that some of the young Indians were using. The
Tribune sensed that the rebellion of the Red Muslims, as the new
Indian leaders themselves called it, was not being staged for laughs.

The Tulsa *Tribune* feared that "Then would come a militant
separatist movement, such as the French-Canadians have in Quebec,
and we're back to the Little Big Horn."

In Tahlequah, back in the hills, Clyde Warrior laughed at these
words. The young Indian intellectual was one of the angriest of
the angry young men of the hills. Not a Cherokee, he had no part
in the uprising. But he was its uninhibited, fiery voice to other tribes.

"We have a Southern social structure in eastern Oklahoma," Warrior said. "The only way you change that structure is to smash it.
You turn it over sideways. And stomp on it. It appears to me that's
what will happen around here. I think violence will come about.
And as far as I am concerned the sooner the better."

> *Ho, you young men, warriors!*
> *Bear your arms to the place of battle!*

Indeed, something had to be done. That winter, under the cold
clouds of discontent, the envoys from Washington had been holding
councils of peace. It was tumultuous enough with the urban Negroes
once again threatening to disquiet the summer solstice with cries of
"Black Power" without rural Indians threatening to do the same with
hunting rifles. Quietly, behind the scenes, the emissaries of the
Justice Department, the agents of the F.B.I., the mediators of the
Interior Department, and the lawyers of the Attorney General's

office in Oklahoma City had gone into the hills surreptitiously, to confer with the armed Cherokees. "To calm the natives down," said Clyde Warrior.

Was all of this because John Chewie had gone hunting? Chewie, an ex-Marine, known as a hard drinker and a hungry hunter, had indeed gone hunting. He had, by killing a deer, become the symbol of the Red Nationalist rebellion.

The rangers of the Oklahoma Department of Wildlife had arrested him for possession of deer meat in his car out of season, and for hunting without a license. He did not deny the charges. He had shot the deer, he said, in the Kenwood Reserve, a region of woodland held in trust by the U.S. Government for the Cherokee Tribe. He was a full-blooded Cherokee and he would not apologize for hunting on land that rightfully belonged to his people; nor did he have to be licensed like a dog by the state. He had hunted because he was hungry, he told the court; to feed himself and his family. It had been the dead of winter and they had to eat.

In the hunter's behalf, Robert Thomas, a sardonic Cherokee anthropologist, testified at the court hearing that these Indians believed that God had put the wild game on earth for the sustenance of man. Were they, believing that, to obtain hunting licenses from God?

Thomas, who directed the Carnegie Corporation's Cross Cultural Project on the Cherokee culture and language in Tahlequah, told the court that the per capita annual income of the Indians in Delaware County was $500. Hardly enough to starve on, he said. He implied that the religious beliefs of the Indians were neither wholly metaphysical nor legally fatuous, but necessary for survival. The diet was simply inadequate, testified Albert Wahrhaftig, the junior anthropologist with the Carnegie Project. So poor was the economic condition of the Indians, he said, that without wild game to supplement their meager food supplies they would have no meat at all.

"I seen my father suffer. I seen my aunt, my own aunt, die of starvation. I seen old womens suffer. I seen the childrens buried in the county coffins." The mourner was a rural Indian, a backwoods dirt church preacher of the Indian Baptists among the Creeks of Oklahoma, the Reverend Clifton Hill, who shepherded a rebellious movement of his own people in a neighboring county. "Sometimes I goes to funerals, and see the poor Indians, I mean *poor* Indians, who don't have a thing they own, lying in the county coffin. And you don't know what I feel when I see that.

"Go down to the depths of the Creek Nation. We have shabby houses. It's nothing like compared in the city. It's worse. When I talk about poor, I mean *poor*."

> *Here on my breast I have bled!*
> *See! See! My battle scars!*
> *You mountains tremble at my yell!*
> *I strike for life!*

"These are very poor people in the midst of a land of plenty," said Finis Smith, one of the religious leaders of the Cherokees and the descendant of Chief Redbird Smith. He believed the "exploitation is accelerating." So was the anger of his people.

"In eastern Oklahoma we have a system of peonage," said Clyde Warrior. "The local politicians and local businessmen find it very profitable to keep these Indians in a state of peonage. They work for people as slave labor; they rent from people off their welfare checks. It has been going on for several years; it is just now coming to a head; the anger, you might say, of the Indian people."

"The life of most Oklahoma Indians is very, very bad," said Warrior, "the sickest, poorest people in the country." Because they were so low economically, and felt so low psychologically, the "Oklahoma Indians had no way of relating to urban America," he said, "just like any other poor people."

The weed roots of poverty in the Indian villages were dug up statistically by Graham Holmes, the former Bureau of Indian Affairs area director for the Five Civilized Tribes of Oklahoma. In a survey prepared for Congressman Wayne Aspinall of the House Interior and Insular Affairs Committee in 1962, Holmes laconically noted:

Of 19,000 adult Indians in eastern Oklahoma, between the ages of 18 and 55, an estimated 10,000, or 52.6 percent, were unemployed;

Of the 10,000 jobless adult Indians well over half received no unemployment insurance, or any other welfare assistance—whatsoever;

Of young Indians, when he was queried "How many Indians 16 or 17 [years old] are now employed? Full time?" the succinct official replied: "Very few, if any."

Yet, having tabulated these statistics of poverty, Holmes's document ended happily. He dryly assured the Congress that all was well:

Question: "How is the morale of the Indian people?"

Reply: "Good."

Question: "Are there any evidences of unusual concern by the Indians?"

Reply: "No."

In rural Oklahoma there is little work for the Indian to do. The economic exodus from the rural towns long since left nothing but a residue of odd jobs and seasonal farm work for those who refused to become city Indians.

John Chewie was a farm laborer. He worked in the strawberry and vegetable crops, when there was work. Most of the time he was unemployed. Hands were more numerous than jobs. Like his neighbors, he hoed a hard row. He was a poor backwoods Indian. A friend in Tahlequah said of him: "He is very Indian looking, with a perpetual scared and timid look on his face. He has no ideological axes to grind. He is a hell of a nice guy, with a great sense of humor, but he is the least likely guy in the world to be in the forefront of an Indians'-rights push that you can imagine. I call him 'The Reluctant Hero.'

"But he is all man," the friend added, "and he doesn't like to be shoved around, bribed, and threatened. So he has gotten real angry about this case. He just wants to hunt."

Hunting to an Indian like John Chewie is not a sport. He does not go hunting and fishing to recapture his lost innocence with mass-produced moose-mating horns. The woodsy disguises of the suburbanite in search of a pseudo-primitive manliness are not for him. Nor is he escaping from the office routine. Like most of the Cherokee hunters, he seeks to escape from the statistics of unemployment. It is not to escape into nothingness, but into Indianness. The woods, the hunt, the wild game, the earth itself represent dignity and pride in the Indian ways. Cherokee tribes hunt to reaffirm their way of life, their oneness with nature, the uniqueness of their Indianness, their treaty rights as an Indian nation. And to eat meat.

Hunting has become a symbol of the new tribalism. Wherever the new Indians gather to reaffirm their rights, the Deerslayer reappears. His rifle echoes and re-echoes throughout Indian country.

Up on the high mountain mesas of the Pueblos of the Hopis the traditional chiefs would not buy hunting licenses for young hunters of the tribe. "We are still a sovereign nation. We have never abandoned our sovereignty to any foreign power or government," they said. Chippewas of Wisconsin's Lake Superior shores demanded their "earth right," as a tribal official phrased it, to fish and to harvest wild rice, without interference, or "okay from outside." The fishermen of the Yakima Indians of Washington State patrolled the banks of the Columbia River with rifles, to safeguard their tribal nets and to enforce their treaty rights. In New York State, the Iroquois, the "native nationalists" that Edmund Wilson wrote of in his book *Apology to the Iroquois,* restated their old religious beliefs by an unfettered and free return of tribal hunting bands to the eastern forests. Deep in the Everglades of Florida the Seminoles were doing the same, while the Red Lake Band of Chippewas in Minnesota fought for and won their "ancestral right" to hunt wild ducks without licenses from the state or the United States.

But why had the movement of tribal nationalism taken on so seemingly archaic a form? Why, of all things, hunting rights?

The wild duck hunters of the Chippewas may offer the clue. For generations the tribe hunted wild ducks on the shores of Red Lake. They ran afoul of game wardens with warrants in their jodh-purs, who arrested the Indians in flocks for not buying migratory bird hunting stamps.

Lo, the poor wild duck became a *cause célèbre*. His unstamped death was fought in the corridors of the Interior Department, until one judicious day the then Acting Commissioner of Indian Affairs, H. Rex Lee, consulted with the wise men of the legal staff and declared: "In an opinion dated June 30, 1936 the Solicitor of this Department pointed out that, while the various treaties between the United States and the Chippewa Indians did not reserve the right to the Indians to hunt and fish within unceded lands of the Red Lake Reservation, it was not necessary to reserve such rights because of the larger rights possessed by the Indians in land occupied and used by them, and such rights remained in the Indians unless granted away.

"In view of the foregoing, it is our view that members of the

Red Lake Band of Chippewa Indians are not required to obtain a Migratory Bird Hunting Stamp to hunt wild ducks on the Reservation."

Whether to buy or not to buy a migratory bird hunting stamp? It may not have seemed of historic importance. But it was. The Indians by defying the proclaimed rights of the states were proclaiming their right to govern themselves. And they were protecting their ancient way of tribal life, with rifles ready. The Chippewas and the Yakimas and the Cherokees were issuing declarations of independence.

The Navajo Tribe had spoken of this independence when one Fourth of July in the early sixties their tribal newspaper editorialized: "Perhaps, for the Indian, the celebration is a bit premature. . . . The day will come, and it is rapidly approaching, all the time, when the part of Webster's definition of Independence which reads 'self-maintenance' will become a reality. We call it self-determination in Navajoland, but it means the same thing."

In any event, the defiance of Stamp Acts ought to have had a familiar ring. In the Boston Tea Party of 1773, when the liberty-minded colonials fought the King's Stamp Act, they masqueraded as Indians. Now the Indians were taking off their masks of timidity and defying the latter-day Stamp Acts that denied them their independence.

In the definitive *Handbook of Federal Indian Law* the late Felix S. Cohen had recognized that "tribal rights of hunting and fishing have received judicial recognition and protection against state and private interference, and even against interference by Federal administrative officials." But the words did not persuade the deeds. At the Chicago Conference of American Indians held at the University of Chicago in 1961, a resolution on "Hunting and Fishing Rights" noted the "increasing concern" of the tribes that state governments were "encroaching on the rights of individual [Indians] hunting, fishing, trapping, and harvesting wild rice on Indian reservations." The four hundred Indians from fifty tribes who gathered at that anthropological powwow petitioned the Secretary of Interior for "a favorable ruling on the rights of Indians to hunt, fish, trap and harvest wild rice, and other vegetation on their own lands."

John Chewie had hunted for more than deer meat. He had

hunted for his self-respect and for self-determination in his tribal way of life.

He had not gone into the woods by himself. The men of fifty villages in the hills had come together that winter and talked of their hungers for food and pride. Led by Finis Smith, these men had secretly met in snowbound cabins and in backwoods towns. They founded the Five County Cherokee Movement, a society of full-bloods—the silent men with rifles. And in the dark of winter, yet unheard in the noisy towns, they voiced what was to be their declaration of independence—the Declaration of the Five County Cherokees:

We meet in a time of darkness to seek the path to the light. We come together, just as our fathers have always done, to do these things. . . .

We, the Five County Cherokees, are one people. We stand united in the sight of God, our creator. We are joined by love and concern for each other and for all men. . . .

We offer ourselves as the voice of the Cherokee people. For many years our people have not spoken and have not been heard. Now we gather as brothers and sisters. . . .

We use our right to freedom of speech. This right is the ancient custom of our people. This right is guaranteed by the Constitution of the United States of America. We insist on equality under the laws of these United States. We act now, peaceably but firmly, to carry out the wish of our people. . . .

We do this for the benefit of all Cherokees. We do this as a good example to all men. Already we have gathered to protect our rights to harvest fish and game to feed ourselves and our children. . . .

These men went into the woods together. In bands of hunters as in the old days, they hunted for game as their fathers had. Chewie was one of many. He was caught, but he was not alone. The hundreds who stood by his side with their rifles on the day of his trial were his blood brothers. In their tribal oath they had pledged to one another:

"We will go on until our lands and our homes are safe. Until we live within the full and just protection of the law. Until we live as the American authors of the Constitution and the Declaration of Independence intended each of the nationalities in this country to live. As dignified men. As free men. As men equal to all other men.

"From this beginning we will go on until the job is done. . . ."

O Great Terrestrial Hunter, I come to the edge of your spittle,
*   where you repose.*
Give me the wind.
Give me the breeze.
Yu!

Inside the courtroom the hearing itself was dull. Hardly was there need of legal evidence to determine what had happened. Even the cross-examination was mostly repartee:

PROSECUTOR: "How many times have you been arrested?"

DEFENDANT: "I don't know. I haven't counted."

PROSECUTOR: "John, do you drink whiskey?"

DEFENDANT: "Don't you?"

Jokingly the State of Oklahoma's Assistant Attorney General, D. L. Cook, invoked his constitutional right not to answer under the Fifth Amendment. The laughter in the courtroom was, on this cue, more polite than prolonged; it was somewhat nervous.

One of the defense attorneys, Stuart Trapp, who had come from Memphis, Tennessee, to represent the American Civil Liberties Union, then took the stand. He did so, the lawyer said, because he sensed that the tension in the town of Jay was about to flare into bloodshed, unless the Case of the Deerslayer were taken out of the State of Oklahoma's jurisdiction. It ought to be judged by the federal courts. The courthouse square was "an unhappy place of considerable tension," Trapp said. He had listened to the Indians talk of injustices for hours, while fingering their rifles.

In deference to the rifles of the silent, and uninvited, witnesses, the Case of the Deerslayer was held over for the federal courts. And, as quietly as they had come, the Indians withdrew from the town.

Once again the town was peaceable. There had been no violence. No shooting. No riot. Not a window shattered. No shouting. No slogans. The young men with rifles had gathered up their rifles and slipped away. It was as though they had never come. By their silence they indicated their disdain of the whole proceeding.

"The Cherokees and the Creeks are a very legal-minded people. They want to try everything that is right and proper," Clyde Warrior said, "because they believe that if they do everything that is legal and proper then justice will prevail. What they fail to see is that in the American system nothing is done legally, honestly, and truthfully. Now, when they find that out, they are going to be pretty damn mad. If that [the legal way] fails, then violence will take place. The country should take heed."

His wrath voiced the frustrations of not only the young, educated Indians. In the hills the country Indians were more and more vocal. And their pent-up angers, so long frustrated by their feelings of hopelessness, upset the rural calm. "These people are becoming more and more aggressive. I do not use the term 'aggressive' lightly. In many areas it is on the verge of militancy," Warrior said.

These views provoked much headshaking among the local officials, especially since the views were supported by hundreds of rifles. In the cities community leaders were troubled.

When the Council of the Five Civilized Tribes of Oklahoma met to discuss the uprising in the hills, there was much dismay. The Reverend James L. Partridge, a Creek tribal councilman of Sapulpa, advocated that the U.S. Congress and the State Legislature pass laws to "stop all this marching and all this violence." It ought to be a federal offense "to lead an act of violence," Reverend Partridge said.

W. W. Keeler, the principal chief of the Cherokee Nation, was more conciliatory. One of the distinguished Indian citizens of Oklahoma and vice president of Phillips Petroleum, Keeler had been a spokesman of the "task force" on Indian affairs appointed by the late President Kennedy. He thought it wiser to soothe, rather than restrict, the dissident full-bloods. "Now is the time to forget these differences" and past "mistakes," Keeler said; let the Cherokees "join hands and work together."

The principal chief was appointed by the President of the United States; he was not elected by the tribe. In the hills they called him "the President's chief"; he was rudely rebuffed by the full-bloods. He was a "white Indian" to the backwoods, dirt-farm rebels.

Finis Smith, the leader of the Five County Cherokee Movement, was blunt: "We do not need to be called to assemblies to be berated for not cooperating in our own destruction. In a strict sense, there are no alternatives to Indian wants. There is no alternative to having

control of our own destiny and having our voices heard and taken
seriously. . . . We certainly need to strike bargains with the general
society, but we do not need to help whites become big shots in
Indian affairs [by being] 'good little Indians.' "

The old tribal leader talked in a tone different from that of a
young "hot-blood" like Warrior. But his goals differed little.

"The 'best of all possible worlds' for the Cherokee people would
have been for the Cherokee Nation to have continued up to the
present," Smith said; "for the Cherokee people to live as an *independent republic of Indians,* closely tied and friendly to the United
States, under the treaties—as a *modern Indian state* of small communities of kinfolk, taking part in the present industrialized economy
of the world, but with a Cherokee government, and legal system
in the Cherokee language, with lands held in common, and educational system in the Cherokee language, and with industrial work
as an addition to farming and hunting.

"However, we are willing to compromise and modify our aspira-
tions to accommodate to the presence of our white brothers who
now live among us."

> *You have brought me down the white road.*
> *There in mid-earth you have placed me.*
> *I shall stand erect upon the earth.*

In the words with which Finis Smith described the old Cherokee
Nation there was a description of the tribal nationalism of the new
Indians. What had been forgotten, or merely suppressed, was no
longer spoken of as the past. It was to be enlarged to a "Greater
Indian America."

Finis Smith, being a traditional chief, had a power in his words
that the younger man did not. Wherever one went in the hills of
eastern Oklahoma, asking what was happening, people said, "Have
you talked to Finis? You have to talk to Finis." The merchants of
the hill towns whispered that he was "the redskinned Malcolm X";
to the local newspapers he was a "dupe" who was used "by outside
agitators." He was a "menace to the peace of the community," said
a police officer. "He is working the Indians up to no good," complained a small-town mayor in Cherokee County. "But if you

quote me, don't use my name. I got Indian voters." The Reverend Lindy Waters, himself a cousin of Smith's, talked of "his brilliant mind [that] is being channeled in the wrong direction."

The man was revered and reviled, heard and feared. Yet no one talked of him in the old stereotype of the taciturn, the inscrutable, the enigmatic Indian.

He was an old Indian. But he was an outspoken new Indian. In the personnel files of the local office of the Bureau of Indian Affairs the folder on Finis Smith revealed that he had lost several jobs for "trying to stir up Indian workers to stand up for their rights"—as a government clerk confided. Smith had been fired from the Tinker Air Force Base, in Oklahoma City, for what was said to be organizing activity among the Indians.

"We do *all* the compromising, and our white brothers have drawn the arena and made the rules by which life must be lived, and we have no choice but to go along, whether we like it or not," Smith said. "But a compromise must go both ways. To begin with, whites must recognize our existence as a modern and permanent part of Oklahoma; as a *people*. . . . It follows that whites must be willing to modify many Oklahoma institutions, laws, and procedures so that we can participate in a common society with them."

> *You have put me in the white house.*
> *I shall be in it as it moves about.*

"The Cherokees have always led the way in every revolutionary concept [in] Indian affairs. Whatever happens in eastern Oklahoma will have a terrific impact on all Indian tribes," said Clyde Warrior. "I've heard it said that whatever the Cherokees do, that's what everyone else will do. I've heard it said, in my travels around the country, that Indians are just waiting for the Cherokees to do something. And then it will be like a snowball rolling down a hill."

The Indian tribes throughout the country were waiting to see what would happen to the Cherokees, Smith thought. It had traditionally been true. History supported this belief, wrote John Collier, the former Commissioner of Indian Affairs, in *Indians of the Americas:* "More than any other tribe, the Cherokee Nation furnished the crystallizing thread of the United States government policy and acton in Indian affairs."

It may have been with this vision of the past and the future in mind that the Declaration of the Five County Cherokees was written. For it beautifully and prophetically and simply said what the new Indians, everywhere, believed:

Now, we shall not rest until we have regained our rightful place. We shall tell our young people what we know. We shall send them to the corners of the earth to learn more. They shall lead us.

Now, we have much to do. When our task is done, we will be ready to rest.

In these days, intruders, named without our consent, speak for the Cherokees. When the Cherokee government is the Cherokee people, we shall rest.

In these days, we are informed of the decisions other people have made about our destiny. When we control our destiny, we shall rest.

In these days, the high courts of the United States listen to people who have been wronged. When our wrongs have been judged in these courts, and the illegalities of the past have been corrected, we shall rest.

In these days, there are countless ways by which people make their grievances known to all Americans. When we have learned these new ways that bring strength and power, and we have used them, we shall rest.

In these days, we are losing our homes and our children's homes. When our homeland is protected, for ourselves and for the generations to follow, we shall rest.

In the vision of our creator, we declare ourselves ready to stand proudly among the nationalities of these United States of America.

> *I stand with my face toward the Sun Land.*
> *No one is ever lonely with me.*
> *Wherever I go*
> *No one is ever lonely with me.*

And so in the hills of Oklahoma the Indians hold on to their rifles. They sit in their wooded villages, in their highway shanty-towns, in their forest cabins, with their rifles between their knees, waiting to hear if justice will absolve them from the burden of blood that the white man's inhumanity and greed have cast upon them. They wait to see if the white man's democracy and rich abundance, taken from their lands, will be shared with the Indian.

They sit silently, doubting and waiting. They squat, and they clean their rifles. They have waited patiently for a long time, but they are no longer patient.

Somewhere in the hills Clyde Warrior, the Ponca, spoke: "I say there will be an uprising that will make Kenyatta's Mau Mau movement look like a Sunday-school picnic."

Clyde Warrior grinned. He, too, was waiting.

2

THE WARRIORS RETURN

The youth, in his Eisenhower jacket, bowed his head.

In solemn arcs of the old man's hand the sacred cedar bark was waved back and forth above the boy's crew cut. The priest of the Newekwe, the Clown Society, purified the Zuñi GI. Until this rite of purification—the Hanasema Isu Waha—was performed the pueblo would not welcome home the warrior. High on the mountain plateau of New Mexico, on the rutted banks of the Zuñi River, where the rite was traditionally held, the family of the youth nodded in approval. He was no longer a soldier in the white man's army. He was a Zuñi.

It was the spring of 1946. The rite of Hanasema Isu Waha was performed repeatedly that year. Literally it meant "Bad luck, get rid of it."

Two hundred young men of the Zuñi pueblo had come home from the battlefields of World War II. Religious belief of the elders prescribed that these young soldiers, who had been contaminated by contact with "The War of the Whites" and by the world beyond, be cleansed at once. One Pueblo mother refused to touch her homecoming son, it was said, until he had undergone the rite of purification; for without the Hanasema Isu Waha the returning warriors could not dance again in the Kiva, nor know the peace of being Zuñi.

The Zuñis have a war prayer:

17

May your way be fulfilled.
May you be blessed with life.
Where the life-giving way
Of your Sun Father shines
May your way be reached.

Not a very warlike prayer, it was a prayer for the peaceful return of the warrior, for the peace that restores the warrior to his people, to his community.

In the farm village of the Rama Navajos, down the road, the returning warriors were similarly purified. These Navajo GI's were psychologically cleansed of their battle traumas and their urban traumas by the ceremonials known as the Blessing Way and the Enemy Way: the traditional rituals of welcome and blessing for returning soldiers. Life in the Navajo way had to be restored to those who had come near to alien death. One of the Navajo war veterans of Rama recalled: "The ceremony was arranged by my grandfather. He said we needed it because we had seen lots of dead Germans. Not only seen them, but stepped on them, and smelled some dead German bodies. He was afraid that later we might go loco if we don't have this ceremony."

The grandfathers said, "Let The War of the Whites be now forgotten. Let the white way of life, and death, be now cast out of you."

The grandfathers said, "Let The War of the Whites be now exorcised." In saying this it was not merely the enemy dead that the priests of the Navajo religion thought of as a threat, but everything that was foreign to Navajo ways. "This exposure to alien ghosts involved not only the Germans and Japanese, but also contact with white Americans," said the anthropologists John Adair and Evon Vogt in their study of the war veterans of Rama and Zuñi.

Rites of purification were widespread. Everywhere among the tribes the rituals were different. But everywhere the aim was the same: to purify the warriors of The War of the Whites and to celebrate their return to the Indian way of tribal life.

Homecoming Teton Sioux veterans of World War II journeyed to the Wind River Reservation of the Arapahos of Wyoming, late in the summer of 1946, to partake in the sacrificial sun dance.

Later, when the once torturous ritual of rejuvenation was revived on the Sioux reservations of the Dakotas, in the 1950's, a young man of the Northern Cheyenne of Montana offered himself in symbolic sacrifice for the return of the warriors of his tribe, who had fought in the Korean War.

Yet the rites of purification were inadequate. The young warrior who fought in World War II, or the Korean War, may or may not have brought home with him the ghosts of the alien dead that his elders feared. But he did bring home living ghosts. The war veteran— there were nearly 25,000 Indians who served in the armed forces— was a veteran of life, as well as of death, in the world beyond his reservation.

He was a "culture bearer" of the nomad caravans of the old hunters—the Marco Polos of the Indians—who brought home enticing tales of the modern world's curious beliefs and strange customs. When the warrior of World War II talked of the battles he had fought he talked not only of those fought on foreign battlefields but of those fought in the barracks of his own army, and on the streets of American cities.

A young Navajo remembered those years. He had been in the Marine Corps, and he had come home to edit his tribal paper. One day, sitting in his modernistic office, years after the war, Marshall Tome began to reminisce; but his war story, like that of so many Indians, was not about his heroism in battle. It was about his being an Indian in a white man's army. He said:

"When I went into the service I was told: 'Remember, you represent us, you represent the Dinés, you represent the Navajo, you represent the Indian. Not the rest of the country. Not the white man.' I remembered that. When I went overseas, to Asia, some of the fellows would be rough, you know, with the girls. And they would hit an old man with their rifle butts. But I would never do that.

"If a boy fell off a bike, I would pick him up. If an old man was hit with a rifle butt, I would pick him up. And people would say, 'He is different from the others. He has a brown skin.'

"And I would say, 'That's not why.'

"And people would say, 'Why are you different then?'

"And I would say, 'Because I am Indian.'

"I lived by that. I believed in that. The Indian, you see, looked at being in the services a little differently."

The Navajo artist Beatien Yazz—Little No Shirt—told his war story with more imagery. But it was the same story. He too had been in the Marine Corps during World War II. He had tasted the water of the far ocean, had tasted it with curiosity, and had found it "tasted salty." He had "to spit out the Pacific Ocean," Yazz said.

Yazz told of the initiation rites of the Marine Corps with similar disenchantment: "They say, 'How old are you?' I say, 'Old enough.' They say, 'Why do you want to be a Marine?' I say, 'I want to see the world.' So I pass my physical, then start taking fingerprint. Oh, my finger was thin, the man say. 'Papoose, go back to your ma.' . . . Two other men talk together about me. One say, 'You think he's tough enough to kill a Jap?' The other say, 'I think he kill several Japs. He's an Indian.' They just laugh at me. So they say, 'Okay, Chief.' "

"Chief"—the word was an endearment to the ears of the Indian equal to "kike" or "nigger." Yet this was the GI dogtag that invariably was hung about the neck of the Indian GI. In the barracks humor the Indian became the butt, or the teller, of wild jokes. He was portrayed with satiric accuracy as Chief White Halfoat in Joseph Heller's *Catch-22*. But, at the same time, on the battlefield he became known as a good man to stay near to. He was cool in combat, the legend said. He was a good soldier.

The "Noble Red Man" lived on; but the two roles he played, as clown and hero, were both white images of the Indian. He was neither.

Eyapaha, the tribal paper of the Upper Brûlé Sioux of the Rosebud Reservation of South Dakota, editorialized on how these attitudes he met in military life affected the Indian soldier: "Ask any Sioux serviceman serving his country in outposts or military bases or on ships or in planes what it feels like to live in a world surrounded by people of other races. He still feels like an Indian, and *he is the envy of all the others who want to, but cannot be, Indian.*" [Emphasis added.]

The Indian soldier had not imitated the white soldier, said the Sioux editor. He had become stronger, not weaker, in his Indian self-esteem because of the insults; what were the insults but a hostile expression of envy?

For all that, he was lonely. The Sioux editor wrote: ". . . the Sioux serviceman stands and feels alone until he returns to his own people."

Coming home from the war, the young warrior brought little with him in his hands. A silken pillow bought in Tokyo, decorated with an embroidered wigwam, and inscribed: GOD BLISS YOU HAPPY HOME. The souvenir of the Statue of Liberty, in a feathered head-dress, whose stomach opened to reveal a pencil sharpener.

He came home also with memories and ghosts. It was these ghosts that the elders feared. It was not that they thought the young men of the tribe had become white. "In four hundred years of fighting, no Indian has turned white," Peter La Farge was to sing. But they feared that, hidden in the warriors' souls, out of sight, was the em-bodiment of the white world, lurking there like a ghost that had to be exorcised. The young warriors had fought in two wars at once. One was military; one was cultural. Both left their wounds.

For the first time since the military defeat of their forefathers, the young warriors had left the reservations by the tens of thousands. Would they return to the ways of their forefathers? Would they re-turn at all? Would they see themselves against the backdrop of the white world, as in a shadow play a puppet is defined against the white screen, and be able to redefine their unique Indianness? Would they become a shadow of themselves? Would they be more clearly visible as Indians? Would they disappear in illusion?

The elders were fearful.

Who knew what thoughts were in these young men? It was not easy for them to talk of these things. Many of them hardly knew the words for their thoughts; for there had been cases of boys on reserva-tions who enlisted, or were drafted, though they could not read or write English. Life in the white world had overwhelmed them with experiences for which there were no words in their own languages. So the warriors were silent.

The upheaval in the life of the Indian was not, however, wholly due to the returning warriors. On the reservations too World War II had brought the white world home—to the doorstep.

In those years there were forty to fifty thousand Indians hired by the war factories. During the wartime labor shortage jobs were offered reservation Indians by industries that had not before, and have not since, needed to hire them. These too were war veterans, in their way, who came home with experiences, and the memories of incomes, that stirred the dust on the somnolent reservations. Jobs in town meant living in town. And radios. And cars. "The war years," chronicled the *Navajo Yearbook,* "opened up new sources of livelihood to the Navajos in the form of wage work on the railroads and in industry, and during that period the social and economic structure of Navajo society underwent important changes. The reservation agricultural base ceased to figure as the principal source of livelihood for a majority of the population, becoming instead a source of supplementary income."

The *Yearbook* noted: To a people to whom cash income was peripheral even soldiers' dependency payments "given to families of Navajos who joined [the armed forces] were a factor in this regard. . . ."

Hunting and herding and farming were still the sources of tribal prestige, but no longer were the sole source of tribal well-being. "We now have a wage economy," Maurice McCabe, the Navajo tribal manager, was able to say within a few years. And the scattering of industries that came to the reservations during the war and postwar years reflected, and intensified, this trend.

One old longhair, on the tribal council of the Navajos, was perhaps a bit premature, but he spoke of the new fear. "Soon we will not be Navajo any more."

It was the first time in history that so many—almost 100,000—Indians had participated in the world of the conquerors. The wars that had been fought for this continent, that had ended less than one hundred years ago, had been fought as against enemy nations. Since their military defeat they had been quite literally imprisoned, under guard, on the reservations. One of the Apaches who fought with Geronimo had called the tribes "prisoners of war." In many ways they had been prisoners-of-war generations after the wars had ended.

War, this time to save the civilization of the conquerors, was ironically what had unlocked the reservation doors. The years of social imprisonment were ending. Peace brought new hope that the Indian would walk out of his isolation, into the triumphant society. He would be free "to be white." He would join the twentieth century. He would be beguiled by its wealth and progress. The vanishing Indian would vanish, as a tribal Indian, and become a sunburned suburbanite.

"We were looked down upon as a backward people, and the assumption was made that we must be like white men to find peace of mind," said the Paiute youth Mel Thom: "No one ever asked us what we wanted. There was always someone to put words in our mouths."

Historian William Hagan, in his *American Indians,* wrote hopefully: "The returned veterans did their part to hasten the end of the old way of life. Wartime incomes and experiences accelerated the detribalization process." The old ways were doomed.

The cultural conquest of the recalcitrant red man, by cajoling and by assimilation, was at hand. He was measured for the melting pot. It was with this hope in mind that the Hoover Commission on postwar governmental reorganization, which had been appointed by President Truman, recommended "complete integration." The Indian had, after all, proven himself, in war factory and on the battlefield, to be the equal of the white citizenry. "Complete integration" was to be his reward.

In its Task Force Report of 1947 the Hoover Commission proposed "a policy of rapid integration into American life" [*sic*]. Further, the commissioners urged the terminating of federal social services to the tribes and the transfer of these treaty obligations to the states. These thoughts were a muted echo of the Senate Indian Affairs Committee report of 1943, which had called for the liquidation of the Bureau of Indian Affairs and the termination of its services. Commissioner of Indian Affairs Zimmerman, in the Truman Administration, had similarly told a Senate hearing in 1947 that he believed the time had come to terminate federal services to the more "advanced" tribes. Evidently it was thought that if the Indian could fight and work like everyone else then he must be like everyone else.

However, it was not until the appointment of Dillon Myer, the former head of the Japanese-American Relocation Center camps during the war—a latter-day "prisoner of war" expert—as Indian Commissioner, in 1950, that these recommendations became policy. Myer was their loudest spokesman. It was under his aegis that the plans to terminate federal services and to relocate the reservation Indians were drawn up. That is, get them off their lands and into the cities.

Later, during the Eisenhower years, when the attempt was abortively made to put these policies into effect, they provoked an anguished outcry from the Indians, especially from the returned war veterans.

In the years after the war the economy of the country boomed, but not for the Indian. He was to rediscover that the Indian was not merely the last hired—he was not hired at all. The war heroes and the war jobs were too soon forgotten. If the young warrior had a brief dream of a new life, it quickly became a nostalgic reminiscence, to be bitterly swallowed in the bars of the reservation towns.

The *Navajo Yearbook* observed the desolation of the dream:

With the close of hostilities and the sudden change to a peacetime economy, these sources of [wartime] livelihood disappeared. And the erstwhile wage earners, finding themselves without employment, were forced back to the Reservation, where there were no resources available to them beyond such meager aid as kinsmen might provide. As a result their plight became critical to the degree that it drew national attention.

Hunger, stark and unbelievable hunger, befell many of the tribes. The Hopis and the Navajos were particularly hard hit; for during the winter blizzards of 1947, at the very time that the Hoover Commission was recommending their "complete integration," these destitute Indians were suffering a famine. Food had to be airlifted to the starving Indians, much as it was airlifted to Berlin, that bitter winter.

On the reservations life was mired in hunger. Again. But the war veterans were no longer willing to endure stagnation as a way of life. Nor were they stoic in their misery, in fear of the dominant society, as their forefathers had been.

These Indian youths took to the roads, but there was nowhere for them to go, and nothing for them to do. On the reservations, the interest in cars was a symbol of their unrest. In those postwar years, the use of cars eclipsed that of the horse and wagon; and this expressed the need to "get somewhere," to "get going," to escape the despair. Still, these restless youths hardly carried their discontent outside their reservations, into the outside world. The youths' angers rarely left home.

The hero of the U.S. Marine Corps, Ira Hayes, who had raised the flag at Iwo Jima, became the symbol of the defeat of the Indian war veterans. Hayes had been feasted and feted and bemedaled. Then he was forgotten. When he wandered home to the Pima Reservation, in the bleak and stark deserts of Arizona, he was destitute—without work, without hope.

> *Just a Pima Indian—*
> *No water, no crops, no chance.**

Hayes had been an exemplary soldier. It was not merely his courage, which had been honored and decorated, that indicated the kind of young man he was, but his behavior. He had been "a good boy"; he had been "a good Indian"; he had been "a good Christian."

The young Pima had abandoned his Indianness for the values and promises of the white society. It was this that rendered him defenseless and unprepared for the betrayal of his beliefs. He had nothing to sustain him in defeat. So he become "the drunken Ira Hayes," the "whiskey-drinking Indian." He drowned in a drainage ditch, in two inches of water, in that waterless desert wasteland in which he sought refuge. To the young warriors who returned from the glory of World War II, the fate of Ira Hayes was the final betrayal.

The betrayal and bitterness that the warriors felt was voiced by another Marine Corps veteran of Iwo Jima. Dennie Hosteen, a Navajo who fought in the Korean War as well, wrote some years later: "Today as I sit at home without a job I think of those Innocents in the Vietnam War that will be returning home soon, saying: What's our benefit? to their Fathers, Mothers, husbands, wives, children, friends. For us poor Indians there are none on our reservations lands and within our reservations."

---

* Copyright © Edward B. Marks Music Corporation. Used by permission.

"For the Deads," Hosteen wrote of his comrades, "surely there are none!"

Liquored dreams, the solace of the inertia and nothingness of jobless and hopeless days, became an obsessive disease of these defeated warriors.

The Paiute youth Mel Thom, who was to become a leader of the new Indians, remembered similar days of bitterness after the Korean War: "For a long time we were just angry. So angry that we would get drunk for five days at a time, you know. What else could we do?"

Into the restless group of new Indians came several thousand new recruits. The Korean War veterans deepened and accelerated these upheavals in tribal life. Even less than the warriors of World War II were they willing to play the stoic, long-suffering Indian. It was a new era.

"Ten years ago you could have tromped on the Indians and they would have said, 'Okay, kick me again. I'm just an Indian,'" said the young Sioux Vine Deloria, Jr. But those days of acquiescence were gone, he thought.

Deloria, Jr., was of the new generation. He was as well the director of the National Congress of American Indians, the United Nations of more than one hundred tribes, the most influential of all tribal federations: he spoke not merely for the young, but for tribes that represented four hundred thousand Indians. He was the Rousseau of the new Indians. He talked of a turning point in tribal history.

"Listen," Deloria, Jr., said, "since World War II the Indian people, everywhere, have gotten out of the era where they were taught a set of [non-Indian] 'truths.'

"Now they are thinking for themselves, and they are going to decide, 'What do *I* choose? My Indianness and Indian culture? Or this myth that the rest of the country lives by?' "

Said the Paiute Mel Thom: "Awareness of our situation had brought out anger. With anger and concern 'hope' was born. We were aware [that] if we did not take action, in our time, future generations of Indians would be denied the right to share our own heritage. This was a direct threat to us, and we knew it. It was a matter of how to set up action to fight this threat and how we [would] rally our Indian forces together."

There was "a new Indian" war, Thom said. It fittingly had begun with the return of the warriors from "The War of the Whites." It was these warriors, disguised by their khaki fatigues, who had gone back to the villages of their forefathers from the alien and urban battlefields. It was these warriors who represented the traditional greatness of the Indians.

Warriors were of the tribal past. If the heritage of the tribal way of life was to be fought for, who better to do so than modern warriors?

3

THE POWWOW OF
THE YOUNG INTELLECTUALS

A few years ago, in the tribal newspaper of the Navajos, there appeared this classified advertisement:

SWAP, SELL, OR TRADE
Well trained roping horse. Rodeo
experience. Weight 1150 lbs. 14
hands high. Excellent condition.
Will sacrifice. Owner in college.

He put his cowboy boots, his worn jeans, his one tie, his high school diploma, his rock 'n' roll records in his broken suitcase. He tied his suitcase with a rope—perhaps the lasso he had used in bull-dogging calves in the Indian rodeos.

He walked in bare feet, one last time, down the dirt road to the blacktop road and onto the crossroad of the superhighway. Then he put on the new shoes he had bought. He looked back at the open country, he turned his back on his indecision, and he walked down the superhighway toward Albuquerque and the University of New Mexico.

The cowboy who had sold his horse was one of thousands of an entire generation beginning a journey between two worlds. Until then he may have been just another "invisible Indian," his thoughts, like himself, kept within the confines of his reservation. Now he was on the open road, where the white man could really see him. He had become visible.

He was the new Indian.

He might have been the Navajo boy Herbert Blatchford, one of the pioneers-in-reverse who journeyed from the reservation to the University of New Mexico in the early postwar years. The young Navajo was to become the scholarly voice of the university-educated, twentieth-century Indians. The quiet voice of the college Indians, articulate and confident, he was the founder of the National Indian Youth Council and is now the executive director and the editor of its journal, *The Aborigine*. But, like the cowboy's his was a long journey.

Young Blatchford is the descendant of an ancestral headman, the grandson of the brother of the great chief Manuelito. He had ridden, as a boy, to the summer pastures with his family's flock. Sheepherding was the old way of the Navajo and he had grown up in a tradition of which he was not the contradiction.

He had been educated in not one, but two, church schools: those of the Methodist and Christian Reform missions. He had entered what he termed the "no-man's land" of education. He had traded his sheepskin bed for a sheepskin diploma. In that unpresuming way he has—in the way of the Navajo—Blatchford said of himself, not modestly but impersonally: "He had experienced about all any sheepherder would. In retrospect he might be classed as a literate sheepherder."

The life of a young Indian, like Blatchford, on the reservation, before his journey to a university education, has been earthily described by a Navajo girl, Carol Bitsui. She was a student at the High School of St. Michael's and the president of the class of 1967, when she wrote of her "feelings of being a Navajo":

I was raised on the reservation in a hogan with neither a running water, not a button to press for warm heat.

My bed was cradleboard, a sheepskin and the earth. My food was my mother's breath, goat's milk, berries, mutton, and corn meal. My play partners were puppies, the lamb and the lizards.

I ate with my fingers. I went barefoot at most time. I washed my hair with yucca roots. I combed my hair with strawbrush. I wore a hair knot.

I had to rise early. I herded sheep in the blazing desert of Coyote

Canyon. I carried water from the water pit. I ground corn for my food. I carried wood on my back and in my arms. I carded wool for my mother.

I sometime went without eating because there was no food in the dish cupboard of my hogan.

I wore clothes that were made out of flour sacks. I sang songs as I tended my sheep. I rode a horse without a saddle. I rode in a wagon to the Trading Post.

I prayed to the Great Spirit of my people. I respected nature because it was sacred to me. I took part in my people's ceremonies. I went to squaw dances, fire dances, and Yei Bi Chai dances, not for fun, but to be the patient's guest. I listened to the legend been told by my grandparents. The medicine man was my doctor. The herbs were my medicine.

I did not speak English, for it was a strange language to me.

Going down the rough dirt road, from the earthy and easygoing tribal life on the rural reservations to the middle-class upmanship of university life in the cities, these young Indians were like refugees in an unknown country. The university was more than strange. It was foreign and alien.

"Very few of us crossed the gap between the two cultures," Blatchford said. "Those who found it difficult to indulge in the new culture developed into a hybrid group, belonging fully to neither culture."

Listening to the young Indians talk of pop sociology, the Beatles mystique, and "the lonely crowd," and seeing them dressed in properly improper collegiate costumes of tight jeans and loose shirts —the native costume of modern Indian youth—few of their classmates could have imagined the depths of the cultural abyss they had to cross to reach the campus malt shop. Journeys of this kind are too hazardous and frightening to talk about. The students do not often talk about them.

The rites of passage are treacherous. But these youths have one advantage their forefathers did not have; they are lonely but not alone.

"In the old days an Indian youth was singled out for education, as an individual, 'to divide him from his tribe,'" Blatchford said. "The Indian boarding schools divided and conquered. But we were a group. There was group thinking. I think that surprised us the most. We had a group world view."

In the years after World War II and the Korean War formal education in the white man's universities, long frowned upon by the tribal elders and skeptically ignored by the governmental educators, became a necessity. Youths who had seen the modern world in military service wished to know more about it, how it worked, where they, as Indians, would fit in. So, reluctantly, did their parents.

Educators of the Indians were now prepared to build elementary and secondary schools, in more than token numbers, for the tribal elite, and to encourage the graduates to go on to college. In the hope that the Indian youth would leave the tribal reservations at last and enter the "mainstream," the government made education the top priority in Indian affairs. The "social-cultural integration of Indians [is] a primary goal of formal education," the Assistant Commissioner of Indian Affairs, James Officer, told a university conference on "Research in Indian Education." He was echoing in the jargon of the academe what an Indian Bureau report in 1882 stated with cruder truth: the schooling of "the savages," it said, was to assure that "the children are taught to speak English, taught the manners and ways of the whites; in a word, Americanized."

The Americanization of the Indian began once more, but this time in the high schools and universities. Within ten years—from 1950 to 1960—the number of Indian high school students increased from 24,000 to 57,000. In that decade the Indian youth attending college for one year or more went up from 6,500 to 17,000.

Nowhere was the cultural trek of the young Indians to the schools more dramatic than among the Navajos of the Southwest. The "Long March" of Navajo children to the schools zoomed from 5,308 (in 1939) to 13,883 (in 1951) to 30,650 (in 1961). In a single decade, after World War II, the number of high school graduates of this tribe increased from 185 to 1,840 annually, while the number of Navajo college students went up from a mere three dozen to more than 400 yearly in the early 1960's.

University education is, in a sense, the Indian's postgraduate course in education in the ways of the white man begun in the army barracks. In the barracks the GI Indian was often a loner. He was a stranger in the midst of strangers. He had no tribal way of understanding the exotic life of the military, and the experience was socially disturbing, no matter how individually rewarding.

In the universities the Indian student is one of many. He rooms with Indian youths like himself, and he belongs to an Indian club. There are even Indian "cultural evenings" to wash off the whiteness of the antiseptic classrooms.

Still the young Indian is troubled. The college dropout rate is high. It is not his academic rating but the academic life that unnerves him. Forty percent of the Indian students who dropped out of one college came from the upper third of their high school graduating classes. In fact, "Indians with high academic aptitude drop out of college as frequently as Indians with moderate academic aptitude," reported Dr. Bruce Meador in a study of Indian college students at five Southwestern universities, prepared for the U.S. Office of Education. "More intelligent Indians drop out of school (percentage-wise) for emotional reasons than non-Indians," Dr. Meador reported.

Blatchford was more specific. The anxieties of the university students, he thought, were not due to their tribal past, or university present, so much as to their fear of the educational "no-man's land" between the two cultures.

"The feeling got around that we students were not sure about our college and tribal future. We weren't," Blatchford said. "We decided to find out whether we were in, or out, or on the borderline, of our people. So we decided to hold a meeting and invite the tribal elders. And our parents. And to ask them.

"There wasn't a room to meet in at the University of New Mexico, in Albuquerque. 'Booked up,' they said. So we met in the auditorium of the Cathedral of St. Francis, in Santa Fe. That was in 1954. That was a historic year, remember?" he added.

Under the blessed hands of Saint Francis of Assisi the powwow of the young intellectuals gathered. It was an ironic setting for the creation of the modern movement of new Indians—the Red Muslims. On the site of the old church of the conquistadores of Spain, built in 1622 by Indian slaves, where the ground was bloodied with the history of Pueblo revolts, the students met.

The governors of the Pueblos came, wearing their tunics and jeans, and bearing their thousand-year-old dignity The leaders of the Navajos and Apaches came, in business suits and sunglasses. The wizened, and sometimes wise, old men, in traditional dress, soothed by age, came together with the nervous young Indian col-

lege boys and girls, with their anthropology textbooks in their suit-
cases.

The young spoke first. And Herbert Blatchford spoke first among
the young:

"In our early childhood, we, as American Indians, have been
taught the distinction between the living and the lifeless. We have
been taught to value the spirit of man as a significant factor in human
environment. We are a deeply and uniquely religious people.

"We, as Indian students, have been indoctrinated to the importance of education many times and by multiple measures. We have
been educated to affirm one proposition: American cultural education. On the other hand, we have, under false pretenses, been encouraged to obliterate our own cultural values.

"Our problem is: How can we, as young people, help to solve
conflicts between cultures? What happens when a person graduates
from college? Where can he go to further his training before attempting to hold tribal leadership? Can we, in some small way, fill this
need?"

Let the elders tell us what they say, Blatchford said; we have
heard the professors, but they are not Indians. "Because of our
cultural heritage, we, under the guidance of our elders, have
become tolerant of all circumstances. And we have relied on the
essence of time to give us proof of all encroaching sincerity."

The elders listened to the young. And then they said: Education
is necessary. We will support you, if we can. We will send you
dancers to perform in your Kiva Club at the university, to raise
money for your scholarships.

The elders said: Come home when you are educated in the white
man's ways. Your people need to know what you know.

> My child, come this way,
> My child, come this way,
> You will take home with you a good country—
> Says the Father,
> Says the Father,
> Ate heye lo! Ate heye lo!
>
> I love my children—Yeye!
> I love my children—Yeye!

You shall grow to be a nation—Yeye!
You shall grow to be a nation—Yeye!

Harmony between the old and young was unlikely. In the meeting of tribal minds the Indians did not close the gap between the generations. But they bridged it.

Wendell Chino, the president of the National Congress of American Indians, was to say five years later: "We are realizing the emergence of young, educated Indian leadership so that the reins of tribal destinies are being transferred to the college-trained, college-educated young leaders [who are] still availing themselves of the sage advice of the older people. . . ."

It had been so from the beginning. "We owe a debt of gratitude to the youth" had been almost the first words of the keynote speech of the Choctaw leader Ben Dwight, at the founding convention of the first National Congress of American Indians in 1944. These young Indians "who have come from tribal schools, who have gone to colleges," the Choctaw had said, were responsible for that movement too.

The patriarch of that founding convention, Attocknie, the elderly longhair and religious man of the Comanche tribe, had nodded: "I am ignorant, but I have the interest of the young and educated Indians at heart. There are Indians like myself who are not educated, who are restricted, and who cannot exist under conditions that will work well with the young and educated Indians. Now, we are very proud of you, our children, that are so highly educated."

"It started with the old people," Blatchford said of the movement of new Indians. "It was never a disjointed venture. The youth, when they get together now, always meet on Indian land, always with the old tribal people. And we came from that very first meeting with the feeling that by going away to college we were not going away. We would be welcome home. So this gave us confidence. Let's start more Indian clubs in the universities, we said. We drew in kids from other colleges. The idea spread like wildfire."

These university clubs were the tribal fraternities of the collegiate Indians. Once they had set them up, the youth wished to bring the far-flung clubs together into a council—a powwow of all the young tribal intellectuals.

Enthusiastic but inexperienced, they sought the advice of Charles Minton, director of the Southwestern Association on Indian Affairs. He was a fatherly, if fitfully arbitrary, friend of the Indians, a refugee from corporate law, given to recitation of romantic poetry of the West, who had helped the youth hire their hall at St. Francis.

Minton, a white-haired iconoclast of the old school, had "gone Indian." Once a Pueblo governor had invited him to a religious ceremonial, but Minton curled his lips, "You know I am a pagan. I can't come." The old man was as enthusiastic as the young Indians about the idea and guided the formation of the Southwestern Regional Youth Conference.

Once more the Indians were to be saved from cultural oblivion by the holding of another conference. It was not exactly what the young Indians had in mind, but it was a beginning.

Conferences were held yearly. One of the largest was held at the University of New Mexico in 1960—then a gracious host to the 350 Indian students from 57 tribes. There were by then even foreign visitors: "the young African from Tanganyika" was mentioned in the conference notes, "who came to observe and take back with him a similar program for African youth."

The "sponsor," as the fatherly Minton thought of himself, was happily harassed. He described the "sponsor" as the one "who does the ground work, much of the leg work, acts as backdrop, fills in the gaps, and does what no one else has time for." He did not, however, speak at the conference. Instead, he sent lists of "suggested" topics to the would-be delegates, who were, in turn, selected, not elected, by school administrators. Nonetheless, the sponsor insisted that the Youth Conferences were "not directed, influenced, or censored. It was 'free,' " the sponsor said, " 'speech.'. . ."

"His Indians," as Minton affectionately called the youth he chaperoned with paternal concern, were beginning to chafe under his fatherly strictures.

"There is a need for a freer movement," Blatchford told the faculty advisors of the Youth Conference in the spring of 1960. Let us have "whatever sparks enthusiasm and interest; rather than [this] more formal agenda," he pleaded.

The uprising of the new Indians was about to break out of the academic reservations. It was at yet another conference—the conference on Indian affairs was "our Western cultural rite," said Professor E. Roby Leighton, of the University of Arizona—that the emerging tribal nationalism of the youth was to crystallize into direct action.

In the summer of 1960, the turning point was reached. The unwitting host to this tribal explosion was Professor Sol Tax, the editor of *Current Anthropology,* who had organized an American Indian conference at the University of Chicago. The Indian establishment had gathered. Few of the venerated tribal leaders and government officials in Indian affairs were missing. There were so many anthropologists with portable tape recorders that they convened their own conference-within-the-conference to compare tapes.

Most of the young Indians who went to Chicago did so on their own. They were not invited. They represented nobody. They thumbed their way. "I was curious [to see] what Indian youth were doing nationally," Blatchford said. "We met for the first time as a group in Chicago," Mel Thom said.

The youthful ardor that they brought to the conference was dispelled by the routine rhetoric of those they called the "Uncle Tomahawks"—the official Indian leaders. "Just out of college, we were very young. So we looked on. We saw the 'Uncle Tomahawks' fumbling around, passing resolutions, and putting headdresses on people. But as for taking a strong stand they just weren't doing it," Mel Thom recalled. His restive voice was echoed by Clyde Warrior: "It was the old song and dance to a slightly new anthropological tune." Herbert Blatchford dismissed "the whole show": "There was a lot of rigmarole about procedure and all that. We weren't interested."

The oratory of the Uncle Tomahawks droned on and the tape recorders of the anthropologists whirled on. But the youths had heard it all before. Little by little the young Indians began to voice their own opinions—at first to themselves. Hundreds of pages of conference notes, memos, committee reports, and meeting agendas poured out of the mimeograph machines. And on the backs of these sheets of "instant anthropology" the young Indians scribbled furious words of annoyance and disagreement.

In large, angry letters one youth wrote to himself: "Fellow American Indians, we the younger Indians are deeply concerned about the outcome of this conference. Within the years to come we will be directly affected by its result." His notes were passed from hand to hand. "It is agreed among ourselves that we [the youth] take a united stand," the handwritten message went on. "With due respect to our elders' learned expression and honorable deliberation . . ."

Neither the official Indians nor the university sponsors were aware of the youthful rebellion. The anthropologists were busily and happily "applying new methods of applied anthropology," as one said later. Conferees enthralled with their own eloquence did not hear the rumblings from the floor. But the conference was about to be host to the birth of the movement of Indian nationalism, the new tribalism.

The disquiet of the youth was voiced by a Navajo girl, Vivian One Feather. She said one day: "We're wondering what youth are doing at an adult meeting. Let's have a meeting of our own."

"We got together in a youth caucus," Herbert Blatchford said. "I chaired it. I told them, 'Look, you can't run and hide. You came all this way. You ought to talk about what you want.' So they talked all night! They talked for four days! I didn't get any sleep for four days! None of us did."

There were twelve youths in that "youth caucus." But these few were soon chairing many of the conference committees. So strong did this band of political warriors become that when the "Statement of Purpose" they wrote was almost tabled they talked of halting the conference by urging a "strike" of the committees they chaired.

"We had a battle. But the 'Statement of Purpose' the conference passed had mostly what we wrote," Mel Thom said.

Into the statement were written the first demands of the new Indian nationalism. "We, the majority of the Indian people of the United States of America," it began, have "the inherent right of self-government" and "the same right of sovereignty." The tribes "mean to hold the scraps and parcels [of their lands] as earnestly as any small nation or ethnic group was ever determined to hold to identity and survival," it declared.

"Our situation cannot be relieved by appropriated funds alone," it continued. "The answers we seek are not commodities to be purchased, neither are they evolved automatically through the passing of time. . . . What we ask of America is not charity, not paternalism, even when benevolent.

"The effort to place social adjustment on a money–time interval scale which has characterized Indian administration has resulted in unwanted pressure and frustration," the statement said. It reaffirmed tribal values—"a universe of things they knew, valued and loved." And it requested technical and financial assistance like "any small nation."

Word for word the incipient nationalism of the "Statement of Purpose" of the conference was identical to the scribbled thoughts of the youth caucus.

As soon as the Chicago conference ended the Indian youth were scattered to the four winds. Throughout that summer letters flew back and forth from reservation to reservation. Those who found letters inadequate tape-recorded their thoughts and air-mailed these. "Boy, the air was thick with tapes as with arrows that summer," one recalled. It was Herbert Blatchford who suggested that the young Indians gather once again, by themselves, and form their own youth movement.

Let us all gather "to maintain our unity" and talk of "possible circumstances for our destiny," Blatchford wrote in a round-robin letter. He suggested that the Inter-Tribal Ceremonial held in Gallup, New Mexico, in early August would be a symbolic and practical time for the young Indian intellectuals to powwow.

"We must use the moon as our mirror."

4

THE RED MUSLIMS

It began in a too small and stuffy room on the wrong side of the railroad tracks in the highway town of Gallup, New Mexico. On that August 10, 1960, the nondescript and dusty Indian Community Center was suffocated by the unbelievably hot, burnt morning air that seemed to evaporate in one's mouth. Ten young Indians, who were to be known as the Red Muslims, sat in a circle like a modern war council.

Whistles of the wailing freight trains drowned their words. In the streets tens of thousands of tourists and Indians milled about. They had come to see the ceremonials. Hour upon hour the ten young Indians talked—a Paiute, a Mohawk, a Ute, a Ponca, a Shoshone-Bannock, a Potawatomi, a Tuscarora, two Navajos, and a Crow. These university youths had come from diverse and distant tribes. One had written, "Of course I'll go into hock to meet with you. . . . I may be forced to travel by oxcart, but I shall be there." But, once there, seated in a circle of decision, with their angers and determinations, they were uncertain. This was not the Cathedral of St. Francis or the University of Chicago. Now their destiny was their own to decide.

"If we organize are we really trying to help our people, or are we going to seek status for ourselves?" asked Clyde Warrior.

The Mohawk girl Shirley Witt was troubled by this too: "Is there any way by which this organization can guard against political climb-

39

ing? Can we prevent its being used as a lever to gain high position?"

The university Indians talked of their desire to "find a place for themselves, *as a group,* within the Indian world. Some of the members stated that, though their training in school would not be of direct help to the Indian people, nonetheless they felt a very strong need to serve those at home. Several members added their voices to this.

"Most of all," the minutes of that meeting concluded, "the group felt that it was vital to retain the beauty of the Indian heritage."

Little by little the image of the new Indians emerged. A Winnebago girl, Mary Natani, said that they "must identify themselves as Indian and still adjust to another culture. But not leave behind what is really Indian." The new Indians would be "hybrids," Blatchford said, and would create a synthesis of the two cultures in their Indianness.

On that day the idea of a new tribalism—red nationalism—began to take form. (One girl, at the meeting, admitted that she had never been to a "regular powwow.") The form was, however, still uncertain; the leaders were yet unchosen; and the organization was nonexistent.

It was the Paiute Mel Thom who proposed the organizational principles of the new Youth Council. He thought that "political climbing" was a concept of the white man that was inherent in the structure and goals of his society. It was not tribal nor Indian. Let us organize "in the Indian way" on the "high principles derived from the values and beliefs of our ancestors," he said. "[And let us] consider rules based on Indian thinking as being sufficient."

Thom later elaborated on these beliefs: "The movement grew in the Indian way. We had decided what we needed was a movement. Not an organization, but a movement. Organizations rearrange history. Movements make history. That's what we decided to do. That's what we did.

"Long ago the Indians knew how to use direct action. You might say that was the traditional way that Indians got things done," Thom went on. "We were concerned with direct action: Indians moving out and doing something. The younger Indians got together in the Youth Council because they didn't feel that the older leadership was aggressive enough. And we felt that Indian affairs were so bad that it was time to raise some hell.

"But it had to be done in the Indian way," he added.

In the bold and innocent conceit of youth the ten young Indians proclaimed themselves to be the National Indian Youth Council. They elected one another the officers—all ten of them. They were its entire membership. Within a few years they were to number thousands. But at that moment they were all chiefs.

The movement needed a leader. Mel Thom, who had been president of the Southwestern Youth Conferences, was elected to the council presidency.

"Little Bear" some have nicknamed him, and "Smokey, the Bear." There were friends—he thought they were friends—who named him "Mao Tse Thom." Physically he fits these nicknames. He is sturdy, short, and stocky. He has a tenacity and hard wit that are discernible in his intense dark eyes. There is something rocklike and unrelenting about him.

He "was born and raised" on the Walker River Reservation in Nevada. The land is a rocky wasteland, a desolate, dismal region of thorny undergrowth and scrawny trees. The barren land is inhabited by ghost towns and geological prehistory and by his Paiute people. Growing up on the desert, he had eaten "everything from jackrabbits to potatoes to chow mein." He had worked at everything from "cowpuncher to construction work through swampland and deserts to assistant resident engineer for the Federal Aviation Agency."

"Just a reservation Indian," Thom said of himself. He had left a "successful career"—he was a graduate civil engineer—to return to his reservation and become tribal chairman of his Paiute people, without pay.

"When you say, 'Did I go back to the reservation?' you are being a little naïve," Thom said. "Does that mean to physically go back and work? This is hardly the case. Our Indian community exists at every level of society—in the universities, in the cities, on the reservations, in the government. It doesn't matter where Indians are any more. They remain Indians. They are, in fact, becoming more consciously Indian. They are very much part of the larger Indian community. So we're finding a new type of young Indian. He fits into this total community.

"The young Indians travel around a lot more. And there's an awareness coming among these young Indians, the more they get around, the more they travel, the more they see and understand how the white society and government work," Thom said.

"In the country today we are undergoing some kind of revolution. The young people in the whole country are not satisfied. Being an Indian and being young means you are twice as dissatisfied. You can hold a people down just so long. Then, pretty soon, they are going to kick back. And that's what's happening with some of the Indian tribes. It has already happened with the young Indians."

Young Thom, as the leader of the Youth Council, and as tribal chairman, combines within himself the new and old tribalism. He was one of its political architects.

"The Indians are the only tribal people, really tribal people, in this country, who don't have the same system, the same values as urban America," Thom said. "And even though what exists in the Indian world is inconsistent with urban America, we've got to recognize this different way of life. If we continue to look at the Indian as a 'problem' that can be worked out by making him look like any other American, well, it wouldn't work.

"The Indian way, or what you might call Indian culture, is the way the Indian people live today. The government and the people of this country seem to feel that the Indian heritage, or Indian culture, is the way we look, or dance, or sing. But Indian culture is the way people live today.

"And there is a way! The young, educated Indian people know this way, this tribal way, and they like it."

Generations ago, in the last gasp of the "Indian revivalists," it was the Paiute prophet Wovoka whose religious visions of the rebirth of the old tribalism inspired the Ghost Dances. In the fading years of the nineteenth century his prophecy swept the defeated reservations like a prairie fire. Wovoka was a tribal ancestor of young Thom's on the Walker River Reservation. The old prophet's grave, where he was buried under his Christian name of Jack Wilson, lay not too far from the office of the new tribal chairman.

In his belief in a new tribalism, Mel Thom is heir to tradition. The Paiutes of Walker River were one of the last tribes to lay down their arms. It was not until 1911 that the final "battle" of the old Indian Wars had been fought on the alkali flats of the Nevada desert.

It was known in history books as the "Paiute Outbreak," but the tribe itself called it "The Massacre of the Black Desert."

"My father knew two children who were caught by the U.S. Army in that massacre. They died. They died of heartbreak," Thom said. Like the tribal memory of Wovoka, these inheritances were in young Mel Thom's thoughts and in his bones.

He even spoke of modern "Indian Wars." His voice had that defiant, unflinching, but calm tone of a modern warrior: "Let us take a look around our great country and see what the red man of today is fighting," Thom said. "There is definitely a battle going on, no question about that. This is not a fictitious 'nothing fight' like that on TV and in the movies. This is a different kind of war—a cold war, one might say. Fortunately, for someone, this is not a hot war; otherwise the Indians might not have so many friends and experts.

"The opposition to Indians is a monstrosity which cannot be beaten by any single action, unless we as Indian people could literally rise up, in unison, and take what is ours by force. We see, however, that our Indian is small, confused, and regretfully does not include all our Indian people. We know the odds are against us, but we also realize that we are fighting for the lives of future Indian generations.

"The weakest link in the Indian's defense is his lack of understanding of this modern-type war. Indians have not been able to use political action, propaganda, and power as well as their opponents. Enemy forces have successfully scattered the Indian people and got them divided against themselves. The enemy has made notable gains; they deployed their forces well. But there is increased activity over on the Indian side. There is disagreement, laughing, singing, outbursts of anger, and occasionally some planning. Given some time, it looks like an effort can be put forth. If we can hold our ranks together, our chances of gaining in our modern campaign are good. There is growing hope.

"We are convinced, more than ever, that this is a real war. . . . No people in this world ever has been exterminated without putting up a last resistance," Thom said. "The Indians are gathering."

Like a familial father the Commissioner of Indian Affairs, Robert Bennett, reluctantly acknowledged this youthful turbulence. He was tolerant of it: "The attitude of the young Indians might, to some extent, be equated to the attitude of a lot of young people in the United States, as manifested by their strikes at universities, their burning of draft cards, their resistance to Vietnam. A lot of us like to indulge in this sort of thing once in a while."

Yet the Commissioner was cautionary. His paternal patience went just so far: "I hope the young people are not misguided in this. We still have reality to face. And the realities that the Indian people have to face require that they have a good education so that they can make a proper adaptation." His official attitude was one of patience—up to a point.

The revivals of old tribalism had lost their way in the labyrinths of nostalgia. Religious leaders of the past had looked to the past. When the reservation life offered no promise for the future and the present was empty and stagnant, it was inevitable that tribalism meant a desperate attempt to hold on to a disappearing heritage. Nostalgia was not a luxury. It was a necessity of nothingness and defeat.

But the young university Indians foresee a future. They do not wish to preserve the past as a museum culture, but wish to recreate their Indian way of life in a modernized twentieth-century version. "They are creating this culture," said Vine Deloria, Jr. These youths were born into an era of resurgent nationalism among dark-skinned people the world over. Having conquered their awe of the technology of Western civilization, the young wish to master it, but not be mastered by it.

The new Indians seek "proper adaptation." But to them it means adaptation of the non-Indian society to their modern Indianness. It means rejection of the melting pot. It means, most of all, rejection of assimilation by the consuming maw of mass urban society. And it means creation of what Mel Thom named "the Greater Indian America."

It was prophesied by Herbert Blatchford, the young Navajo who helped found the Youth Council, that the time of the new Indian had come:

Perhaps it is a remnant of the "Warrior Society" whose job it was to be aware of all threats to the tribal group. Well then, rise up—make haste—our people need us.

It was prophesied by young Richard McKenzie, the Sioux who led the "Raid on Alcatraz" to claim the abandoned prison as a site for a University of the American Indian. Sitting in the board room of the San Francisco Indian Center, the young man said:

Kneel-Ins, Sit-Ins, Sleep-Ins, Eat-Ins, Pray-Ins like the Negroes do wouldn't help us. We would have to occupy the government buildings before things would change.

It was prophesied by Guy Okakok, the Paitot leader of the Alaska Eskimos at the polar village of Point Barrow, who said almost in a whisper:

Eskimos still want to be peaceful and like and trust everybody, but the time has come when they must take a stand.

It was prophesied by the old leader of the Blackfeet of Montana, Walter Wetzel, an honored former president of the National Congress of American Indians:

We Indians have been struggling unsuccessfully with the problems of maintaining home and family and Indian ownership of the land. *We must strike*. We must have a new policy.

It was prophesied by the young leader of the Tuscaroras of New York State who turned back the bulldozers of Robert Moses when a dam was planned on Iroquois land. Wallace "Mad Bear" Anderson was thought by many to be a modern prophet, and his prophecies were revolutionary:

Our people were murdered in this country. And they are still being murdered. They used germ warfare against us, when they drove us into Kansas. My people crossed the rivers and waited. They promised us land, homes, tools. Wagons came filled with blankets and clothes. They were infected with smallpox. My people took them and died and they died and died. We do not want to be absorbed by a sick society. There is an Indian nationalist movement in the country. I am one of the founders. We are not going to pull any punches from here on in.

It was prophesied by Robert Thomas, the Cherokee anthropologist, who wrote in *Indian Voices*:

The Indian picture isn't any blacker than it always was. It is just that American Indians are trying to do something about their problems and injustices. They are speaking out more and making their wish known. They aren't laying quiet and doing nothing any more. Maybe a new day is dawning for the Indian.

It was prophesied by Robert Burnette, the leader of the American Indian Civil Rights Council and former director of the Indians' Congress. The fiery Sioux, of whom it has been said, "If he had been a war chief one hundred years ago the white man would have never crossed the Mississippi," declared:

There is a new mood. In the last few years there has been an upsurge of young Indians. And the old Indians are joining them. And they will drive the corrupt out of their lands.

It was prophesied by the Ojibwa Francis Le Quier, the chairman of the Great Council Fire, who in 1963 posted this proclamation on reservations throughout the country:

To the Chiefs and Spiritual Leaders of the Indians of the North and South American Continents: . . . This is the day when the Great Spirit calls to all men. This is the day all our Great Chiefs spoke of. This is the day when all Indian prophecies will be fulfilled. This is the day when all the tribes shall come together and be one nation. This is the day when a new race of men shall be raised up by the power of the Great Spirit. This is the day of the Great Justice.

You shall hear the voice of the Owl, the Fox, the Bear, the Coyote and the Eagle.

The young Chickasaw Kenneth Kale wrote:

> We know all about
> Our redskinned counterpart
> Of Martin, Gregory, and Stokely
> Rolled into one—
> Like an angry "Red Muslim"
> With work to be done. . . .
>
> I've often wondered why it is said
> That the Indian Spirit is broken and dead
> When in their midst like a grizzly bear
> Is the sleeping redskinned giant
> Now on the prowl. . . .

The voice of the new Indian was heard in the land. What he had to say was a choral chant of tribal resurgence that was articulated in the themes and words of modern man. Yet what he had to say was old.

In the beginning there had been an educational explosion. Now the young Indians were lighting the fuse of a political explosion. "We in the National Indian Youth Council were looking for a target area. We were looking for a target area for direct action," Mel Thom said.

On the wild rivers of the State of Washington the new Indians found their target.

5

THE FISH-IN WITHIN THE FISH

In childhood the fishing began. What else was the nursery of a young fisherman?

The Makahs had a lullaby:

My little son,
You will put a whale harpoon,
*   and a spear,*
*   for seals in your canoe,*
Not knowing how to use them yet.

A young girl of the Yakimas, Irene Goudy, remembered when her family had "followed the salmon":

"Long ago my mom used to smoke, salt, and dry fish. Fish would be all over. The aroma always made me hungry. Dad built a smoke-house near our shack. Mom built a fire in it, and let the little house get smoky. Then she put slices of the fish on the racks in there. After the fish had been in the smokehouse for two weeks or so, and was thoroughly smoked and dry, it was ready to be stored away in baskets for the winter. Fish were salted raw as soon as they were caught and cleaned. When the barrel was filled, it was then sealed and shut and not opened until winter.

"I remember walking along the trails of Celilo Falls when the fresh aroma of fish filled the air."

That was "long ago," the teen-age girl remembered, maybe ten years ago, when she was young. It was changed now. The memories of her childhood were gone.

"Over ten years ago, a dam was built in The Dalles, Oregon. Before this dam was constructed, ten miles upriver was Celilo Falls. The Yakimas and Indians of many tribes went there to live, stock up on fish, and earn a living.

"Today, fish are getting scarce. The Indians are rapidly losing all their fishing rights. The Dalles Dam forced us to abandon our homes at Celilo Falls. Even after the dam was built, the Indians continued to fish in various spots along the Columbia River, but the white man became hostile.

"The Indians were thrown in jail, and fined, for fishing. It should have been the other way around. Indians should put white men on reservations and give them only certain privileges."

Up the Pacific Coast the Tlingit sang a mourning song:

The nation's drum has fallen down,
My Mother—
Play the drum so it is heard again,
My Mother.

The Yakima girl said: "But, as fate has it, the Indians are losing their own ways of life, and much that they love. Despite the Indians' great loss of our fishing rights we are still able to go up into the mountains. The berries still grow and ripen. No one, as yet, has taken them away."

The Tlingit sang:

My own mind is very hard to me.
It is just as if
I were carrying my mind around.

On the white waters of the rivers of the Northwest, where the salmon leaped upriver on their way to the spawning grounds, the boats of the fishermen once more set out. The waters were unfriendly that cold day in March. But it was not the onrushing waters, burgeoning on the banks with the spring thaw of the snows of Mt. Rainier, that threatened the fishermen. The warrants and the guns of the game wardens and state police, who had come to halt the fishing of the Indians, threatened them much more.

The Fish-Ins had begun. . . .

Hundreds of Indians stood on the banks of the river, watching the fishermen row out. The winds of Puget Sound tore at them. On the Quillayute River the Indians were uneasy. The tribe was small. It had never done anything this bold; for fishing off the reservation, without licenses, was an act of civil disobedience to the game laws, and to the State Supreme Court decisions that confined net fishing by Indians to their reservations. And the wardens were white with wrath.

The Indians were not fearful. But they were troubled. One who shared their apprehension was Mel Thom, then president of the National Indian Youth Council, which had organized the Fish-In as their first direct action.

"In the beginning the Indians just watched," Thom said. "The riverbanks were crowded. It was tense. The tone of the crowd was rather tense. You could feel the hostility build up against the game wardens. The authorities, the people with the law, were really mad at us for being there.

"We knew the game wardens would make arrests. They did. This was not going to be a cowboys-and-Indians story.

"And then a funny thing happened. The Indians began to enjoy it. They were happy to see some direct action. Then the tenseness broke. You would see kids running back and forth on the riverbanks and laughing.

"And some of the Indians took out their cameras and began taking pictures of the game wardens. Most times you see white people taking pictures of Indians, but this time it was Indians taking pictures of *mad* white people. That made them madder. It was our turn.

"You could feel there was a squaring off," Thom said; it was "the first time in recent history that we were publicly demonstrating what we privately felt."

And before it had ended the hundreds of Indians had swelled to thousands. There were Fish-Ins on half a dozen rivers. There were dozens of arrests, war dances on the steps of the capitol rotunda, an Indian protest meeting of several thousand at the state capitol. There were Treaty Treks on the streets of the cities and Canoe Treks, of sixty miles, through Puget Sound. There was a gathering of more than one thousand Indians from fifty-six tribes throughout the country who came to join their brothers.

Seminoles of Florida, Winnebagos of Nebraska, Navajos of New Mexico, Blackfeet of Montana, Potawatomis of Michigan, Iroquois of New York, Shoshone of Wyoming, Sioux of the Dakotas, Kiowas and Poncas of Oklahoma, Nez Percés and Coeur d'Alenes of Idaho. . . .

"We were ending the government's divide-and-rule system among Indians," said Mel Thom.

"It was the first full-scale intertribal *action* since the Indians defeated General Custer on the Little Big Horn," said Herbert Blatchford, then executive secretary of the Youth Council.

The Quillayute River and Puyallup River and Yakima River and Nisqually River and Columbia River and Green River became political battlefields. And there was fighting on the rivers. Women and children stood on the riverbanks and threw sticks and rocks at the state police and game wardens who came to arrest their men. The men in the boats fought back with their fists. Jails became familiar to the Indian fishermen. There were several arrested for the Fish-In on the Quillayute. Later, more were arrested on the Puyallup. Half a dozen were arrested on the Nisqually; four more on the Green. And these jailed fishermen joined the more than forty Indians arrested in the previous eighteen months.

"I think the State of Washington will fill the jails with Indians. But the Indians have no choice," said Bruce Wilkie, one of the young leaders of the Fish-Ins.

Mel Thom quietly said: "Laws or not laws, if people are downtrodden, if your treaty rights are violated, if there's police brutality, and these are things you feel and know, then, regardless of what the penalty is, any group will defy the law to correct a wrong. All I know is that when there is a problem the only thing that takes care of it is direct action!"

On the coastal rivers and along Puget Sound up to 75 percent of the Indians earned much of their livelihood, and obtained much of their food, by fishing. It was estimated that 25 percent of the income of the Yakimas and the Columbia River tribes depended on their fish catches. Without fish their families would not eat.

One of the Nisqually who was jailed, Don McCloud, said he pulled in about $20 a day fishing when "the fish were running." But much of the year his family of nine children was on relief. Let the state feed them if they jailed him, he said angrily: "They can eat what the governor told them to eat—sympathy."

The temper of the Indians was voiced by another of the Nisqually tribe, Alvin James Bridges, who had been arrested twice. He had failed to appear in court, and in response to a court order "to show cause" why he should not be jailed for contempt he blurted forth the anger his tribesmen felt:

"I went to jail last year to test the state's jurisdiction and was treated by the Supreme Court of Washington State as an animal with no rights whatsoever, e.g., 'Menagerie Theory'—which in essence means that we (like the deer and bear) reserved within the treaty the rights to go to the river for a drink of water, and not to fish.

"New devices are dreamed up to place us in jail, further impoverishing and humiliating our position. Our boats have been confiscated, supposedly for evidence. Yet they never appear in court. The State of Washington is attempting to deprive us of our fishing rights, using illegal chicanery, political-minded judges and the militant Nazi-like Game and Fisheries Departments as weapons against us.

"For these reasons I feel compelled to avoid the courts who are avoiding justice. . . . If I were ignorant of my rights, perhaps I would not feel so bitter toward the judges, who I know are not ignorant of my rights."

More than a dozen Yakimas were then arrested on the Columbia River. And the Yakimas took up arms.

The conservative Yakimas had refused to join the Fish-Ins. Located in the fertile bend of the Columbia and Yakima rivers, on the orchard lands of Washington's famous "fruitbowl," their huge reservation is one of the richest in the state. For years they fished from the banks of the Horse Heaven Hills across river from the Hanford Project of the Atomic Energy Commission. The Yakimas seemed unconcerned —at first. Besides, the U.S. Government, desirous of keeping the tribe amiable in view of their precarious location, had offered them $15 million in payment for the destruction of their ancient fishing sites by the construction of the Dalles Dam on the Columbia.

So the tribal leaders counseled moderation. When the jailings began, the Yakimas felt betrayed. They took up arms. Young men of the tribe put on their discarded Marine Corps and Army uniforms and shouldered their old M-1 rifles. The armed Yakimas patrolled the banks of the rivers, guarding the tribal fishermen. There were guns along the rivers for the first time since the Yakima Wars, one hundred years before. Rifles in hand the Yakimas cast their nets.

The upheaval wrought by the first tribal direct action of the ten young university Indians who had met that sultry day a few years ago surprised even them. It was they who planned, launched, organized, and guided the Fish-Ins. The response of the tribes had astounded the youth, and everyone else.

It had all begun one day in February of 1964. The tribal council of the Makahs had decided that the small and scattered tribes of Washington State could never win their fishing rights until they got together.

"As one, we can win," the Makahs said. The elders of the tribe sent word to the university boys and girls of the Youth Council to come. Let us organize the tribes everywhere in the state, they said, and do something together that the white men will not forget. The Red Muslims among the younger members were eager for direct action, any action. "Just a little field study of some of that sociology we had learned in college," one of them said.

Urgent messages were sent to fifty tribes to come to a council meeting. More than forty came. There, in that meeting of tribal elders and young university Indians, the Fish-Ins were planned. It was the first time in the history of the tribes that so many had come together for a modern political battle.

And the youths were asked to lead it. In proper academic jargon the university youths named the tribal direct action the "Washington State Project." Mel Thom said of it:

"Long, too long, the State of Washington had been denying the Indians their treaty fishing rights and the Indians were never able to do much about it. Whenever the Indians got into federal court they won, but in the local courts they never took the federal treaties and laws into consideration. It looked hopeless. And the Bureau of Indian Affairs and the Department of Justice were very relaxed; they would not protect the Indians.

"Someone had to do something about it. And the Youth Council decided to go in with the Northwest Indians and stage the first tribal direct action in modern history."

It was an unprecedented task. The more so because of the lethargy and disarray that plagued the tribal spirit and structure of the scattered and disunited thirty thousand Indians in the state. Remnants of the tribes in the Pacific Northwest were so dissipated and divided that some were tribal skeletons. The government had recognized twenty-six tribes in the state, though the Indians spoke of dozens of scattered bands. A few had some acreage, but there were others who owned nothing more than a tribal anthill: the Puyallups' reservation had thirty-three acres of tribal-owned land; the Nisquallys had two acres; the Snohomish had sixteen acres; the Suquamish had forty-one, while the Muckleshoot tribes of three hundred members shared a tribal-owned reservation of one-quarter of an acre. The tribes were pathetic. Politically the scraggly bands of Indians, on a pittance of land, were incapable of resisting the powers of the state. If the last vestiges of their heritage, their fishing rights, were to be denied them, they seemed too weak and powerless to do anything.

"In the beginning tribal support was a little difficult to get" was the laconic understatement of Mel Thom. "Being a conservative people, as they are, the tribal leaders had never had the opportunity to be aggressive. For long they had been dominated and run by the government. So action, direct action, was something they were not sure about. These tribes had never used direct action.

"Was it 'the Indian way'? What would happen to them if they protested! Would all their rights be taken away?

"The Indian had been stereotyped to act in certain ways; he was not supposed to take direct action, or to picket, or to demonstrate. People were curious to see if the Indians could do these things. So were the Indians!"

Could a handful of tribal Indians undo the stereotype of the communications industry and the image machinery of a society? Could these Indians who "had been stereotyped to act in a certain way" break free of their image of themselves?

"If we were going to make any headway the stereotyped image had to be done away with," Mel Thom said, "so we decided to do something dynamic and different. We decided on the Fish-Ins.

"Up there fishing was part of tribal life. If we didn't do something the tribes would be destroyed. They knew it. We knew the odds were against us. We were small in number. And we had to make every effort count. The tactic best used by the Indians was to hit strategically. We decided to take direct action. We decided to show this country, and ourselves, that the Indians had guts. Not all the tribes went along with this thinking. But the majority did."

It was a century-old struggle. The Treaty of Medicine Creek, signed in 1854 by the United States and the Indians, had deprived the tribes of Washington of most of their lands. But it had guaranteed their "right" to fish in the rivers, in the "usual and accustomed grounds." In the coastal regions of Puget Sound the tribes had signed some ten treaties, besides that of Medicine Creek, giving up eleven million acres of land. Here too they had been left with little more than the "right" to fish.

"This right of the Indians was purchased by them very dearly, through giving up two-thirds of the State of Washington," said Senator Magnuson.

Janet McCloud, of the Tulalip Tribe, one of the Fish-In leaders, quipped: "They promised us that we could fish—'Long as the mountain stands, the grass grows green, and the sun shines,'" but now the State of Washington had decreed that the steelhead trout "is a white man's fish." She said, "They must think that the steelhead swam over behind the *Mayflower*."

Fishermen of the tribes had the "right" to fish, yet they had nowhere legally to cast their nets, so little had been left them of their reservations. It was disingenuous of the State of Washington, the Indians said, to jail them for fishing off their reservations when most of their tribal lands had been taken from them, and they had nowhere else to fish. The "usual and accustomed grounds" were beyond the reach of their nets.

When in the old days, in the old ways, they had fished with hand-hewn spears, and crude-twined nets, and long poles, no one had complained. But, of course, their catch had been small. And the picturesque tribesmen along the rivers were a tourist attraction. Using the modern method of gill netting the tribal fishermen had increased their haul—so much so that they had become commercial fishermen and were threatening to make a living by fishing. In recent years the Indians had taken up to 30 percent of the fish caught on the rivers. The Yakimas alone netted 15.4 percent of the catch on the Upper Columbia. It was no longer picturesque; it was profitable.

There was an uproar of protest by non-Indians. Especially by the commercial fishing companies.

Judicially, 109 years after it had been signed, the Supreme Court of Washington State decided to take a look at the Treaty of Medicine Creek. And, in effect, it nullified the treaty. "None of the signatories of the original treaty contemplated fishing with a 600 foot nylon gill net, which could prevent the escapement of any fish for spawning purposes," the court decreed, in December, 1963. It was that decision that led to the decision of the tribes, three months later, to begin the Fish-Ins.

Legally, "the treaty must be broken. That's what happens when progress pushes forward," declared Thor Tollefson, the director of the State Fisheries. He was merely obeying the law by breaking the treaty, he said.

Ever since the treaty had been signed, the State of Washington had bit by bit been denying the fishing "rights" of the Indians. The Quinault Tribe, back in 1929, had been barred from fishing at their "usual grounds" at Peacock Split, on the Columbia, so that the state could lease the fishing rights, for $36,000 a year, to the Baker's Bay Fishing Company.

The sun was no longer shining upon the Indians' treaty rights, and the grass was no longer green.

"We were dying too," a Fish-In leader said.

Conservation of fish eggs was the justification given by the Supreme Court for its decision. The trout and salmon, devotedly swimming upriver during the spawning season, had to be protected from the nylon nets of the tribal fishermen.

"It wasn't the Indians who killed off the buffalo" was the reply of the Fish-In leaders. "The Indians do have conservation laws. It should be pointed out that tribal governments support only those fishermen who follow tribal-imposed conservation methods [to] preserve the salmon runs."

In any event, much of the conservation outcry was a smoke screen, the Youth Council said, to protect not the fish eggs, but the commercial fishing interests.

"Salmon runs must survive Japanese, Russian, Alaskan, and Canadian fishermen before they reach our Northwestern streams and rivers. Upon entering Washington water, the salmon must pass through flotillas of commercial fisheries and sportsmen. At the end of the line are the Indians," the Fish-In leaders said. "We will stand with the tribes on the riverbanks."

"Justice," declared the Youth Council, "[must] no longer be prostituted to the growing demands of non-Indians fishing and commercial interests upon fishery resources."

The young Indians did more than stand by the side of the rivers. Leading the tribesmen, by the hundreds, by the thousands, they went on a pilgrimage to see the Governor in Olympia. Not to march or to demonstrate or to picket, but to dance.

In the headdress of the whale, and the wolf, the Makahs stomped on the steps of the state capitol. The Makahs did a war dance. And, incongruously, the tom-tom resounded in the marble rotunda. And thousands came, how many only the newspapers guessed. It was the occasion for a feast. Yet, to smoke the salmon and roast the venison and cook the hot dogs from the supermarket on the cold granite steps would have been unseemly. So they danced for hours.

Instead of a feast of peace, there were speeches of protest. Robert Satiacum, Bruce Wilkie, Mel Thom—the Fish-In leaders—talked of the "Proclamation of Protest" that they had brought to the Governor. In it they said the State of Washington had "unconstitutionally assumed jurisdiction over Indian tribes and lands . . . without prior consent of the tribes involved." That, they said, was the source of most of the conflict. That, they said, had violated their treaty rights. And there was a speech by the Hollywood Indian Marlon Brando, who had cast his net on the rivers, lumberjacketed, waiting for jail. Brando too spoke of the treaties that the government had signed:

"Not one of them has been kept. In every case money has been the ruling factor in the dispute with the Indian, and every time money has won out. These treaties were made in perpetuity. For 'as long as the grass grows and the rivers run.' The Indian wants to keep what he has. It is only a handful of dust and a trickle of a stream. But it is his."

And the dancing went on. Until, at last, the word came that the Governor would talk to the Indians.

Donning an ornate war bonnet for the news photographers, the then

Governor Albert Rossellini met with the Fish-In leaders. He listened carefully, declared his sympathy, and shook his head. He offered to form a commission that would study the clash between the tribal fishermen and the defenders of the fish eggs, that would talk to him— at a later date. He then turned down the plea that the state relent:

"We cannot, in the face of all these existing hazards, add or condone a new one in the form of uncontrolled or unregulated fishery by the Indians, at such times and at such places, as they, and they alone, may choose."

The Indians took their tom-tom, and the headdresses, and their "Proclamation of Protest," and went home.

Incoming Governor Daniel J. Evans, who upset Rossellini in the next election (he did not get the Indian vote), was to reiterate this position: "The law must be enforced."

The State of Washington, though shaken, was unmoved. Under the law of the Congress, known as Public Law 280, said the officials, they had the right to decide what fishing "rights" the tribes did, or did not, have. Nor did they have to ask the tribes. Indeed, Public Law 280 had given any state that wished it the right to assume control of law and order, jurisdiction on any Indian reservation—without prior consent of the Indians. Under the campaign to end federal services during the Eisenhower Administration, what some called the "Indian States' Right Bill" had become the source of bitter battles.

"Congress had defined the goal as 'termination' of the reservation system," observed the *Daily Olympian* of Puget Sound, but the "Indians have called it 'Cultural homicide.'" It was a "life and death" conflict, Bruce Wilkie said; for the "survival of the tribes" was at stake, on the rivers.

The Fish-Ins were in pursuit of more than fish. The Reverend John J. Yaryan, Canon of Grace Cathedral of San Francisco, one of those arrested for fishing-in alongside the Indians, sensed this deeper purpose when he declared: "These Indians want to remain twentieth-century Muckleshoots, Puyallups, and Nisquallys, and not become twentieth-century Anglo-Saxons."

"Living in the suburbs, in tract houses, is not attractive to them," the Reverend Yaryan said. "They want to live by their streams."

Thom was explicit: "Our whole interest was to build communities,

Indian communities. The Youth Council is dedicated to modernizing and preserving tribal society. Not only for today, but for the future. Because, you know, the basic government policy of doing away with Indians, as Indians, is not working, never has worked, and it will never work.

"Some of the tribes who opposed us have now begun direct action on their own. I hear that the year after the Fish-In the game wardens rowed their boats out to where some old fishermen were netting, to stop them, and there was a fist fight, right on the river. Just some old Indian fishermen . . .

"The Indian never fought back before. He just folded his arms and went away angry. In the past he was defeated before the fight began. That's changed. We changed that. Little tribes you hardly ever heard of are still fighting by themselves. They just stay in there and keep fighting."

Along the waters of Puget Sound the Indian fishermen banded together in the Survival of American Indians Association. Through this group they hired lawyers, notably Jack Tanner of the Northwest Area of the NAACP, to defend the fishermen who had been arrested on the rivers. In the meetings of the Survival Association they planned their own direct action, community support, and the sharing of boats and gear.

It was these fishermen who should be honored, said Hank Adams, chairman of the Washington State Project of the Youth Council. Talking before a meeting of the fishermen on the Nisqually Reservation he called the Survival Association's fight "a chronicle of courage."

"You have stood alone for the most part. You have stood alone against the most formidable odds facing Indian people anywhere today. And you have had the opposition of other Indian people," Adams said. "There are those who say that your demonstrations and direct action are 'wrong.' There are those who say you are nothing but a group of rebels and renegades.

"On the contrary. It is wrong to surrender our rights in silence," the Youth Council leader said. "It is true that you are rebels and renegades, but because you must be. You are rebels with a cause and renegades only because you are right."

The youth spoke of reliving the "proud heritage" of their warrior ancestors in modern life. "Some say that Indians should not demonstrate or engage in direct action, 'because Indian people are a proud people.' We are not born with pride," Adams said. "We cannot cite pride and be content to relinquish our rights and witness the loss of our lands. We cannot declare our dignity while prostituting ourselves to the politics and power that would leave ourselves nothing.

"We are fortunate to have received such proud heritage from our fathers, but what shall we pass on to our children?"

Were the youth challenging the elders? It was something new in tribal life. Yet, at the same time, it was something old, rooted in older ways. It recalled the days when the young did lead the tribes in battle with the world outside. Heirs to a tradition, the university students of the Youth Council were building their image of twentieth-century tribalism on the inherited ways of the old tribalism.

"I look upon these young people as a new warrior society," said an old tribal chairman.

He leaned back in his swivel chair, in his modernistic, air-conditioned office, built with government funds. He mused: "We, publicly, don't acknowledge their existence. If we did, our government liaison and finances would suffer legal thrombosis. The government, you know, holds the purse strings on all our money. Our money! So don't say my name loudly. But it's a joy to see these kids raise hell." He smiled.

Father and son: to the tribes this was more than an individual matter. It was communal. It was tribal. And that meant it had a built-in influence in their communities and was a prefabricated part of a political family. Whether covertly or openly, the elders recognized the young Indians as an important part of tribal life.

It was because of this that a handful of university Indians, from diverse tribes and colleges throughout the country, could become leaders of the Fish-Ins. The young Indians knew this tribal strength. For they had fought with the elders of the tribes many times, arguing over their newer, bolder approach to the whites, but they did so from within the security of the tribes. In spite of these disputes, Bernadine Eschief, a Shoshone-Bannock girl and a Youth Council leader, said, "We should nevertheless heed the wisdom and experience of the elders." The Mohawk student Shirley Witt, who like her youthful colleagues had come to be part of the Fish-Ins, agreed: "We should listen and respect and honor the experience and advice of our elders." So too Clyde Warrior, the stormy petrel of the new Indians, while urging bold, outspoken leadership, had said, "It should be done with great deference to the elders."

It was uniquely Indian: the respect for the elders by the youth; the recognition of the youth by the elders. And it was what enabled the once politically apathetic tribes of the State of Washington to influence the federal government in defending their treaty rights and their fishermen.

The Fish-In had caught, to the surprise of everyone, most of all the Indians, the biggest fish of all.

Nearly two and a half years after the fishermen cast their nets upon the waters the Department of Justice, in Washington, D.C., declared it was ready to uphold "the solemn obligations of the government" in the defense of the fishing "rights" of the tribes of the Northwest. The federal government appeared before the Supreme Court of Washington State "in behalf of a tribe which had been enjoined from exercising its treaty fishing rights." In the long memories of the tribal elders there were no memories of such a thing. For the government to defend the tribes' rights in a treaty made with the government was unprecedented.

Yet Edwin L. Weisl, Jr., the Assistant Attorney General of the United States, had written to the National Indian Youth Council:

The Department of Justice is determined to defend the treaty rights of the Indian tribes, since federal treaties are solemn obligations of the government, whether they are with foreign nations, or Indian tribes. Thus, in the case of Indian fishing, it is our policy to defend, on request, individual Indians, who fish in accordance with the treaty and tribal regulations, in the event they are charged, by a state, with violation of its fish and game laws.

We plan to use other legal avenues to insure that the various tribes are able to pursue their treaty fishing free from outside interference.

Hank Adams welcomed the Justice Department's legal intervention. The "displaced Assiniboin-Sioux," as he called himself, who had grown up on the Quinault reservation, requested more than legal aid, however. He requested "technical assistance and fishery management

services to the tribes." And funds for tribal fish-conservation programs, for "scientific information and data of [fishery] resources," for
tribal development of "commercial and sports fishing," and a federal
appropriation of $100,000 for these programs.

Such a fishery program, with federal aid, would put the tribes on a
firm economic footing, Adams said. He envisioned the employing of
"qualified Indian personnel, from fisheries biologists to regulatory
enforcement officers." The educated youth of the tribes could fill these
jobs, the "displaced" youth said.

"We are dismayed to learn that almost twice the $100,000 we were
seeking for the tribes . . . was being made available by the Federal
Bureau of Commercial Fisheries to non-Indian commercial fishing
and industrial interests," Adams said. "The only difference is that the
Indian people of that area are extremely impoverished, and the non-
Indian interests are economically well-established."

One of the obstacles that the Indians faced in obtaining their
fishery programs, said the Fish-In leader, was that "officials invoke
the priority needs of the Vietnam war."

Ruefully the youth replied: "We were surprised to learn that the
Civic Action Program in Vietnam is assisting the Vietnamese in a
fisheries development program that dwarfs the needs of American
Indians." He did not begrudge the fishermen of Saigon this aid. But,
he commented, with as much awe as irony, "While the State of Washington was confiscating hundreds of fishing nets and scores of boats
and motors of the Indians, the United States was supplying nearly
10,000 outboard motors, 50,000 sets of fishing gear, 27,000,000
fingerlings for stocking purposes, and building 16 fishing piers for the
Vietnamese."

The Indians were patient people, Hank Adams said; but he thought,
as the first Americans, they might have a higher priority than the
Vietnamese.

"Up until now we've always been on the defensive, but now we've
reached a point where it's life or death for the Indian culture, and
we've decided to take the offensive," another of the Fish-In youth
leaders told the *National Observer.*

Hunter S. Thompson, the author of *Hell's Angels,* who reported the

Fish-Ins for the Washington journal, went on to say: "Throughout the country Indians are doing battle with the Federal and State governments over a variety of causes. And even though Fish-Ins and assorted protests have resulted only in a stand-off, the attitudes they represented could have wide-reaching repercussions. As the Indians press their fight, the Youth Council will probably do much of the fighting, and its emergence here was a major event. . . ."

The mood of the youth, as the battle subsided, was voiced by a young Indian who was studying for a degree in sociology at the University of Washington, Patrick Hamilton: "The past decade has shown us the power of civil disobedience. Wake up! Remove your rose-colored glasses of egocentricism. Wake up! And see what your people have done to us and then decide if breakage of a few fishing laws is justifiable."

Mel Thom was as defiant: "We demonstrated that the Indians were not afraid. We proved that the Indians had enough guts to stand up."

In a reflective mood, Thom thought of the future: "We intend to stay right in there and keep up canoe trekking and treaty trekking and fishing-in. There's no backing off. This was the first time we ever tried direct action. We did not have a backlog of experience to go on. But the next time we try direct action we're going to be better prepared."

"Sure we made a lot of mistakes. Now we know what to do next time," chortled Clyde Warrior. "This was just our beginning. Wait till we get rolling."

It was said:

"Kwatee, the Changer, had created the Quillayute River. It happened one day long ago, when he was having a fight with the Wolf family. And the Chief Wolf had chased Kwatee down the shores of Neah Bay.

"When the Wolf reached to grab him, Kwatee stuck his comb in the sand. The teeth became the hills and rocks at the point.

"Then Kwatee ran down the coast. When the Wolf came close he poured hair oil on the beach, and he made a river. That is how he made the Quillayute River.

"And then Kwatee escaped in his canoe. When he got in his canoe, Kwatee pulled it into the ocean, out over the breakers. So the Wolf family gave up the chase.

"Out in his canoe, Kwatee sang a song about a man-eating shark. He would kill the man-eating shark out in the ocean, he sang. But the man-eating shark swallowed Kwatee and his canoe. From inside his stomach Kwatee killed the man-eating shark."

It was said by an old Quillayute Indian.

Was it, perhaps, the first Fish-In? Was it, perhaps, told as a modern parable of the Fish-In within the Fish?

6

THE ACADEMIC ABORIGINE

On the beach of Neah Bay is the most northwesternly land's end of the State of Washington, a fingertip of rock and sand. There the rough whalers and four-masted schooners came to rest, sunk in the storms on those wild waters. There the tribe of Makah Indians, the few who have survived, have been forced by history to cling to footholds on the rocks. On the edge of the Pacific Ocean an atomic scientist lay on the beach, asleep.

He was vacationing from the manufacture of nuclear death that was his job at the plant of the Atomic Energy Commission at Hanford. He was hiding from himself, trying to get as far from the anxieties of the atomic age as he could. He had come through the primeval rain forests of the Olympic Peninsula to seek the ancestral peace of the Makah Indians, who were, he thought, ignorant of the twentieth century.

Nearby, on the beach, a group of young Indians were talking. Unlike the scientist they had come to Neah Bay to attend a conference. The executive board of the National Indian Youth Council was meeting to discuss the political results of the Fish-Ins. And to plan the next step in the defense of the fishing rights of Indians on the Columbia River, where the scientist made his bombs.

The scientist awoke and heard them talking of the abysmal poverty and despair of the Indians. He wished to do something for them. But what?

"I want to help," the scientist pleaded. "Tell me what I can do to help."

When they heard what he did for a living the young Indians were quiet. The leader of the group, Clyde Warrior, who was soon to be elected president of the National Indian Youth Council, then grinned. "Show us," Warrior said, "how to make the bomb!"

The huge living room of the old, majestic house on the hill of Tahlequah, where I met Clyde Warrior years later, was a far cry from his surroundings at Neah Bay.

He lived in the incongruous past. The mansion, with its rambling porches and gracious rooms, was a monument to the Victorian tastes of the Senator, one of those Cherokee legislators of the early years of the century, who had built it to enshrine his success. Everything in it was an ostentation, from the too-long, unwieldy kitchen to the once opulent parlor, where we sat. In the parlor were two or three worn, somewhat stuffed chairs, the inevitable hi-fi, a tape recorder, and a television set—all else was emptiness. The furniture was sparse, and typical of the poor urban Indian, or the young intellectual.

On the lawn, unkempt now but once a Roman garden, there were stately and spacious trees, a bit frayed about the leaves. Under the trees was a second-hand car—"It needs a new battery"—that was an anomaly, like the refrigerator that stood in the once palatial parlor.

The young Warrior was an up-to-date, contemporary, hip, and fashionably angry youth who compared himself to the new generation of rebellious college students. "I am an academic aborigine."

He had earned his university credentials of irony. Working with the University of Chicago anthropological team on the Carnegie Project among the Cherokee, and then as a researcher for the studies of the University of Kansas, he had been initiated into the scholarly fraternity. Co-editor of *Indian Voices,* he had written for several publications, lectured to the usual seminars, and had learned the scholarly jargon well enough to use it and mock it.

He was the young intellectual voice of the new Indians. Yet his voice was uniquely his own—bold, blasphemous, saying what no one said in public, certainly no Indian, fiery, articulate, too outspoken for his quieter friends; he was the prophet of "Red Power."

Warrior had sounded his battle cry in his comments on the "Angry Nationalists." It was published in *ABC: Americans Before Columbus,* the newspaper of the thousands of young Indians of high school and college age who belonged to the National Indian Youth Council. His words had unleashed a re-echoing war cry:

"I am fed up with religious workers and educationalists incapable of understanding, and pseudo-social scientists, who are consciously creating social and cultural genocide among Indian youth.

"I am fed up with bureaucrats who try to pass off 'rules and regulations' for programs that will bring 'progress.' "

(Elsewhere he had written to condemn those bureaucrats—the "narrow-minded, middle-class Anglo-Saxons who are bent on stamping out Indians because they pose a threat to [their] way of life. . . .")

"And I am disturbed to the point of screaming when I see American Indian youth accepting the horror of 'American conformity,' while those who do not join the great American mainstream of personalityless neurotics are regarded as 'incompetents and problems.' "

(Elsewhere he had written to condemn "these foreign institutions" and "this world created by a foreign society.")

The young Indians, Warrior wrote, "must introduce into this sickroom of stench and anonymity some fresh air of new Indianness, a fresh air of new Indian idealism, a fresh air of a new 'greater Indian America.' How about it? Let's raise some hell!" But "This will not come about without nationalistic pride in one's self and one's kind."

In the words of Warrior the tribal society had found its university-trained voice. He was hailed, somewhat facetiously, as a Sitting Bull with a university degree.

He consciously played the part of the "academic aborigine." The game was one of double entendres of cultural charades, in which he acted the acculturated Indian who had "gone Indian," laughing at his own performance as he went. But in his mannerisms he betrayed the bitter irony and angry contempt he felt for those he was putting down. Nonetheless he enjoyed the game. He joyed in the mockery he made of the society by using its language against it.

Even his personal appearance was a mockery of the society he despised. Warrior, of "the peaceable Poncas," as Helen Hunt Jackson had described his tribe, sprawled in a beach chair. He was wearing

Bermuda shorts and a Hawaiian sports shirt of loudly flowered print, with a straw hat jauntily tilted back on his head, with his feet spread to receive the breeze of an electric fan by the window. A young man of massive build, he had a sensual nonchalance that delighted in natural and physical enthusiasms. Not the least of these were joyous Elizabethan belches, for which he was famous. He would listen critically to his belches, and belch once more in encore.

He was ready to talk. In urbane accents he intoned his belief in a "new Indianness" of "tribal values" that would revolutionize our urban "foreign society."

Laughing, then, he talked of his "Indian revolution." His laugh was a peculiar laugh, as uneasy as it was angry.

Revolution will come, Warrior began. "What it amounts to is that the Indians are getting fed up. It's just a question of how long the Indians are going to put up with being took every day," he said. The uprising of "rising frustrations," he said, had been going on for several years. It was just now coming to a head—the anger, you might say, of the Indian people.

Society had banished the Indian, he said. He was supposed to have vanished, become invisible and assimilated. What had happened was that the Indian was a refugee on his reservation—exiled in his own country; he was so downtrodden and so disheartened that he could see no way out. He was said to be "stoic," Warrior said, but that was because he was defeated and hopeless.

"What can you do when society tells you that you should be nonexistent?" Warrior asked. He answered himself: "As I look at it, the situation will not change unless really violent action comes about. If this country understands violence then that is the way to do it. Some of the young Indians are already talking revolution. 'We have tried everything else,' they say. 'The only thing we have left is our guns. Let's use them.' "

Like the warriors of old the young Warrior spoke of his vision as though magic were reality. Warrior is known as a war dancer. He is especially fond of the fiery rhythm and manly stomp in the rituals of the warriors of the Plains tribes. In his full regalia, plumed with feathers and brilliantly costumed, his dynamic dancing presents an impressive and powerful figure. He does not dance for tourists.

Like so many of the young intellectuals among the new Indians, when he dances he means it; it is not for show. He dances to renew his tribal heritage within himself.

And yet Warrior's words are rhetoric. The rhetoric is not that of the old warriors, mythic and religious. It does not have that harmony of word and deed by which his ancestors expressed belief and action in one breath. By saying what is his truth he cannot lead his tribesmen over the hill, into battle, by the power of his words alone. He does not possess what the Indians called "the power."

Warrior is an agitator. He is a young activist, knowing in the ways of political organizing, modern and hep. He uses the logic of the social sciences to voice the tribal ethic.

In spite of this there are old Indians who believe that Warrior's words have a power of their own. "He may not have the power in the medicine way," a Cherokee said, "but he knows how to talk to those who do have the power and can't express it in a modern way. Some of the young Indians don't know how the old Indians *feel*. He knows. One of the greatest things is to see him talk to the old Indians in the back-country towns. The old Indians dig him."

"He understands the tribal ways," said another. "I mean he really feels it."

It is an interesting distinction. The power to talk to the modern world for those who have the power with the tribal world is being recognized as a new form of expanded tribalism. Political agitators are updating the warrior societies. In the young Ponca's own life there was an incident that revealed how integrally the old and new ways are meshed. When the war in Vietnam had intensified, Warrior had grown restless for action. He did not at that time approve or disapprove of the war, but simply wanted to fight.

A friend described how Warrior debated with himself whether to enlist. "One day he went to Mississippi instead to enlist in the Freedom Fight there," the friend said. "It was on an impulse that he decided. So, instead of joining the Marine Corps, he spent the summer with the kids in SNCC. That was a typical Indian way of doing an Indian thing."

The new tribalism of young men like Warrior has come face to face with the twentieth century. Boldly it confronts and embraces the ways of contemporary life, and yet it does so by donning the appearances of social change while seeking to remake them, and incorporate them, in the ways of tribal life.

Nostalgia for the tribal past is not enough, Warrior said; the tribal society "no longer exists" by itself. "In the place of the tribal world is today's complex, neurotic, urban world," he said. If the way of the Indian is to survive, it will have to use the ideas and techniques of contemporary politics. "Until we do that, it's all a lot of wishful thinking. We have to fight in modern ways for the old ways."

Warrior said, "The 'Angry Nationalists' want to stop the trend toward personality disappearance [among Indians]; for this they are termed 'radicals.' "

But wasn't he radical?

"Radical! Radical! Radical!" he erupted. Sometimes he had been cursed as a Communist. He was not. He had campaigned for Goldwater. If there was any political philosophy for which he had sympathy it was that of the conservatives. Though to him the political label was incidental. Warrior said, "Those who try to pin political labels on Indians don't understand that when we do not accept the values of society, when we reject them, then we cannot be measured by them. We are not radicals. We are not trying to revolutionize society. If society would leave us alone, we would leave it alone."

He prophesied nonetheless that there would be an "Indian revolution." But his prophecy was a curious mixture of tribal beliefs and modern sociology that had the tone of a religious chant. It sounded more like a sermon on morality than a political incantation.

"I believe that what is at the heart of this Indian revolution is bureaucracy out of control, over-institutions, alienation of individuals, exploitation of people—our friends and neighbors," Warrior began. "And the Indian suffers these things more than most people. He is the worst victim. But when the powers-that-be look at these people they say it's all their fault: what they should do is 'get educated,' or 'they don't have any morals,' or they're 'racially inferior.' Which doesn't mean nothing. It only justifies their being.

"And American Indians are fed up with this. They know that's not the problem. They know it's the system: the social, political, economic structure of this country is such that it causes these things. And we Indians are beginning to see that the only way to change it is to destroy it. And to build something else.

"And this isn't unique, this type of thinking, to Indians. This is what the students at Berkeley are mad about. There's not that much difference in their thinking, or their anger. This is what people are screaming about in Vietnam. This is what Fulbright says, and Morse: that maybe we should stop and re-evaluate ourselves as a person, as a group of people, as a community, as a nation. And see what we're doing not only to each other but to ourselves."

In the house of bourgeois splendors, Clyde Warrior leaned back in his lounging chair. And he cursed the degeneracy of Western man. He dreamed of tribal revolutions. He prophesied the world of his dreams.

It was a sullen summer day. The humid wind of rural Oklahoma hovered in the room. All afternoon there had been the threat of a rainstorm. Now it came. Lightning hit the hills with that vicious suddenness so common in the Ozarks.

Warrior smiled; he was comforted by the thunders that were companions to his angers. He wet his lips with a cool drink and he cursed.

"Uncle Tomahawks," he labeled those tribal leaders who had acquiesced to the society of the white man. He was vehement about those who, he thought, "were bought off with government jobs, or jobs of Indian do-gooders." Finks, "Indian finks," Warrior muttered, were holding back the uprising of the tribes.

"Is this an American way of hollowing out the insides of people?

"And, as I see it, before we change, things are going to get worse. There are going to be more riots. And if it doesn't change, then the students and the Indians might just smash it, and change it themselves. These people are going to get so angry, so mad, that they're going to destroy the American society, without any thought of what to replace it with.

"If American society is so goddamn great, then how come it creates social movements like this? If everything is really ducky, then how come we have things like this happening? Maybe we're not those good, pious people we project to the world; maybe we, as Americans, are really bastards. If America is so good, if America is so great, if America is so charitable, then why are we forcing people to behave like this? Why are we warping and twisting them to where the only thing they can do is come out with volcanic eruptions of violence?

"Can it be, perhaps, that we are wrong?"

Warrior had resigned from the National Board of the Youth Council he had helped found and direct because he thought that it too had become "a political springboard whereby [young Indians] get sucked into the system." But before the summer had gone to dust "the unpeaceable Ponca" had been elected president of the National Indian Youth Council that he had condemned. Were the young Indian leaders ready to accept his wraths? Or had he moderated his "revolutionary, but not radical," views?

His inaugural press conference, in Washington, D.C., was his angry reply that shocked the assembled press corps: "White colonialists, racists, fascists, Uncle Tomahawks, and bureaucrats" staffed the United States Government agencies dealing with Indians, he thundered. These officials were "concerned only with procedure, progress reports and regulations, and couldn't care less about the average Indian.

"How long will Indians tolerate this? Negroes, Mexican Americans, and Puerto Ricans could only take colonialism, exploitation, and abuse for so long; then they did something about it. Will American Indians wait until their reservations and lands are eroded away, and they are forced into urban ghettos, before they start raising hell with their oppressors?"

Warrior, in the angry voice of the new Indian, for whom he was now the elected spokesman, made it clear that as far as he was concerned the time had come.

7

THE GREAT
WHITE FATHER MYTH

. . . In the Beginning

There is a joke the Cherokee tell:

"An old Cherokee was given an allotment of land, good land, up near Claremont, by mistake. He settled on it and was just about getting ready to be happy when he found out he had a tenant farmer on his land, who was white. Well, they got along fine, for a few weeks. Until the haying began. The tenant farmer did the haying, since he was the tenant farmer, and the old Cherokee just sat around and told him what to do, since he was the landowner.

"Now the tenant farmer thought that was peculiar, because it was. Everyone knew Indians sat around because they were lazy, not because they were bosses.

"Well, they got the hay into the barn, where it belonged. You know how hay gives off a gas when it's new cut. Well, they got to sitting around in the barn after the haying, and the white tenant farmer was smoking. So the old Cherokee said to him, 'Better not smoke in the barn.' The white tenant farmer he grunted, and he nodded. But after the old Cherokee had left the barn he stood up and he said, 'Hell, I ain't gonna let no Indian tell me what to do!' And he lit another cigarette. Well, poof! The hay lit and the barn exploded. 'Serves him right, all right,' the white tenant farmer snorted.

"The old Cherokee's dogs heard the explosion and they come running and the white tenant farmer, he shot them. And the old Cherokee's wife come running, and he shot her too. He was getting real mad by then. So he cut the old Cherokee's cows' throats, he set fire to his house, he cut the old truck tires, and he lit out, to make his way in the world.

"When the old Cherokee come home and seen his hay gone, his barn burned, his dogs shot, his wife shot, his house set on fire, his cows dead, and his old truck's tires cut, he was pretty annoyed.

" 'I will get that man for this, if it's the last thing I do on this earth,' the old Cherokee said.

"So for the next five years the old Cherokee roamed the earth in search of the white tenant farmer. One day he saw a man who looked just like him sitting under a glacier, up near Fairbanks, Alaska, just outside of town by the Dairy Queen stand, where the road forked. He walked up to him and he sat down beside him and he said, 'Ain't you the bastard who lit my hay, burned my barn, shot my dogs, shot my wife, set fire to my house, slit the throats of my cows, and cut my old truck's tires?'

" 'Yep, that's me,' the white tenant farmer snorted.

"The old Cherokee he looked him right in the eye for a long while, and then he said, 'You better watch that shit!' "

It was not a tobacco-chawing, hay-sucking, floppy-hatted, illiterate back-country Cherokee farmer who told me this. The joke was told by a Cherokee with a university degree. He told it to show, he said, how little of what he thought the Indian really communicated to the white man.

The elder Indians, no matter what he thought, or wished to do, did not communicate it, or do it, when face to face with his conqueror. He would be self-effacing before the Great White Father. It was dangerous to speak the truth. It was safer to act the mute, the tongue-tied and sullen Indian, "with an ugh-ugh here and an ugh-ugh there" as the Pueblo musicologist Manuel Archuleta had said.

It was an ingrained way of talking to whites. Or rather, of non-

talking. Calvin O'John, a young Plains Indian, wrote of the deceptive silence:

> *You smiled, I smiled.*
> *So we're both happy.*
> *But deep down inside*
> *There is hatred between us.*
> *Let us not show our inside*
> *Feeling to one another.*
> *Just keep on smiling*
> *Until we smile away our hate.*

The false face, the stoic smile, the self-perpetuation of a stereotype.

Kahn Tineta Horn, a young Caughnawaga Mohawk girl, indicated
the false face Indians often felt forced to don: "We are really a happy
people. But in front of whites we are serious and self-conscious. We
feel we are on trial and what we say will be turned against us. The
Indian will remain mute until this stigma has been lifted from him."

So it was that the tribal elders kept their beliefs about the white
man hidden in their hearts.

Elders of the tribes, in years past, talked of their thoughts to the
white man obliquely—by evoking legends, by reminiscences of lost
glories, by clothing their anger at contemporary life in historical
parables. In these stories the elders were voicing, in the only way they
knew how, their contempt for, and rejection of, the Great White
Father myth. The white man thought these stories picturesque and
happily primitive. He was reassured to hear about the noble red
man—who was gone.

The elder tribesmen would talk for days and days about the past.
"Unprepared as primitive man [*sic*] is to give a well rounded and
complete account of his culture," wrote Paul Radin, in his *The Autobiography of a Winnebago Indian,* "he has always been willing to
narrate snatches of autobiography."

Yet strangely, in these libraries of reminiscences, the old tribesman
rarely, if ever, expressed what he thought about the white man to
the white man.

His thoughts were not heard in English. To the face of the Great
White Father he was silent, he smiled, he was polite. And he said
what he thought the other wished to hear. In high cravat and top hat

and cutaway coat, the elders of the tribes, the chiefs and priests, would be brought to the White House in unending delegations. (One government school for Indians in the nineteenth century awarded its graduating students top hats with their diplomas.) Posing for the news photographers, the elder would sign the treaties of peace with his meaningless X, and present the Great White Father with a war bonnet. Then he would return to the blanket of silence that fell upon his reservation.

It was a ritual that the Great White Father seemed to enjoy. So the elder of the tribe acquiesced; he often still does—even for the tourist.

> *Niathuau Ahakanith!*
> *Niathuau Ahakanith!*
> *The Whites are crazy!*
> *The Whites are crazy!*

The Sioux sang this song of Sitting Bull in the circle of their Ghost Dances. But they did not say this to the whites.

Under the blanket of the hogan, or the pueblo doorway, behind the flap of the wickiup, in the intimate circle of kin, within the tribal council, the elder might bemoan his fate, or curse it. But he kept his counsel to himself.

In the beginning it had been different. When the white man first came the chief of the Southern Arapaho, Left Hand, had sung a different song:

> *My children, when at first I liked the Whites—*
> *My children, when at first I liked the Whites—*
> *I gave them fruits.*
> *I gave them fruits.*

The precolonial Indians had welcomed the European with an openhearted curiosity and innocent friendliness. He had offered his guest, as he thought of the visitor, the hospitality that was an extension of his tribal ethic. Powhatan, the father of Pocahontas, had said to Captain John Smith: "Come not thus with your gunnes and swords, to invade as foes. . . . What will it availe you to take that perforce you may quietly have with love, or to destroy them that provide your food? . . . Lie well, and sleepe quietly with my women and children, laugh, and [I will] be merrie with you. . . ."

Christopher Columbus had discovered the same hospitality. He was so awed he thought he had come to the garden of a new Eden, where, he marveled, the Indians were "so entirely our friends it is a wonder to see. Anything they have, if it be asked for they never say no, but rather invite the person to accept it, and show so much lovingness as though they would give their hearts." So too, Amerigo Vespucci observed, with equal enthusiasm: "They are so giving that it is an exception when they deny you anything. . . . They showed themselves very desirous of copulating with us Christians." And Vespucci thought this "the full extreme of hospitality."

On the Great Plains of the West, in the beginning of the nineteenth century, it began all over again. Lewis and Clark, in their *Journals,* wrote: "Those people are Durtey, Kind, pore & extravagant, pursessing national pride, not beggarly . . ." and they gave of themselves with "civilities." "The Sioux," Clark wrote in wonder, had "a curious custom . . . to give hansom squars to those whome they wish to Show acknowledgement."

"The Indian was too kind. He helped his enemies. And they killed him," Alan Cottier, a Sioux from the Rosebud Reservation, was to say ruefully, generations later. Cottier was president of the San Francisco Indian Center, where he sat in the board room and ruminated about the paradox of history. "But," he sighed, "kindness to strangers *is* the Indian way."

"We welcomed you with open arms," a Pawnee-Otoe woman, Mifanway Shunatona, said. "Maybe that's where we made our mistake."

It was not tribal kindness alone with which the Indian welcomed his guest. It was as well a verbal eloquence that overwhelmed and awed the European; for it seemed incredible to these men educated in the oldest universities of Europe, that the unlettered and illiterate "savages" spoke with a rhetorical skill that they could compare only with the classic orators of antiquity and with the biblical texts.

William Penn, an Oxford scholar in his youth, who had made it his business "to understand the Indian language," wrote in amazement of this eloquence: "I know not a language spoken in Europe that hath more words of sweetness and greatness, in accent, or emphasis, than theirs. Their language is lofty, yet narrow; but like the Hebrew, in significance, full. . . ."

Equally impressed was James Adair, who in his early work *The*

History of the American Indians (1775) wrote, with as much bewilderment as delight: "Their words and sentences are expressive, concise, emphatical, sonorous and bold. . . . The Indians express themselves with a great deal of vehemence." That feeling was conveyed as well by the early philologist Du Ponceau, who marveled: "Whether savages have or have not many ideas I do not determine; but if their ideas are few, their words to express them are many. I am lost in astonishment at the copiousness and admirable structure of the American languages."

So eloquent was the oratory of the Indian that Thomas Jefferson remarked that he wished that the men of Congress could orate half as well. H. H. Bancroft, one of the founders of American historiography, in *The Native Races,* published in San Francisco in 1886, had a similar comment upon the grandiloquent eloquence of the Indian. Bancroft wrote: "Indeed, throughout the length and breadth of the two Americas aboriginal tongues display greater richness, more delicate gradations, and a wider scope than the uncultured conditions in which the people were found, would lead one to suppose."

What muted this Hebraic eloquence?

Following the idyllic days when the earliest explorers rhapsodized upon the garden of a new Eden, and the Indians greeted them with bouquets of words, there intervened three centuries of bestial wars. Known more comfortably as the Indian Wars, never as the White Man's Wars, they are too well known to be retold. Not known as well, not remembered, not retold by most of the histories of our country, certainly not by the history textbooks, was the savage bestiality with which the white man, not alone the Indians, fought. Inherent in the bestiality of these wars were hatreds and fears that have to be understood if the subsequent silence of the Indian is to be understood.

One hundred years, almost to the day, after the signing of the Declaration of Independence, the *New York Times* reported on July 7, 1876, that there were those in the War Department, mostly "high officers," who advocated "the policy of extermination of the Indians and think the speedier, the better, its accomplishment." The Indian Wars were "wars of annihilation" to these officers, wrote the *Times.*

Upon the battlefields the results of this military policy were ghastly. Two instances will suffice.

Paul Steiner

Log and mud hut on the Assiniboin Reservation in Fort Peck, Montana. This old type of dwelling lives on, and is lived in, on most Indian reservations, where an estimated 90 to 95 percent of the housing is "substandard."

Paul Steiner

An outhouse and an old hand-pump are typical of the sanitation facilities on the Bad River Reservation of the Wisconsin Chippewas.

Three women oracles: Sculpture by young Indians at the Institute of American Indian Arts, Santa Fe, New Mexico.

Paul Steiner

Electric washing machine side by side with still-used outdoor bread ovens: Courtyard of Governor Abeita's house, Pueblo of Isleta, New Mexico.

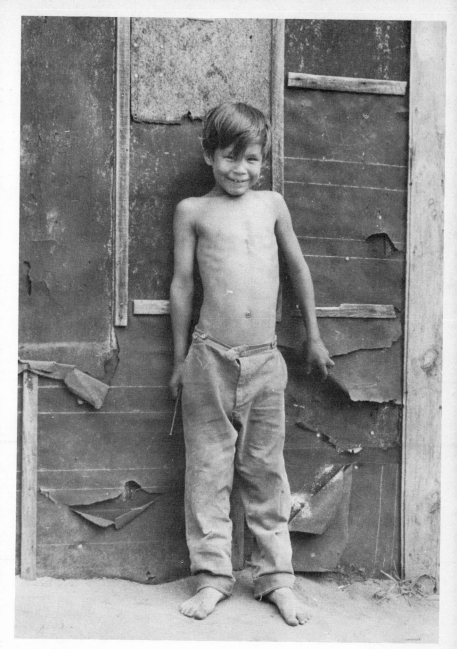

A child of Ponemah ("Old Village"): A grandchild of the religious leader Dan Rain Cloud. Chippewa Reservation, Red Lake, Minnesota.

Stan Steiner

A cafe and gas station and trading post and used furniture store, all in one, on the desolate desert reservation of the Maricopa tribe of Arizona. The wasted land of the Indians is surrounded by some of the richest, irrigated cotton crops in the whole country.

Lieutenant James D. Connor, of the New Mexico Volunteers, has described what happened to the Cheyenne at the Battle of Sand Creek. His testimony before the U.S. Senate said: "In going over the battlefield the next day I did not see a body of [an Indian] man, woman, or child but was scalped, and in many instances the bodies were mutilated in the most horrible manner—men, women, and children's privates cut out, etc. One man [said] he had cut out a woman's private parts and had them for exhibition on a stick. . . .

"I heard of numerous instances in which men had cut out the private parts of females and stretched them over the saddlebows, and wore them in their hats while riding in the ranks. . . ."

Of the same battle, a Lieutenant Cramer told the U.S. Senate: "The women and children huddled together, and most of our fire was concentrated on them . . . no wounded fell into our hands and all the dead were scalped."

North in the Sioux country the Battle of Wounded Knee was described by Private Eugene Caldwell of the U.S. 7th Cavalry: "After it was all over it was an awful sight to see. It made me sick to look at it. There were about one hundred and fifty buck and seventy-five women and children killed. . . . Some of the men went wild; they would shoot men or women."

Wrote another soldier in the U.S. 7th Cavalry: "The women lay thick. One girl about eighteen was supporting herself on her hand, the blood spurting from her mouth as from a pump. Near her lay two others, and all around, like patches on the snow, were dead squaws, each in a pool of blood. Colonel Forsyth looked very white as he gave orders to see if any of the women who lay thick were alive. From the blanket of one we took a boy five years old and a baby about as many months—both unhurt, but the mother was dead. She must have been shot with a revolver held not five feet away, as her hair was burned and the skin blackened with powder.

"Of course the camp-liar (the next day) was in his glory, but who shot the squaws was not known, at least no one boasted of it."

These men were obeying attitudes, if not orders. General George Custer expounded the commonly held belief that the Indian was "savage in every sense of the word," and had "a cruel and ferocious nature [that] far exceeds that of any wild beast of the desert." The "beautiful romance [of] the noble red man" who was a "simple-minded son of nature" was "equally erroneous with that which regards the Indian as a creature possessing human form." And these "wild beasts" need not be "judged by rules or laws [of warfare] applicable to any other race of men," Custer wrote.

Brigadier General James H. Carleton, commander of the U.S. Army's Department of New Mexico, proclaimed it his policy to "exterminate the Indians." His orders to his troops read: "August 3, 1863: Kill every male Navajo and Apache you can find."

As I wrote of this history a letter came in the mail one day—one of many—that bore witness to the recentness of these horrors:

Who can blame the Indian who wants nothing to do with the paleface's culture? He has vivid memories of limitless wrong. The scars are still vivid. Can the Apache, whose people never practiced scalping, forget the bounties on Apache scalps collected by the White Men: or, the Sioux forget the unspeakable desecration of the bodies of their murdered wives and daughters, whose 'scalps' [sexual organs and public hairs], as with euphemistic ribaldry they were called, were, in many an Army Post and frontier saloon, tossed from hand to hand amid obscene laughter?

And there was an old Navajo at Fort Defiance who told of how the "Long Knives of Kit Carson," so named by the Indians because of their bayonets, would also cut off the breasts of Navajo girls. These heroes of the West would then toss the severed breasts back and forth like baseballs.

"That was a soldier's game," the Navajo said.

It bears remembrance. There are tribal Indians whose mothers and grandmothers, fathers and grandfathers were scarred by such bestiality, and who from childhood had lived with the memory. Yet there was even a Boy Scout troop on the Navajo Reservation named after Kit Carson.

It was not because the white man was a "savage" any more than the Indian was that the wars between the two were fought so cruelly. These wars did not consist of battles fought by the armies of nations. On the one side were the armies of Europe, and later the United States, but on the other side were the whole of the Indian people— men, women, and children. Since the land belonged to the Indians, the armies of the white man were invaders before they were conquerors. The Indians for their part had the vastness of a continent to retreat into and hide within. And the invaders could not confront and conquer the tribal warriors when they were forever escaping into the wilderness. The brunt of the bayonets thus repeatedly fell upon Indian women and children, who were innocent targets and easily slaughtered.

So the savagery of the wars was caused not so much by the na· ture of the men involved as by the nature of the wars. The Indians of course fought the invaders with a ferocious futility. In the chronicles such as *Indian Horrors, or Massacres by the Red Men, Being a Thrilling Narrative of Bloody Wars with Merciless and Revengeful Savages,* by Henry Davenport Northrop, a doctor of divinity, the nineteenth-century reader was terrified by the gory details of these tribal counterattacks. And these bloody accounts continue on film and television.

Yet the "revengeful" horrors of the Indians were just that. They were defensive attempts to halt an invasion. Dr. Frederick J. Dockstader, director of the Museum of the American Indian in New York City and chairman of the U.S. Department of Interior's Indian Arts and Crafts Board, has succinctly said: "These wars were courageously, ferociously and savagely fought by both sides. But it must be remembered that the Indians were fighting for their land against a foreign invader."

Even so the invaders in battle after battle had to seek out, give chase, and entrap the tribesmen to force them to fight. General Custer, for instance, attacked the families of Sioux and Cheyenne who were gathered for their summer powwow on the green banks of the Little Big Horn. It was not the Indian families—mostly women and children, who far outnumbered the warriors in that camp—who attacked the U.S. Army.

The troops were therefore not merely invaders of what became known as "enemy territory," but they found themselves at war with an entire people. It was for this reason that the anthropologist Paul Radin wrote, "The winning of the West meant the annihilation of the Indian." And the elders of tribes, remembering this history that was as recent as their youth, were understandably inhibited from speaking out, honestly and openly, to the sons and daughters of the invaders.

Something else inhibited them. When the tribal Indians did speak they spoke truthfully. It was not merely their morality that made them truthful; but in a society without written languages, without signed agreements, and without licenses a man's word had to be his bond. There was no other. If men lied, the tribal society would not function. And the "forked tongue" was the snake's.

"What we say is from our hearts. We speak truths that are based upon our tradition and religion," the hereditary Hopi chiefs of the pueblos of Hotevilla, Shunapovy, and Mushongnovi wrote in their "Prophecy of Peace" message to President Truman in 1949.

The words "We speak truths" were the clue to the tribal use of words. Words were literally truths. Words were not abstract symbols, but represented real things that they had the magical power to evoke. Words were therefore to be spoken religiously, not lightly. The wrong word would make the ritual a failure. The lying word would endanger the life and harmony of the tribe.

Under the surface layer of English these tribal meanings of language persist. And so the tribal Indians talk carefully and sparingly and quietly.

Quiet is a tribal characteristic. "We communicate by listening and being quiet," Kathryn Polacca, a Navajo teacher, said. "I think sometimes too much belegona [white] speech is hard for us. Sometimes we feel that we need to be alone to think, and to decide." Yet this too, as was eloquence, is a tribute to the power of words.

The Indian would not talk of his deepest emotions to those he thought had betrayed him. Hatred was, in any event, dangerous to talk about, and one spoke of it warily, if at all: to talk of hatred was to evoke its consequences. It was better to talk of "the good way."

Kathryn Polacca said: "It was thought in the old ways that to talk of danger was to invite danger upon oneself. My people prefer to think about the 'Yateeh' way, the good way."

The years of silence between the Indian and the white man were broken only by the anguished outcry of the defeated warriors, like Chief Joseph. And by old men who helped the anthropologists earn their doctorates. It was generations before the tribal Indian would again talk honestly, openly, and directly to his conquerer.

From the end of the Indian Wars to just before World War II the tribes were thought of as defeated nations, and were so treated and so held captive. The stringent military occupation did not end until little more than a generation ago. On one Western reservation the U.S. Army was not withdrawn until the 1920's. Neither side, during that time, had a great deal to say to the other. It would have been conversation between prisoner and jailer.

The tribes were not, however, merely defeated nations. Unique in modern history, they were wholly surrounded by the nation of their conquerers, who, because of this untenable blot on their geographic map and because of their Puritan ethics, set out zealously to "convert the heathen" and to "civilize the savage." Henceforth, the Indians were "wards," and the government was their "guardian." Psychologically this "ward of the government" status was more injurious to the tribes than had been their military defeat. It further inhibited any truthful communication.

The Great White Father's decision to be the guardian of "his children" was guided by what the United States Commission on Civil Rights (Report of 1961) termed the belief in "the superior rights of civilized men." It was definitively expounded during the last century by Commissioner of Indian Affairs Francis Walker, who in 1872 said of the guardianship doctrine: "There is no question of national dignity, be it remembered, involved in the treatment of savages by a civilized power. With wild men, as with beasts, the question whether in any given situation one shall fight, coax, or run, is a question of which is safest."

Walker believed that the purpose of guardianship was to assure that the Indians would be "reduced to the condition of supplicants for charity." He would then "rejoice."

To the reservation Indian this meant an assault on his dignity, his self-respect, and his belief in his tribal integrity. He was reduced, if not to supplication, then to self-abnegation, in order to receive the handouts that enabled him to stay alive. For he had been denied his ancient way of living, but had as yet learned no other.

The Youth Council leader Mel Thom said that "Indian birthrights and self-respect [went] down the drain for a few bits of 'progress' to show the 'Great White Father.' "

In the process the last hope of communicating with his conquerer was lost. The years on the old-style reservations sealed the lips of the tribal Indian. His thoughts then turned inward, and his stoic resignation became his image. His voice was not listened to when he tried to speak and those agency Indians appointed by the government spoke for him.

"Our Indians in the Creek Nation were fearful, they were afraid," the Creek prophet, Reverend Clifton Hill, said. "It seemed as though they couldn't speak for themselves. Or do anything. Because all through the ages, all through the years, the white men were always telling the Indians they couldn't do nothing."

Reverend Hill thought that the Indian was not mute; he had been deliberately rendered voiceless: "Any time an Indian spoke up for himself and his justice, the white men, and the white Indians, who worked for him, they stood up and said, 'We don't want it that way.' They were the ones that always smothered what Indians really thought and wanted. That has held us back. That has been going on for years. That was a Great Giant. That was a Mountain.

"Like that Tower of Babel, that had to fall. It had to come down. It could not go on. Our Indians had to learn how to shake up that Tower of Babel. And they will. They have."

The awe of the Tower of Babel no longer overwhelms some of the young Indians. Some of them have climbed the tower. Some speak the languages of confusion. "If someone asks me, condescendingly, whether I talk 'Indian,' I usually answer in French," said the Cherokee girl Mary Lou Payne. From the top the tower does not loom so large as it did from the bottom. And some of the elders of the tribes, seeing their youth climb upward, are no longer as fearful of it; it does not seem so formidable an obstacle.

Has the Tower of Babel fallen? Not quite.

Coming home from the schools and the cities and the military services the Indians of the new generation loom larger in their own self-esteem. It is this contagious pride that they have brought back with them to the reservations. Moreover, they now know more than merely how to speak the language of the conquerors. They know how to speak it in a way that the white man knows how to listen to. And it is this, their articulate voices, in swinging and university-toned

English, which they have brought to the tribal elders, that more than anything else has scaled down the size of the unmountable mountain.

The effect of this change on the Cherokees of Oklahoma was told by Clyde Warrior: "The unrest and resentment has always existed through all the age groups of Indians. But the elders did not think anything could be done.

"Now they have young people coming home who are somewhat verbal [in English], who have some knowledge of how the mechanics of government and American institutions work. They have begun to utilize these rebellious young people. It's a kind of happy meeting of elders, with power in the community, and these young people who have some idea of how urban America works."

In this way the young Indians are becoming the spokesmen for the unspoken thoughts of their fathers. So many things unsaid and uncommunicated for years have begun to be voiced with that "vehemence" and that "expressive, concise, emphatical, sonorous, and bold" eloquence that James Adair heard two hundred years ago.

And yet the white man, long soothed by the seemingly supplicant and seemingly stoic Indian, is reluctant to give up that comforting image. He prefers, of course, not to listen.

The tribal Indians are undergoing so intense and complex a process of rediscovery of their beliefs and strengths that they do not know how to make their voices heard. Nor do they know what to say. Young Vine Deloria, Jr., of the National Congress of American Indians, thought his own path of self-discovery that had led through two universities and governmental offices and Congressional hearings and national politics was not atypical.

His path "was just a little longer," Deloria, Jr., said: "In the college where I went there was a professor who had just discovered the 'crisis of identity.' He would sit in seminars and ask us: 'Do you have this "crisis of identity"?' What he meant was, 'Do you have a crisis in identifying with the mainstream of my way of life?' He should never have asked that question!

"There were a number of us, young Indians, who thought about it and discovered that we did not identify with his way of life. We identified with *our* Indian way of life.

"Lots of young Indians have been educated in this way, in colleges, in the last ten years. They understand the so-called mainstream. They look at the mainstream, and what do they see: ice cream bars and heart trouble and neurosis and deodorants and getting up at six o'clock in the morning to mow your lawn in the suburbs. They see that in the mainstream the urban and suburban men are trapped; once you get a job it's climb, climb, climb. If you get heart trouble it's the price you pay.

"It's a strange thing. When you get far enough away from the reservation, you can see it's the urban man who has no identity. So he gets money. Or power. To feel secure, to protect himself. But he hasn't any roots, any land, any soul.

"In the beginning, when the Indians first went on the reservations, they were brainwashed by do-gooders, people who taught them Western culture. For a long time the older people accepted these things as 'truths.' These were the 'truths' brought to them by the missionaries, by the Bureau of Indian Affairs. And the Indians adjusted to this. But, at the same time, these people in their urgency to get the Indians into the mainstream began to educate them.

"You can educate a brainwashed Indian just so far. And then he begins to think for himself. He decides that he can accept, or reject, these 'truths.' That's where they made their mistake.

"The young Indians know these are not 'truths.' It is a pattern of behavior you are forced into because you live in a certain way. So you find lots of Indians, educated Indians, rejecting this way of life, and going back to the old people and saying: You have kept the tribal values under wraps, and you've never dared express them. Well, it's all right to express them. We have been out in the white man's world. We have been educated. We have read Plato and all his philosophers. And we see that the Indian ways are better. So the old people shouldn't be afraid to be really Indian."

Deloria, Jr., thought it was not just the younger Indians who spoke of these changes. Their fathers, so long silenced by hopelessness and the burdens of the past, were becoming as outspoken. In the once somnolent reservations more and more of the elders of the tribes were beginning to say, truthfully, in public what for so long they said only in private.

His own father was one of these.

When the Reverend Vine Deloria, Sr., thought of the white man, he thought of how it all began; he thought of the coming of the white man to the Dakotas. He thought of the old ways of the Sioux. He thought of *his* father, a Yankton Sioux chief.

"Oh, my father said, Why did they have to come and steal our life from us? Before they came we lived happy lives. We lived with nature. The heat was not too hot and the cold was not too cold. Now they have made us weak, my father said; too weak for the heat, and too weak for the cold, and too weak to live with nature. He loved the old ways, my father did.

"Oh, I remember how it was when I was a boy on the reservation. The feather dress. The paint on the horses. The horsemen riding ten abreast. The circle of tepees between the hills.

"Oh, I remember how it was with all our neighbors sharing their lives—our people as one people."

The governor of the Pueblo of Isleta in New Mexico, Andy Abeita, relived the same reverie. When the governor thought of the white man, he thought of the very beginnings, of the conquistadores of Spain. He thought of history as yesterday. He thought of *his* father:

"The old people had a saying: From the rising sun will come white men, with skins white as the sun. They will be greedy. From the setting sun will come yellow men. They came, it is said, but no one remembers them. From the South will come men with beards. They will conquer us. You know the men of Coronado had beards. The Spaniards.

"My father, Pablo Abeita, he was an old-timer. He didn't see much college. He was governor of the pueblo before me, in 1940. There was a dedication for a statue of Coronado that year and they invited my father to speak. He spoke last. When he spoke he said: The Indian people don't have anything to celebrate about Coronado. He raped, he stole, he killed. The Indian people will celebrate, my father said, when the descendants of Coronado depart. And then my father sat down."

Up in Minnesota one of the Seven Hereditary Chiefs of the Red Lake Chippewa, old August King, thought these tribal thoughts, but he thought them differently. He thought of history as irony, like a Rip Van Winkle who had perverse delight in telling the white man that he had merely been feigning sleep:

"In the beginning we bothered no one. The white men came to us, we did not go looking for them. Then the white men wanted to make peace with the Indians and they laid down their muskets. And they told the Indians to lay down their bows and arrows. So we did. And then the white men said: You must never kill white men again. So we didn't. Very much.

"When the wars of Europe began, the white men sent Indians to kill white men. I ask you, Was that right? That was the white men's wars against white men, whom we promised not to kill. It proves you can't trust white men, what he says. He is very treacherous. He lies."

The Chippewa chief said mischievously, "Lenin, that red man, knew that. He was a wise old geezer, that Lenin. I mean for a red man who was a white man." He laughed. "But they say he was a 'savage' too, you know."

In the Pueblo of the Taos Indians no one laughed at memories of the past. History was not a joke, but was religiously revered. Like those of feudal Japan the log corrals were impassive along the River of Taos, where the ancestral dust of the ten-centuries-old dung heaps stood like ruined shrines. Here in the tiered and classic pueblo made famous by D. H. Lawrence and the calendar photographs history was worshiped. Every stone in the pueblo had its history. And it too was worshiped. The Taos Indians talked of the past with hushed and troubled words.

Paul Bernal spoke for them. He was a determined and hard man, it was said, the interpreter for the governor of the pueblo. He had seen many Great White Fathers in the White House, face to face, and he was angered by them. Yet, in the twilight chill of a Taos evening, he stood in moccasins in the grass, in his darkening corral, and talked of cruelties with a gentle voice:

"It is said that years ago, many years ago, when the Indian was alone in this country, he cherished every little thing. Every living thing that grew from the green earth of nature he cherished.

"But the white man cherished nothing. He destroyed everything. The Indian was conquered. He was overrun. He was dominated. His lands, his best lands, were taken from him. His religious shrines of nature were taken from him. His culture was taken from him. Why? Not because the white man cherished them. No, the white man wanted to destroy them. He wanted to destroy the Indian, to exterminate him. He wanted the Indian to die.

"The Indian was left naked. He has nothing left but what he can hold in his hands. The earth where he stands. And what he has in his heart. No man can take these things from the Indian. Only God can take these things from the Indian. And the white man is not God.

"It was so and it is so. The white man will not let the Indian live as he wishes. He should have died, the white man thinks. Then there would be no 'Indian Problem.' "

Of the Great White Father myth, Bernal said: "My friend, someday there will be only one key in this big country. And that key will lock all the banks. That key will lock up everything. And do you know who will own that key? That one key will belong to the man in the White House. He will lock up everything.

"I say the Government of the United States in Washington has been crooked. It is now rotten. It lies when it says it wants to help the Indian. It has never helped the Indian."

Bernal spoke of these things quietly. He was a gentle man with soft eyes who had been thoughtful and patient for years before he had decided to speak.

"For fifty years I have been learning how to speak for my people," he said. "I did not speak sharply at first. I did not say the things I thought to the white man. Now I will speak sharply! I will not speak loudly. I will not speak quickly. That is not the Indian way. That is not the sensible way to speak to the white man. The Indian is sensible. He will always do the sensible thing. We do not fool ourselves."

It would have been unheard of a few years ago for these words to be spoken so sharply, however softly, to a white man. Unheard of for an elder of the tribe to talk in this way in public. But the young men have freed the older men of their fears. And both are beginning to speak truthfully of what they have hidden in their hearts.

. . . *In the End*

"I hate the whites!" She spoke with a smile, but in her defiant young eyes there was an old judgment.

Lieutenant Patricia Jackson, a "full-blooded Assiniboin," was in her twenties, outspoken and brash. She had been to college and had enlisted in the U.S. Army to find out "how whites think." She was "a mean Indian," she said. Coming home on leave to the ranch of her family on the Fort Peck Indian Reservation in northern Montana, she was suspicious of the white man sitting in her mother's kitchen.

"I don't trust whites. I don't trust any white man. I don't trust you," she said.

One thousand miles to the east, on what once had been the reservation of the Menominee Tribe of Wisconsin, a seventeen-year-old girl reiterated these words.

Laureen Waukau stood behind the counter of the Indian store where she sold trinkets to the tourists she hated. It was a summer job. Like many of the Menominee youths she had been away to school for several years in a large city and had just returned home to discover "that I want to be an Indian. I have to learn how." But "I am a fake Indian now.

"Just recently I realized that I hate whites. When the tourist buses come through and they come in here and stare at me, that's when I hate them. They call me 'Injun.' Like on television. It's a big joke to them. You a 'drunken Injun,' they say. 'Injun' is a degrading word. I hate it.

"I am not human to them. I feel that I am an image, not a human being, not a girl, not even an Indian. You know what I am? I am a buffalo!"

Her sister, Lisa, who had had three years of college and had worked on a newspaper in Chicago before returning home, was less hurt, less bitter. But her words were harder.

"You don't think most Indians hate whites?" the elder sister said.

"I do. The whites are hypocrites. Why do the whites always talk
about what Hitler did to the Jews? They don't know what they are
talking about. They did the same thing to us. They slaughtered most
of us, but that didn't satisfy them; now they want to steal what we
have left, and they are stealing it. They terminated the Menominee
Reservation, and they're buying up what's left."

"Let's stop them," Laureen said.

"Can you?" her sister asked.

"If we don't, what future do we have?"

"We have no future."

"You're too cynical."

"Didn't you say you were a buffalo?"

"Yes."

"The buffalo are extinct."

"No, they're not. They're coming back." Laureen laughed in
triumph. "It's just that the Menominee are too white. We've been
surrounded by whites for too long, and we're too white."

"Listen, people around Indian reservations hate Indians," the
elder sister said. "It doesn't matter how white an Indian is. We
are like foreigners to them. Like when you fill out a job application,
and it says, 'Foreign Language,' and I feel like saying, 'Sure, English.' "

"The whites are the foreigners," the younger sister said.

A busload of tourists descended on the Indian store. One lady
gently touched the young girl's wrist. "Dear, are you a real Indian?"
she asked. "I hope you don't mind my asking. But you look so
American." There was a stony silence.

"I am a buffalo," Laureen said.

> We are making reservations,
> That will be just for whites. . . .
> We are going to be the tourists,
> We'll come to see you dance.*

The threnody of anger was heard throughout the country that
summer as young Indians came home from schools and city jobs. It
echoed in the stodgy solemnity of the Grecian post office architecture

* Peter La Farge, "Hey, Mr. President," copyright © 1965, United International Copyright Representatives, Ltd.

of the hall in the Interior Department Building in Washington, D.C., the anger of the new Indians. There, at one of those inevitable conferences on "the Indian problem" before a distinguished audience of the Commissioner and lesser dignitaries from the State Department and the Department of Agriculture, a slight Wisconsin Indian girl, Nicki Barnett, who was a coordinator of that state's Governor's Commission on Human Rights, told the assemblage: "The little Indian blood I have in me becomes thicker the longer I work with white agencies. I am losing my white outlook."

West of the Rockies in the gaudy and ornate state building of the city of Reno, Nevada, another conference was in session. Hundreds of Indians from tribes in the Western states had gathered in those marble halls at a Youth Council meeting when two California Indians rose to the podium.

"We have arms and legs and eyes, as the white men do," said the Yurok Indian leader, Alyce Williams. "But we have hearts. And I have yet to find the white man's heart." He sat down. There was nothing more he had to say about the white man.

Ralph Moranda, his fellow California Indian, was as brief: "We have been looking for a white god. My fellow Indians, there is no white god. Get off your knees and walk tall, walk ten feet tall."

In the old capital of the Cherokee Nation at Tahlequah, Oklahoma, that summer, Clyde Warrior brooded: "One of those token Indians will stand up and spout off a speech about how all Indians are great Americans and how we love our country because it has been so good to us: That is an absolute lie! This country hasn't been good to us. All this country has meant to us is exploitation and watching greedy people come in and take advantage of inarticulate and inexperienced Indians. I despise what the white man has done to us."

The Reverend Clifton Hill spoke with the same trepidation. He used almost the same words: "One of the deadliest things the white man has brought us is greed. The tumor of greed has spread to the Indians." In biblical tones he raged against the immorality of the white society. He likened it to Sodom and Gomorrah, to Goliath, to the Philistines; this civilization of the white man was, he intoned, "a great monster."

"The enemy," said Mel Thom, in his more politically-reasoned way, was "a great monster . . . a monstrosity." But, reflecting his leadership of the National Indian Youth Council, Thom tried to view "the white problem" less emotionally. He attempted to achieve an objective, politically useful view. "The enemy," he thought, was not the white man, as such, but "the poisons of the dominant society."

"These poisons are greed, abuse of power, distrust, and no respect for people who are a little different," Thom said. It was not the white man, but the "American system," that produced "these poisons." It was not how "the present American system deals with the Indians" alone, but how it deals with the world. The Indian, Thom said, was just as "appalled by the way he [the white man] treats other white men."

Was this not due to a whole "system of values"? Thom's objection was that this was being forced upon the Indian, so that "Indians learned how to cheat. In the American way it's called 'competition'— free enterprise," Thom said. This had "eaten away at Indian ranks."

"A sad note is that many Indians have been destroying themselves with the poisons of the dominant society," he said. Let the white man live by his "system of values," if he wished; but let the Indian rebuild his own tribal values, build his "Greater Indian America."

It was not liquor and unemployment, poverty and disease, that were "the poisons" that were destroying the Indian, Thom thought. He had been tribal director of the Office of Economic Opportunity on his reservation, and he had been to the War on Poverty conferences and "consortiums." Thom believed that the tribes would solve their economic and social problems, in their own tribal way, if the Great White Father would let them and help them. "The poisons" that were destroying the Indian were spiritual and moral, not statistical, Thom thought. It was the way of life of the white man, "the American way of life," that was "the enemy."

Rebellion of the youth; but with a difference. The temper, the mood, the philosophy, of the new Indians voiced no rebellion against their fathers, the tribal elders. Rather it was their guardian—the Great White Father—they were rebelling against, and they were returning home, to the home of their fathers, their spiritual fathers. "You *can* go home again" was their motto.

One of them was Professor Jim Wilson, an Oglala Sioux. He had a doctorate in education, but he was thinking now of going home to his reservation. He remembered when, as he was growing up on the Pine Ridge Reservation in South Dakota in a back-country hut, "the yellow school bus had kidnaped him"; and he began his wandering in pursuit of education. He was one of "the select club" of Indians, he said, who "had made it." Wandering the nomadic trail of academia in search of a career, he had encamped at various universities before becoming chief of the Indian Division of the Office of Economic Opportunity in Washington. Where could he go from there? His odyssey was leading him, it seemed, back to his people. His tribal trek was, he thought, typical of his generation.

"I am enough of a Red Muslim to think I've got to speak out!" Dr. Wilson said. "Many of these young people who are getting educated and finding employment are going back [to their tribes] and reviving some of the things that were almost lost during the past generation. The young Indian finds in going back for the second time, with more time to devote to it, with a better understanding of the learning process, that he can take his heritage back into himself to a greater extent than if he had grown up in a condition of poverty. He might have had these things around him before, but to a large extent they were unnoticed. It is like studying something new.

"Many of the concerns of the traditional Indians about the changing values of the young Indians were relieved when these young Indians found that they could be productive members of this society, and still be Indians in every sense of the word. This was the real breakthrough for a lot of us."

And the "breakthrough" was growing wider, thought Vine Deloria, Jr., who like his fellow Sioux tribesman Dr. Wilson had spent several years in Washington, D.C., as the director of the National Congress of American Indians.

The cultural turnabout of the young Indians had begun to affect even the student elite, Deloria, Jr., said. Recently the United Scholarship Fund of Denver, Colorado, under his direction, had assisted more than forty Indian boys and girls in attending exclusive prep schools.

"When I was working with the prep school program," Deloria, Jr., said, "and getting these kids accepted, their first reaction to the testing and all that was to be as good white Indians as the missionaries and local school districts had taught them to be. These kids weren't in prep school for six weeks before they were the most violent nationalists you ever saw. These kids began to write me all the time: Send us books on Indians. We want to learn the legends of our tribe. Here they were, in the perfect setting for painless acculturation, and they were racking their brains, twenty-four hours a day, to remember the Indian words they used to know. They began to write the old people at home to find out the Indian words they had forgotten.

"I think these kids suddenly realized that outside of hula hoops and Cadillac fins, the white society had nothing, absolutely nothing, to offer them spiritually. They became really proud to be Indians. They had a culture, something of their own that their classmates did not have. Holden Caulfield was a sad cat to them."

"These young Indians have their sawdust leaking out," said the Cherokee anthropologist Robert Thomas. "And they are going to build the barricades on which to fight out the battle of their Indianness, out of their own sawdust, if they have to. But they are going to make themselves Indian. Every three years there is a new generation. And every new generation is more Indian than the last. Youth leaders of the National Indian Youth Council, who were hotshots three years ago, are considered by the *new* new Indians to have cooled it, to be conservatives."

The older generation of new Indians, the generation of a few years before, sensed the change in the newer generation. Clyde Warrior said: "Five years ago those of us who started off the Youth Council were called the most radical of radicals. Those of us who headed the movement five years ago now are considered Uncle Tomahawks. There is a more and more angry bunch of kids coming up. Which I like. When we started five years ago I said: It wouldn't be us that do anything. It'll be the ones that come after us. They will be angrier and madder. It's happening. It has happened."

Herbert Blatchford, in his calm Navajo way, reflects: "It is time to face the fact that the Indians are skeptical of the Anglo-American culture."

8

THE CHRIST WHO
NEVER CAME

"We Buried Jesus Christ"

In the clearing in the forest of tall pine the hut of the old priest leaned on the earth. The hut was held together by tarpaper and old boards; it was as durable and tenacious as its owner. Winter left the snow high upon its roof. The summer sun melted its tarpaper walls. But the strength of the hut was rough-hewn, uncouth, undeniable. On the door was a neatly lettered sign: "Knock, please."

The hut was the home of an old man, Daniel Rain Cloud, the village carpenter, fisherman, and priest of the Chippewa's old religion. He was what was known as a "medicine man."

Ponemah, the traditional village where the hut stood fast against the forest, was on the far shore of Red Lake. In the wilds of Minnesota under the Canadian border, the scattering of shantytown huts was beyond the tourists; only one Commissioner of Indian Affairs had ever visited Ponemah. The village was, in many ways, a modern version of a Chippewa encampment.

White men, they said, did not often come to Ponemah. On the village Main Street the stores were mostly empty, burned out, abandoned. Poverty had claimed them like weeds. The children played in the bankrupted buildings. But the tribal ceremonial ground in the village center was well kept.

In the hut's yard it was a hot, dusty wait for the old man to come. He had promised. He came in a pickup, driven by his son who was on the tribal council, and waving a bag of groceries. "I am hungry. I will eat." And he disappeared into the hut.

One hour later he reappeared, picked up a fishing crate and set it under a shady tree. Then he sat down with his back to me. I went and sat beside him with my back to him, not looking at him; listening to the grasshoppers in the tall weeds.

Then, after a few minutes, he said, "You want to talk?"

His grandchildren were playing with wornout tires in the dirt about the hut, as they had been for hours. Jeffery, the oldest, had told me, "He has medicine. My grandfather has good medicine." The boy did not say he was a "medicine man," or that he "made medicine," but that he "has" it. So I asked him about it.

"Yes, I have medicine," Rain Cloud said. "I have it. I have cured many people—many. But I think I am getting too old to cure any more. Not many have it any more.

"Shall I tell you about it? I tell about it many times. It will take thirty-two years to tell. And cost you half a million dollars. Cash. The university people come to me, always, and I tell them about it. But I don't tell them anything. In the house on the road is an old man who knows too. He knows but he will not tell too."

He was not just old, but had the wizened look of wisdom, with a face like a spruce knot. The deep-set eyes laughed at his joke, but he hardly smiled. If it had not been for his vague and far-off look, his eyes would have had a blinding intensity.

"Let's not talk about your religion then," I said. "Let's talk about all religion. Religion itself. Who is God? What is life?"

Rain Cloud peered at me. "I never heard that one before, from a white man.

"I have to think about. I have to begin long ago, before the white man came. I have to think a long time to give a long answer to that. Come back in two months." He laughed. "I will be sitting right here. And I will have thought of the answer to that."

He thought for a moment. "When I was a boy there was a boy in

Ponemah who went away to the Carlisle Indian School. You know, with Jim Thorpe. The boy came home and talked about Jesus Christ. He was the first one who talked about Jesus Christ in Ponemah. And so we named him Jesus Christ.

"Jesus Christ! He didn't like that. But that was his name after that. He died. On his grave we wrote, 'Jesus Christ Died.' We buried Jesus Christ. He was not resurrected.

"I have never understood it, why Indians go to the white man's religion. Jesus Christ, they say, He was born far away, over the far water." (The old man pointed to the eastern sky, which was darkening.) "That was two thousand years ago, they say. God sent Him to the white man, they say. I say, two thousand years ago the Indians had their own religion. I say, God must have given us our religion then, for us to have it.

"You know who God is? In Chippewa we say God is 'The Kindhearted Spirit.' "

Rain Cloud made no comparisons. He said no more. But to him "The Kindhearted Spirit" of the Chippewa religion was not the wrathful Jehovah of the Old Testament. He was a more humane God. The tribal religion was not one of forbidding codes, guilts, original sins, prohibitions, and confessionals. It was a celebration of nature and natural man.

"Paganism is quite laissez-faire," said a missionary on the Red Lake Reservation. "It permits everything, so it does not have to forgive anything."

Yet Rain Cloud merely said: "We believed in one God. Why did we need two?"

In the north woods the old religions of the tribes of the Great Lakes have decayed as badly as their reservations. Not everyone has accepted the new religion as philosophically as the old priest. There are some, especially among the youth, who are embittered.

"The missionaries came with Christianity not to convert us, but to defeat us. That's what I think," said Lisa Waukau. "I was baptized Catholic, but I don't go to church any more. Religion is a farce to the white man. Christianity? He doesn't really believe in it himself."

Rain Cloud merely shrugged.

There are many churches on the Red Lake Reservation. In the

town of Red Lake, the modern town where the schools and government offices and tribal industries are, there are half a dozen churches. Each sect has its own altar. It is the old story of the confused Indian who asks the missionary, "How many Gods is your one God?"

Even in Ponemah, up the road from the hut of the old priest, there was a new mission. It was bedecked with "Revival" signs.

However, the village is largely traditional. It holds on to the old religion by hiding itself in the woods, away from the churches and industries and tourists. For this it has paid in the coins of poverty and neglect. Perhaps this was why Rain Cloud was dismayed; for the religion of the Chippewa is peripheral to the modern lives of the people. Every year the old priest blesses the ceremonial and rodeo. Yes, he said, but how do you "bless a highway"? Should he invoke "The Kindhearted God" to okay the OEO-CAP program? Should he bless the plumbing in the housing project of the tribe where he worked as a roofer?

"The Indian religion is dying now," Rain Cloud said. He did not sigh, but he was resigned.

Was there no revival of the Indian religion?

"Not here," he said. "I have not heard that. I do not know young Indians who speak of that. Here it is the old who keep the old ways. Years ago when they beat the tom-toms on the Point of the Lake, we heard them in the village. That was before the white man came. He ruined it somehow. I don't know how. We don't hear the tom-toms any more. We have lost the way. Now I think I will spend my time with my grannies. And go fishing."

The old religion could not be revived? Was it too late?

"It is never too late. Unless the Chinese invade us. Like grasshoppers. Then we will have new churches. Chinese churches."

Long ago, the Lakota chief, Shakopee, had bemoaned, "The white men are like locusts"; now Rain Cloud spoke of the "grasshoppers." In the weeds about our feet, as he talked, the grasshoppers were swarming. "You see."

Now he had to tend his nets which were hung up to dry beyond his hut. He had finished talking and got up to go. He said, "I will think about what we have said. Come back in two months." He walked away.

"Going fishing?" I called after him.

"Yes, before they convert the fish."

"If There Is Anything Left, Let It Be for Me"

In the Pueblo of Isleta the people had been Catholics for three hundred and fifty years.

One morning the monsignor was led from the old church. He was led down a winding road by the houses of muted mud in the cold dawn to the outskirts of the pueblo. He was told to get out. "Do not come back. We do not want you here," the governor of the pueblo, Andy Abeita, told him. The monsignor made the sign of the cross. He went silently. He had thought it would be worse.

"I took him by the hand. Hand in hand. I led him out of the pueblo," the governor said. "He said we were pagans! He said we were infidels! He said we were hypocrites! He said that from the pulpit of the church. He criticized the people, the customs, everything. He was caught taking down the ropes in the plaza that we had put up for our ceremonial dances. He was caught doing it.

"Why? We danced in our ceremonials on the Holy Days. We keep our customs. But he wanted to destroy our customs. We will not stand for that," the governor said.

The monsignor had come to Isleta ten years before. He had come like a penitent, at first.

Into the quiet pueblo he had walked, washed by the eternal sun and immersed in the dust of history that sifted through the ancient plaza. He was, perhaps, awed by the peace of Indians, and overwhelmed by the calm of the church he then saw, which arose from the mud of the centuries-old town, like St. Augustine's City of God, in whitest adobe. So many had been becalmed by it before him.

St. Augustine's at Isleta Pueblo was built in 1613. The conquistadores of Spain built it well. "One of the oldest, if not the oldest, church in the United States that exists on its original site and with the original walls," the sign in the churchyard says.

Inside the church is a long and narrow corridorlike hall. Log beams hold up the old ceiling. The walls are as white as the desert sand. It has a classical simplicity that is startling in its stark purity.

Under the nave the Christ is crucified on a huge cross on the white wall. There is lettering, "I am the Bread of Life." That is all. No gaudy rococo saints. No pews were here until a generation ago when the Pueblo Indians would come to kneel on the dirt floor in their tunics; kneeling beneath the urns of incense that hung from the log beams, as they had for centuries.

Isleta means "island." It was so named, maybe, the old men said, because when Coronado came in conquest of the Seven Cities of Cibola, he did not attack the pueblo. He went around it, like an island. "We were fierce fighters in those days," the governor said. Yes, the old men said, we still are!

The farmers of the village have tilled the Valley of the Rio Grande for uncounted centuries, and time moves through the pueblo unendingly like the water of the muddy river. In the old plaza there is no town clock. No one counts the hours. Who counts the days? The years?

The monsignor had placed the sign next to the huge wooden doors:

TALKING ABOVE A WHISPER IS IMPROPER

—Monsignor Fred Stadtmueller, Pastor

Quiet is a way of life. On the roofs of some of the adobe houses are the inevitable television antennas, and in one courtyard a washing machine stands beside the old-style outdoor bread ovens. But most of the people work as they always have, if they work (two out of three men have no work), and live as they always have (90 percent of the houses have no running water or electricity), and keep to themselves, keep the peace.

"We are a conservative people," said the governor.

In the beginning, the monsignor respected their ways. He "made friends in the pueblo," the governor said; then he "began advocating reform of pueblo politics." He made "public statements deriding the Indian religion." That created anger though the people of the pueblo did not anger quickly. The pueblo council in 1962 asked the monsignor to appear before it "to answer for statements about the pueblo government."

"He was specifically asked by a member of the pueblo if his ultimate aim was to destroy the pueblo tradition and religion," the governor said.

"I will spell it out for you so that you will not misunderstand. Y-E-S," the monsignor told the pueblo council. "Y-E-S. It is my duty."

The elders of the pueblo went to see the archbishop in Albuquerque. Led by the governor, they requested that the monsignor be removed and another priest be assigned to their church, because, they said, of "the admitted policy of Monsignor Stadtmueller to eliminate the native religion by any means possible," and because they feared for the "safety of his life and limb."

But the archbishop "did not keep his word" that the priest "would be transferred in the immediate future," the governor said. So the Indians voted to remove him. "We are removing an individual, not the Catholic Church," they said.

"I am a Catholic. I am not a fanatic," the governor said. "My people were Catholics before the Pilgrims landed, before the forefathers of this man, this priest, came, before there was any United States of America. We are still Catholics. We are not fanatics. Long ago, when the Spaniards came, they got our corn, our wheat, our land. And what did we get? The Franciscan fathers gave us their religion. Wise men of the pueblo took that in. The old people had a meeting. 'What can we give the Christ?' they said. 'We are poor. We have nothing to give Him. We have our customs, but that is all we have. We will give him our dances then. We will dance in His church for Him.'

"And that's what they did. The old people danced the Indian dances in the church for Christ. You know, the church is the symbol of the manger.

"In those days they did not take the saint into the fields. One year there was a drought. The governor of the pueblo, at that time, he said, 'We will take the saint into the fields, into the plaza, into the community center. And we will dance before him.' That is what they did, in reverence. That is what we do now, when we dance in the plaza, before the church. That is our reverence.

"Hand in hand, that is how religions should be. I respect any faith. Catholic, Presbyterian, Baptist. Who am I to decide what is the true religion of God?

"If a man believes in that rock over there, that is his religion. Then I cannot say to him, 'No! You're a hypocrite. You're a pagan.' If he believes it in his heart then that is his religion."

Pueblo Indians are the oldest Catholics in the country. But, at the same time, they hold on to their old religions. A Laguna Pueblo Indian, Anthony Purley, who was a director of the State of New Mexico's Division of Indian Education, sought to explain it:

"In my mind the missionaries do not ever convert the believers in 'primitive religions.' Religion is too strong to be converted, to be changed, like clothing.

"Catholicism is the religion of the Pueblo Indians. However, if you see how the Pueblo Indian thinks, you see that Catholicism means something different to him than to the Anglo. He sees it in his own way. Look at the green bough on the white cross. You know how the Pueblo Indian thinks of that? He says the white cross is the white man's. He says the green bough is the Indian's.

"The 'religious bit,' what is it? Why the conflict? In the religion of the Pueblo Indians the values of Christianity are there, the Supreme Being is there, the baptism is there. Why do they always try to change that? But when you question that the missionaries become uncomfortable. Why should they be?"

It was that way at Isleta. The governor said: "We believe that our customs are good. This is one thing we stand firm on; we have a constitution and we have our customs. You can revise our constitution, but you cannot revise our customs.

"Catholicism is not like that. The Catholic religion has changed to fit the desires of the human race. In Rome, they are changing it again. The Indian religion is not flexible like that. He did not understand that, that man, that priest. That was why he tried to destroy our customs. That was why he said we were pagans.

"He did not understand. I am just as human as anyone." The dark face of the governor had hardened. It was the one moment that there was anger in his eyes. Andy Abeita, the governor, was a cattleman.

He is short, built like a small bull, with a hard, abrupt manner. He has the manner of a man who is embattled, with a guarded yet necessary severity. He had come, the day I visited him, from branding some calves. Blood was smeared on his trousers. "A calf kicked me," he shrugged, "that's why I was late."

In truth he was four days late. That week I had come to the pueblo to see him several times, but always seemed to miss him. He did not know I had come, I thought. No one seemed to pay any attention to me. Of course, I was wrong.

"You bought some bread on the plaza the other day," the governor said. He knew I had been there. He wanted me to know he knew. Strangers were watched. The village had been the scene of so many battles that there was suspicion of outsiders, especially near the church.

The calm of Isleta was deceptive. In the quiet adobes the faith of the people had erupted into anger; there was a religious battle being fought in the pueblo.

"Inquisition!" one of the former governors of the pueblo, Lawrence Jaramillo, had charged. Jaramillo, who supported the monsignor, had journeyed to Washington to testify before the U.S. Senate Judiciary Committee that was investigating violations of the constitutional rights of American Indians. He told the Senators of midnight arrests; of being held in jail, incommunicado, for two days; of "a large amount of dissatisfaction and defection" in the pueblo; of talk of impeaching the governor, whom he termed "despotic."

Some of the Pueblo Indians were "becoming solid, prosperous men of property," Jaramillo told the Senators. These had "adopted the economics and ways of the white man, as well as his clothes and speech."

What did the governor say to these accusations? What did the people of the pueblo, the peaceful people, the conservative people, feel about all this?

The governor leaned back in his easy chair. He peered about his modernized home, with the crucifix hung over his television set. On the coffee table were photographs of his children, in college. There was a filing cabinet in one corner of his living room, for tribal business and his cattle business. "I have been re-elected to be the governor for another year," said the governor. "You see how it is. I believe the customs of my people are religious and good. We want to keep them. We are good Catholics. But we are Indian Catholics. Let me tell you what that means. Let me tell you one thing.

"When the Anglo prays, he prays for what *he* wants, for *himself*. When the Indian prays he prays for other people. The last words of the Indian prayer are these: *'If there is anything left, let it be for me.'* That is what the Indian prays: *'If there is anything left, let it be for me.'* You do not hear Anglos pray that way. It is our way. We shall keep it that way."

"God Is Red"

"I live in fear! I live in fear!" the minister leaned forward in his easy chair. "Yes, I live in fear of the white man!"

On the quiet corner of the tree-shaded street the white stucco house was the picture of peace, hedges trimmed by Norman Rockwell. Suburbs are everywhere the same. In the town of Pierre, South Dakota, they were merely more so. It was a comfortable feeling, the neat and easy conformity of the house on the pleasant street.

It was the suburban home of Reverend Vine Deloria, Sr., an archdeacon of the Episcopal Church.

Hymnals were on the organ in the living room. The frayed pages of *Dakota Odowan (Dakota Hymns)* were opened to the church hymn *"Jesus Christ Wanikiya De Anpetu."* Beside it, on the music stand, was the hymnal *Wakan Cekiye Odowan.* Upon the mantel of the fireplace were two chrome basketball trophies and an old calumet, the peace pipe.

The minister is a Sioux. He is the son of a Yankton war chief, who was one of the earliest Christian ministers among the Plains tribesmen at the time of Sitting Bull. He is by heredity both a war chief and a minister. In his thirty years in the Episcopal Church he has brought the faith to hundreds of hamlets and back-country villages of the

Dakota Sioux. The minister has devoted a lifetime to proselytizing Christianity. From parish to parish he has journeyed to preach "the Gospel of the white man to my Indian people."

He had come to rest in a corner of suburbia to ponder his own preachments. He had come to doubt, not the Gospel but the white man, and his thoughts returned more and more to the Gospel of the Indians. The minister had retreated behind the curtains of his suburban home to prepare for the religious battle: "With my own soul," he said.

"I live in fear! I live in fear!" he said once more. "There is no man I hate, no matter who he is, or what he is. But I live in fear of the white man. I fear the death he possesses. I fear the violence that is in him. And I would not be surprised if one day the white man killed himself, and all of us. I live in terrible fear of that.

"The white man hates himself. And he hates the Great Spirit. I think of that sometimes. Why else would the white man do the things he does? The things he has done to the Indians? To everyone? I do not believe that the white man feels guilty, as they say; he is too full of hate.

"Can the white man be saved from himself? I wonder. Will he have to be damned? I wonder. Will he have to go to hell before he is saved? I wonder.

"The white man is going to hell right now!"

High churchmen were perplexed by the minister's words. One fellow churchman, a long-time friend, said gloomily: "I just do not know why old Deloria says things like that. He's half white, you know."

Deloria—the name *was* French. It is the Siouan way of saying a name long forgotten; many of the Sioux in the old days had intermarried with the wanderlusting fur trappers who sought skins along the rivers of the Northern Plains. The Frenchmen were acculturated by the Sioux maidens. "French Indians," these fur traders were contemptuously known as. One of the Deloria family ancestors was one of these "French Indians." He was "found" on a riverbank, half dead, by Deloria's maternal grandmother, the minister said: "Like Moses, the babe, in the bulrushes." Ever since, the Delorias have been bicultural, or perhaps tricultural.

The minister's sons are university bred. One, Vine, Jr., had become director of the National Congress of American Indians. The youngest son, Sam, worked with the Office of Economic Opportunity at the University of South Dakota. And his sister, Ella, was an anthropologist at the university.

In the suburban home talk journeyed with sophistication and religiosity through the realms of philosophy—from Plato to Crazy Horse.

"He is a white Indian," an old Sioux tribesman had said to me. "His grandfather was a French. His wife is a white. His church is the white man's. That Deloria, he is not blue-eyed. He is a white-eyes."

When he heard that, the minister smiled ruefully, as if he had heard it before.

"I can act the white man." He nodded. "Now I am pretty good at it. You know, at church conferences. But I am not comfortable when I do it. After thirty years in the church I am still not comfortable when I do it."

He had accepted Christianity easily, he said. It was easy for the Indians to do, because philosophically they believed in Christianity, long before the missionaries came.

"Christianity was not new to the Sioux; the Sioux had their own kind of Christianity. We just did not call it that. We believed in one God, the Great Spirit. We believed in our own kind of Ten Commandments. And we behaved as though we believed in them. That's why it was easy to change to the white man's religion. It was there to start with."

Historically it made sense, he thought. The tribes of Israel, who peopled the Old Testament and who were prophetically rewarded by the New Testament, were communal and rural groups, like the tribes of Indians. And like the Indians they decried the urbanites, of the cities of Sodom and Gomorrah and Rome, who crucified Christ, who defiled the communal and Christian idyll of simplicity as a way of life, purified by sacrifice, few in possessions and idols, sharing one's life with one's neighbors, coveting not.

"Yes, the Sioux had all that," he said; "The Sioux was a Christian whether he ever heard of Christ or not. But the white man did not *practice* his religion. He did not *behave* as a Christian. He lied to himself, and to us. He tried to destroy our religion and leave us with promises of heaven."

The white man had betrayed his own beliefs, the minister thought. He came from an urban, industrial, covetous society, that was acquisitive and un-Christlike; so that his Christianity was only for heaven, not for his life on earth. He could not live by it.

"Religion is an intellectual abstraction to the white man," his son, Vine, Jr., said. The younger Deloria had studied for the ministry; had he been ordained he would have been the third generation of the family to have donned the cloth. But, he had not been ordained. He too had lost his faith, not in religion, but in the white man. "It's all in their minds," the minister's son said. "Religion is something they *talk* about. It's not spiritual to them. They hold it out there, and study it." He held his right hand, with his palm upward, away from his chest. Then he touched his chest. "It's not something they feel in their heart. Religion, to the Indian, is in his heart. He feels it.

"The Indian didn't talk about his religion because he didn't have to. He lived it," the son said.

It was the minister's son, Vine, Jr., who had thought of the taunting slogan "God Is Red," in rebuttal to the new theologians' existential metaphysics that was expressed in the concept "God Is Dead." Vine, Jr., mused: "The white man has lost his soul. But he is so smallminded that he has confused his soul with God."

His father, in his own way, said something similar: "Missionaries always told the Indians that they had the only path to the Great Spirit. That there was only one path. The Sioux did not believe that the Great Spirit was as small as that. If there was only one path then the Great Spirit would have to be as small as a church. The Sioux believed that the Great Spirit was as large as the world.

"That disillusioned the Indians. Churches, the denominations, are like fraternities; yes, they are. Except that the fraternities don't steal each other's members."

And there was another reason why the white man's religion conflicted with the Indian's Christianity:

"The white man cannot stand a peer. He believes no one is his equal. Yes, oh yes, he loves to help the downtrodden, to pity the

Indian, to convert the heathen, to save the sinner. But he would not permit the Indian to look him in the face and say, 'I am your peer,'" the minister said.

In the nineteenth century it might have been possible to establish a national Indian Christian church. Had an Indian liturgy been written, had the rituals of the tribal religions been encouraged and embraced by the Christian churches, had an Indian saint, a Guadalupe of the United States, been sanctioned, as in Mexico, the history of Christianity among the Indians might have been quite different.

The Reverend Deloria doubted that the white man would have permitted it. He doubted, even now, that he understood it.

"The clergymen," wrote Stephen Ferara in his study of Sioux religious beliefs,

seem to have assumed two attitudes toward the native practices and beliefs—either ignore them, or stamp them out. . . . [And] every assistance was rendered the missionaries in suppressing the Indian religion. Dances, of all types, were officially banned by the government, whether religious or not. . . . Shamans and herbalists often practiced secretly, and were sometimes arrested.

The Sun Dance was officially banned in 1881 . . . the last of the torture [sacrificial] dances were actually held in 1883.

Yet, in spite of this religious suppression, the tribal beliefs of the Sioux "were strong as ever," the minister said. Ferara too, in his *Wakinyan: Contemporary Teton Dakota Religion,* commented upon "this tenacious hold of tribal religious practices." The older Sioux had never given up their beliefs, he wrote; and the younger generations "have lately taken an interest in things Indian." He thought this "religious revival" reflected a political interest in "Pan-Indianism," a multitribal "nationalism."

"Religious concepts of the Teton Dakota Indians of South Dakota are basically unchanged," Ferara concluded, "and pre-reservation beliefs, practices and cults, are by no means stagnant, but in many cases are flourishing."

The rituals of tribal religion are integral to the day-to-day life of the Indian. He is not "a Sunday Christian." He does not go to church "to absolve himself of sins committed during the week." For the Indian rituals are not merely prayers to God, the Great Spirit, but are part of his daily life, and are necessary to keep his tribe, his communal society, together.

So the white man cannot destroy the rituals without destroying the tribal life. That he has not yet succeeded in doing. On the prairies the Sun Dance is being danced once more. It was revived, surreptitiously at first, in the early twenties and thirties; but nowadays it is danced openly by many Sioux tribes, both socially and religiously—"with skewers," that is, by piercing of the dancers' skin, as one tribal leaflet announced it.

"The ways of our forefathers have not passed away. My father is in my heart often these days. Religion is strong in the hearts of my people. It is in my heart, too."

In his easy chair, with a Bible on his knees, much penciled with marginal thoughts, the Reverend Deloria leaned back and closed his eyes. He is a man of the prairie, lean, clear as the wind, his eyes sharp, his words hard. There is a Sioux's resilience, unflinching and severe, beneath his dignified warmth.

"Once the white man thought he was chosen of the Lord. He knows now that three-quarters of the people of his world are not white. He knows that the Lord created most people with dark skins, like Indians. He knows this. But I still do not trust him.

"Sometimes I despair of the white man's ever becoming a Christian. Sometimes the Holy Bible does not seem to teach people anything. And the Lord seems to have forsaken us. I go down to the cellar of my house when I feel that, where I have my drum, and I beat my drum quietly. Quietly so the Lord will not hear me, so that the Lord will not be offended. Though I think the Lord would not mind the drum.

"I feel better then. I feel Indian."

"Prophecy of the Four-Legged Man"

"I am not saying I am the Messiah, or the Savior." The young man was muscular and towering. Powerful of body, he had the physique of the heavyweight fighter he had been. He had fought in the Golden

Gloves. He was the Reverend Clifton Hill, barely out of his twenties, who is thought by many of his people to be a prophet; and there are those who swear he is the Indians' Messiah.

He has a booming laugh. "The Indian is always looking for a Messiah, or a Savior, to lead him to prosperity. I am just a poor, stupid Indian."

He is a Baptist preacher. Just as his father had before him, the young Reverend Hill walks the muddy roads of the Oklahoma hills to the back-country churches of the Creek Indians preaching the gospel. But his is a new, yet old, gospel. It is the gospel of the resurrection of the Indian people, so often prophesied. On his treks he founded and now leads a dirt-farm, grass-roots, backwoods movement of thousands of his tribesmen toward that vision—known by the prosaic, nonvisionary name of the Creek Tribal Centralization Committee. He is *its* Prophet. He is *its* Messiah.

"I always tell my people we are like Little David in the Bible," the minister began.

"The Biblical story goes that Israel was fearful of the Philistines. These Philistines were giants; they had the powers and authorities. I can hear the giants of this Philistine army saying, 'We belong to the Methodist Conference. We belong to the Southern Baptist Church. We belong to the Bureau of Indian Affairs. We got the power. We got the United States behind us. We can do anything. We can steal and rob and lie—anything.'

"And here comes Little David, our organization. Poor, but stands for justice. And the Israelites were expecting their Savior to be mighty and strong and intelligent. But God looked around, He saw a little shepherd boy out in the field, just with a little sheep clothing on, a little satchel of pebbles, and a little slingshot on his side. And God said, 'I'm going to send you out to deliver your people.'

"Well, at the great front lines the Israelites were fearful, they were frightened, they were ready to run. They were so shocked and the enemy was so strong, and there was nothing they could do. And Little David, he came on the scene, and he said, 'I am the man God sent!' The Israelites said, 'Oh, my God! Why in the world did He send something like that? So young and not strong. He couldn't be our Savior.'

"And Little David, here we see him. They put the helmet on him. He took it off. They put the breastplate on him. He took it off. They wanted him to be connected up with the Bureau of Indian Affairs, or some big Christian movement. And the Israelites were so ashamed, they said, 'He couldn't do nothing. There is nothing he could accomplish for us.'

"But the little shepherd boy he come out of the trench. The Bible tells me that the giant's shadow overshadowed him. And I can hear Little David say, 'In the name of the Lord. The Lord is Justice.' And as he began to walk in the shadow of the great Philistine the Bible tells me he destroyed him!"

On the porch of his white frame house beside the highway, with two medicine feathers stuck in his door jamb, the Reverend Hill stood like an Old Testament prophet. He retold the Biblical tale as though it were a tribal lesson in politics. But that too was in the tribal tradition.

Throughout our history every movement of the Indians against the encroachments of the white man was preceded by, and accompanied by, a religious prophecy. The prophet did not stand behind the warrior; he stood beside him, or, more often, he led the way.

It was a Delaware prophet in Tuscarawas, Michigan, who in 1762 had a vision of intertribal unity, the defeat of the white man—by supernatural and natural catastrophes—and the return of the Indian to communal and tribal life (the three elements of all Indian prophecy) that inspired Chief Pontiac to launch his united tribal war to wipe out the frontier posts. It was a Shawnee prophet, Tenskwatawa, who in 1805 had a vision that inspired Chief Tecumseh's attempt to halt the invaders west of the Ohio. It was Smohalla, the Wanapum prophet, whose vision inspired the Nez Percé War in the Northwest, and the courageous battle of Chief Joseph. It was Sitting Bull, the Sioux prophet, whose vision inspired the defeat of General Custer.

The Reverend Hill is in this tradition. His prophecies are a mixture of Biblical tales, bread-and-butter economics, and practical politics; but underlying these is the belief in mystical prophecy that causes many Creeks to call him by the name of their last war chief. And he calls himself, at times, by that name:

"We needed a leader. Someone. Lots of these Indians, they were looking for a man with a great intelligency, vast amounts of money, a very educated man. They were always looking for someone like that. That's why I tell my people the story of Little David."

He was just "a country Indian," the Reverend Hill said, "just a poor, stupid Indian"; he had "nothing but country schooling," until his father, himself a Baptist preacher, went to Tulsa and sent him to high school. Even so, the Reverend Hill had to earn his living with his hands, chopping cotton, and with his fists, in the prize ring.

"Love is what combined our organization," he said. "Not money or intelligency, but love of the poor. I am proud of being poor. Like I went to Washington and talked to those Senators and Congressmen and I had a hog ear in one hand and cornbread in the other. I wasn't ashamed because I was there speaking for my people.

"Got to let you meet the poverty Indian, the real Indian. He is the real Savior. He is Little David."

He got his family into his car, and we drove off into the night, forty miles through the hills, up dirt roads, through backwoods towns; into the black night past fields of cotton, darkened farm huts.

Where there was a country store it was little more than a dilapidated shack. The huts of the farmers were no larger. The barns had few silos; few tractors were in sight. The fences were crudely split logs. The muddy road was a wagon trail for cars. Up any of the back roads in the Indian country, from Okemah, and Henryetta, and Wewoka, it was a journey back into the nineteenth century.

"I was raised around here, on my daddy's farm. I was born up the road. Got folks hereabouts. Everywhichway."

On a stomped-on knoll of grass an Indian Baptist church suddenly loomed out of the darkness. We drove up, and were welcomed by a farmer who introduced himself as "Geronimo"; he led the Reverend Hill inside. There was going to be a cakewalk, he told us.

The church had a dirt floor. Its walls were patched with cardboard cartons and discarded signs, but even so the holes were visible. Hung from the ceiling was a single bulb. The insects swarmed about it, until they fell stunned into the pot-bellied stove in the middle of the dirt floor, a reminder of the winter winds that would pierce the paper-thin walls. Looking about the church one was struck by how long and narrow it was; it resembled a long house, an earth lodge. But, built of makeshifts left over by the white man, it was not as sturdy as the old lodges of the Indian religion.

In the summer night the windowless hut was steaming in the heat. Sweat ran down the dark faces of the Indians who had gathered.

"Lord, forgive us for not having more to offer our people." The local Indian preacher placed an armful of cheap cellophane-wrapped cakes on a pew. It was a short sermon; to the point.

The cakewalk began. On the dirt floor was a circle of numbered boards; for five cents to be contributed to the parish the walkers could win a cake. A young Creek girl put some Bingo tokens in a coffee tin and rhythmically began to shake them to the beat of an unseen tom-tom. And the Indians walked the circle on the dirt floor of the church, as if in a tribal dance.

Into the night, out of the church, the Reverend Hill stalked, his indignation in his ponderous tread. "Poor!" he muttered. "Why, they won't raise but a couple of dollars."

"The way a person ought to do it," the minister cried to the sky, "is take it from the rich! Like the Kennedys and the Rockefellers. Get something from them. And give it to the poor. The Bible tell me, 'There was a rich young leader came to Jesus, and said, What must I do to be saved? And Jesus said, Sell all that thou have. And give it to the poor.'

"I see myself as a Robin Hood. I take from the rich. And give it to the poor. That's what we need, a Robin Hood type. That's how I see myself.

"Some of the half-breed and mixed-blood and educated Indians, they've always wanted to rob the poor, the full-blood, the country Indians. They're just like the 'tares in the wheat.'

"If I was a half-breed or mixed-blood or educated Indian I could make it in the world. I could go to New York, I could go to California, I could go anywhere. And I could lie and cheat and steal just to get by—if I had any white blood in me. But you take the full-blood. They have always put him behind. They always put him way in the back, never in the front. And that's the reason our organization wants to put real Indians, the poor and full-blood Indians, up front. And let them run the show. And let them dominate. And be the head of everything. And let them do whatever they want to achieve, to do."

The Creek prophet has a dream; but it is not a dream of equality and integration. His is the wrathful dream of justice as told in the

Old Testament. The Reverend Hill divides the world into good and evil, poor and rich, Indian and white; he preaches the gospel of the triumph of righteousness. He is no prophet of compromise; was there ever a holy vision of compromise?

"The day of the poor will come," he said. "Long as there's breath flows through my veins, long as I am alive, I am going to try to spearhead that. I don't know how in the world I will. But I will.

"I got the odds against me. Some people say to me, 'You can't win.' Maybe I can't. I don't care. I like the odds against me. I fought that way when I was in the Golden Gloves. I like to fight the hardest man. But I speak what I see and I speak the truth and I never am going to stop speaking it.

"The day of the poor will come."

He did not really believe, did he, that these poor Indians, these Little Davids would defeat the Goliaths of society?

The Reverend Hill replied with a parable, but not from the Bible. He told of a prophecy of the old religious leaders of the Creek Nation. It was a tribal tale of ancient belief, he said; yet it sounded like a modern political speech:

"Way before 1500, way before the contact of the white man, the elder council used to sit around and prophesy into this age: That a four-legged man would come out of the sea unto this continent, and through his intelligency he would surpass the Indian. He would dominate him. He would strip him of everything. And then he would destroy him. The four-legged man would destroy the Indian almost to nothing.

"And the elder council prophesied: When the four-legged man had done all the damage he could he would return back to the sea and disappear. And then the Indian would come back. He would call his children together and teach them and admonish them and they would reconstruct their laws and traditions. And they would live forever. That is the story of what will happen."

The young man stood tall in the black cornfield.

"I do definitely believe that we will," he intoned in the soft but deep Southern tones, every word measured and weighed, "we will defeat Goliath."

9

THE TIME MACHINE

One day in the spring of 1965 Ambrose Gravelle, the chief of the Tobacco Plains band of Kutenai Indians, just north of the Canadian border in British Columbia, told a story.

He told of two trappers who came years ago. One was known as "Good Fire" (K! isuking! uku), who made roaring, huge fires. And one was known as "Bad Fire" (Sahaning! uku), who made meager, weak fires. One of these trappers married the daughter of the old Tobacco Plains band chief Kulsmayuk, who was Gravelle's forefather. The newlyweds went into the White Swan Lake country to trap furs —with the wife's relatives. There tragedy came to them.

In the third year the daughter of Kulsmayuk gave birth to a child. They lived happily. Life was good, the furs were plentiful, the rivers ran fast. Every year the trapper went over the high passes to the Rocky Mountain House trading post with his furs. He came home richer.

But in the fifth year he was murdered.

Journeying down the Old Man River, a fork of the Flathead River, the party ran into a bellicose group of Stony Assiniboin Indians who were "out for scalps." They deceived the warriors and fled. The Assiniboin then came upon the Kutenai camp of Chief Kulsmayuk, when the men were away hunting, and they killed several of the women and children. Kulsmayuk blamed the trapper for the massacre. The grieving chief murdered his son-in-law in vengeance. In his rage he tried to kill the trapper's child, his grandson. His daughter begged her father to spare the child, and the old man relented. Later, it was said, the son of Kulsmayuk convinced the chief that the trapper had been innocent. It was too late.

It was not an unusual story of the mountains. Except for one thing. Gravelle told it in detail, from memory, in the spring of 1965, but it had happened one hundred and sixty years before, sometime around the spring of 1805!

Gravelle was illiterate. He had not read in the history books the old tale he retold. It is mentioned in the history books, but in nothing like the detail that he told it. He retold the story of his ancestors from memory, but not from his memory. He retold it from the memory of his tribe, his tribal memory.

"I have long been impressed by the historical sense of the Kutenai and their ability to transmit orally events of more than usual interest to posterity," said the anthropologist Claude Schaeffer, to whom the old tale had been told: "This faculty is certainly present among other Indian tribes, but the Kutenai seem to possess it to an uncommon degree."

Is it that uncommon? There was the Creek who told me of the prophecy of the council of his tribe in the 1500's, and retold how and where that council had met. There was the Pueblo Indian of Laguna, a university graduate, who told me exactly how his village had greeted the Spanish conquistadores. There was the governor of Isleta Pueblo who described to me how the elders had debated Christianity in the 1600's. There was the religious leader of the Sioux who recounted for me the coming of the first white men to the Dakotas and a prophetic dream of his great-grandfather, as if he himself had dreamt it the night before.

The word-by-word reliving of the past by the Indian was extraordinary. It still is. One of the university-graduated leaders of the Youth Council told of the last battle of his tribe with the white men, but no history book would verify his version. "It was 'told history.'" He shrugged. "You won't find it in the library. My father told it to me. And I told it to my children. We don't have to write it up in a Ph.D. thesis to remember it."

In this way the Reverend Clifton Hill of the Creek Tribe told how the U.S. Army troops rode through the cornfield to confront the old chiefs, how the sunlight hit the tassels of the corn, how words were exchanged between them and then shots, and what was said on that day of Creek defeat generations ago. His story too, in all the detail he told it, was nowhere known in written history.

"We do not forget these things," said the Reverend Hill. He relived what he told so vividly he told of it in the present tense—as Indians often do. He called himself by the name of the old chief as he did so.

Modern man—book-weary, literate, multilingual—has been baffled and fascinated by the ability of the Indian to recite from his tribal memory. He has lost that ability himself. In his mind memory is a mystery that he long ago forgot how to fathom and had to confine to computers and mechanical time machines and books. But the illiterate Indian knew the unwritten history of things that had happened hundreds of years before as he knew his daily life.

The mind of the Indian was a time machine. His memory was his reality. It was as well a tribal necessity. The tribes, except for the Cherokees for whom Sequoyah devised a syllabary in the 1830's, had no written languages. Every man had to be his own history book, his own walking archive.

On the Colville Reservation in the woods of Washington, an old woman, Mrs. Clara Moore, recalled that in her youth stories "were unwritten texts in history, geography, nature study and ethics." And William Shelton, a chief of the Snohomish, wrote: "My parents, uncles and great-uncles told me, in days gone by, stories that would create in me the desire to become brave, and good, and strong, to become a good speaker, a good leader." The Indian way was to teach children by telling stories, the chief said. "Where we propound a scientific theorem they construct a myth," wrote John Fiske in his early work, *Myth and Myth Makers*.

When the leaders of the Cherokees prepared a primer and textbook for their schoolchildren, in the summer of 1966, with the aid of the Carnegie Corporation Cross Cultural Education Project of the University of Chicago, one of the first things they did was to publish a book of *Cherokee Stories*. In these stories, told in Cherokee and English, the history of the tribe was retold to instruct the young by use of modern "myths."

One of the typical stories that were told by the old to the young was "The Pretty Colored Snake":

A long time ago there was a famous hunter who used to go all around hunting and always brought something good to eat when he came home. One day he was going home with some birds that he had shot, and he saw a little snake by the side of the trail. It was a beautifully colored snake with all pretty colors all over it, and it looked friendly too. The hunter stopped and watched it for a while. He thought it might be hungry, so he threw it one of his birds before he went home.

A few weeks later he was coming by the same place with some rabbits he had shot, and he saw the snake again. It was still very beautiful and seemed friendly, but it had grown quite a bit. He threw it a rabbit and said "hello" as he went on home.

Some time after that the hunter saw the snake again. It had grown very big, but it was still friendly and seemed to be hungry. The hunter was taking some turkeys home with him, so he stopped and gave the snake a turkey gobbler.

Then one time the hunter was going home that way with two buck deer on his back. By this time that pretty colored snake was very big and looked so hungry that the hunter felt sorry for him and gave him a whole buck to eat. When he got home he heard that the people were going to have a stomp dance. All the Nighthawks came, and that night they were going around the fire, dancing and singing the old songs, when the snake came and started going around too, outside of where the people were dancing. That snake was so big and long that he stretched all around the people and the people were penned up. The snake was covered all over with all pretty colors and he seemed friendly; but he looked hungry too, and the people began to be afraid.

They told some of the boys to get their bows and arrows and shoot the snake. Then the boys got their bows. They all shot together and they hit the snake all right. That snake was hurt. He thrashed his tail all around and killed a lot of people.

They say that snake was just like the white man.

In the story the "myth" of the past became a parable of the present. The story, like so many Indian stories, was living history.

History as such did not exist for tribal man. In the old Indian's words the past was as alive as though he had experienced it himself. The past had never ended. When he told of what had happened to his forefathers, whether in realistic detail or in mythic abstraction, he did not merely recite it. He relived it.

In the winter of 1966 when the Five County Cherokees of Oklahoma wrote their "Declaration of Purpose" they began it: "We meet in a time of darkness to seek a path to the light. We come together just as our fathers have always done to do these things."

And 236 years before when the Cherokee Chief Ketagustah uttered the tribe's verbal "Declaration of Purpose" at a conference with the British, in 1730, he began it: "We are come hither from a dark mountainous place where there is nothing but darkness to be found, but are now in a place where there is light."

Tecumseh, the Shawnee warrior—he was commissioned General Tecumseh by His Majesty's Army—in his speech to Governor W. H. Harrison in 1810 began with the words: "The Being within, communing with the past tells me . . ."

He was not conjuring up a fanciful figure of speech. He was evoking the tribal memory within him in order to explain his tribe's contemporary needs.

In speech after speech the tribal leader of today begins with homage to "our forefathers." The rebellious Red Muslims of the National Indian Youth Council in their first statement based themselves "on the inherent strength of the American Indian heritage." And their demand for a "Greater Indian America" was founded upon the expanding of that past heritage. The words were not Fourth of July rhetoric, Indian-style, that paid lip service to nostalgia. It was the university youths' way of "communing with the past" that Tecumseh had spoken of, by which the new Indians expressed their belief in the essential harmony of tribal life and the indivisibleness of time.

Einsteinian in his way, the Indian thought of time not as a mechanical tool to be utilized by man, but as part of the process of life. Time had a dimension of its own.

"Time decides. When something has to be decided it is good to wait," said Herbert Blatchford. "If you act too quickly then you do not give time a chance to act. We believe that time will help the decision to be made."

Blatchford did not say that time would give a man the chance to decide, as the non-Indian might; but that "Time decides," by itself. "When the Youth Council meets that's what happens. They sit around for four days and everybody talks. Everybody listens. It seems like nothing is happening. Then on the fourth day, though nobody says so, the decision has been made, and it is decided without further talk. Now, what has happened? Time has decided. It's not something you can see, that you can hear, but it's there. Time has its own ways. It's something the white man doesn't understand about Indians. He has to measure everything by his immediate knowledge. But that's the way most Indians decide things and the white man can't figure out what happened. He can't understand 'Indian time.' "

If the tribal Indian did not decide at once, sat still, seemed stoic and impassive, he may have been waiting to see what time would do. He might say he had decided, to appease the white man's impatience. But in his mind nothing was decided. He was measuring his decision by a "time dimension not linear," as former Commissioner of Indian Affairs John Collier has written.

In the mind of the Indian there was a larger time dimension, Collier wrote, "which was of ancient man" and "bestows the power to endure . . . to outlast." The Indian, therefore, had "the capacity to wait, to endure, to possess things that seem gone. . . ."

"That possession is a time sense different from ours, and happier," Collier wrote. "Once our white race had it too, and then the mechanized world took it away from us. . . . We think now that any other time than linear, chronological time is an escapist dream." For we escape it only "in solitary, mystical experience [where] many of ourselves do enter another time dimension."

"We bow to clockwork time. We think we must yield to it our all —body, conduct and soul. The Indians tell us otherwise, and their message and demonstration addresses itself to one of our deepest distresses and most forlorn yearnings."

It has been said that the Indian behaved as though time stood still. He lived with one foot in the grave of his history. He existed for the moment. He understood only the past and the present, was not "future-orientated," and could not plan for future goals. Any such view was naïvely primitive. By unifying the past, present, and future within himself, the Indian created a highly sophisticated and integrated sense of history. He thought that it was the white man who lived for momentary gratification. For the Indian, "the Being within" expanded his thought beyond himself.

"Wherein no past is wholly gone and no future wholly inert," wrote Collier. . . . "Life has an inner spaciousness greater than yours or mine."

The new Indians have taken this way of life and created a theory of life out of it. It is not their purpose to recreate the history and time sense of the old tribalism. Rather they wish to remake them in such a way that a new tribalism can be built upon them.

"I say, enjoy life right now. Live a full life, right now. Be really human, right now. Share with your neighbors, right now," said Vine Deloria, Jr. "What a man does with his life right now is what he will do in the future. That's the Indian way. So you might say the Indian is 'future-oriented' in the present. The urban man says he lives for the future. He doesn't really. He lives by the time clock and the calendar and the bank check. As a result he hardly lives at all. Now or ever.

"No man can live one way in the present and then retire and become a different sort of man. He will be whatever his history has made of him while he was living his history. Who has no goals? It's not the Indian. He lives for today the way he would like to live in the future. He believes that the history of his tribe is the guide to both. He doesn't want to inherit the earth, just to live on it, as he has done throughout history."

History is eternal. It is present in each day that a man lives, in the way he lives, in the way he remembers his forefathers.

Every year the flowers of man grow from seed to seed. The Indian lives within these continuous circles of harmony, as they live within him. And he has learned through the centuries to respect these things. Where the unity of time is shattered he too is at the mercy of the time clock. Where his tribal memory is forgotten he too has lost his history and has to depend on the pages of books written by strange hands.

Black Elk, the holy man of the Oglala Sioux, lamented long ago that the cycle of life, the sacred hoop, was broken:

"With tears running, O Great Spirit, my grandfather, with running eyes I must say that the tree has never bloomed. A pitiful old man you see me here and I have fallen away and have done nothing. Here at the center of the world where you took me when I was young and taught me, here, old, I stand, and the tree is withered, my grandfather! Again, and maybe the last time on this earth, I recall the great vision you sent me. It may be that some little root of the sacred tree still lives. Nourish it then, that it may leaf and bloom and fill with singing birds. Hear me not for myself but for my people; I am old. Hear me that they may once more go back into the sacred hoop and find the good road, the shielding tree."

10

THE FACTORY WITHOUT
A TIME CLOCK

In the reeds along the banks of the Missouri River, up the bend from Running Water, in the town of Greenwood, is a unique factory.

The factory on the old Yankton Sioux Reservation is a fantasy of the Yankton Sioux. It is a tribal dream that has been industrialized, like a prophet's vision of what the twentieth century could be. And yet it is as real as the electronic components it manufactures so idyllically—without a time clock.

Every Sioux in the factory has his own desk. He comes to work when he wishes. He goes home when he wishes. He will work for twenty-four hours, round the clock, if he wishes; and then he won't work for a week. He will go fishing in the river, or take a correspondence course in missile engineering, or make love, or dance in the sun. He is paid at the end of the month for the work he has done, if he has done his work. No one asks him how, or when. He does not have to punch a time clock. There is none.

There is not only no time clock in the factory, there are no time-study engineers. There are no management-labor problems; for management and labor are both the same tribal entity. There are no traffic jams.

Is it real at all, or one of those visions of the Sioux, who love to dream? It is not a Sioux's vision at all. One day an Episcopal Church missionary had a way-out thought; he would bring harmony between the discordant tribal way of life of his parishioners and the industrial demands of the twentieth century. He opened the doors of his church community hall to build a visionary factory.

It would not work, everyone said. It worked very well, to everyone's surprise. "That little factory is highly respected by electronics firms in the Midwest that have subcontracts with it," said Vine Deloria, Jr., whose forefathers had been Yankton Sioux. "It started with twenty, twenty-five men. And now it's expanding to twice that many."

The community had been dying. Once the Yankton Sioux Reservation had been one of the most populous on the plains. Five thousand Indians had lived where now there were less than fifteen hundred. There were ghost towns all along the Missouri River. Greenwood was hardly a town at all. The inhabitants said they had numbered "about fifty." It was so small a settlement that its population had not been a statistic on the map of South Dakota. Not only had there been no post office, but there had been no grocery store and no gas station.

"Folks down there are rebuilding the Greenwood community," Deloria, Jr., said. "They have petitioned to reopen their post office. Soon they will have stores, owned by Indians."

Once the tribal factory was a success the Yankton Sioux sought to expand it. The tribe sent a spokesman to Washington to request $8,000 for new tools. "Why do you want to expand?" they were asked.

"So that in the wintertime when the Santee Sioux have no jobs they can cross the ice of the river and we can put fifty of them to work. And they can go back and forth across the ice," the Yanktons said.

It was not the customary way of commuting to work. But the government was interested. The Commissioner of Indian Affairs sent an industrial expert from the Chicago office to investigate what these Yanktons were up to. He was so enthusiastic about what he saw that he proposed the government build a $115,000 electronic plant.

"My God, we don't want that. That's just what we *don't* want,"

the Yanktons said. "We can do what we have to in the church community hall. We don't want to urbanize the countryside. We just want
to help our brothers."

Laughing, young Deloria recalled the dispute. His father, the
Reverend Deloria, had been the tribe's spokesman: "My father
talked to the Commissioner all afternoon, trying to get that $8,000.
He was told the government has no way to give a tribe that little
money for equipment. It has to be a monstrous program: On the
Job Training Centers, Capital Funds for Industrial Expansion, Ten-
Year Development Projects, and an investigation as to who is on
welfare. He was told: Okay, those crazy Indians want to live in
Greenwood way down in the weeds on a dirt road eighteen miles from
nowhere. We will build them a great big two-lane highway so the
trucks can get in and out. We will build them a huge plant.

"It was incomprehensible to the government. Soon as an Indian
got good on electronic work the Bureau would try to send him on
relocation to Los Angeles. They would say: 'You can earn $3.75
and $4 an hour out there.'

"But the Indians would say: 'We have been to Los Angeles. We
didn't like it. We rather live on the Missouri and earn $1.25 an
hour. Here there are no freeways. Here no one pressures us to conform to the white man. Here we are free to be ourselves. We can hold
our dances and sings and church services and live simpler and come
out ahead. We are happier.'

"The tribe had to go ahead on its own. The Episcopal Church of
Boston gave them the $8,000. And they are doing it in their own
way. What they are doing is putting the old Indian society together
again with the white man's economics. And it works."

An old Sioux said: "The white man works like a slave all his
life in order to retire, to be able to loaf and hunt and fish. We already
have this for which the white man is working. So why should we
adopt his ways and work all our life for what we already have?"

The editor of the *Navajo Times* who quoted this commented:
"How does one go about providing a job for a Navajo who likes
to herd sheep and has no desire to substitute his relative *freedom of
choice* for the regimented clock-punching job of the White Man?"

Work for the tribal Indian was, and is, secondary to living. His has been the "reverence for life" that Albert Schweitzer spoke of in tribal men in Africa, not the reverence for work. His has not been the Calvinist belief that work is the source of goodness, or happiness, or success.

If he had the need to see the sunrise at home, or someone in his family was sick, or his job was boring, or there was a religious sing, or he had enough money to quit—he would quit. Human needs and desires took precedence over commercial needs and demands.

And many manufacturers were, for years, as loath to hire tribal Indians as the older Indians were to work in the assembly-line factories. Their attitude toward work played havoc with the work schedules and production quotas of industrial routine.

The hard-working, self-made, rugged Calvinists of the last century were appalled by the Indians' disdain. "Lazy Injuns" was a politer term they used to describe the tribesmen. In an interview early in the 1890's the crusty "Old Indian Fighter" General William Tecumseh Sherman blurted out with "detestation and contempt" the then prevalent belief that Indians couldn't, or wouldn't, work. The old warrior voiced this view with unabashed bluntness, refreshingly so:

"Injuns must either work or starve. They have never worked. They won't work now. And they never will work," said General Sherman.

"But," the interviewer ventured, "should not the government supply them with enough to keep them from starving?"

"Why should the government support two hundred and sixty thousand paupers? No government that the world has ever seen has done such a thing." He spoke, the interviewer wrote, "in crisp, even gruff, sentences about Indians." "They look for the return of the buffaloes. Then they can eat without working. But the buffaloes don't return. They have all been killed."

Then the old man went back to reading his book. He had retired after a lifetime in the military and devoted himself to reading and hunting.

Hunting was not work. It was not productive in that it did not produce a product for the market. The industrial man had converted the labors of the tribal man into a pastime; he hunted for sport, for the kill. Whether he believed that soldiering was work

General Sherman did not say. But there was no doubt in his mind that the attitude of the Indian was immoral and immaterial.

While the Calvinists of the Industrial Age believed that industrial work was a moral necessity, the social scientists of the Technological Age believed it was historical fact. Indians had to accept norms and "goals of economic and social compatibility with the other peoples of the country," declared Commissioner of Indian Affairs Robert Bennett. They had no choice. It was all a matter of environmental cause and effect; for if "properly motivated" the tribal Indian could be taught to have the incentives of competitive, not communal, ways of work. "Operation Bootstrap" came to the reservations.

"Moccasins have no bootstraps," said a Kiowa Apache university student. "They got the wrong culture, man. They are so far out of it, the way the Indians think, that it's pathetic. They don't have to 'motivate' us to work, just to work for them. Man, we know how to work. Who do you think built those Pueblo apartment houses and irrigation systems in the 1300's and those Cherokee roads and schools and mills in the 1800's? But we want to work for ourselves.

"And, man, when we work for our own 'self-actualization' you watch us. That isn't the scene they swing with. That's all."

Of all the conflicts between the cultures, those concerning attitudes toward work have been hardest to resolve. Schooling has been widely accepted by the tribes. The diseases brought by the white men have been diminished. At least epidemics are rare. Culturally the Indians have absorbed many of the white men's artifacts and customs. But on reservation after reservation from 45 to 95 percent of the tribal populations still do not work in offices or factories. In technological terms they are unemployed.

These Indians may work hard at survival, but not in the labor market. Many work at the seasonal job, the odd job, as much by choice as by economic inevitability.

Still, the tribal Indians have been more practical than is usually recognized in attempting to resolve this conflict. The tribes have sought a compromise, often more realistically than their uncompromising conquerors. And several of the tribes have built unique and imaginative tribal enterprises that combine the old ways of communal sharing with the demands of the market economy.

In the deep forests of central Arizona live the descendants of the band of Geronimo. Led by a newly elected, young university-educated tribal chairman, Ronnie Lupe, the White Mountain Apaches have consciously tried to incorporate their old culture in the new economy.

"Now on our reservation today, and much to our dismay in a way, modernism from the outside has complicated our everyday life," Lupe said. "Our slow transition from reservation life as we know it to modern times, with the introduction from the outside of new scientific development and technology, further complicates our otherwise simple home life and community. In many instances confusion has set in and our behavior shows attitudes of defiance and depression." Lupe nonetheless told the Apache Tribe to "accept modernism as part of our everyday life [in order] to attain certain goals and a better standard of living." He quickly added that this had been done "without elimination of our age-old traditions, customs and Apache language."

On their reservation the White Mountain Apaches have in fact successfully developed cattle ranching, modern farming, recreation and tourist facilities, gas stations and motels. And these innovations, for the most part, are tribally owned and run in a communal way. The herds of cattle are managed by a democratically-elected cooperative of tribal ranchers. Most of the farms are cooperatively administered. But they are neither collectives nor kibbutzim. Each plot is farmed by an individual family. And yet they are irrigated, the produce is sold, and the financing done by the communal guidance of the tribal council.

It is a unique combination of tribalism and free enterprise. The four thousand Apaches at White Mountain are "almost 100 percent full-blooded, and primitive in their mode of life," said a tribal publication. Half, or more, live "in straw huts called wickiups." But there is nothing "primitive" in the complex social system, which combines "modernism" with tribal traditions of communal living, that these descendants of Geronimo have devised.

High on the mesas to the north, the Hopis' Arts and Crafts Guild has been built on the same unity of old and new. Each of the tribesmen is paid *the same* for his work, whether it is well or poorly made, whether it sells to the tourists or not. "The Hopi craftsman gets money for his work even though it has no market value," the guild director said. "We can't sell it? We display it anyway. We charge the tourist more for good work, a certain percentage, so that we can pay for the bad work. We mark the things in code so the poor craftsman won't be hurt and the good one won't be jealous. We have to be fair to every Hopi."

In New Mexico on the reservation of the Mescalero Apaches, the individual herds have been brought together in a "Cattle Corporation," run by the tribe. The profits from this tribal herd are divided among the tribesmen. Each is paid in proportion to the number of his cattle and his work. "It's an adaptation of the tribal economy to the economy of the country," said Wendell Chino, the tribal chairman.

Not all of these economic weddings of the tribal and the technological, the communal and the competitive, have been happy unions. There have been some deformed offspring.

The Menominee story was tragic. In years past the Menominee Tribe of Wisconsin had run a huge and productive tribal sawmill, where hundreds of tribesmen were employed. Men were kept on the payroll whether they worked well or not. And they were paid regularly for irregular hours.

"If a man had a family, his family had to eat," said the old former tribal chairman, Jim Frischetti, shrugging. "What could we do? Punish the children because their father was a poor worker? That would be inhuman."

In spite of this, the sawmill was so successful that the government decided that the Menominee Tribe had made it in the ways of the business world. Congress voted to terminate the reservation. The tribe's members, promised an inducement of a few thousand dollars per family, agreed. The Menominee Reservation became Menominee County, the tribal sawmill became a business corporation, and the communal hiring system was updated by a time-studied, cost-accounted personnel policy. In the process the sawmill was placed in the hands of non-Indians; five of the nine new board of directors members were bankers and industrialists. Laggard Indian workers were fired and production was speeded up. The sawmill, having dissipated several million dollars, has since been reported nearing bankruptcy.

"We were fooled," Frischetti nodded with melancholy. "But we are not fools. We were fools, maybe, to vote for termination. We have learned to respect our own ways again. Our way of work worked better for us than your way. We forgot the Indian way."

In the past there had been tribal sawmills and fisheries, woodworking and crafts industries, banks and tribal motels. Most of these were, however, imitations of the business folkways of the white men. The tribal Indians, who had no experience in modern economics, knew no other way to operate these enterprises. So they imitated the successful industries they saw about them. Often as not the results were ludicrously sad.

The university-graduated new Indians have both a knowledge of the workings of the outside world and a dream of a modern tribalism. Now the tribes have a wider choice. And they are freer to seek their own way of working.

The young Indian poet David Martin Nez, a student at the Institute of American Indian Arts in Santa Fe, voiced the vision of the new generation in his poem "New Way, Old Way":

> We shall learn all these devices the White Man has.
> We shall handle his tools for ourselves.
> We shall master his machinery, his inventions,
>   his skills, his medicine,
>   his planning;
> But we'll retain our beauty
> And still be Indian.

"Romantic but unrealistic," scoffed one of the anonymous officials in an area office of the Bureau of Indian Affairs. "Our economic system is competitive. It's not a charity. It's not poetic. You got to be hard as nails to be a success in this world of business.

"These Indians have got to leave their dreams back there on the reservations, and get into the real world," he said.

Enticing the Indians off the riverbanks and into the industrial mainstream has been the goal of the government ever since the early days of the Vocational Training Schools. Yet half of the tribal Indians have resisted the temptations of the urban ghettos and suburban developments. These stubborn ones who have clung to their lands and beliefs have been the visible sores of poverty and unemployment; for those who have made the trek to the cities have been mercifully lost amid the invisible poor.

Unsuccessful in its attempt to bring all of the tribal Indians into the competitive economy, the government has sought to bring the competitive economy to the tribal Indians. In one decade—from the mid-1950's to the mid-1960's—the Bureau of Indian Affairs cajoled, persuaded, and helped finance the relocation of seventy-six outside corporations onto the reservations. The Commissioner's report for 1965 declared that in that year alone twenty new plants had begun operation. And these industrial and commercial enterprises employed three thousand workers, of whom, it was said, 60 percent, or eighteen hundred, were Indians.

Yet the triumphant statistics faltered. Of these seventy-six plants "52 are presently operating," said the report. That is, twenty-four had ceased operation, closed, or were temporarily bankrupt. And that was 30 percent; one of every three plants.

Still the factories are encouraged to settle on the reservations. There is a pickle factory at the Isleta Pueblo. There is a manufacturer of battery chargers for electric toothbrushes at the site of the Custer battlefield on the Crow reservation in Montana. There was a missile plant of the General Dynamics Corporation to be built on the Navajo reservation. There was a diamond-cutting plant of Harry Winston on the Pima reservation.

These industries are owned by outside corporations. Although the tribes have often financed them, in whole or part—the Bureau's inducement has included the prospect of "Financing by the Indian tribe"—the plants are not tribally owned. Some of the tribes have invested substantially. The Crow Tribe was "skeptical" at first, the Bureau said, but was persuaded to make a "heavy investment" ($300,000) in the electric toothbrush business in order to lure the reluctant manufacturer into the beautiful wilds of Montana. It was such tribal generosity that softened the hard facts of factory production far from railroad yards, commercial centers, and markets.

"The paleface businessman is beating a path to the Indian teepee," exulted the Area Redevelopment Administration during the brief spate of "project studies" it conducted in 1964 "to help generate job opportunities on Indian Reservations." Like the Bureau the agency of the Commerce Department sought to tantalize corporations with the promise of "a new source of industrial financing—tribal funds."

Not to be outdone, the Bureau undertook 107 "feasibility studies" of its own "to determine the feasibility of various economic endeavors using Indian Reservation resources."

Recommendation for even more factories like the electric toothbrush plant on the Little Big Horn have resulted. The Indians have, however, become wary, critical, and selective. Many millions of tribal funds have been lost in the one out of three factories that closed.

When the J. R. Simplot Company, a huge commercial farming outfit, sought to lease the lands of the Isleta Pueblo for a factory-in-the-fields farm operation, the Indians were hesitant. They "were in no mood," reported the *New York Times,* "to sell Manhattan Island all over again." Ex-Governor Andy Abeita sarcastically said: "I much prefer industrial development. Farming is too much like work." But he cautiously added, "I'm not about to tie up [our] land for ten cents an acre."

In his testimony before the Senate hearings on urban poverty of the Ribicoff subcommittee, Mel Thom, speaking for the Youth Council, was equally sarcastic: "It doesn't take all kinds of experts, social scientists, or government bureaucrats to figure out what Indian communities need. Any Indian will tell you he needs a steady income; he needs a job.

"For the last decade many studies have shown there are resources to be developed on Indian reservations," Thom testified. ". . . however, the government has not been willing to significantly subsidize economic development in the Indian communities. Neither has it been willing to embark on the kinds of public works programs that would employ Indian people. It has spent immense amounts of money to treat the symptoms of Indian poverty, but has not really tried to create the forty thousand permanent jobs which are needed to put Indian communities on their feet."

Jobs created in ten years by the expenditure of millions of dollars in tribal and federal funds to lure outside corporations onto the reservations totaled 1,800. That meant 180 new jobs each year. It would be another 240 years before Indian unemployment would be eliminated at that rate—if the population remained static. But the youth were coming of working age many times faster than these jobs were being created. And the birth rate on the reservations was increasing.

"Hypocrisy!" Thom said. After the hearings the Youth Council leader's frustrations seemed to be smoldering. "Hypocrisy that we pay for. If they are going to use tribal resources and tribal financing for these industrial plants why can't they at least be tribally owned? And run in a tribal way?" Thom said. "Let us try to work these things by ourselves, for once."

Deloria, Jr., was as critical: "Instead of starting where the tribal people are, from how they think, and trying to develop industries they understand, the government brings in these multimillion-dollar projects. The government takes an urban ideology and they try to put it into a rural, tribal setting. Consequently they cause disastrous social problems.

"Sure we want electronics factories on our reservations. Sure we want IBM's. But the Indian wants economic opportunity in his own tribal way.

"That's why our National Congress of American Indians talks about acculturation. But we mean the acculturation of your technological society by our tribal society. That's why we say: Let us take a look at your culture and see what we can use for our economic development. Let us rearrange your science and education to the best interest of our people. Let us adopt those things that you offer that *we* consider of value."

> *He yoho ho! He yoho ho!*
> *The yellow skin, the white skin—*
> *I have now put him aside.*
> *I have now put him aside.*
> *I have no more sympathy for him.*
> *I have no more sympathy for him.*
> *He yoho ho! He yoho ho!*

When the prairie winter comes and the ice floes clog the waters of the Missouri the Santee Sioux who live on the Nebraska riverbank will come across the ice to work in the tribal electronics factory without a time clock in the tiny church community hall of their Yankton Sioux brothers.

In the summer the factory will once more be surrounded by fields of flowers. And in the reeds along the riverbank the Sioux will work in peace.

11

THE LOST TRIBES OF
RUGGED INDIVIDUALISTS

WIND RIVER, FORT WASHAKIE, Wyoming, (UPI), Dec. 30, 1966—Wanted: Residents for a new $225,000 low-rent apartment building on Wyoming's Wind River Indian Reservation. A federally-financed 20-unit apartment was built to help take Shoshone and Arapaho Indians out of their log shacks, but officials are finding difficulty in getting anyone into the building. Embarrassed officials extended a deadline for housing applications from December 23, after only one family requested a unit in the new building.

The horsemen of Wind River toured the model of suburbia on their wild Wyoming reservation. And smiled politely. Then they went home to their log huts and ranch houses, and sat around the corrals laughing. "A spokesman for the Indians said that Indians like to live apart from other Indians," reported the *New York Times*.

"It's absurd," said Vine Deloria, Jr.

Upon the vivid green prairies of the reservation of the Oglala Sioux in South Dakota, there was nothing to be seen for miles but the unending horizon. The government, however, had built another suburban housing project. It looked like Long Island, or the outskirts of Cleveland. The bemused Oglala, who lived far off in log huts on the hills, peered skeptically at the little neat rows of houses. And walked away shaking their heads.

"Lots of those houses are vacant, too," Deloria, Jr., said. "The people lived in them for a while, and they were too close together, so they cut out. Why is it that practically every housing program the Indians have with government funding is an adaptation of urban programs? Why don't they ask us what we want?"

In the town of Pine Ridge there was a bright, new, beautifully equipped old-age home for senior citizen Sioux. An elderly Indian lady, who managed the St. Francis Sioux Museum, said wonderingly: "It is like a hotel. Everyone has his own room! They say. Everyone has his own heat! They say. But the old people, we don't want to live there," she said. "I guess we rather stay out in the country and die in the country. They had us go up there and look at it. I went too. But I won't go inside. Some did go. I guess it is warm inside because there is no dirt floor in there. But I don't want to die in a hotel."

The housing project the government built on the Lower Brûlé Sioux Reservation faced similar tribal disdain. "People refused to live in it for a long time. They said the houses were too close together. And we've never lived close together," Deloria, Jr., said. "If some live there, it's because they have nowhere else to live. They said, 'If we want to live like that we can go to Chicago. Why do you bring Chicago to us?' "

On the rolling hills of the North Dakota wheatfields in the rural town of Belcourt, population 450, 150 miles from the nearest city, there is still another suburban housing project. Horse corrals and goatherds and deer fences surrounded these garden apartments. The huts and shacks of a shantytown of leantos were on one side with cheap bars and highway roadhouses on the other.

"Why did they build suburban housing way out here?" The young Chippewa, Harry Peltier, wagged his head with incredulity. " 'It's to improve Indian housing,' they said. 'Wonderful!' I said. 'But we don't need suburban housing at $25,000 per unit. You could build a dozen times as many units if you built $1,500 two-room houses.' 'But,' they said, 'the government don't build houses that cheap.' 'Well,' I said, 'at least spread them out. Our tribe has at least 35,000 acres.' But they won't listen."

A young man in his early thirties, Peltier was Tribal Community

Action Program Director on the Turtle Mountain Chippewa Reservation. He decided to try a little direct community action of his own. He would demonstrate to the government what tribal housing ought to be like by building his own house—Indian-style.

Up the road were dense forests and lovely lakes. It was a region of quiet beauty. One summer, Peltier and a few of his friends built a house in a field of flowers on the lake shore, with a wide screened porch looking out at the water. The cost was less than $1,500. He went to the builders in Belcourt in triumph, and told them of his private housing project:

"I said, 'Look, if the government can't build houses for $1,500 our tribe can. Let us have the money you are spending through the Community Action Program. We'll build our own housing project in our own way. In the woods. Away from the highway. And at one tenth the cost.'

"You know what they said?" Peltier grinned. " 'No!' "

The Chippewa was chagrined. But hardly surprised. "Just because we do not do things the way they think we should do things they think we cannot do anything," he said. "We have no 'initiative.' We are 'unrealistic.' If they just let us really do things our way for once, then individual 'initiative' would be no problem."

"We are the world's worst individualists," Peltier said. "Life ought to be free."

The old-fashioned individualism of the new tribalism was confounding the experts. Especially those in the government. Hardly had the city planners of the prairie gotten a blueprint for paving the grassroots off their drawing boards when some group of Indians was threatening to stomp on it. The housing projects of urban relocation kept rising on the reservations, but it was only the city Indians back from Chicago who would live in them. The factories kept coming to the reservations, but often the unemployed men would only let their wives work in them.

"I believe in the integrity of the individual," said Mel Thom. "Our Indian people should be made of strong individuals, with sound principles of our own thoughtful choosing. No government, federal, state, or tribal, should take the place of individual thinking."

Legendary was the willful, independent spirit of the old Indian.

He had to be "a man for all seasons," self-reliant and self-suffi-
cient, to survive in the wilderness. The image of the lone rider—
the one man against the forces of nature, the hero of the country's
most favored myth—was modeled upon the way of the Indian. The
individualism of this Indian was not that of an iconoclast; he was
obeying the beliefs and necessities of tribal life. It was celebrated
in his sacred songs. "Grandfather, hear me! I will live! I have said
it!" began the Opening Prayer to God of the Teton Siouxs' Sun
Dance. "I am making you a spirit," sang the Chippewa in the Death
Song. "I am poor," sang the Assiniboins; "I have suffered. I will
sacrifice. I wish to live." "I am very handsome," sang the Cherokee
lover; "I take your soul. Sge!" While the Omaha prayer simply
said, "Wa-kon'da, here needy he stands. I am he."

That was the old way of the Indian. That had to be the way of
the new Indian, Thom thought; for if the new tribalism was that
of "strong individuals" who lived by their own truth, then, "The
Indian people are going to remain Indian people for a long time to
the future with *every right to that identity*."

It is still so. "No one tells an Iroquois what to do," an Onondaga
young man said. "You can tell him. But he won't do it unless he
decides to." A Kiowa who worked for the government lamented:
"I talk to one of these country Indians all day. Sometimes all night.
They nod, they smile, and they do what they want to." A Kiowa
country Indian in Oklahoma said: "I can't speak for anyone but
myself. No one can speak for another Indian but himself." A Navajo
smiled. "We believe that no one should tell anyone how to think."

The Indian is fiercely and proudly individualistic. He is defiantly
so. What is there in tribalism that has brought about this seeming
paradox?

"What is the source of this? The spirit is the force behind the
psychological drive of the individual Indian," Herbert Blatchford
said. The Navajo youth leader believed, "If you take away the
Indian's religion and his tribal community you destroy him as an
individual. And as an Indian."

Individualism and tribalism? Aren't these two words contradictory?

The member of the tribe is at the same time a very private person.
He is a "whole man" within himself. He accepts his limitations as

well as his abilities. That is, he knows what he knows and what he doesn't know. He is sure of his identity, his place within the community, and his human and therefore humble ignorance before the power of the Great Spirit and the mystery of life. Knowing, not believing but knowing, the nature of his world makes it possible for the Indian to explore and express his own individuality with ease and freedom.

He lives within himself, but not for himself. The distinction is vital. Everything in tribal life is based on the community's protection of the individual. The tribe shelters a man's family with the umbrella of the kinship family. The tribe nourishes a man's well-being in time of failure with its built-in brotherhood and neighborliness.

"The Indian has a free spirit," Deloria, Jr., said. "And his tribe is his source for that. Like home base."

Communality of tribalism does not diminish the Indian's individuality. On the contrary it protects him socially and thus frees him individually. The stubbornness of the Indian was born of his bond of oneness with his community and the feeling of security that it offers him. The more secure his tribe is, the more secure the Indian feels —and the more independent and self-confident he is. Where his tribalism has been weakened the Indian tends to be unsure of himself, conformist and immobile.

Repressive, restrictive, ritual-dominated communities of passive individuals—these are some of the ways that tribal life has been described by those on the outside looking inside.

The young Indians protest that these words may describe the lives of those who studied them, but not the lives they know. It is the urban man in his mass society whose individualism is denied, they insist; it is technology that is the enemy of the individual. "Technology has as a basis the creation of the inhuman human," said Deloria, Jr. Technology has turned the individual into "The cog who fits into a certain gear mechanism and performs a certain 'function' as part of a machine. . . . Technology makes people feel an obligation to live but does not give a reason for acting or the feeling of having done something that is important to the person himself."

The individual is vital to the tribe. He has not been displaced by a machine. He participates in the life of the community by doing what he knows best and does best. "Participatory democracy is nothing new to tribal Indians," said Deloria, Jr. "Maybe we didn't invent it, but we sure practiced it. And I mean democracy of deeds, not words."

Nowadays the young Indian often feels less overwhelmed in his tribal society than in the massive structure of the industrial and technological complex of the city. He may feel he has more elbow room to develop his individuality. "There can be little doubt that technology has contributed to this yearning for old ways," Deloria, Jr., said. But this yearning has not been left to chance. It is the natural outgrowth of the upbringing of the Indian child.

He is encouraged to be a strong individual. From his early childhood his parents and grandparents teach the Indian child to take care of himself, to do things by himself. It was once necessary for his survival to learn ways of self-reliance. On the rural reservations it still is. And children are still taught in the old way.

"We do not restrict children the way non-Indians do," said Shirley Witt, the Mohawk youth leader. "Let the child learn about the world. Let him stumble and fall and learn to get up. If he needs help, help him, but don't stand over him with a psychological test and punish him every time he disobeys Dr. Spock. That is the Indian's usual attitude. Some people say it's too permissive. But the child grows up to be strong and independent."

His schools and social failures have often suppressed the "free spirit" of the young Indian. But where his individuality has survived these tests his boldness and independence have been the source of many a modern legend. The heroism of the young Indians in the armed forces is well known. So is that of the Mohawk high steel workers. So is that of the Zuñi forest-fire fighters. So is that of the Cherokee and Apache rodeo cowboys. So is that of native hunters of Alaska and the Makah fishermen of Puget Sound. These have been exceptional only to the extent that the dominant society has restricted the individuality of the tribal Indian.

It has been said that tribalism is a rigid and unbending way of life. But the new tribalism of the young Indians is showing itself to be more flexible and freer than the white man had imagined because of the rugged individualism that is inherent in tribal man's view of himself.

A young Red Lake Chippewa, Ronald Head, reflected this when he said: "I feel freer on the reservation. Ever since I came home I feel no one is telling me what to do, how to act, where to go. Tribal life is freer. Who is not Indian cannot feel it."

The young Navajo girl Roberta Harvey discovered it in a different way. Roberta was attending the Abbott Academy in Andover, Massachusetts, two thousand miles from her home in New Mexico. She wrote in a letter:

One summer away, away. A chance to see living as it is. A mirror image of myself and what I am. I have found myself and I have found [my] people. A gratitude for what I have. A gratitude for my heritage and culture. All I know is that I am myself and this I value as true, and the highest of all knowledge.

That one can cry, that one can laugh, that one can love, in a world of strangers, and yet be Indian. It is beauty.

Hundreds of odysseys of contemporary Indians have told of this individualism based upon tribalism. In the modern world the "home base" of kinship families, cultural roots, and tribal homelands has given the new Indians a freedom of movement that is unique. "We are nomads of old on wheels," Deloria, Jr., said. "You see, we can always go home again and have a home to go to." But it is not only the young who were free to roam without uprooting their individual psyches.

Old August King was one of the Seven Hereditary Chiefs of the Red Lake Chippewas. For thirty years, on and off, he had wandered in the world of the white man. The old man had come home. He had worked everywhere, from the chicken farms of New Jersey to the gourmet restaurants of New Orleans. "In Lousy Anna," he said. He was sophisticated in the folkways of the twentieth century. "I had five wives," he said, "all of them good."

"I was white enough to forget that I was Indian. But I never forgot it," the old man said.

King had been put in charge of the smoking of the fish in the Red Lake Tribal Fishery. It was a quiet job. Wearing his yellow rubber apron like a royal robe, but with a debonair flair, he had settled into tribal life. He smoked the fish "in the old Indian way, with pussy willows," he said. "Just for the Indians. The white man, he doesn't know the difference between a burnt fish and a smoked fish."

He had forsaken the city life, the gourmet restaurants, the sophistications of the white world, and his wives. All five of them. For what? To smoke a golden fish. But why?

"I heard the beat of the tom-toms," the old man said. "Here, in my heart."

He had not been able to dislodge his tribe. It was not separate from his self. A people within his mind. "Wherever I went I was a Chippewa," the old man said.

"My tribe is within me," a University of Oklahoma Indian boy said. "It gives me strength."

12

GO IN BEAUTY

One Sioux youth was an alcoholic. He hated alcohol, and he hated himself for drinking. He cried and he cursed himself. But he could not stop. Then one day when he could not stand it any more he went to his brother in tears, and he said to his brother: "My brother. You see how miserable I am. I cannot live this way. My brother, if you love me like a brother you will kill me." He said, "My brother, take my rifle and kill me."

And his brother who loved him like a brother took his rifle and killed him.

The brother was tried for murder. In court he told the judge what had happened. A friend who had been with the brothers at the time testified that the story was true. But there was much skepticism. The police had tried for days to break the friend's story and to force the brother to admit that the killing was the result of a fight. Neither the brother nor the friend would say another word. The district attorney now tried to shake their story. Still they would not say anything further. They refused to speak.

In exasperation the judge asked them, "Why do you refuse to speak? Don't you realize that you are on trial for your life? Don't you realize that you can be given the death penalty?"

The brother just looked at the judge. He quietly said, "We told you once." That was all he said.

He was acquitted of the murder of his brother. He could not be acquitted of his brother's death, though, any more than his brother could be acquitted of his wish to die.

The tale is a modern parable. It was told by the Reverend Vine Deloria, Sr. He leaned back in his chair and his eyes tightened to close out the memory of the murder trial; for the parable was the truth, the minister said.

Who was his brother's keeper? It had been the literal truth to the tribal Indian, the minister said, that everyone in the kinship family was responsible for the life and death of everyone else. The belief had merely been perverted by the alcohol and the rifle of the white man's society. Beneath the ugliness and the violence of their lives the two brothers were trying to keep alive the brotherly ways of their tribe. "Unto death he *was* his brother's keeper."

"Go in beauty," say the Navajos in parting. That too is a way of expressing the brotherhood of kinship. It is the blessing of one tribal brother to another. For life, not death. But can one "Go in beauty" into a world where brother kills brother in the name of brotherhood?

"I sorrow to see how our kinship loyalty has been turned against us," the minister had said. "We destroy ourselves."

Many have thought the kinship family was doomed. It was dying. The economic strains and psychological tensions of contemporary life had rendered it impotent and self-destructive of the very values it sought to preserve. Rather than keeping tribal society alive kinship was dragging Indian families to their demise. Kinship no longer functioned.

D'Arcy McNickles disagreed. "Kinship systems and lines of descent still function, often at variance with Government record systems and legal procedures," wrote the anthropologist, who was a member of the Flathead Tribe of Idaho. "Indeed, American Indian groups still retain many aspects of their own distinctive ways of life and have in only rare instances become 'Americanized.' "

Actually the kinship family has simply changed. It has been loosened up by the population explosion, it has been scattered to the four winds, and it has become almost intertribal. So many Indians have married into tribes other than their own that the expansion of the forms of kinship was inevitable. The old clans are rarely intact.

In many families, through intermarriage and movement, the related kin are spread through several states. "If I ever figured it out on paper," said an Arapaho boy, "my family would probably be two hundred people. Living God knows where! They are probably in at least nine states that I know offhand." The kind of work so many young Indians do—seasonal jobs and odd jobs—further extends the geography of kinship.

The National Indian Youth Council in its "Glossary" of new Indian words put it this way: "Integration" means "marrying into another tribe."

Little is known by non-Indians of the jet-age functions and modern forms of the kinship system. The anthropologists who have studied its ancestral history in minute detail have largely ignored its contemporary existence. Yet the young Indians often say that the modernized kinship system is one of the most vital elements of the new tribalism. It sustains them in their intellectual wanderings. It offers them the mobility to explore and experiment with new ways of revitalizing tribal life.

The young Indians have referred to the kinship system as "the Indian Social Security System." Mel Thom said: "It's like Social Security with direct action. And there is no government form to fill out."

His family, the kinship family, in which uncles are like fathers and cousins are like brothers, extends beneath his wanderings to universities and urban jobs, much like a huge and safe net. Relatives, as the tribesmen traveled and intermarried, have extended the benefits of the kinship system throughout the country. And these intertribal families help and feed their relative members as the tighter, much smaller non-Indian family does its immediate members.

Kinship on the reservations is still based on the clans. But in the cities it has been broadened to embrace a larger community of Indians.

"It works like this," Vine Deloria, Jr., said. "When I go to Standing Rock, I always have a place to stay, even though I don't live there. And my family doesn't live there. But I have relatives there.

"And in my home in Denver I'll always be perfectly happy to have relatives stay with me," he said. "But even Indians who are not 'family.'"

In his large, rambling house in Tahlequah, Oklahoma, with its many rooms, where Clyde Warrior lives with his wife and child, he insists that there is no wasted space. "My relatives and friends are always coming to stay a while," Warrior said. "That's the way I like it."

Children have been doubly protected by this kinship system. The Indian child and old person have always been special beneficiaries of "the Indian Social Security System."

"In your kinship system, there really are no orphans because everyone is more or less related, and you feel compelled to take in children without parents," Deloria, Jr., told a Subcommittee on Constitutional Rights of the Senate Judiciary Committee. In the hearings on the constitutional rights of the American Indian he said: "In *Look* magazine (June 1, 1965) Attorney General Katzenbach advocates 'substitute parents' as a means of handling juvenile delinquents. The kinship system did just that," Deloria, Jr., told the Senators. "In this social system there has been, until recently, no need for juvenile delinquency programs."

But the kinship family does more than care for the child. It recognizes his participation in the life of the larger family; he has his work to do, and his contribution to the communal well-being is appreciated and rewarded. He is not babied.

S. Gabe Paxton, Jr., guidance officer of the Sherman Institute for Indians in Riverside, California, observed these effects of the kinship family upbringing upon the Hopi students: "The Hopi child is never allowed to feel isolated or abandoned, for he always has several groups of relatives to whom to turn for comfort and reassurance. The tendency to treat children as a group apart from adults, strongly developed in White American culture, does not exist among the Hopis. A child is regarded as an important member of the community."

At the same time the Indian child is brought up with a natural ease and unusual freedom. Early educators, in an era when the teacher's ruler was a tool for punishment as well as measurement, thought the child-rearing methods of the Indians showed a "barbaric lack of discipline."

"The aversion of these Indians to restraint" in bringing up their children provoked consternation in the Victorian mentality of Indian Agency superintendents in the nineteenth century. Roswell Wheeler, who served at the Pima and Maricopa Agency, observed: ". . . although they were not in the habit of punishing their children, it was their custom to talk to and to lecture them a great deal at home, teaching them the difference between right and wrong" by personal example.

Young Indians who have had college training have commented on the similarities between the kinship families' way of bringing up and educating their children and some of the modern theories of child rearing and progressive education. "It was a mixture of John Dewey and Dr. Spock," said Shirley Witt, the Mohawk anthropologist.

"The larger society [is] beginning to adopt Indian social forms," Deloria, Jr., said. If that was so, the kinship family might be a starting point for study, he thought.

Unhappily, the kinship family is in trouble. It has been overwhelmed by urban tensions and ghetto poverty. The reservation Indians have been journeying to the cities in such numbers in search of jobs that the kinship family has been stretched great distances. It is being called upon to cover a multitude of urban sins for which it is ill-equipped. And it strains to the breaking point.

When a sojourning Indian finds work and an apartment, the word of his good fortune soon spreads to his relatives. He will be besieged.

Deloria, Jr., told the Senators: "Let them become spot welders, mechanics and the like [but] they are still Indians, whether on the reservation or in the city. And so relatives or some Indian in need would come to them, and immediately they would take them in, and pretty soon they did not have the earning power to support these people. Everybody then went down together, and you had a failure . . . because of the Indians' natural way of sharing.

"So [the Indians] are caught between—between wanting to continue to be Indian and take in these homeless children (and relatives), and turning them over to State institutions or foster homes. So tribes are having to let some of the kinship systems go by the board because they do not have the economic base to continue to provide for these people."

Poverty is not the worst enemy of the kinship family. The way of life of the dominant society, with its enticements and pressures, and the competitiveness of urban living, make the tribal way of sharing difficult.

Kathryn Polacca, the granddaughter of Hopi and Navajo headmen and a teacher in the Bureau of Indian Affairs' Adult Education Program, talked of the stresses and strains on the kinship family that have been created by the influence of "the white man's way."

"For this system to work well, everybody must believe in sharing food, money, or whatever the others need that you may have at this time. If some don't want to share, if some want to go to the white man's way, and just take care of the immediate family, the plan doesn't work so well, and there will be misunderstanding and hardships. It isn't easy; if you share too much, you can't save for your own needs; if you save enough, you can't share."

Eyapaha, the Sioux tribal newspaper, was equally sorrowful: "Generous as the Sioux are, it makes it mighty hard for the ones who are getting ahead to try to make a go at it while supporting others with no income."

Deloria, Jr., thought: "If we could get a better economic base, we could take care of some of these problems, the problems of orphans. . . ."

However, the Bureau of Indian Affairs, together with the Child Welfare League of America, resolved the problem of the weakened kinship families differently. Those who could no longer care for the children of their kin were helped by having their children offered to non-Indians to adopt. In nine years, 325 of these Indian children were adopted.

Seeing the newspaper advertisement that pleaded, "Adopt an Indian Child," Deloria, Jr., was reminded, he said, of the Christmas appeals of the Humane Society "offering puppies for adoption." The young Sioux shook his head sadly. "It may be humane, but it isn't human."

"Look at what your society does with orphans and old people," he said. "You have a society that would rather institutionalize an orphan or old person than take them into your homes. You would rather someone else took care of them. You give to the federal government and it gives it to someone else. You give to the church and it gives it to someone else. You have taken the human element out of it. The Indian shares. But your society has introduced 'giving.' If you see a human being in need, you take him into your house and help him. That is the Indian way. You don't give fifty dollars in taxes so that

the government can build a brick building fifty miles away to institutionalize him. That is the inhuman way."

It was a "return to Indian values," to "Indian humanism," that
Deloria, Jr., proposed. "The tribe," he wrote, "is the group within
which people are allowed to express themselves and realize they are
truly people."

The revival of Indian humanism had been the visionary hope of
every tribal prophecy since the first defeat of the tribes. It had never
been realized. Until this generation of university-educated Indians,
it had been no more than a nostalgic dream.

Writing in *Poor Richard's Almanac,* in 1775, in his "Remarks
Concerning the Savages of North America," the philosophically
hard-nosed Benjamin Franklin had wondered why the Indians thought
their life a "perfection of civility." The thought was to many all but
incomprehensible. But Franklin, with uncanny insight, touched the
core of "the great order and decency" in tribal life.

"The Savages," wrote Franklin, had a society where "There is no
force, there are no prisons, no officers to compel obedience or inflict
punishment." He left it there, went no further to explain this odd
phenomenon, and he was too honest to attempt what he could not
comprehend.

It remained for the Indians to tell of it. They tried for years to
explain that tribal life was built upon human and natural needs and
values. But they were not listened to and they were not understood.
Until, at last, they became silent.

Thomas Wildcat Alford, a Shawnee tribesman, was one of those
who tried in the nineteenth century to tell the country something
about the humanism of tribal life. He quoted at length from the unwritten codes of justice of the Shawnees. It might be remembered
that these were the willful people who had fought fiercely, under the
genius of Tecumseh, and had almost stayed the invasion of their
lands by the white men. Yet, in his recitation of the codes of these
warriors of the Appalachian Mountains, the Shawnee leader cited
two Christian-like commandments:

"Do not kill or injure your neighbor, for it is not him that you
injure. You injure yourself.

"Do not wrong or hate your neighbor, for it is not him that you wrong. You wrong yourself. Moneto, the Grandmother, the Supreme Being, loves him also as she loves you."

If these warriors sought to live by love how did they punish the transgressors? These "standards of conduct were just as rigid as the laws of any other people," said Alford, "but force was seldom used to enforce good conduct. *Each person was his own judge.* Deceitfulness was a crime. We lived according to our own standards and principles, not for what others might think of us. Absolute honesty toward each other was the basis of character."

So deeply were these codes ingrained in tribal life that when they met the "cunning and deception" of the white man, said Alford, these were ways of behavior "for which [the Indian] had no name." Many of the early Indian leaders uttered the same plaint.

Justice to the tribal man was human. Human needs were the measure of wrong and right. The values that industrial societies place upon property, money, status, and the manufacture of products for the market were almost nonexistent in tribal societies. And to this day these are secondary values in the minds of modern tribesmen.

The Indians therefore dealt with transgressors humanly. In the codes of tribal justice punishment was not necessarily humane—"an eye for an eye"—but it was personal and immediate. Whoever stole from his neighbor, or injured him, had to repay the debt of his theft or injury to the neighbor he had wronged. He did not pay the tribe. He "owed no debt to society," as such. Indemnity was not thought of as punishment of the wrongdoer, but as justice to the wronged.

The Legislature of New York State in 1965, under the direction of Attonery General Louis Lefkowitz, sought to codify the tribal concept of indemnity into criminal law. But its humanism was oddly eliminated. Indemnity would serve as an added burden of punishment. The law professors thought it might be a preventive threat against those who committed crimes against property, not as the Indians had viewed it, as the affirmation of the individual's responsibility for his brother's keeping.

When this inversion of the Indians' belief was pointed out to the Attorney General's office the reply was that it was "most interesting." It would be "looked into." But indemnity to affirm human brotherhood, rather than to punish human beings for violating the laws of property, was unknown to nontribal lawgivers.

Long ago these laws of the ancients ceased to govern the Indians. The legal codes of the modern tribes are ruled and judged by the rituals and laws of the white men, or by imitations. Economically and politically the needs of the dominant society have been successfully imposed upon the tribes—and the tribal morality has had to accede to these. It seems to do so. Laws, in any event, are enforced that require the Indians to conform to the necessities of technological life. And they do, at least on the surface.

"What do you expect?" exclaimed Robert Thomas, the Cherokee anthropologist. "Men have been tribal for hundreds of thousands of years. Men have been technological for barely four hundred years. Do you really think that the history of tribal man can be wiped out by laws?"

Humanism is persistent. The young Indians think it has merely been submerged, though words belie it and laws supersede it. But the humanism of tribal man is not a philosophy that another philosophy can undo by logic, they insist.

"This is real tough for non-Indians to see," Vine Deloria, Jr., said. "Because Indians think like Indians unconsciously, without projecting a rationalization or goal to fulfill, or 'pilot project' of logic. You look for it and you don't find it. But it's there. If you recap the tribal past, but in a modern way, you can't see it unless you have a tribal past and know where to look. But it's there. I *feel* it."

It hides under new forms. It is visible in the gusto, unadorned honesty, *joie de vivre* and camaraderie of some of the young Indians. That is, when they are within a tribal atmosphere. Then there is an uninhibited naturalness in the way that they share their enjoyment of life. "Enjoyment" is too mild a word. "Celebration" is truer. For the essence of tribal humanism has been its glorification of man in his natural state, to whom no experience is alien. "The whole man with a whole view of life," Deloria, Jr., said, "is the ideal of the Indian."

Love of life to the tribal Indian means the love of every living thing. His passions are specific, down to earth. His love, be it for a stone or a star, is real. It is not that he endows these things about him with human qualities so much as that he treats them as human beings. Once again the modern meaning of the word "love" is inadequate.

Paul Bernal, of Taos Pueblo, said it this way:

"It is said, years ago, many years ago, when the Indian was alone in his country, he cherished every little thing. He cherished the auger, the bow, the stones, the buffalo hide, the deerskin to make moccasins with. He cherished the corn, the kernel of corn that he planted with his hands to make his flours, his bread. He cherished the trees. He believed the trees had a heart, like a human being. He never cut down a living tree. A tree was a living thing. It was not to be cut, or hurt, or burned.

"Every living thing that grew from the green earth of nature, he cherished.

"In the skies he cherished the king of the flying species—the eagle. He cherished the little birds as well. He cherished the skies and stars as well.

"He cherished human beings, all people, most of all. He cherished himself."

If "every living thing" was to be cherished and worshiped equally, it was then natural to the humanism of the Indian that "every living thing" was to be shared. Humanism that extended beyond the human being, that extended beyond the kinship family, was bound to conflict with the values of the society that conquered it.

The Council for Christian Social Action of the United Church of Christ, in seeking to explain the tribal origins of Indian humanism to its non-Indian parishioners, wrote that the "basic difference in cultures . . . is in our value concepts. We memorialize 'rugged individualism' and free enterprise. The more we get the better we are. Materialism is our way of life. For the American Indian (and many other 'folk' cultures) the opposite is the highest value. The only reason for having something is to give it away."

Herbert Blatchford would agree. Like so many of the young Indians he no longer lives on his tribal reservation, or in a hogan, but rents a house in town, and possesses a car, a television set, a tape recorder, and an office with a desk. Yet, he casts dubious eyes upon most of these possessions. What value do they have?

"I feel that the Anglo-American is continually striving to satisfy

his spiritual desires by acquiring material means. His belief is that
the way to the Ultimate State is through acquiring riches. But I feel
the Indian does not have a great attraction to material means. I do
not mean by this that the Indian has no use for material things. He
has. But I am attempting to say that the Indian is trying to reach the
Ultimate State by living in harmony with the spiritual universe. The
Indian is trying to satisfy his spiritual needs by spiritual means."

Robert Thomas thought that this difference between living in nature
and the conquest of nature is the difference between enjoying life and
consuming life. "Americans confuse consumption with experience,"
Thomas said.

He described the two attitudes this way:

"When I go fishing with [white] friends of mine, they go out in a
boat and they're going to fish. And they fish. And they've got just so
much time between two and five to get this fishing done. They've got
only three hours to do it in.

"And they're supposed to be 'recreated' at the end of those three
hours so that they can go back and produce some more.

"So they go out and they've consumed those three hours. They
don't want to sit in the boat and not catch fish, because you can do
that at home. That's nothing; it's nonfishing. You're out to fish. So
you want to get the biggest fish, and you start the motor, and you
go over to that part of the lake, and you don't get any. So you consume fishing.

"Incidentally, a lot of American men seem to consume their women
in the same way—the sexes consume each other."

Man's love of life is the center of the Indian world, and the
harmony of man with his spiritual and physical world is the circle
that enlarges that humanistic belief. "Where does this come from,
harmony in the soul of the Indian?" said Anne Wauneka, the great
lady of the Navajo tribe. "It comes from nature. It comes from everywhere. It comes from Indian way of being. It comes from beauty.

"Beauty is really used with nature. You see beautiful things when
you look about.

"Beauty is the Navajo way of life. They are not looking for bad
things, but the bad things are always hanging around, too.

"In the prayer it's always beauty. In every direction: to the east, to the south, to the west, to the north. A medicine man always says and feels that every Navajo should walk in beauty.

"It is very hard to express what it means. To us it is significant. And I believe we should keep it to ourself. When there is going to be beauty there is going to be beauty.

"We feel that nature is beautiful. The world is beautiful that you are living in. The blue sky, the rains that fall should all be in beauty.

"Every Navajo should be walking in beauty. Beautiful thinking. Beautiful image. Beautiful children. Whatever they do must be in the sense of beauty."

But tribal society and technological society are hardly in harmony. They are often in violent conflict. His inability, in the past, to reconcile this divisive state that foreboded evil and death demoralized the elder Indian.

It remained for the younger generation of educated Indians who have lived in both worlds and who understand both worlds to balance the improbables. In the late 1950's Bernadine Eschief, a Shoshone-Bannock girl, spoke at the Third Southwestern Youth Conference the thoughts of her fellow students: "Indians should retain their traditions while integrating into the dominant culture, by choosing the best of both, coupled with a belief in the Great Spirit."

These thoughts were reiterated by a young Oglala Sioux with the fittingly fiery name of William Fire Thunder. He spoke boldly of what the young Indians have most often preferred to speak of among themselves: "When civilization is ready to destroy itself, Indian youth can rise up and again teach the science of [spiritual] survival to the white world. If, that is, the Indian remains an Indian. I believe that the Indian can master the techniques of the whites and still remain an Indian."

The young, educated Indians are not seeking to hold on to the tribal past. Living in fading nostalgia as walking museum pieces does not appeal to the youth. Rather they wish to live as contemporary Indians in the modern world, to modernize the old tribal ways so that they will not only survive but will be revitalized.

"I suggest that tribes are not vestiges of the past, but laboratories of the future," Deloria, Jr., said. "The tribal groups are in transition, but to a new form of social understanding. If understood by other people, their way might help solve some of the pressing social problems of today. As we see the larger society beginning to adopt Indian social forms, we feel impelled to suggest that tribes be allowed maximum flexibility in developing their own economic, political, and human resources. In that way they might bring the best of Indian understanding of life to the rest of this country.

"I think you might learn something from us. How to be happier. How to be more human," Deloria, Jr., said.

In the face of these beliefs the new Indians have chafed at being called "culturally deprived." More and more of the youth believe that their own culture will not only survive but is superior to much of the way of life they see about them in the country.

"Culturally deprived," scoffed the Youth Council in its "Glossary": the "Culturally deprived" child, they wrote, was "The suburban white child!"

"Who is culturally deprived? Not the Indian." Mel Thom laughed angrily. "We resent being called 'culturally deprived.' We are not. You might say we are the only people in this melting pot who have kept their culture. And we aim to keep it. The Indians are the only tribal people in the United States. Tribal people have a unique culture that will exist as long as there are tribes.

"It's the urban white American who is culturally deprived. It's the tourist who is culturally deprived," Thom said. "What culture has he got? The culture of the mass media that is fed to him. He doesn't have any culture he can say is really his."

Thom believes that tribal life is so rich, so cultured, so human that it could contribute to the cultural void that he feels the urban and suburban man lives in. "The culture I am talking about is not something like a war bonnet and a powwow dance put on for tourists. It's something that the Indian has in the way the Indian lives. Not as he lived in the past, but as he lives now. That exists in his *being* an Indian."

The love of life, the love of every living thing, the joys of nature, the harmony of man with the natural world, the communal brotherhood of the tribe, the free spirit of the individual, the loving—not prohibitive—care of children, the larger love of the kinship family, the concept of justice, not punishment, the wholeness of man, the eternity of the present, the root and identity of the soul—these are some of the things that tribal society might bring to technological society in spiritual payment for its material goods and services.

Now that the young Indians are reviving the tribal beliefs of their forefathers they are seeking to modernize them. In doing so they are changing them to fit the needs of the day. Where the ancient ways would not yield to the twentieth century, or were hopelessly lost, the youth are creating a new Indianness out of the old.

It is true even of the war dances. The young Indian is in some ways personified by the way he dances. Not by the religious dance, or by the tourist dance. These are not dances that the individual does for himself. He dances then for the gods, or to pay his grocery bills. But when he dances for himself in university Indian clubs, in urban powwows, or on the reservations during the summer nights, then the old rituals take on new meanings. And the ancient dances become a personal chronicle of the journey to the new tribalism.

Some of the new Indians are ardent dancers. There are not many who are champion war dancers like Clyde Warrior. Yet in no other youth movement in the country are so many of its intellectual firebrands given to stomping down the imprint of their ideas on the earth. The SDS collegians did not dance on the campuses, nor do the SNCC militants dance around the courthouses.

But the young Indians dance with a purpose.

When the National Indian Youth Council began it might be said to have begun with a war dance of Indian college students. It was the Nizhoni Dancers of the Kiva Club at the University of New Mexico who in 1954 provoked the discussions that were to lead to the creation of the Youth Council. "We built our club around that dance group," said Herbert Blatchford, the council's first director. When the Fish-Ins climaxed with a protest rally at the Washington State Capitol the Indians symbolically did a war dance on the steps of the rotunda. When a group of Sioux decided to picket the White House they brought along a drum to do a war dance at the East Gate. When an Indian leader suggested the tribes demonstrate before the state legislatures to make their needs known he urged that they "do war dances on the floors of the chambers! That might wake them up!"

The young Indians do not dance merely to amuse themselves. Or to pass the time. In the dance they rediscover and remake themselves; for though most of them no longer know the religious beliefs that shaped the rituals of the dance steps, the youths create an individual, contemporary, and living Indianness as they dance.

In the Institute of American Indian Arts in Santa Fe, there was a young and talented painter, Phil George of the Nez Percé tribe, who described how he came to do the war dance, and what it meant to him. "I was once asked to wear a warrior's robe, like a Roman senator. I'm not a great warrior, or a chief. But I am the descendant of some great Indian leaders and I obeyed the request." He watched how the others danced and he imitated them. He danced and he thought: "To war dance is to pray to Tahmahnewes, the Great Spirit. When Indians of long ago practiced this ritual they did not put on a show. The people did not applaud." In his boyhood he had never thought about these things, he said. Now dancing the war dance the past he had never known came to him.

"The war dance was a prayer for courage in war," the young man said. "Today the war I fight is life. I want to defeat my greatest enemy —myself. It is a tough war, a real challenge. To win I need the help of Tahmahnewes.

"Yes, the fancy war dance is attractive and the timing is difficult. This form has derived from the wishes of the white man to see an exciting and colorful spectacle. White men have encouraged Indians to show off, to entertain them. I must dance traditionally.

"My greatest thrill," he said, "is the war dance." When he danced he was "mentally and physically refreshed." He was an Indian again. He danced to make himself "more human, more loving, more peaceful." In this way the old war dance had become a dance of inner peace.

There are three dances. There are three cultures. One is for the gods to know, one is for the tourists to see, and one is for the new Indians to feel.

Sang the Nez Percé youth as though in a trance:

> *Carry me in regalia of bygone days,*
> *Plumed by the morning breath of Appaloosas,*
> * I'll drum.*
> * I'll sing.*

Hold me without bruising, as in embrace,
Carpeted on palms of loving hands.
Move through the camps from west to east,
For my sun rises, does not set. . . .
> *I'll drum.*
> *I'll sing.*

13

AS LONG AS THE GRASS
SHALL GROW

". . . no Mohawk has ever been buried in Brooklyn."

In the gutters of the skyscrapers twenty minutes from Times Square, where the longshoremen of the duchy of Anastasia, the late prince of the underworld, lived, on the sprawling waterfront of New York City with its many-cargoed freighters from around the world, there have long been secluded the most famous urban Indians in the country. The Mohawks of Caughnawaga have been coming to work and to live there for fifty years. And for fifty years the coffins of their dead have been shipped home to be buried.

The Mohawks of Caughnawaga are the high structural steel workers, the acrobats of the skyscrapers, the "jockeys of the clouds." It is their skill and courage that have built the fabled towers of Manhattan: the Empire State Building, Rockefeller Center, the Waldorf-Astoria, the George Washington Bridge, and those numbered and nameless steel and stone peaks that are the feats of modern architecture. It is daring work and dangerous. Ever since the days, in 1915, when the first tribesmen came to tightrope-walk on the beams of the early skyscrapers, many have lost their lives in building the symbols of modern cities.

Why then were their coffins sent to the weedy old dirt of the

Caughnawaga Reserve of Canada to be buried? Four hundred miles by hearse. Not one of the Mohawk steel workers who died building New York has ever been buried in New York.

"In a fundamental sense," wrote anthropologist Ruth Blumenfeld, "though the Caughnawaga Mohawk ironworkers have succeeded in and are part of the white man's city—they never left home." They go home every summer while they are alive and, when they die, forever.

Why does their land call the Mohawks even in death? It is best to begin at the beginning. Once the Indians of America lived on what the real-estate entrepreneurs have since decided was 1,905,000,000 acres. The country was theirs. Of those almost two billion acres barely a remembrance—56 million acres, or 2.9 percent—of the land has been left in their hands.

The legend of the theft of Indian land has been a romantic myth. Eskimo leader William Hensley said of this vanishing land: "It was by the use of laws that our people have been deprived of their land." Most of their land was taken from them with unscrupulous legality by treaties ratified by the Congress and signed by the government. Treaties of peace they were called. But they were little more than real-estate deals. From 1778 to 1868, in ninety years, there were 370 of these treaties signed by the federal nation with the Indian nations. The Cherokees signed twenty-two. The Delawares signed twenty-five. The Sioux signed thirty-nine. The Chippewas and the Potawatomi signed forty-seven each. There were so many treaties not because there were so many Indian Wars, but because there were so many Indian lands that the tribes were forced, or enticed, to sign away.

"We are the only people who have a history of getting the shaft from the federal government," Vine Deloria, Jr., said. "I mean, you don't have federal laws taking away anyone else's land, or destroying anyone else's communities. But we have been *legally* given the shaft. The treaties were *legalized* theft."

Roger Jourdain, the tribal chairman of the Chippewas of Red Lake, in Minnesota, reflected upon the duplicity of history: "Lincoln—the 'Great Emancipator'?" Jourdain scoffed: "He emancipated the slaves and he emancipated ten million acres of our land at the same time." The "Great Emancipator" not only signed the Homestead Act of 1862 that opened the West for settlement of Indian lands, Jourdain said. It was during Lincoln's presidency that the Treaty of Red Lake was signed, which stripped the Chippewa Tribe of much of their ancestral land.

An Oklahoma Cherokee joked about this. His humor was trenchant: " 'Course, in the Historys, Wars always start 'for patriotism's sake,' but you read on, then get down to the Peace Conference and you find that the historian has to write pretty fast and veil things over very cleverly, or the reader is apt to discover what changed hands at the finish besides a mere satisfying of honor. You look at all Wars and you will find that there is more new deeds for land signed at these peace conferences than there is good will."

The caustic humorist was Will Rogers. "So, you see, in Wars the Slogan is Honor, but the object is Land," Rogers said. "They are always fighting for Independence, but at the finish they always seem to be able to use quite a snatch of the defeated opponent's land to be Independent on."

Rogers was born on a ranch north of Claremore at a time when Oklahoma was still Indian Territory. He was, he once said, "an ornery Indian boy," who grew up when the Cherokee Nation still ruled: "We then had our own Government and the name Oklahoma was as foreign to us as Tooth Paste." So there was more than a touch of personal history in his historical comment: "I doubt if there is a thing in the world as wrong or unreliable as History. History ain't what it is; it's what some Writer wanted it to be, and I just happened to think ours is as Cock-eyed as the rest.

"It is funny, what a respect and National Honor a few Guns will get you, ain't it?" Rogers added. "It all depended on which end of it you were—on the sending or receiving end."

By the time the Congress had halted treaty making in 1871, the Indians had about 140 million acres left—of the nearly two billion. Unsatiated by this triumph in land wars—the real Indian wars—the Congress in 1887 passed the Allotment Act, which facilitated the acquisition of most of the rest. Supposedly, the Allotment Act was aimed at "civilizing" the Indians, by breaking up tribal society and communal land and offering each family 160 acres to convert the tribesmen into New England farmers. But as the minority report of the House Committee on Indian Affairs said at the time: "The real aim of this bill is to get at the Indian lands and open them up for settlement. The provisions for the apparent benefit of the Indian are but a pretext to get his lands and occupy them." That was what happened. In one generation the Indians lost an additional ninety million acres.

And it was the worst land that was left to them. If the Indians were to be exiled to reservations, on the periphery of society, it followed that the land they would be permitted to hold on to would be marginal and submarginal. So it was.

The Branch of Soil Conservation of the Bureau of Indian Affairs has estimated that the reservation lands consist of 14 million acres that are "critically eroded," and 17 million acres that are "severely eroded," and 25 million acres that are "slightly eroded." Of the 56 million acres of land left them, the Indians are the proud owners of 56 million acres of erosion.

Little good for anything but grazing nearsighted cows, some 61 percent of that acreage is scrawny grassland. And most of that is leased to white ranchers. The tribal Indians farm barely 6 percent of their own lands. Of those 3,500,000 acres of farmland, 2,900,000 acres are in dry farming; that is, farms where there is no irrigation, and little—or no—water.

In the Hopi villages these dry farms have been called miracles of agriculture. The corn has grown tall in the white hot sands of the deserts for centuries, nourished only by the ceremonial rain dances and prayers in the Kivas, and the sacred scarecrows.

"Only the Hopis could have grown anything in those deserts," said a government agriculturist at Keams Canyon. He thought it miraculous, but had too much faith in his scientific soil analyses to be quoted as saying anything so blasphemous. "Just say it *seems* miraculous," he said.

Miracle or not, it need not have been. The waters of the Colorado River, which flows to the north of the Hopi pueblos, pour millions upon millions of gallons into the green fields of the white farmers in several states, while these Pueblo Indians, who had devised vast systems of irrigation long before the thirteenth century, have to depend on prayers to their gods for rain.

In his "Voices Out of Utah," a passage in his morality play *The*

Dervish and the Offensive Stranger, Mark Twain had a trenchant comment, as he would, on this paradox:

The White Chief (to his people): This wide plain was a desert. By our heaven-blest industry we have dammed the river and utilized its waters and turned the desert into smiling fields whose fruitage makes us prosperous and happy, a thousand homes where poverty and hunger dwelt before. How noble, how beneficent, is civilization!

The Indian Chief (to his people): This wide plain, which the Spanish taught our forefather to irrigate (sic), was a smiling field, whose fruitage made our homes prosperous and happy. The white American has dammed the river, taken away our water for his own valley, and turned our field into a desert; wherefore we starve.

Where the Indians had water, as did the Paiutes of Pyramid Lake in Nevada, efforts were made to take it from them; and where the Indians had land, as did the Senecas of New York, efforts were made to flood their land.

"Rather than shooting Indians, it is now more fashionable to drown Indians by building dams," said Mel Thom. "The 'Army' is still at work to destroy Indian life. Now they are called the Army Engineers. Indians have 'dam' problems in New York, Montana, Arizona, and now we hear something about a dam up in Alaska. And 'dam' Indian land isn't worth much these days. The title 'Indian' seems to lower the value."

The land of the Indians has been dammed up, bled dry, eroded and flooded and stripped, leased out, wasted, and legally stolen. On the reservations are pockets of poverty and erosion of hopes, the reminders of defeat and degradation, where the poorest of the poor subsist on one-third to one-half the poverty-level income, in substandard huts and shacks, beset by the highest disease and youngest death-age rates in the whole country.

If this is so—and it is more so than ever—why do the Mohawks want to go home again? Why does any Indian?

Land to the tribal Indian is not the source of his food alone. It is more than his ancestral home. It is more than the root of his uniqueness as an Indian, his identity, and his psychological security. It is all these things; yet it is something more.

In a way that is vaguely understood by the logical and technological society, the Indians' religion is rooted in the land.

"To be blessed with nature," said Anne Wauneka, was how the older generation of her people, the Navajos, expressed it. She tried to tell what this meant to them: "What made the Navajo? What happened in the beginning? What is it, let's say, this corn pollen, which is very sacred in the beginning of life of a Navajo—what is it? What are the sacred mountains? What are the connections with nature? Why is the corn planted—the yellow corn and the white corn.

"And the Sacred Songs are pertaining to these corns. And the Sacred Songs are sung to the Sacred Mountains. To the Sun. To the Mother Earth. To the Great Bodies of Waters.

"And the prayers are performed at a certain hour of the day, or a certain hour of the night. Not usually at the hand of the clock. But it's at the movement of the stars. Or the movement of the Sun. Or the movement of the Moon—the Half-Moon, the New Moon.

"These are connections that are made. There are long stories connected with these things. Many connections. And the stories are long.

"There are many sacred things within the Navajo country. Very sacred to them. It is very hard for a non-Navajo to understand some of these beliefs. It is very strong."

She was talking of the religious beliefs of a tribe with a sophisticated and modern educational system, hundreds of university students, highly astute political leaders, that owned tribal industries and banks capitalized at tens of millions of dollars, and that had a complex IBM in its tribal offices. She was talking for the elders of the tribe, but she was not talking of a dim tribal past. Until a few years ago the industrial complex of the Navajo had as its vice chairman an old medicine man—Scott Preston.

The educated youth as well believed in these religious ties to the Mother Earth, though many denied it. Many were embarrassed by it.

A boy of the Yakima Tribe told how he was initiated into manhood. His mother was dying. His time had come to leave his childhood. Ted Palmanteer, who was studying at the Institute of American Indian Arts in Santa Fe, told how he had gone into the forests of Washington State in his rites of passage, during the Eisenhower Administration. His initiation took place in the 1950's, not the 1850's.

"I, a boy, have come into the forest to win my spirit and become a man. My pure white heart quickens with waiting. I listen, sniff the air, smell the damp odors; look and see the green sights. I yell, scream, and hear my own deep echoes."

Four days and nights he wandered in the forest seeking the spirit of his manhood. But it did not come to him. He cried out: "Nature, give me a spirit. I need a spirit. Send me one tonight, for I am yours. You are my mother. You must take care of me. I lay my soul to your mercy.

"Nature! Pity me for I am of you. I need a strong mountain spirit. Give me the wolverine. Give me the bear. Give me the wolf, or sly coyote. Maybe the swift deer, the sneaky cougar, or the never-seen bobcat's spirit. Here I fast, waiting, waiting. Listen!"

Then, on his fourth day in the forest, his uncle came to him and told him that his mother had died. He had to come home to her funeral.

Someone at the coffin began to sing the old Yakima war song. It was then he felt the spirit within him: "It moves in my body, in my soul. I can feel it fighting in me. It tears at my heart, my throat. It shatters my whole being. What can it be?

"That song! It is the old Kamaiakin song. Kamaiakin, the most powerful war chief of the Yakimas. His spirit lives and is mine. He was great, and now his ruthless spirit is mine. His charmed, reckless ways are mine. I can use them as I wish. The world is mine with all its good and bad, for I am a man."

The Earth Mother was now his mother. She was the catalyst of his manhood.

Of this religious feeling of the tribal Indian for the land Mary Lou Payne, who left her homeland to become assistant director of the Association on American Indian Affairs, said: "The Oriental contemplated nature; the white man conquered nature; but the Indian lived in nature." She, though she had lived in New York City for several years, went home every summer, to the Cherokee Reservation, for what she thought of as "earth therapy."

"The Indian interacts with nature," Mary Lou Payne said. "A lot of people can't understand why the Indian wants to hold on to the reservation. It is more than just land to him. There are religious ties to it."

Said Vine Deloria, Jr.: "It gives him his life. It gives him his identity. He treats the land just like he treats the people around him. He is not so much interested in speculating on that land, as he simply wants to live there and preserve his way of life, his community. The Indian does not understand the 'value' of land in American terms. He is not a speculator on a piece of the ground.

"Society's justification for stealing the Indians' land has been, 'Well, they had this land, but what did they do with it?' As if everything in life was to be 'done with.' But the point that the white man has missed was that the Indian lived on it."

One hundred years before, the old chief Standing Bear of the Sioux had uttered a similar plaint: "The white man does not understand the Indian for the reason that he does not understand America. He is too far removed from its formative processes. The roots of the tree of his life have not yet grasped the rock and soil. The white man is still troubled by primitive fears. . . . The man from Europe is still foreign and alien. And he still hates the man who questions his path across the continent.

"But in the Indian the spirit of the land is still vested. It will be until other men are able to divine and meet its rhythm. Men must be born and reborn to belong. The bodies must be formed of dust of their forefathers' bones."

From the old chief Standing Bear to the young university-graduated Vine Deloria, Jr., the attitude of the Sioux toward their lands had not greatly changed.

In the eerie Badlands of South Dakota is the habitat of the coyote, hawk, and rattlesnake. Humans cannot survive in its dry gullies and alkali flats. Yet, to the Oglala Sioux, these Badlands evoke a physical ecstasy and metaphysical reverence.

Jake Herman, an Oglala who had recently been elected to the Todd County school board, said, "Way out in the valleys of the Badlands, far away from the river and seas, there is one royal campus for me. When I am in the Badlands, I feel like a king. When I am away, I feel like a bum."

Herman went there in the spring. "When the green grass and birds come back, I want to go to the Badlands just to wonder and walk around. I want to sit under a well-balanced, spreading cedar tree, embedded in rocks and clay, where the agates glitter like the snake that glides and glitters and goes into a Badland rift. I want to sit on the green below, gaze into the blue above, to see Kola Wamblee [the eagle] soar and sail."

What was it that he felt when he sat there by himself? He heard the drums of history: "Sioux legends tell us that these Badlands have seen many summers that shine, and winters of snows, where once the throbbing of drums vibrated over the sagebrush flats, and the jangle of roweled spurs made Western music over the cactus flats," Herman said. "Mother Nature's gift to mankind stands in the Badlands. . . ."

Love of nature does not explain this. The truer word is "reverence"; in the belief in the Mother Earth there is a religiosity. The intensity with which the tribal Indian expresses these emotional ties to his land has lately taken on the quality of tribal nationalism. And that has strengthened the older religious belief with a modern dimension.

These beliefs are not incomprehensible to the white man. But they make him somehow uncomfortable—especially the thought that there are university-educated young Indians who might worship, if with nothing more than an awe of the unknown, a Mother Earth. In a time of the Freudian anti-woman, such a thought is disturbing.

The new Indian is a religious man. His religion is still rooted in beliefs in the life of the land, the Mother Earth. It is less overt, more internal, but it persists within his emotions. Matthew High Pine, a tribal leader of the Oglala Sioux, talked of these roots of his tribe in their land.

"We, the Oglala Sioux, have chosen this way of life, and I am sure the other reservations across the state have chosen also to be left alone—'to live and let live.' The majority of the Indian people are content to remain 'status quo' on a reservation. We are not isolationists and we do not think of ourselves as an island. Neither do we advocate a socialist kind of government. But we are content now to live on the reservation, the wide-open spaces, where hospitality still reigns and the atmosphere is friendly."

Land is the measure of life. In his view of the land the tribal Indian denies the values placed on it by the white society. His own values are to him more eternal and essential to the human spirit, having existed before the advent of the barbed wire and commercial fence.

The tribal council of the Northern Cheyenne Tribe of Montana, spoke of this traditional view:

"Our reservation is more than a reservation to us Northern Cheyenne. Our land is the home of our people, and that is why our grandfathers broke out of prison in Oklahoma and died and starved and froze and fought all the way back to this good place.

"We want to hold every foot of our land. We do not want one foot sold out of Northern Cheyenne ownership. Once our land belonged to the whole tribe and no Cheyenne could sell away a piece of it. That was good. Then the land was allotted. Every Cheyenne was given a piece of it. Today we children of those Cheyenne are very poor, and God will forgive us for selling our pieces of our homeland to buy food and clothes. But it is not good for our people to do that. When they have eaten and worn out the clothes or spent the money childishly, they live right here among us on relief, and a part of our community is gone forever."

William Hollow Breast, a vice chairman of the Northern Cheyenne tribal council, lamented: "With the cooperation of the reservation's government officials, and with the help of lots of liquor to help talk Indians into selling, they [the white man] might get our land. But we are hoping to stop them."

It was the old conflict. The clash over the two views of land value had led inevitably to a clash over the land itself. But with the decline of the reservation land that age-old struggle has reached toward its final solution.

Up in Alaska, the Eskimos and Indians are facing the old conflict, which has reached its last stage. In the tundras and woodlands of that vast territory there are more than 103 million acres of native lands whose fate has yet to be legally decided. The bill by which the Congress voted the statehood of Alaska empowered the government of the new state to select acreage from these "federal lands." But the native people objected: "These are not public lands that you can give away. These lands are ours." Eskimos and Alaskan Indians had been trapped as the tribal people always had been in a conflict not of their making.

The Eskimo legislator William Hensley described how once again the native land was being lost: "We don't 'use' and 'occupy' land. We don't have 'deeds,' like everyone else does. Nor do we understand town-site surveys and things of this sort. This is because we don't understand the use of land as you know it. Of little squares and triangles. And lines on paper.

"It's a very large state. And there's land enough for everybody. But, naturally, the land they want is where we are. They come into the villages with groups of surveyors, and start auctioning off the lots. And the native people don't have the money to buy their own land. Or more probably they are out hunting. So they don't obtain land in their own villages, which are auctioned out from under them. We are unable to get land in our own country."

It is not politically necessary or legally possible to sign treaties of peace with the Eskimos and Indians of Alaska to acquire their land. "We are no military threat," William Hensley said, half smiling. "Once we might have been. But we are not now." The tribes of Alaska and elsewhere had long since been defeated, had surrendered to the sovereignty of the government, and had been rendered politically impotent.

Even so, the *Tundra Times,* the newspaper of the Eskimo, Aleut, and Athapascan Indians of Alaska, reported the native people were resisting the loss of their lands: "There is a silent struggle that is going on in northern Alaska that most people are unaware of. The struggle is the interchange of two cultures. What is unique is that the ancient culture is resisting the onslaught of civilization."

The policies of the government had to change, as they do with every era and every administration. But the basic design has remained the same. "Civilizing" of a tribal society meant the acceptance of "the full responsibility of citizenship." That, as the Hoover Commission reiterated, meant eventual "full integration" in the mainstream of the dominant society.

And those who envisioned this as the final solution for tribalism thought it required the dissolution of tribal land. Legality moves in mysterious ways.

In the "lower forty-eight," as the Eskimos and Alaskan Indians call the older states, the problem is more complex and less obvious than an open acquisition of tribal lands. The treaties of peace have the effect of protecting those reservations that are still left.

And there is the city Indian to contend with. Citifying the tribal

Indian seems a hopeless task as long as he has the tribal reservations to return to. He, with typical Indian stubbornness, has begun to use his urban residence to set up extension services of tribal life, and to reinforce the economy of his reservation kinship family with the proceeds of his city job. William Hagan, in his *American Indians,* reflected the dismay this caused among the advocates of the melting pot: ". . . as long as the ties with the reservation exist, any relocated Indian who encounters difficulty in adjusting finds it easy to take that way out." That is, to go home. He thought this "depressing."

"The ultimate aim [of the white man] is to bring about the breakup of the Indian tribes throughout the country by doing away with the reservations," said *The American Indian,* the publication of the San Francisco Indian Center. Society sought to accomplish this, the magazine said, by forcing the tribal Indian "into [its] big melting pot, which they so fondly refer to. This is to quit being Indians, give up your customs, and act like a white man."

Year by year there has been an attrition of tribal land. Some of the tribes have been reduced to a fraction of their former reservations. And there are others that have accepted the enticements of the government and voted for termination—as did the Menominee and Klamath—and have given up their tribal lands.

These measures created a sorrowful mixture of distress and determination. Something more sweeping was needed if the final solution was to be effective. The Indian Omnibus Bill of 1967 was that government solution. "Rumor is that the latest legal twist is to have the tribes mortgage their reservations. It's the main proposal in the bill," said Vine Deloria, Jr. "Ostensibly it would be so we could raise capital, but many tribes think it's just another scheme to get their land."

Are the reservation lands then doomed to extinction? Are the tribes to be doomed with them?

"The Indian will wake up one day to find he has been converted into a white suburbanite. And all the land that he will have will be a ticket to a parking lot," Deloria, Jr., thought. "They are trying to make us into white suburbanites. They will only create another social crisis. They don't understand Indians."

In reservation after reservation, the tribes are seeking their own way out of the economic erosion of their land problems. They have begun to use the real-estate methods of the white man to buy back the tribal lands that have been lost. "We have to beat the white man at his own economic game," Deloria, Jr., said. History would be re-written by deeds.

These "land consolidation programs" are a peculiar combination of communal tribalism and modern real-estate methods. One of the most successful is that of the Cheyenne River Sioux. The destitute reservation of this tribe was hidden in the wastelands of prairie grass and lonely buttes on the banks of the Great Bend of the Missouri that poured through the expanse of central South Dakota. It was a forgotten region of towns with picturesque names —Whitehorse, Green Grass, Iron Lightning, Red Scaffold, Glad Valley, Firesteel, Eagle Butte. A land of blue skies and red sunsets, glorious history and inhuman poverty.

In the squalor of one generation ago it seemed as though the tribe would never rise again. Before World War II, a visitor had described the Cheyenne River Sioux Reservation as "The Black Hole of Calcutta of the Prairie."

The tribe had barely forty thousand acres of tribal land left when in 1940 it began a "land consolidation program."

Now the tribe owns 1,100,000 tribal acres. And among the many tribally-owned enterprises there are a telephone company, a laundromat, two supermarkets, and a tribal bowling alley. The Cheyenne River Sioux have tribal assets in excess of $15 million. And the yearly income, per family, for the four thousand members of the tribe is above the poverty level of $3,000—a rare accomplishment for any Indian tribe.

Using their tribal land as a home base the tribe bought into the neighboring countryside—small businesses and service industries— with the profits feeding into the communal treasury.

"If the other tribes would use their tribal land as the Cheyenne River have," Vine Deloria, Jr. said wistfully, "we could solve our own problems in a tribal way, and preserve our tribal way of life. . . . [Tribes] could control the service industries on, or near, their reservations. They could control the funds for investment, and be the largest money source in their areas. They could buy up all the small businesses along the highways. They could train Indians to keep books and run these.

"What's the sense of having these Indian dances for the tourists and charging fifty cents a head? Tourism right now is dancing for tourists. But owning all these tourist services would be much more profitable.

"Suppose a tribe did a survey of everything within three hundred miles of their reservation. Suppose they started buying up all the gas stations along the highways, and the motels, and the cafés. One by one.

"The tentacles of the tribal community would extend for a few hundred miles. And the wealth would be brought back to the reservations, instead of going out as it does now. The Indians would work outside. But they would live and spend their money at home.

"It would reverse the whole economic process. The tribal asset would grow because of their investment in these off-reservation, but Indian-owned, businesses. And the Indians, instead of being punished for being Indians economically and wanting to live in a tribal way socially, would have a secure financial base. And their children wouldn't have to be ashamed, or jobless, or run to the city skid rows."

Young Deloria, Jr., in addressing a National Conference on Manpower called by the government, reiterated this tribal program of self-help. He told the two hundred tribal leaders who had gathered that though the industrial programs of the Bureau of Indian Affairs had brought some dozens of factories "on or near reservations," in recent years, he doubted that this would answer tribal needs.

"I think this is one place we are going wrong. We're talking about tribes as they are today. Eighty percent of them are small tribes that don't need much. A lot of them just want a filling station, a laundromat, or a restaurant. They'll employ maybe eight or ten people. That's what they need. They don't need those million-dollar showcases."

Returning to the Cheyenne River Sioux, Deloria, Jr., talked of the vision of the tribe's future: "In twenty years the members of the tribe who can't work, who would rather stay on the reservation, will be able to do so. And the tribe won't need any outside welfare program. They will be able to take care of their own in the tribal way.

"And those tribal members who were working off the reservation, in the tribal businesses, would know that the land was theirs. The reservation would always be their home, where they could go to hunt and fish. Where they could go to retire. Where they could go just to live. Where they could always be as Indian as they wished.

"That, as I see it, is our only economic alternative. I mean, our tribal alternative. That is the only way we will survive as a tribal society."

14

THE CEMENT PRAIRIES

In Billings, Montana, there is a hill. In Sioux it is called Place of Many Sorrows. There a child dies every week. A wife dies too young. A man he is old and sad at 30, and the sick are too many. The dead songs are singed there till a tall man runs from his shack, from all his family, and he drinks not to hear. Now he sits, drunk so much he cannot talk, and too sad to not sing the same hard songs. He cannot go away. There is no place to go. These men, these people, are Indians who have sold their land.

The unlettered Indian had written his anguish on the back of an unused government form. He had not signed his name. He had mailed his outcry to the Denver *Post,* which sent a reporter, Robert W. Fenwick, to find the Dantesque inferno—the Place of Many Sorrows. Fenwick found not one but several.

One of these, known as "Hill 57," in Great Falls, Montana, was typical of the rest:

"It's an Indian village of shocking filth, poverty and degradation. Its outstanding features are the frail huts, the battered hulks of automobiles, the ever-present outhouses, a hand-pump which is the sole water supply for the entire community, and an almost unbelievable sea of junk resembling a city rubbish disposal," Fenwick wrote.

"Now, the Indian sits on the White Man neck," the nameless Indian had written, "and the White Man is saddened because of this. We are both sad because only grief has come to both of us because of sale [of Indian land]. Soon, if this goes on, all Indians must come to town.

"What town want one more Place of Many Sorrows? Who will fight this thing? What man is so brave? Now something must be done. Who will do it?"

One young Sioux in San Francisco, who was shown a copy of the pathetic letter, scoffed at it. "Man, I think that letter is a put-on," he said. "For one thing that's not how a Sioux thinks. There's no Sioux I know of who would say, 'He cannot go away. There is no place to go.' He can go home to his reservation any time. If he can crawl, they'll take him home. For another thing living in towns, lousy as it may be, doesn't scare us into writing gibberish. Man, we been doing the towns ever since Sitting Bull laid down the tools of his trade on the Little Big Horn and joined the touring Wild West Show of Buffalo Bill.

"Every town has a hellhole like that. Every town in the West has its 'native quarter,'" the San Francisco Sioux said. "That's not the problem. You see, living in the city is your problem, really. We just come visiting to make a little money. Our problem is making it."

Interestingly enough, when the Denver *Post* reporter searched Billings, Montana, asked everywhere, he could not find the Place of Many Sorrows.

Are the city Indians invisible?

The tribal Indians are unquestionably coming to town. Half of the Indians in the country may be city Indians, Vine Deloria, Jr., has estimated. There are a quarter of a million living in the metropolitan areas alone, thought Mel Thom. And the San Francisco Indian Center publication *The American Indian*, has reported that the Indian adults living "off-reservation"—estimated at 198,000— outnumbered those "on-reservation"; for many job-seeking parents left their children at home with grandparents.

One decade ago, The *Harvard Law Review* estimated that "about 100,000 Indians [reside] in American cities and towns" ("American Indians: People Without a Future," by Ralph Nader, May 10, 1956). Even if the statistic was a reasonably inaccurate guess, the urban population of tribesmen has doubled within ten years.

But the city Indians have always been invisible statistics. The

U.S. Census Bureau counts Indians only when they so identify themselves, or are identifiable. And the city Indians often "pass" as whites, when it is economically necessary, or socially desirable. Those who don't "pass" have been usually counted as "nonwhite"— a nearly invisible shade, it seems, when they happen to be Indians.

The statistics of the Bureau of Indian Affairs have been as equalitarianly invisible, for the Bureau's concern has traditionally been the reservation Indian, and the cajoling of him to leave the reservation. Once he goes, however, the Bureau no longer counts him.

So the city Indian has been an invisible man. He has not even become a statistic.

"Chicago does not realize they have a 'reservation of Indians' right in their own backyard," commented an official of the American Indian Center on the near North Side. "There are better than ten thousand Indians representing seventy tribes in Chicago." Half of these are wedged into a few-block area between the Puerto Rican ghetto and the luxury apartment houses on the Lake Shore Drive.

"We don't riot," said Nathan Bird, one of the Chicago Indian leaders, "so no one knows we're here."

Brooklyn, New York, Cleveland, Detroit, St. Louis, Minneapolis, Omaha, Denver, Phoenix, Los Angeles, San Francisco, and Seattle all have their own "native quarters" of Indians. Many of these have more than ten thousand tribal residents. And in the smaller cities of the Rocky Mountains, the Plains, and the Southwest, there are repetitious "Hill 57's." "The Cement Prairies" was what some of the city Indians nicknamed these homeless homes away from home.

In a tongue-in-the-throat article entitled "The Indian in Suburbia," *The American Indian* offered its own tourist guide to tribesmen coming to town:

When an Indian family first comes to Oakland, or San Francisco, they will find thousands of cement streets running in every direction.

On these streets will be tens of thousands of automobiles. These automobiles are filled with people who are trying to kill each other off with these steel monsters as fast as the white man killed off the Buffalo.

To find his way around in this cement prairie, the white man uses a map, and so must the Indian.

All of the houses have numbers and some of the streets are called by numbers. Some streets have other names, and in many cases streets are are not called streets but avenues, places, boulevards and freeways. Freeways are the most dangerous and no one walks on them, and sometimes it is even hard to drive on them. . . .

"This may sound confusing to some of our people on reservations who have never been to California," laconically commented *The American Indian,* "but, it is." In the words of Calvin O'John:

> *A dirt road begins at the highway*
> *And ends at our front yard.*
> *I walk on dirt roads,*
> *But never will I walk on highways.*

And yet they come, in bemused bewilderment, and in growing migrations.

In the eyes of an Indian what does the city look like? He has seen villages and he has seen towns. Nowhere has he seen one million people, five million, living in houses like great tombstones, row upon row, and running about like little mechanical ants, to and fro, on streets full of cars like plagues of grasshoppers. He has lived most of his life without a sidewalk, without a subway, without a superhighway, and often without a supermarket.

He has lived beside the still waters.

Living in the city is then not something he can adjust to with a street map, an orientation course, and a job. It is beyond his imagination, beyond his emotion.

Within a few miles of the metropolitan areas of Los Angeles and New York City more human beings live than in the more than one million square miles of all the states of the Western mountains and plains and deserts, where most of the tribal Indians come from.

So the tribesmen come into the metropolis with its glass and steel office buildings, where the twentieth century is on perpetual display like a living museum piece.

How exotic are the artifacts of the urban civilization! Its rituals of folk-rock chants, commercial ceremonials, and automobile worship were fascinating. The tribal Indians come with the curiosity of tourists. It is like visiting a circus in a foreign country.

Richard McKenzie, a young Sioux who lived in San Francisco for several years—successfully—and was a leader of the Indian

Center in that city, cast a dubious eye on this citifying of the tribesmen. "The reservation Indian has not been prepared to make his way in the city of 1860's—much less the demanding fast-paced and cold-blooded city of 1960's," he said.

Life in the city whetted the Indian's curiosity, McKenzie said, but he faced a "hopeless situation." Most of the Indians he met were lost. "The simplest facts of life in the city were new to them: gearing your entire day by a clock, when to go to work, when to eat lunch. They don't even understand where you board a bus, how to pay, and how to open and close the doors.

"Because they have been sent from the reservation with the lack of training, information, and money," he said, they would be victims of "the hardships and loneliness of the disillusioned Indian in the city."

Why then, if the city Indian faces a "hopeless situation," do more and more rural Indians come to the cities?

"Lots of the younger kids want to leave the reservation and get a job," said Mary Lou Payne, a Cherokee girl who made the journey to the city herself. "It's not that they really want to get away from the reservation, but that they want to have an income. Everyone is *encouraged* to go away. To leave. To become a working American. To join the 'rat race,' really. What they call the 'mainstream.'"

The exodus has been not wholly voluntary. "It reflects a policy the Bureau of Indian Affairs has had and still has: to get the Indians off the reservation," Mary Lou Payne said.

"Relocation" is the term given to this trek. It was instituted by Commissioner of Indian Affairs Dillon Myer, who, as has been noted, was director of the Relocation Centers where Japanese-Americans were imprisoned during World War II. Thus, the term had a disquieting connotation to young Indians, many of whom had fought in that war. Nonetheless, tens of thousands of tribal Indians have been "relocated" since the early 1950's.

Vice President Hubert Humphrey has written optimistically about the "Relocation" Program: It is aimed at "encouraging Indians to move off the less promising reservations and into industrial centers where work opportunities are more plentiful. . . . A package program—vocational training and job placement, with all expenses paid for trainee and family—has lured 50,000 Indians into successful urban living."

The former Commissioner of Indian Affairs, Philleo Nash, who guided the program during the administration of the late President John F. Kennedy, was more cautious and less optimistic: "Relocation by itself solves nothing," Nash said. ". . . As long as relocation was merely a program to transport people from one pocket of poverty to another, little was accomplished. Not everyone likes city living— not everyone is suited to it. To combat poverty successfully will require programs that relate people to jobs wherever they choose to live."

Some of the relocated Indians were even more skeptical. The Sioux Richard McKenzie said that when a reservation Indian arrived in San Francisco he was referred by the Relocation Office to "the few boarding houses available to Indians under the Bureau program [that were] usually ill-run, often short on food, and in bad districts—especially for girls."

The jobs that the Bureau found for "the usually unskilled Indians" were often with "fly-by-night outfits who enjoy getting as much labor as possible from their workers, while paying them as little as possible," McKenzie said. Since the Indians did not know union rules, many were working up to twelve hours a day without overtime pay. When "the pitifully small cash given him to make the trip" ran out, the relocated Indian was often penniless and lost.

His own family, McKenzie said, had housed and fed "many Indians who were in dire need, but somehow did not qualify for aid from any [welfare] agency."

"Mr. Indian," said the irate Sioux, "your 'Green Pastures' in the city will be even worse than what you have now at home. Sending Indians [to the city] on a sink or swim basis is the way to guarantee most will sink."

"It was shameful," Mary Lou Payne said, "to force rural Indians into urban ghettos. It's no answer to poverty to dump these people into the cities. They are so unprepared for city life, paying bills every month, going to work every day, that they filter out to the very bottom of society.

"This shipping out of unprepared people is just shameful. It doesn't work out. They just go back to what they did before. Which is picking up odd jobs. But doing it in the cities."

Vice President Hubert Humphrey sounded an official note of concern: "Most of them [those Indians who go on their own] have never held jobs of any duration and are almost totally unequipped for industrial work. They seek to escape from poverty on the reservation without realizing that they may be making another and worse trap for themselves. Unless we take measures to help this group, we will find new ghettos being established in our cities and towns, new slum children growing up, a new breed of unemployed unemployables, taxing our welfare services."

Measures had to be taken immediately. . . .

Relocation had become a fancy word for "dumping the rural poor into the ghettos," said Mel Thom. The idea of urbanizing and integrating the tribal Indian was forgotten, momentarily, and practical reality was recognized by changing the name of the Bureau of Indian Affairs, Branch of Relocation, to Branch of Employment Assistance.

The Vocational Education Act for Indians was intensified when Congress increased the appropriation from $12 to $15 million. Under this act, originally part of the Relocation Program, tribal Indians were job-trained and paid to leave their reservations. Yet, in the first ten years of its operation, but thirteen thousand of the tens of thousands of Indians who went to the cities benefited from its largess. "Usually Indians must leave the reservation to take advantage of it," *Eyapaha,* the Rosebud Sioux newspaper, complained.

Mary Lou Payne was less polite: "I have gripes about the on-the-job training programs. On the Cherokee Reservation back home we have two factories. One of them is a stitching plant, they make bed clothing; and the other is a bobby pin factory. They run the Indian kids through the training courses, the government picks up part of their salary while they're training, and then when they're through training, the company employs them for a month, or two months, and drops them, and hires another crew for training.

"How many jobs are there on the Cherokee Reservation where they can go and make stitched bed clothing? It's so impractical.

They should be trained to become plumbers, carpenters, electricians, television repairmen."

Joe Maday, a young Chippewa boy on the Bad River Reservation in Wisconsin, had just come home from an on-the-job-training project, two thousand miles from his home.

He sat in his father's gas station, on a muddy river flat, near the wild-rice fields of his tribe on Lake Superior. He reminisced and he cursed the government for sending him to Seattle.

"Couldn't they send me to Milwaukee?" the boy said. He had gone wide-eyed and eager to see the country, on a $130-a-month government allowance, paying $90 a month for boarding-house rent. "Who could live on what was left? That rent for a dormitory-type room," he said. But it was exciting, anyway, being with Indians from a dozen tribes he had never heard of. "It was like a big powwow all the time. It didn't ever stop."

What did he learn? "Nothing!" he shrugged. "They wanted to teach me mechanic. But I didn't want to work as a mechanic way out there. So far away from home. And mechanics are a dime a dozen around here. So I come back. I'm going to learn electronics this time. If there's a job around here, I rather stay. But maybe I will go away. There's no work here. No one stays."

In spite of the newer urban-orientation course that had been started the tribal Indians still seemed disoriented by city life. So it was decided to urban-orientate them twice. Upon their arrival in the cities, the Bureau of Indian Affairs began to offer them a secondary education course in the rituals and customs of urban living.

Dr. Sophie D. Aberle and the late William A. Brophy, in *The Indian: America's Unfinished Business*, described one of these advanced courses:

"Orientation courses for Eskimos and reservation Indians unfamiliar with the manners and customs of life outside their villages have been started in Seattle, Washington. The three-week course is based on the assumption that the quickest way for students to adjust to modern life is to let them use up-to-date conveniences. . . .

"The training center is, therefore, located in a modern motel. Seven furnished apartments are rented for the trainees and their families. . . . All accommodations have carpeted floors, draperies, an all electric kitchen, private bath and living rooms.

"It is too early to evaluate the results of the orientation or pre-vocational training courses," the authors wrote. "However, methods of teaching have been developed and are being studied by psy-chologists, psychiatrists, linguists, and other specialists, so that im-provements are being constantly made."

When oriented the Indians were moved out of the all-electric kitchens and the wall-to-wall-carpeted motel suites into the nearest ghetto. The transition was jarring. "One Indian woman in Cleve-land didn't know how to light a gas stove," Mary Lou Payne related, "and a welfare worker who visited her walked in and found this woman standing in the middle of her kitchen and throwing matches into the oven."

In the ghetto of Puerto Rican Harlem, the Barrio of Nueva York, lives a very different sort of city Indian. Her name is Princess Wa Wa Chaw—Mrs. Bonita Nuñez.

She was one of the earliest of the city Indians in New York, and she is now one of the oldest. In the cluttered memories of her rooms, high in a municipal housing project, are stacks of boxes full of history: souvenirs of the days when she danced with Isadora Duncan; her painting of Joe Gould, the Greenwich Village poet and eccentric; invitations to the White House; mementos of the vaudeville stage; books on the mysteries of the occult; and news stories of tours and arrests in the Indian-rights fight of fifty years ago.

"When I came here I was one of the first," the old woman said. "I 'came out' [off the reservation] so long ago. I lived on the Lower East Side for some time. The Jews from Europe had never seen an Indian before. There was quite a commotion. But we became good friends. Sometimes I don't know who has had it worse—the Jews or the Indians.

"The Negroes talk about discrimination. In those days there was worse discrimination in the cities against Indians. 'Savages' they called us then."

The old woman is very old, how old she would not say. She was born a Rincon Indian, in California, and was adopted by a white family at birth. "It was before the earthquake in San Fran-

cisco," was all she would say. She was on the stage at the age
of ten. She lived all her life in the world of the white man. She
knew no other life.

"Oh, I had friends everywhere. I could sing and act and dance
and paint. I was not afraid," she recalled. "But you see I am still
an Indian. Should the Indians be afraid of the city? No, the 'mainstream' should not frighten us. I am an existentialist," the old
woman said.

Huddled under a shawl, in her modern apartment in the New
York City housing project, she looked out on the defaced walls
of the cold slums below her window and thought of one day long ago.

"One day I was walking down the street when a lady stopped
me. She looked me in the eye. Then she hit me in the face. 'Go
back where you came from! You foreigner!' she shouted. She was
Italian, I think. But I was a brown Indian, you see." She sighed:
"I am aware that [we] can become victims of the 'lonely people.' "

Who are these "lonely people"?

The "lonely people" are, of course, "the lonely crowd." It is the
remoteness and coldness and self-interest of the harassed urban
populace that has created the "cold-blooded city" of Richard Mc-
Kenzie's image. And it is this that is so strange to the tribal Indian.

*"That lonesome path that leads to Nowhere is taking me away
from this lonesome place"* was the lament of the Plains Indian boy
Calvin O'John, who had come to a very different city, in a very
different era. He too had felt the cold hand of the "lonely people."
So did his fellow student at the Santa Fe Institute of American
Indian Arts, Donna Whitewing, who thought of the city as a "blank
cold wall":

> *Against a blank cold wall*
> *room enough for many flowers*
> *to grow and bloom.*
> *Feel the heart hesitate*
> *as flowers and buds*
> *will and die with pain.*

Where was the warmth and love of the kinship family? In the
impersonal and cold efficiency of the city there is no such human
touch. The "lonely people" do not touch one another.

Donna Whitewing wrote:

*The essence of death
is the untouched sense
of being felt.*

Loyal Shegonee, another of the young city Indians, poignantly cried out: "Where are my friends? What is there to do? Would someone, anyone, please come and talk to me?" He heard, the young man said, "the deafening tick-tick of the clock." He felt "the dark room crowding its silence upon me."

"Oh God," he cried out. "Someone, please come and talk to me!"

Who in the city talks to strangers? The "lonely people" prefer to talk to their machinery; for didn't they say "the medium is the message"? Kathryn Polacca, a Navajo teacher who has been to many cities, said: "Your people have so many ways of communication: IBM machines, telephones, newspapers, telegraphs, radios, and television. In the Navajo ways the most important communication is still person to person. This is the way we solve many of our problems. This is the way we enjoy life." The Indian way of talking and living, she said, was based on human values, not on mechanical or monetary values.

Unlike so many newcomers to the cities the tribal Indians "are not with it," Mel Thom said. "He doesn't think of making money. He just wants to make a living and live." That is why, though there are an estimated twenty thousand Indians in the environs of San Francisco, and perhaps thirty thousand in Los Angeles, Thom said he knew of only two or three Indian-owned establishments in either city. One was a bar.

"Money! Money! Money! That is all the white man thinks of when it comes to the Indian," said a Pomo Indian of California. "The only thing they see is money. For me a heartbeat is enough."

On the icy tundra of far northwest Alaska in an Eskimo village, where the silence of centuries was being broken by a plant of Kennecott Copper, there came the quiet voice of William Hensley. He is a young Eskimo of Kotzebue, who graduated from George Washington University in Washington, D.C., and who has become the executive director of the Northwest Alaska Native Association, the vice president of the statewide Native Federation, and a member of the State Legislature.

For all the vast distances that separate them, the young Eskimo's words might have been those of one of the new Indians: "I would rather be a poverty-stricken Eskimo way up in the North than a wealthy white man in your cities," Hensley said. "Many of our villages are just as they were hundreds of years ago. Very, very slow moving, fairly primitive way of living. I'm not saying it's a bad life; in fact, I think it's a good life. I would prefer for my people not to have to live in the cities that I have seen throughout the country.

"There isn't any comparison. And this is one of the things that native people are thinking about life in the larger, urban society. Many of them don't want to become part of this mainstream of yours.

"Last summer I was up in Point Hope, one of the oldest villages. I was staying with the head of the village. There had just been some mass crime—of a white man in Texas killing a half dozen or more people. And the head of the village said to me, 'If this is civilization, I don't want any part of it.'"

A Chippewa youth, Ronald Head, who has worked in Texas, has similar trepidations: "Come and join the Great Society, they say. I don't know if I want to join. What for? To be killed by a white man in a University tower, in a 'seat of learning'?"

It was not the violence that these Indians feared. Guns and shooting do not frighten them. The urban man lives in terror of a hunting rifle on the ordered, policed, shattering quiet of the city street; the Indian does not. Hunting is a household commonplace to Indian youth. Rather it was the inhumanity of the mass killings that frightened the Indians. The cold-blooded way in which urban man would kill strangers to him for no emotional reason, with no feelings.

"Why do they kill like that?" an Oklahoma Cherokee, who regularly went home to hunt, asked. "I would not shoot deer that way."

Those Indians who chose to stay in the "cold-blooded city" had to protect themselves—politically, economically, and culturally. They were often abandoned by the federal bureaus, with little knowledge of the city agencies, left on their own, uncomfortable with urban life, separated from their tribes, and something had to be done for them, by themselves. The invisible city Indian had to become visible. Where Indians have come, they have built Indian centers. The men and women from tribes throughout the country, with different cultures and different languages, would get together and establish a meeting place where they could meet relatives and tribesmen, reminisce about life back at home, discuss the frustrations of city life, and help and protect themselves. The Indian center might be a tiny, dreary storefront, or an elaborate and well-equipped community hall. But, whatever it looked like, it was run by and financed by tribal Indians, for tribal Indians.

Powwows in the city? A nostalgic attempt to transplant tribal life to the cement prairie? These Indian centers are not governmental or social-work-sponsored, not tribal nor intertribal. In coming to these community halls the Indians come as Indians, not representing their tribes. The city Indians have created something new and independent and yet Indian. They speak of the "Indian language"— "Let's talk Indian," they say; though there is, of course, no such language—and seek to preserve their "Indian traditions," and they dance in powwows, doing "Indian dances," and they fight for their "Indian rights."

In doing these things they are not only building an Indian urban community, but are building an Indian consciousness that is no longer tribal, but is extratribal. It too is an embryo of Indian nationalism.

Chicago's Indian Center, one of the oldest and largest of these urban, extratribal groups, is typical in its goals of most. Its aim is to help tribesmen in becoming "a functioning part of the social fabric of the city," while "sustaining cultural values perhaps uniquely their own."

The Indians of Chicago are seeking, in other words, to become urban citizens outwardly, but to remain Indians inwardly. And these Indians wish to do this not by urbanizing the tribal life, nor by tribalizing the urban life, but by combining both. Fascinating are the combinations. Rock 'n' roll and tribal dances. Potlatch dinners and auto-mechanic classes.

In the San Francisco Indian Center within an ordinary week there was: Tuesday—Indian dancing; Wednesday—ladies' sewing club, Indian arts and crafts, girls' ping-pong and boys' pool tournaments; Thursday—council meeting on job, housing, and welfare problems; Friday—modern ballet class and a powwow (singers and dancers were "paid with gas money"); Saturday—children's health clinic and rock 'n' roll dance (music by The Enchanters).

And on Sunday there was a movie entitled *The Exiles*.

These programs are run with a tribal communality: "Our Center is operated by Indians for all Indians in the Bay Area. All help is voluntary. Everyone just comes and does whatever they think has to be done for improvement. There is no one sponsoring this organization. Indians work here not for profit, but to contribute their time for a preservation of our disintegrating culture and heritage."

In a similar spirit of tribalism the American Indian Center in Chicago declared: "The Center is an achievement of their own [the Indians'], and not something provided for Indians by others. . . . The Center is not a sort of missionary outpost of the urban majority. It is a grass-roots effort."

Yearly the Chicago Indian Center provides services for thousands of tribesmen, but since its members have "never been wealthy people" it is in a perpetual state of near bankruptcy. The Welfare Council of Chicago, to which it is affiliated, suggested that the comfortably endowed and well-known Hull House take over the administration of the Indian Center. Its financial problems would be solved, and it would benefit from professional social work management.

The Chicago Indian Center voted down the beneficent offer, to the surprise of the city fathers. It was like voting not to accept a Congressional appropriation.

Nathan Bird, an Indian woodworker, who was on the board of directors of the Indian Center, tried to explain: "The Hull-House is a fine place. We have nothing against it. We were afraid that we would lose our identity if they took us over. It always happens. It would no longer be an Indian Center. The whites would take us over and tell us what to do. It was a bribe. We could use the money. We won't sell our Indian rights for money.

"That's what happens on the reservations," Mr. Bird said. "The government is always taking things over to 'help us.' We don't want that kind of 'help.' We didn't come all the way to Chicago for some more of that."

City Indians, because they are on their own—neither protected nor restricted by the Bureau of Indian Affairs—tend to be more independent and more outspoken. In Minneapolis the city Indians twice in two years picketed the Bureau's area office. Picketing, in itself, had been unknown to tribal movements; tribesmen would sooner take up a rifle in defense of their treaty rights than take up a picket sign. It was "un-Indian," the elders said.

But the Urban American Indian Protest Committee of the Twin Cities had no such fears. It was organized by two younger Indians, Mary Thunder and George Mitchell. On its first picket line it mustered thirty-five city Indians, who carried signs demanding that the government begin programs to help them. It had none, they said, and they demanded assistance in getting housing, jobs, and education; referral services for medical and legal care; and practical urban orientation programs.

The "Bureau employees shut the window," said Gerald Vizenor, one of the protest committee youth—in shock, perhaps. However, the area director, Glenn Landbloom, proclaimed: "My door is always open," and invited the picketing Indians to come up and talk. None came.

"The Indians replied that the door had been open for more than a hundred years," Vizenor said. "Talk is what the Indians did *not* want to do. They were protesting to change policy, not to cultivate conversation."

One-third of the Minnesota Indians now live in the Twin Cities. There are more urban tribesmen than there are Indians on any reservation in the state. Yet, Vizenor said, "The Bureau has no programs directed to their needs. What is the Bureau doing with its growing budget to serve a decreasing reservation Indian population? If assimilation is the Bureau policy then it seems logical that the Bureau should offer some referral and urban assistance to Indians moving from the poor rural reservation areas to the Twin Cities."

The area director, Landbloom, explained that the Bureau served only Indians "on or adjacent to Indian trust lands." He was not clear how near "adjacent" meant, but he thought the Twin Cities were not really an Indian reservation.

Gerald Vizenor was jovial in spite of the rebuff: "Another picket is planned. Many Indians felt so good about the last one that there are plans for a group three times as large with moccasin games and dancing, if the Bureau doesn't come across with some proposals for adequate programs for urban Indians."

The invisibility of the city Indian belongs to the past. He is becoming visible. He may have been lost in the city; but the longer he has stayed the more he has begun to feel it is the city that is lost—not he. When the city Indian began to build urban tribal communities he discovered the Indian way of life filled the lonely void of "the cement prairies." And he began to wonder if "the lonely crowd" might learn neighborliness from him.

"The very values the Indian represents may contribute to the improvement of our frantic cities," said Richard McKenzie. He thought the values of tribal humanism might "make the cities more human." And one young Pueblo Indian in the Chicago Indian Center said: "Instead of giving Indians these urban-orientation courses, maybe they ought to give Chicagoans human-orientation courses."

Has the "alienation" of the city Indian been too convenient and self-comforting a concept? It has been used by non-Indians to define the feelings of the Indian, but it has described the effect and not the cause. It has placed the onus on the Indian for his failure to conform to urban life and for his return home to the reservation. But, at a time when the disappearance of communities and the demise of neighborhoods are troubling city planners, the communal feeling of the city Indian has something to be said for it.

If the "alienation" of urban life becomes too overwhelming, the city Indian returns to his tribal community, and home to the reservation many had gone.

"The return to the reservations," former Commissioner of Indian Affairs Philleo Nash, estimated, "was about as frequent as the permanent relocation." Mary Lou Payne thought it even greater: "On this relocation the return home is fantastic. I bet it is 60 percent and up who return to the reservations." Richard McKenzie said it was his experience that 90 percent returned home as soon as there were jobs on the reservations.

A young girl of the Laguna Pueblo, Pat Pacheco, who returned to her pueblo from college, where she had studied psychology, said: "It's almost impossible to adjust to the outside world, and many of our people are coming back from Cleveland, Chicago, and Los Angeles, because they can work here now."

Not only are the relocated Indians beginning to go home, the *Wall*

Street Journal observed, but "there's evidence Indians aren't moving off reservations as readily as a short while ago."

Into the Indian Center of San Francisco, up the shabby stairs, one day walked an unknown tribesman. He was welcomed, as every Indian was, a tall man, with a tight face and puzzled eyes. The man was a newcomer; perhaps he had just arrived from the reservation, and was ill at ease.

The stranger was something more, however. He was a relocation officer of the government who had been sent from the reservation to see how the tribal Indians were being urbanized.

"He was told we took a rather dim view of the program," a San Francisco Indian recalled. "I pinned him down about the lack of adequate orientation on the reservation. And he said they did indeed tell people about buses, housing, and so forth. I told him that John Glenn could tell me in six orientation lessons how to fly a space ship and I wouldn't know a thing about it if I got in one."

That broke up the official meeting. "Last three hours of our visit were spent talking about hunting, fishing, and wide-open spaces on the reservation. The cheaper cost of living and better life in general back home," the relocated Indian said. "Naturally, many of the things the relocation officer said, and many of the things he saw, will never be included in his written report to Washington, D.C., or for that matter in his verbal report to his superintendent on the reservation.

"One wonders, after seeing relocation at the other end, if he will not be more reluctant about sending Indian people out. Will the relocation officer relocate himself?" The city Indian laughed.

The most unusual tale of relocation-in-reverse, however, occurred in Los Angeles. In that multiplicity of the Angels lived a group of Cherokees. Some of the families were well established and some were well to do. They were all Los Angeles boosters; for they had done well enough and lived quite happily.

Yet the hills of eastern Oklahoma of the Cherokee Nation haunted them. "Twelve years ago a group of Indians, many of us children, or grandchildren, of Oklahomans, decided to 'put down a fire' in California," said Dr. John Harris Jeffries, a lawyer and chiropractic doctor who was a leader of these Los Angeles Cherokees. He explained that to "put down a fire," in the Cherokee tradition, meant just that. A ceremonial ground was prepared and a fireplace dug in the earth. There the fire was lighted for religious rituals. There a stomping ground for religious dances was established around the fire.

In the city of Los Angeles, the Western Keetoowah Society was founded. The Keetoowah Society is the nativist religious group of the Cherokees. Its traditional worship, with masks and robes and rites, was not only sacred, but in the urban frenzy was an island of the Indian spirit. Though the city Cherokees were separated by miles of freeways, they held regular religious ceremonies and prayers. In the kinship families they kept their matriarchal clans intact. The old customs of the tribe were practiced, and the children given Cherokee names in the traditional way.

One of the Western Keetoowah Society of Los Angeles members was a lawyer. One was an insurance salesman. One was the owner of an electrical firm. One was a professional golfer. One was a professional artist. One was a surveyor. One was a doctor. One was a computer analyst. And yet—business suits off, ties loosened, brief cases left in the foyers of the suburban houses—they were traditionalist Indians.

"Suddenly we began to think about coming home," Dr. Jeffries said. "I don't know with whom the idea originated. We knew we wanted to get out of the rat race in Los Angeles. There just wasn't any discussion about where we should go. It was Tahlequah."

And so to Tahlequah, Oklahoma, the old capital of the Cherokee Nation, the families began to come. In the beginning just seven families moved. Then four more came. Soon forty of the Cherokees had come. Dr. Jeffries expected that in all one hundred and fifty would come home.

"It was home instantly," he said. "No one has mentioned moving back." Somehow it was as though they had never left.

The coals of the sacred fires that they had "put down" in Los Angeles were unearthed. In their cars the coals were carefully carried halfway across the continent, once more to be buried, but this time in the earth of their Cherokee homeland. Once more, the fires would flame.

15

THE WAR ON
HOSTEEN POVERTY

"A long time ago Navajo leaders got together and decided to wage a war of extermination on the three notorious threats to the tribe. Public Enemy No. 1 was Poverty. Public Enemy No. 2 was Disease. And No. 3 was a bedfellow of the others. He was known as Hosteen Louse (Mr. Louse). The tribal council was mapping out its war to rid the earth of these, when the three, who had somehow heard of the threat to their continued existence, suddenly appeared at the meeting and asked to be heard in their own defense.

"Mr. Louse by infiltration entered the council lodge first and was given the floor to present what everybody thought would be his last speech.

"In a humble, friendly manner, Mr. Louse said: 'O great chiefs and warriors of a great people, you rule fairly and wisely. So I plead with you to think seriously before you take drastic action against three of your clansmen. Think how dull and uninteresting life would be without us. Think how you would miss hunting the louse—offering as it does an exciting sport and rewarding pursuit. Without us lice to keep you on your toes, you would become lazy and indolent and you would fall easy prey to your human foes. In your own self-interest, spare our lives.

"Then Disease spoke, and he too pleaded that if there were never any sick people to be cared for physical and spiritual elements of Navajo culture would die and wither. There would be no need for religious and ceremonial rites, and the old culture would disappear.

"Poverty spoke last, but along the same lines. To the effect that Poverty and his lieutenants, hunger, thirst, exposure, ignorance, and apathy, were constantly challenging the people to improve their ways of life, so that more persons might enjoy the benefits of nature and the good life in the world of beauty.

"The war chiefs thought it over and decided that after all their life would be incomplete without their favorite three enemies. So, since they probably could never entirely get rid of them anyway, they would let them be. Then the people would always have something to fight, and this would help hold them together and give them a common purpose."

The old legend, with its language modernized, was retold by Howard McKinley. A former tribal councilman, the blind and dryly caustic McKinley had been one of the first of his tribesmen to graduate from the University of New Mexico. He was a bridge between generations who spoke the language of both the cultures.

He had been a director of the new office of Navajo Economic Opportunity. But he knew the fables of the old tribal war on poverty too. "We still accept these ancient enemies as part of our lives," McKinley said. "We shall probably always have many diseases and a few lice, and we have the Bible's word for it that the poor we have always with us. Nevertheless, they are still enemies and must be fought. The Economic Opportunity Act gives the Navajo people stronger weapons than they have ever had with which to fight their eternal enemy—Poverty."

He did not predict victory. McKinley told the tale with that wariness that the tribal Indian always has when he talks of government programs. He did not reject them; for they might be helpful. He placed them within the tribal tradition. And he withheld his judgment.

The Youth Council leader Mel Thom, who has been a tribal OEO director, expressed this wariness bluntly:

"Another move by our opposition and protector is the declared

'War on Poverty.' War has been declared on our condition. To many of us poverty is a way of life. We do not like to be miserable, but our poor conditions have preserved a way of life for a while. Is this just stepping up efforts to absorb us into the mainstream of American life?"

Long had this been the stubborn, hard suspicion of the tribesmen. Buffalo Tiger, chairman of the Miccosukee Tribe of Florida, talked of it: "A lady asked me, 'Are you poor people?' I said, 'Yes, we have always been poor. But we feel all right.' " In the town of Wounded Knee, South Dakota, a Sioux tribesman, Wilbur Riegert, talked similarly of President Johnson's War on Poverty program: "I am sure, Kola, he had poverty on Indian reservations in mind," but "The Indian has to be content to live in poverty on his reservations."

Is poverty thought of as a tribal virtue? The modern Indian has a certain pride in having survived his hungers. But he is not a spartan. He is not an ascetic. There are deeper resentments and suspicions in his wariness over the War on Poverty.

In the early days of the War on Poverty a Conference on Poverty in the Southwest was held in Tucson, Arizona. From reservations throughout the desert and mountain states tribal leaders came to assure their tribes of a cut of the funds. And to assure themselves that their tribes would not be cut up in the process.

"In our haste, we tend to equate material poverty with spiritual and cultural poverty," the San Francisco magazine *The American Indian* reported that a spokesman had said.

"The Anglo must realize that many who are poor in the Southwest have rich and priceless traditions—a cultural kind of affluence we need badly to share. As we undertake to rid the Southwest of poverty . . . we'll be working in a land of great beauty, among peoples of great beauty. We must be sure that our efforts in no way erode the great gifts of diversity which we enjoy here—diversity of language, art, dance, ceremony, religion."

The mystique of poverty did not persuade the Indian. He did not believe in the Culture of Poverty; he had his own. He lived with its cruel and unforgiving reality. But, if he had learned to live with it, that did not mean he had made a philosophy of poverty. He hated not it, but what had caused it.

"Poverty is a noose that strangles humility and breeds disrespect for God and man," the Sioux Wilbur Riegert said. "Poverty is a stigma of disgrace, especially in this glorious land of ours. It is inexcusable in a land, and of a people, having more than plenty, and a pointing finger of shame on those who govern and regulate 'progress.'

"American Indian family life on reservations is an example of 'progressive' poverty brought about by the powers of force, which have left generations to brood over their inability to stem the overwhelming tide of greedy fortune hunters, to have and to hold all they could possess. They have it now, America the beautiful and the bountiful.

"Think it over, Uncle Sam and industry. And whatever you do, don't give it in the name of Charity, but a return (for what you have stolen).

"Give it a workable plan for past concessions brought about by treaties, some broken, some kept, and through the confiscation of precious lands and our only ways of livelihood. . . ."

The War on Poverty to the Sioux was a hypocritical apology for the misery that the white man has caused. He did not see it as a benevolent and generous plan to uplift the poor Indian. "Poverty is a noose," the Sioux said; he did not wish to be uplifted once more by the hands that held the noose. He thought of the War on Poverty as partial payment for what had been taken from him.

"Where did you get the money for your government programs? And your riches? From us!" said Roger Jourdain, tribal chairman of the Red Lake Chippewas. "You acquired the richest resource we had. It was our land that made you rich."

"You are not giving us anything. You are merely returning a finger of sand for all that you have taken," Jourdain said. "But you act like you were doing us a kindness."

And he too was cynical. Lest the War on Poverty turn out to be but another scheme, like so many in the past, to weaken the tribes in the guise of helping them, these tribal Indians were going to play an old waiting game.

It was this cynicism that Mel Thom testified to at the Senate hearings on the problems of urban poverty in the winter of 1966:

"We observe that the federal government's poverty program is nearly three years old. Gentlemen, the federal government's Indian poverty program is over one hundred years old. What is the result of this hundred-year war on Indian poverty? The result is an Asiatic-type poverty.

"In trying to solve the so-called Indian problem, the government has come forward with one simple-minded solution after another," the Youth Council leader said. "Over the past one hundred years this country has spared little to turn Indians into whites. But all this policy has accomplished has been to shatter Indian communities and obscure the real problems."

The litany of unbelievable poverty was then recited. On the reservations the infant mortality rate was 53.7 deaths per 1,000 live births—twice the rate of 25 deaths per 1,000 live births among the general population. Of those Indian infants who survived their birth one study showed that 500 of 1,700 would die in the first year of life of "preventable diseases."

Death ages of Indians averaged forty-three years. In regions of large Indian populations, like Arizona and Alaska, the death age averaged in the early thirties!

Reservation Indians had a death rate from tuberculosis that was 400 percent higher than that of non-Indians. The death rate from influenza and pneumonia was 300 percent higher. Hepatitis had an incidence rate that was 800 percent higher than the national average. Gonorrhea was 500 percent higher. Strep throat infections were 1,000 percent higher. Meningitis was 2,000 percent higher. And the incidence of dysentery among reservation Indians was 10,000 percent higher than in the rest of the population.

There were diseases that reached epidemic proportions on the isolated reservations that were virtually unknown elsewhere in the country. In the past generations there had been epidemics of diseases brought by the white men. Some of these—syphilis and measles—had a deadlier effect on the tribes than did the Indian Wars.

One nurse in the Public Health Service, a Cherokee girl, said: "If the government doctors improve our health, what's so great about that? After all, it was the whites who infected our people with most of these diseases in the first place."

The health crisis of the tribal Indian was brought about by the untenable dichotomy of reservation life. He lived in a pre-industrial society upon which the diseases of the industrial society descended. In this historical vise, he had been trapped. The ills of the white society were visited upon him without the safeguards it used to protect itself against itself.

It was not merely a medical problem that he faced. Dr. Carruth J. Wagner, chief of the Division of Indian Health of the Public Health Service, testified before the House Subcommittee on Indian Affairs to half of these truths: "The burden of disease is heavy and much of it is associated with the hazards and rigors of the environment in which these Indian beneficiaries live."

If you go into the homes of the Indians, Dr. Wagner told the Congressmen, and see "the types of housing in which they live, you see [why] the [infant] mortality rate is some four times greater in the Indian than in the non-Indian."

The ills of the tribal Indian cannot be measured by even poverty standards. Housing, after years of increasing numbers of federal building projects, is still officially estimated to be 90 to 95 percent substandard. That means not merely rural ghettos. It often as not means tar shacks, dirt huts, adobe mud hogans and grass wickiups. *Eyapaha,* in commenting that many of the South Dakota reservations were "skid rows of the plains," wrote: "Nothing kills the incentive more than to live day-in and day-out in cramped quarters (of one room) surrounded by a dirt floor, a dirt roof, and sometimes, dirt walls."

A survey of the living conditions of 42,506 Indians in eleven Western states by the Public Health Service, revealed that in such homes "The unsafe water supply is a very common cause of many diseases."

Hauling water, by wagon and pickup truck, is not a picturesque exoticism. It is a necessity. These Indians—81.6 percent—have to haul their drinking water for "distances of a mile or more." The running water that is taken for granted in the worst of urban slums is virtually nonexistent in these homes. Families get their water from "irrigation ditches and ponds." And 77.8 percent of this water is "potentially contaminated." That means drinking water used by livestock, that was adjacent to outhouses, that was stagnant. Some 80 to 100 percent of all the drinking water used on fifteen of the twenty-two reservation areas surveyed came from these "potentially contaminated" sources.

There was one reservation—that of the Oglala Sioux at Pine Ridge, in South Dakota—where 100 percent of the Indians had to "haul all domestic water," and where 100 percent of the water they hauled was "potentially contaminated," and where 100 percent of the "excreta disposal facilities" were either "unsatisfactory," or there was a "complete lack of facilities."

"It is almost unbelievable," Dr. Wagner told the House subcommittee, "that the vast majority of these people do not have *any* of the modern conveniences which we just take for granted."

The late Congressman Hjalmar C. Nygaard (Republican, North Dakota) was moved to reply innocuously, "I hope all of these problems someday can be solved." But the nonplused response may be forgiven in view of the depths of Indian poverty.

Employment and income statistics are as abysmal and as "unbelievable." In the winter of 1962–63 the government surveyed unemployment among tribal Indians. The Indian Unemployment Survey of the House Committee on Interior and Insular Affairs reported that on the plains of the Dakotas, the Pine Ridge Sioux had 2,175 of 3,400 tribal adults unemployed (yearly family income was $105), the Rosebud Sioux had 1,720 of 2,996 unemployed (yearly family income, $1,000—though the tribe, four years later, estimated $600 was more accurate); the Standing Rock Sioux had 500 of 880 heads of households unemployed (yearly family income, $190). And so on and on and on . . .

To the north, on the Blackfeet Reservation of Montana, the "permanent unemployment" rate was 72.5 percent. The yearly tribal income was "less than $500 per family."

Down in Mississippi, on the Choctaw Reservation, of 1,225 adults there were 1,055 jobless. Unemployment rate: 86.1 percent.

Where the tranquil and ancient Pueblos of New Mexico stood, seemingly impervious to the economic winds, there were 10,699 jobless out of 13,711. Unemployment among these, perhaps the oldest of the country's inhabitants, was 77 percent. The Hopis too, those idyllic "peaceful people," had a less than idyllic unemployment rate of 71.7 percent.

In the Pueblo de Acoma, the "City in the Sky," unemployment

stood at 89.6 percent. "How is the morale of the Indian people?" the government questionnaire asked. Governor Jerry Garcia, of the Pueblo de Acoma, merely replied, "They want employment."

On the cement snake of Route 66, which winds in and out of the volcanic lava and desert sand that surround the old pueblo, one young man of Acoma was asked, "How do you earn a living? What do you do?"

"Living?" He laughed. "I just live."

In the mythology of the oil-rich Indians so credulously huzzahed by television comedians and popular legend, none are supposedly wealthier than the Oklahoma tribes. And yet, the Five Civilized Tribes reported an unemployment rate of 55 percent, and an annual income per family, including the fabled oil-lease payments, that came to little more than $1,200.

So it went from tribe to tribe. Unemployment rates from 40 to 80 percent; incomes from $105 to $1,200.

These statistics are neither new nor surprising. However, the mixture of the old poverty and the new Indians who have seen the material riches of the outside world, and who are angered and impatient, has created an explosive situation.

"If something isn't done the young men may go to violence," said Deloria, Jr. Economic conditions were so unbearable that they would lead to "a king-sized uprising that will make the Little Big Horn look like a merit badge contest," said Deloria, Jr. Young men of several tribes were talking of taking up arms, Deloria, Jr., warned. The Red Muslims of the National Indian Youth Council were full of wrathful prophecies. One young militant at a government Conference on Manpower said that unless something was done soon "the young men may go to arms." Clyde Warrior was talking of an Indian "Mau Mau" movement.

When, in the winter of 1964, the tribal leaders gathered in the East Room of the White House, for the traditional ritual of official commiseration over the poverty of the Indians, they were not too optimistic. The President had, however, indicated his interest, and they presented a petition in the name of the National Congress of American Indians to the newly elected Chief of State. The tribal petition to the White House began:

We are thankful that the great policies and programs of our late, beloved, fallen President, John Fitzgerald Kennedy, will go forward under your administration. We again express our deep sorrow and grief for our late Chief, known to our people as Chief High Eagle.

President Kennedy twice met with us during his short years in office. We talked about great objectives. . . .

We are delighted that you are going forward with President Kennedy's programs and that you desire to make his hopes for the American Indian come true. You remembered us in your State of the Union message and this gave heart to all our people. Now, in aid of your programs we should like to bring to your consideration our thoughts on some of our problems.

The quiet of the tribal petition was not jarred by the muted tone of misery that they then argued:

Unemployment is our major concern. Almost one half of the employable American Indians are without jobs. On some reservations three fourths are unemployed. Indian reservations are indeed pockets of poverty. . . . A good policy uttered in Washington has no significance unless it is brought to life on the reservation level.

Wearing buckskins, beads, and feathers over their business suits, the tribal leaders then offered the President a wicker basket, a wooden bowl, and a peace pipe.

The government must be compassionate, responded the President. He recalled that when he was a young Congressman his father had admonished him to always ask himself before he acted, "What does this vote do for humanity?" It was his hope therefore to put "first Americans first" in the War on Poverty. "The Johnson administration has declared war on poverty and disease," the President said. Since the Indians "suffered more" than any other people in the country they deserved to come "first."

Less soft-worded and more hard-nosed were the political reasons for the government's concern about Indian poverty that were interpolated by Secretary of Interior Stewart Udall. In his speech behind "the green doors" to Bureau of Indian Affairs officials the Secretary said that Indian poverty was becoming, well, "embarrassing." The Secretary said frankly: "Our country has moved into an unprecedented period of peacetime prosperity . . . yet in that period of rising economy the poverty question of which the Indian people are only a part becomes more and more embarrassing. This is the reason President Johnson, two years ago, declared the War on Poverty."

In the past there had been much commiseration about the "poor Indians." John Adams had been the first President to offer his "commiseration" in so many words. But, since programs for tribal economic development had been singularly lacking, the situation had gone from the worst possible to the impossible.

Hunger rates, disease rates, and death rates were compiled. But they were meaningless to an affluent society where the thought of "Asiatic poverty" in its midst was too exotic to be really believed. The tribal Indian had been cast beyond the economic pale, beyond the periphery of known poverty. He was a statistic so minimal that to most experts he was a non-statistic.

Little was known of the cultural hungers and economic sorrows of the tribes. The Conference on Economic Progress report, *Poverty and Deprivation in the U.S.A.*, in 1962, had wholly ignored the poverty of the Indians. This summary report did not so much as mention their existence. Equally obtuse were the scholarly compendiums and statistical source books that were used as guides in the War on Poverty, such as *Poverty in America* (University of Michigan Press), edited by Louis Fermin, Joyce Kornbluh, and Alan Haber, with an introduction by Michael Harrington. The editors acknowledged that "among the hardest hit of this country's poverty stricken" were the Indians, who were "not a vanishing group." Having said this *Poverty in America* devoted three and one half sentences to these "hardest hit" Americans.

Even this heralded a hopeful advance from Harrington's own discovery of *The Other America: Poverty in the United States* (Macmillan), in which the Indian had not yet been discovered at all. There were, to be sure, "Indian poor" mentioned in that pivotal work on the War on Poverty. But these were, it seemed, Indians who lived in Asia, a linguistic confusion that had befallen other discoverers of America. It was the thesis of that exploratory work that the poor are "invisible." The Indians—American, that is—being the poorest of the poor, were apparently simply more "invisible" than anyone else.

The warriors on poverty thus ventured forth blissfully unarmed.

Into the economic gap that separated the misery of the Indians from the country's knowledge of their conditions the poverty fighters went. And they were promptly ambushed in the Credibility Gap. It was a latter-day moral massacre.

In the Pine Hall of Bemidji College in Minnesota's far north woods one of the first engagements took place. There was a planning meeting on the War on Indian Poverty, and tribal OEO and CAP directors came from reservations throughout the region. Herbert Bechtold, one of the brave emissaries of Sargent Shriver's Office of Economic Opportunity in Washington, suddenly found himself under attack from all sides.

Roger Jourdain, the Red Lake Chippewas' leader, engaged Bechtold in a bit of verbal coup counting:

JOURDAIN: "Who makes policies in Washington?"

BECHTOLD: "Various people. We don't. You do it by letters and requests. I don't know why policies are made."

JOURDAIN: "We are forced to submit to policies we don't make. We are at the mercy of these policies."

BECHTOLD: "In the present world everyone is bound by bureaucratic regulations. This is a bureaucratic society. If you want to play in the big leagues, then you must play, and learn the rules, and work within the framework."

JOURDAIN: "The rules are changed in the middle of the game."

BECHTOLD: "OEO is subject to public opinion."

JOURDAIN: "Then Indians have a bad press."

BECHTOLD: "When you hire a CAP director it will be easier."

JOURDAIN: "You fund us and we'll hire a director. We asked for an administrative component last summer, but you sent it back and said we should come in with a comprehensive program. We sent you a comprehensive program and you won't fund it."

BECHTOLD: "I just don't know."

The old refrain, with the old chorus, so familiar to Indian leaders was then taken up by Peter DuFault, tribal chairman of the Fond du Lac band, and president of the Minnesota Federated Chippewa Tribes.

DUFAULT: "The people who make policy [in Washington] are never on the reservations."

BECHTOLD: "That's true."

DUFAULT: "Then whom can we contact?"

BECHTOLD: "Shriver."

The unconvinced tribal leaders, as they always had at government conferences, sent the obligatory telegrams of annoyance to Sargent Shriver ("Whom do we contact?") and Vice President Hubert Humphrey ("He was once from here, you know"). Lamenting that those who were offering to help them had never asked them what help they wanted the leaders wrote: "THESE POLICIES RESTRICTIVE AND ARBITRARY AND ILL DEFINED, INDIAN RESERVATIONS NOT CONSULTED OR ADVISED." Then they went home.

On the White Mountain Apache Reservation there was a similar conference of tribal CAP directors of Arizona. There was a similar refrain. "Washington has adopted a 'father-knows-best' attitude," said Raymond Kane, one of the Apaches' War on Poverty directors, "when it actually has no first-hand knowledge of our problems." Kane said there were "plenty of communications," but there was "a lack of communication."

Exasperated by the tribal attacks, a non-Indian regional director of an Indian OEO area office burst out: "These tribal chairmen are creeps! Sometimes I argue with them all day and they haven't any idea what I am talking about. They say they want an Indian advisory board on the War on Poverty. Why? What do they know?

"Creeps!" The regional director shuddered.

Into the tangle of confusion the government rushed the experts. University consortiums were established at the Universities of South Dakota, Arizona, and Utah, to see if the expertise of social scientism could get the antagonisms untangled. "Several universities have become very interested in Indians now that there is money in it, to the point of hiring some Indians," said a young Sioux, Sam Deloria, who was one of those hired.

Experts were, however, looked upon with some skepticism by the tribal leaders. The university people had developed projects for rural and urban ghettos which were not acceptable or understood by the tribes. And the communal programs requested by the tribes were not understood or acceptable to the experts on Indian poverty.

In the lull of a regional conference of the Indian OEO, tilting his chair against the hotel-room wall in cracker-barrel style, Sam Deloria talked of this profusion and confusion. He had worked with OEO projects on tribal, university, regional, and Washington levels, Deloria said. He described how the university teams of experts went to work "consorting":

"Say a tribe works out a project proposal. It submits it to the government for approval and the bureaucrats send out some experts to do a feasibility study. What happens? The government decides the Indians aren't feasible. So they assign some more experts to make us feasible. And these university experts then decide who is and who isn't feasible. Usually they decide that they—the university experts—are very feasible. They rewrite the project, and the government funds it, and the tribe says it isn't what they wanted. And, of course, it doesn't work. But it is very feasible.

"By now the government ought to know the Indian isn't feasible. And we're happy not to be," Sam Deloria said.

If a tribe sought in the face of the expertise to work out its own poverty program in its own way it was bound to run into unending delay. "And memos," Deloria said.

Roger Jourdain talked of how this conflict had stymied one of the Chippewas' programs: "Our Tribal Home Building Program was one of the first of its kind in the United States, I think. It wasn't one of those suburban housing projects. It was really tribal, just the way the community wanted—tribally built, and tribally owned, and tribally run.

"You see, we didn't want any outside projects. Washington said, 'No. Can't consider it.' I said, 'Why?' Washington said, 'Not within our legal definitions.' I said, 'Who is the poverty program for? Poor people, or your Harvard lawyers?' "

"The San Carlos Apaches had the same trouble," said Sam Deloria, "but the Apaches are stubborn people. The San Carlos Apaches sent in their program. Washington cut it and funded the cut. The San Carlos Apaches said, 'No!' Washington said, 'All right, we'll give you half.' The San Carlos Apaches said. 'No!' Finally, after some embarrassment, Washington gave in and funded the original program. You know, participation of the poor.

"It took sixteen months," Deloria said.

Roger Jourdain laughed at that. His tribe had had exactly the reverse trouble with the experts, he recalled: "Our tribal OEO people submitted a program. And Washington rejected it: 'Think big. It's too small,' they told us. So we sent for some of the 'Indian experts' at the University of South Dakota to rewrite it. And we resubmitted it. Washington rejected it: 'You'll have to get some experts to rewrite it,' they told us. So they sent us some 'Indian experts' from the University of South Dakota to rewrite it. And then we got it."

Jourdain admitted that the Chippewas had written up their program wrongly: "We wanted a recreation camp for the kids. So we said so. The experts argued against it.

" 'Recreation camp? Oh, no,' the experts said. 'Call it anything but that.'

" 'What shall we call it?' I asked.

" 'Social skills,' the experts told me. They were experts, all right. That's how we got our recreation camp for the kids."

"Undemocratic," "bureaucratic," "politically contrived," and "paternalistic" were criticisms of the War on Poverty that tribal leaders began to make with increasing frequency. Yet in tribe after tribe the applications for projects and funds also increased. There were soon one hundred tribes requesting poverty programs, while at the same time tribal leaders kept up a drumbeat of criticism.

"Jobs are jobs," a tribal OEO director said. "You can't understand what it means. Here we have ninety percent of the men without jobs. So even a no-good job, doing a no-good job, on a no-good project is better than nothing. It feeds someone's kids."

Critics within the tribes began to accuse the War on Poverty of enforcing the tribal status quo and enriching the tribal officials. The Indians at the lower depths of reservation life, they charged, were not benefiting from the poverty funds.

"It doesn't reach to the poor Indians," the Creek leader Reverend Hill said. "The rich Indians get the poverty money. But the real poor Indians, the poverty Indians, the country Indians, do get nothing." Eskimo leader William Hensley had a similar plaint: "We have various programs. Poverty programs, and what not. But they are not reaching into the villages like they should."

Paul Steiner

A tourist "trading post" at the Pueblo of Santo Domingo, New Mexico, which capitalizes on the image of the Indian as a living museum piece.

A bookmobile makes its regular stop at Lake Hawley, on the White Mountain Apache Reservation, Arizona.

Paul Steiner

Abandoned church, Chippewa Reservation, Bad River, Wisconsin. A boarded-up missionary church is the result of the resurgence of native religion.

A jail at Mission, South Dakota. In towns bordering on reservations, arrests of Indians are frequently disproportionate to those of the general population.

MISSION
CITY JAIL

HEART BREAK
HOTEL

A new-style community center, staffed and run by Navajos, in Gallup, New Mexico. It provides rooms, showers, counseling, and a communal meeting place for city Indians, as well as for rural Indians job-hunting in town.

John F. Kennedy Center, Sioux tribal headquarters in Devils Lake, North Dakota. Though the center was built in part with federal aid, the sign proclaims grievances about lost land and the tribe's pride in the Sioux Uprising.

Navajo tribal council building in the shape of a gigantic hogan, Window Rock, Arizona. At the left, the radio broadcasting antenna; at the right, the sacred Navajo Window Rock.

Suburban housing built by the federal government on the Turtle Mountain Reservation, North Dakota. Many tribes have objected to these "garden apartments" as being too urban and "un-Indian," and they stand half empty.

Paul Steiner

New-style hogans, financed by the tribal building program of the Navajo tribe, have corrugated-metal roofs, windowpanes, skylights instead of smoke holes, and huge television antennae.

"Women Strike for Peace": One of the thirty Sioux men and women who came from the Rosebud Reservation, South Dakota, to march in the New York City "Peace Parade," spring, 1967.

The New Indians: On the dais of an intertribal rally of six hundred Indians from Western states, Reno, Nevada, April, 1964—National Indian Youth Council leaders Bruce Wilkie, Clyde Warrior, and Mel Thom.

Canadian and United States Indian youth join hands: Allen Jacobs (center), Chippewaian of Canada, meets with Mel Thom and Herbert Blatchford in Denver, Colorado, December, 1964.

Under the rotunda of the Washington State Capitol in Olympia, the Makah Indians hold a tribal dance in honor of the Fish-Ins.

One of the most critical was Mel Thom. "I worked with OEO and CAP for a year at home, on the Walker River Reservation. The government said they wanted 'maximum participation of the poor,' 'grass-roots people,' and so forth. All nice sayings," Thom said. "But the bureaucracy, so far, hasn't allowed this to happen. Those memos they keep sending. It would take a professional person to run those programs. And there just aren't that many professional people on the reservations. So the poor don't have a chance.

"The War on Poverty is having real difficulty in gearing itself to the poor and less-educated people. And so far I am a little disappointed," Thom said.

In fact, the National Indian Youth Council in its "Glossary" of terms defined a "pilot project" of the OEO as "An old project with a new name" that was run by a "social worker," who was defined as "An overtrained, underexposed professional who helps us solve our problems." The OEO itself the "Glossary" defined as "A state of confusion."

Yet, in spite of these criticisms, the War on Poverty has brought about an upheaval on the reservations. Its sharpest critics began to talk about it. "The War on Poverty hasn't shaken up all the dust, but it's a good start," was the begrudging comment of Mel Thom. And Vine Deloria, Jr., was even more affirmative: "With five men on its Indian desk the OEO has done more in one year to shake up things than the Bureau of Indian Affairs has done in the last one hundred and forty years."

It was not what the poverty programs contained but what tribal poverty contained that caused the unexpected upheaval. The nature of tribal life so altered these otherwise routine programs that they had a politically dynamic effect on the tribes. What happened?

In the urban ghettos and the counties of the rural poor the "representation of the poor" has been a hotly contested political issue. "Percentages of poverty" have been fought about. But on the reservations there is no such problem. Among the Indians everyone is poor.

"Conditions of poverty cut across all lines on the reservations," explained Dr. Jim Wilson, the Sioux educator who is chief of the Indian desk of the OEO in Washington, "because everyone is in the government definition of the poverty group. So that representation of the poor among the tribes we deal with is really one hundred percent of the people. Most tribal councils are elected at large and almost all the people [on the tribal council] are in the poverty class."

There are richer and poorer Indians. Every tribesman's economic status, education, and interests are not identical. But, by and large, they are united by common tribal bonds and purposes to a degree that does not exist among the Brechtian poor in an urban ghetto or dying rural town. There is no suburban constituency, real-estate lobby, ADA, or Birch Society among the Indians. If the poverty programs were to be run by the tribes it meant that the poor would have control of them.

"That's what happened," Dr. Wilson said. It had never happened before in the history of the federal government's dealings with the tribes. The Bureau of Indian Affairs had always devised and planned programs for the Indians. Where the tribal councils had been involved it was to help administer these government programs, or to advise the government on how to make them work. It was rarely to help plan them.

Now, for the first time, a federal agency had requested that the tribes do their own planning. The Indians, with advisory help, were to establish their own tribal OEO and CAP offices, plan their own projects, staff them, administer the funds, and be responsible for their success or failure.

"You can't be responsible if I control what you do," Dr. Wilson said. "The Indian OEO programs provided a chance for a tribal control of responsibility."

Said a young tribal OEO director of a Northwest tribe: "For the first time in history, reservation Indians were given X number of dollars to direct things for themselves." He was so enthusiastic that he urged Indians trained in government by these poverty programs to run for local and state offices. "Young Indian leaders ought to infiltrate jobs in state and federal agencies," he said.

"It was a dream come true for the youth," said the tribal OEO director of the Cheyenne River Sioux Reservation. "These kids have a job to do now. And they don't go down to the pool hall any more. They will fight in every way possible to hang on to these programs."

The poverty programs are most often modest, almost familial affairs in one-room offices. Some are, however, multimillion-dollar enterprises, employing two or three hundred tribesmen.

The Standing Rock Sioux Reservation had stagnated knee-deep in despair for generations, but the poverty program brought new hope. The tribal OEO, at a prairie grass-roots level, set up programs that included: ranch management, with a model tribal cattle ranch to be run by thirty to fifty young Sioux; Headstart classes far out in the rural villages; an old-age project that was aimed at involving the tribal elders' traditional power in the tribe, in community development; and courses in tribal politics. Cost: $600,000.

One hundred tribesmen are employed by the tribal OEO. "They are mostly Indians," said Teddy Jamerson, the local Sioux Headstart director. "Nothing like this ever happened here before. We were never given the chance."

The tiny Makah Tribe, out on the tip of Puget Sound at Neah Bay, Washington, with its one-classroom program, reported similarly enthusiastic results.

Young Sandra Johnson, the Makah OEO director, said that the tribe's Neighborhood Youth Corps (training ten boys and girls for office and community work) and a single Headstart preschool class ("We are moving the community center, picking it up and moving it, nearer the schoolyard, so the kids can play") had worked so well that the tribe of fishermen would apply for programs in adult education and business consultation. Cost: $42,000.

"It's the most exciting thing that's happened out here in years," Miss Johnson said. "We are really doing something for ourselves, by ourselves."

If the Indians were surprised and delighted by these unexpected successes, despite all the obstacles, those in Washington who had fought for decision making for the tribes were exultant.

Sargent Shriver felt that his faith in the tribes had been vindicated: "There were experts who told us, when the War on Poverty got under way, that the Indian wasn't ready for a program based on local initiative, a program that required the Indians to create and manage their own campaign to combat poverty; that the Indian didn't want and wouldn't respond to such a challenge. The experts were wrong."

The successes of the War on Poverty may not have been exactly what the poverty programmers had envisioned. Many of the new Indians used the program as a stomping ground for their political coming of age. It was a coincidence of history that the challenge had been offered them at a time when the new Indians were looking for it and ready for it.

Since the new Indians and Red Muslims had appeared on the reservation scene they had been seeking a political test. If the tribal governments could function, not only within the tribes—that was something they had always done—but to govern programs that were part of the society outside the tribes, then the modern tribalism might be more than a youthful dream. And strangely enough it was the War on Poverty that offered the young educated Indians their first opportunity to test their beliefs.

And the new Indians not only achieved a victory over their doubts but in some tribes achieved tribal leadership. By-passing the old, demeaning dependence on the program of the Bureau, the young Indians emerged self-confident from the battles of the War on Poverty. And with political know-how.

Unfortunately little, if any, change has been effected in the economy of the tribes. Indian poverty has not been perceivably altered by the War on Poverty.

It is true that several thousand Indians have received part-time or full-time jobs. But these jobs are of a training or service nature. And they will end when the poverty program ends. Job Corps programs that send young Indian boys into the forests and train Indian girls as typists have little economic effect when there are no new jobs for these typists, and no lumbering industries.

Harry Peltier, the tribal OEO director of the Chippewas' Turtle Mountain Reservation, sourly talked of the economic dead end he thought the War on Poverty was leading to: "We have been given more than a million dollars. We have a payroll of two hundred to two hundred and fifty people. We have sixteen projects. And what happens when it all ends? We will be lucky to have created four jobs.

"Instead of giving all that money, like welfare, why couldn't they let the tribes put it in capital investment? But no! They wouldn't let us do that," Peltier said. "So we train people for jobs that won't exist. Our people are in such a state of depression they would jump on any bandwagon that offered hope. But the government feeds the wagon before the horse."

But the War on Indian Poverty has itself been poverty-stricken. Its funds in the first year were little more than $4 million, about $10 per reservation Indian. By 1966 these funds had been increased to $12 million. However, they had to be divided among 105 tribes and 58 CAP programs, said Dr. Jim Wilson.

If compared to the $4.5 billion that Congressional experts estimated would be needed to revitalize Appalachia—an area of smaller size—it can be seen that these funds for the tribes could hardly fill the pockets of poverty on the reservations. They barely lined those pockets.

There has been considerable rejoicing and self-congratulation by the government agencies over the improvement of Indian health, housing, job, and income statistics. However, these improvements when weighed beside the booming of the already affluent economy of the country indicate the condition of the Indian has worsened.

The cruelty of any comparison has perhaps frightened off the statisticians of poverty. What sense would it make to talk of the increase of the yearly income of the average Indian family from $1,200 to $1,500 yearly—that is, $300—in a *ten-year period?* The yearly income of the median white family stood at $7,170. And that white family's income increased by $312 in *one year alone*—1965.

Either income—improved or unimproved—of the Indian family barely equals 20 percent of his average white neighbors'. In order to have a slight idea of what it means to live as the Indians do, one has to imagine the average white family's receiving an 80 percent cut in pay. Poverty such as this would be inconceivable to most people.

In the Negro ghetto of Los Angeles' South Side, the average family's income, it has been protested by civil rights leaders, rose only 4 percent in 1965—from $4,497 to $4,669. In view of the rising cost of living this was a relative decline.

Yet those ghetto incomes were more than 300 percent higher than those of the Indians.

Emphasizing the absurdity of any comparison is the Labor Department report that in "poverty areas" one of ten Negroes in the labor force is unemployed: "For Negroes in poverty areas unemployment rates were higher than the worst national rates for the entire labor force recorded since the depression of the 1930's." But on the reservations, after four years of the War on Poverty, unemployment was still estimated at 40 to 80 percent. The advent of a mere 10 percent decrease would be greeted as a millennium.

One year after the War on Poverty had begun the San Francisco Indian Center's *The American Indian* gloomily said, "The very structure of the relation between the rich and the poor, keeps the poor, poor." The publication concluded "that the powerful do not change, and that it is the very system itself that causes poverty, and that it is futile to work within this framework.

"Who knows better than the Indian the bitter division and strife in their communities and the placing of our forefathers in a powerless position. This is the powerlessness of being coerced and manipulated by the very system that excludes them. There are articulate spokesmen for the poor, but there are no articulate spokesmen of the poor on those 'Poverty' programs," the San Francisco Indian group declared. "So the Indians and all the 'poverty' stricken Americans wonder if this 'War' is just another political exploitation, and another bureaucratic program."

Once more the Indian felt his hopes had been betrayed. In spite of all he had achieved within himself, the poverty programs had not changed his outward poverty. He was right back where he had started from. He was more beset than ever with pent-up sorrows.

The tale of Charlie Foot, the hermit of the Rosebud Sioux, that took place in the second year of the War on Poverty, touched the feeling of sorrow:

He lay in a cave of roots. The disfigured hermit lay there crumpled, in an icy corner of the five-by-seven home that he had carved out of the cave floor: a coffinlike nest where he huddled for warmth, to keep from freezing to death. Lying on a bunch of old, torn blankets, he was too weak to kneel or stand up. His food and water were gone. His fire had gone out long ago. He had not eaten in twenty-four days. He was dying of hunger and cold.

It was winter on the prairie. Snowdrifts were deep in the Badlands of Dakota. The temperature had fallen below zero once more. North, in the sea of snow, beyond the blizzard-bound town of Parmelee, on the Rosebud Sioux Reservation, where Buzzard Butte pierced the wintry horizon to the west, and the frozen White River Fork flowed to the east, was the hideaway of the starved recluse. He had lived alone since his mother's death, in his cave of roots. He was feared by some—an evil-tempered bachelor, with a misformed body, who threatened those who came near his cave.

He was witched, some said. Yet, in the town of Parmelee, where he usually came for handouts, the hermit was missed. When he did not appear during Christmas they searched for him.

A fellow Sioux, Sleeping Bear, found the hermit. He found him half dead and summoned the tribal ambulance, which rushed him to the Rosebud Hospital. That was on January 7. Foot had been lying in his cave, without food, without heat, since December 14. The hermit, who normally weighed 150 pounds, had shriveled to a mere 80 pounds. He was suffering from "severe malnutrition and pneumonia," said Dr. Gordon Hollis at the hospital, but "he's going to live."

His tribesmen were enraged. There was angry talk. Some of them, it was said, blamed the War on Poverty for not "taking care of the poorer Indians." Some of them blamed "the society that makes outcasts of men because of physical appearance." Some of them, in tribal shame, blamed the tribe itself for the loss of its communal brotherhood. They blamed the tribal council for not "watching out for a fellow tribesman." They blamed the hermit's tribal neighbors for not "being a brother's keeper."

The young Sioux who edited *Eyapaha*, the tribal paper, Frank LaPointe, was one of those who believed the case was an omen. LaPointe, a soft-spoken, educated young man, thought the source of evil was the dependence of the tribe on the civilization of the white man. He blamed the morality of the white man.

"It is ironical that in this season when Christ was born in a cave to save the world, an Indian almost died in a cave because no one cared," LaPointe said. "As we look at the Charlie Foot case, it is even more ironical that we must fight to keep our racial lives as well as our physical lives."

Was this what the War on Poverty had promised? Was this what had happened to "the hope [that] had crept into the thinking of the Sioux"?

LaPointe was bitter: "We are not the only 'skid row' of the plains. But we pray to God that the government will not let another generation of Sioux die poor, ill-clothed, and without hope for their children."

16

THE CHANGING WOMEN

"We are full-blooded Assiniboins, my daughters and I," the mother said with pride.

The eldest daughter had a tense and hard laugh. "I am a mean savage," she said. She was not joking; there was a severity in her face. "My sister, on the other hand," and she indicated a young girl who was quietly sitting in the corner of the kitchen, with long, light hair and a calm face, ". . . my sister runs with the whites! I run with the Indians! And my mother, she runs . . ."

"Where does your mother run?" the mother asked.

It was the late afternoon of a cool and lucid summer day in northern Montana. The quiet was brittle. In the tall grasses of the high prairie the wind blew autumn from the Canadian border, through the fields of the Fort Peck Reservation. The horses in the corrals kicked up a whirlwind of dust. The horses snorted; the wind in their nostrils had excited them and they had to be tied up.

The women sat around the kitchen table and talked politics.

"Where does your mother run?" the mother repeated.

"You run for tribal office. But where does that get you?"

"It is true. Sometimes I think I am running in circles."

When women led by being women, they held together the tribe and family by their act of being. Unobtrusive, soft-spoken, quiet women did not have to act like men. In those days women did not have to be elected to leadership that was theirs by virtue of their existence as the core of the kinship family. When the men of the tribe were away to hunt, or to war, women held things together.

But the old tribal way no longer held together. In the governments of parliamentary men, the position of women had been usurped by elections and the laws of the white man that came outside of tribal life.

"Whoever heard of a tribal chairwoman?" the mother said.

The mother had been recognized for her political leadership as a vice president of the National Congress of American Indians; but she had not been recognized by her own tribe. She had run for the tribal council and lost.

"Now they say I should run for tribal chairman," the mother said, her hands in her apron knotted at the thought. What should she do? Her uncle, "a medicine man, as you say," had told her that two men would stand in her way in the last election. That had happened. "I lost by two votes," she said, "so I better ask my uncle before I run again. My daughters do not believe these things; they do not understand the old things."

"There is nothing wrong with medicine men," said the eldest daughter, who had been to college for two years. "Psychologically they are quite perceptive sometimes. But there is something wrong with tribal politics."

"What?" the mother said.

"Men!" said the eldest daughter. "For too long tribal politics have been the refuge for yes men. For self-seeking men. For weak men. I think we need women running things once more."

"Like you, I suppose?" the younger daughter scoffed. "You hate everybody."

"Just white Indians."

"Whites are no different than Indians."

"Why do you always side with them?"

"Because you think you are better than they are."

"I am better! I am Indian!"

The squall of words subsided as abruptly as it had begun. The mother smiled at both. Her daughters were strong-spoken; she liked that. Women ought to be strong.

"Mother, if you run for tribal chairman," the eldest daughter said, "I will run against you."

"As long as it is in the family," the mother responded.

The Assiniboins are rural people, ranchers and farmers most of them. On the Fort Peck Reservation they keep to themselves. When the tumult of the outside world enters their lives they like to keep it a family affair, within the tribe.

"If you're so Indian, how come you left home?" the younger daughter chided.

The eldest daughter's eyes flared: "It's the psychology of the whites that I want to learn. To be inside of their psychology. That's something we Indians can do. But they can't learn to be inside our psychology. None of the girls in the army believe I am Indian. They say to me, 'You must be Greek or Spanish or Italian. You are too smart to be Indian.' But I tell them I am a savage. I tell them I am a mean and savage Indian, so watch out. Mother, you are too old-fashioned; if you are too polite the white men will walk all over you. And the Indian men will never elect you. The young Indian girls are different. We're modern." She frowned, biting her lips. "Except, that is, my sister. But, you'll see, in five years I will be tribal chairman."

On the kitchen table lay the shadows of the late afternoon sun that slanted through the window. The three women sat quietly. Listening to the silence that separated them, they were thoughtful. "We live in three different worlds," the mother said.

The men of the family had galloped off, as was fitting, to hunt for stray cows, and the women of the family had stayed home to discuss the social structure of the family, in the modern kitchen of the ranch house. The Assiniboin family had simply modernized the traditional division of tribal labor.

Women had tilled the earth, sown the seeds, and harvested the crops. Women had preserved the tribal unity and maintained the family. In fact, the women had often been what modern man somewhat enviously had termed "the decision makers." In the matriarchal clans that ruled many of the tribes barely a few generations ago—in some tribes they still do—the women were not merely the titular heads of the families, with the inheritance of tribal leadership and family name being given by them. These women were often the de facto powers of government.

That this was but a few generations ago may account for the modernized and traduced form in which it had persisted. Even if only around the kitchen table.

"Someone had to do it," the eldest daughter said. "Those anthropologists say we had a matrilineal family. Actually, all we had was common sense. Someone had to run things while the boys were being boys, and shooting the countryside full of arrows and making widows, instead of babies. Someone had to keep the home fires burning. You know, a buffalo hide was no Social Security system. That matrilineal family talk was about the only survivor's insurance we had.

"Oh, all that Earth Mother nonsense. Those anthropologists ought to write mysteries." She laughed. "Women were just being practical."

The power of women within Indian beliefs may nonetheless have corresponded with their importance in tribal life. In the myriad theories of tribal religions about the creation of human beings— the creation myths, as the scientific mythology referred to tribal theories—there was one recurring theme: the sacredness of the Earth Mother.

The Earth Mother was thought to have created human beings. The theory varied with the teller and the tribe, but it was told that the Spirit of the Sky, or the Grandfather Sky, or the Father Rock, or the Father Sun, or whatever name was given to the Supreme Being, who was male, may have guided the Earth Mother in her act of creation. However, she, not he, was the creator. The female origin of humanity was self-evident to tribal man. It was woman's work. She was the Creator, the Source, the Womb.

So there were: The Grandmother Cedar, of the Arikara Tribe of the Plains, who was the "Grandmother of life," and who "Led the people out of the Underworld." The Mother Corn of the Pueblo Indians, who "gave" life and led "the people to the surface of the earth." The Mother Corn of the Pawnees, who "taught the tasks of mankind," and who "gave the breath of life," and speech itself. The Grandmother Earth of the Winnebagos, who, like the creator God of the Sioux, was feminine and who was the symbol of women. "Our Grandmother Earth is a woman, and in abusing your wife you will be abusing her," an old Winnebago man told Paul Radin. "She it is who takes care of us."

The Zuñis had a prayer:

> *Mother Corn caused movement.*
> *She gave life.*
> *Life being given we came.*
> *Out of the Underground.*

It was the Navajo Goddess of Creation who was, however, the most vivid. The Changing Woman, said the Navajo religion, created the Diné—the people—by molding them from the skin of the underneath of her breasts, the tenderest and most sensitive part of a woman's skin, it was said. Human beings were the only creatures created from the breasts of the Changing Woman, it was said.

Whichever way she created life, and whatever her form was, the Earth Mother was not merely a holy woman. She was thought of as a living deity. She was an earthy goddess, indeed, for she was the biological, as well as the agricultural, as well as the spiritual giver of life.

In a time when the power of women in tribal life had diminished, and the attitudes of men toward these women had demeaned them, why resurrect the belief in the Earth Mother? The historic and religious background of tribal women is of importance in understanding the self-image of the modern young Indian girls, and the source of the strengths that they draw upon to become the contemporary Changing Woman.

Nowhere was the power of women in tribal life more dramatically shown than in the shaping of the Iroquois Confederation of Nations. It was the women of the Iroquois tribes who fought what may have been the first successful feminist rebellion in the New World. The year was 1600, or thereabouts, when these tribal feminists decided that they had had enough of unregulated warfare by their men. Lysistratas among the Indian women proclaimed a boycott on love-making and childbearing. Until the men conceded to them the power to decide upon war and peace, there would be no more warriors. Since the Iroquois men believed that women alone knew the secret of birth, the feminist rebellion was instantly successful.

In the Constitution of Deganawidah the founder of the Iroquois Confederation of Nations had said: "He caused the body of our mother, the woman, to be of a great worth and honor. He purposed that she shall be endowed and entrusted with the birth and upbringing of men, and that she shall have the care of all that is planted by which life is sustained and supported and the power to breathe is fortified: *and moreover that the warriors shall be her assistants.*"

The footnote of history was curiously supplied when Susan B. Anthony began her "Votes for Women" movement two and a half centuries later. Unknowingly the feminists chose to hold their founding convention of latter-day suffragettes in the town of Seneca, New York. The site was just a stone's throw from the old council house where the Iroquois women had plotted their feminist rebellion.

But, as the white women were gaining power, the Indian women were losing theirs.

Ironically, it was the very power of women within tribal life that led to their powerlessness in modern society. The women were trapped within the confines of the kinship families and tribes. In political affairs their influence was limited to the tribal world and went no further. The white man was ignorant of the tribal women, or ignored them.

Because of this ignorance, or because of the masculine conceits of "Western Man," the government in its official dealings with Indians did not recognize the power of the tribal women. The matriarchs of the tribes were not invited to sign the treaties of peace, though it may have been they who had decided upon the peace. It was a disastrous oversight. The headmen, or the heads of the warrior bands, were summoned to these X-signing ceremonies, but never the women.

One observer knowingly noted: "The Indian Service has made the mistake of dealing exclusively with the men, only to wonder or to be annoyed when agreements reached with men are not carried out."

Women were as conspicuously absent from the hundreds of tribal delegations brought to Washington by the government in the late 1800's. Perhaps the government could not comprehend a society where women held the power to influence peace and war so decisively.

It was a moot question. The U.S. Army in that period had reflected the attitude of white men toward Indian women by naming the sitting target on their shooting ranges "The Kneeling Squaw."

When the power of the tribes began to disintegrate in the nineteenth century, so did that of the women. The men were confined to the reservations and could no longer hunt in the old way or do things that men did. In frustration they turned their energies inward to tribal affairs. And the tribal councils of men and tribal chairmen that were established by the government to carry on official business further diminished the older tribal ways of governing and the political role of the women. The men then began to adopt some of the white man's attitudes toward their women.

Mrs. Anne Wauneka, of the Navajo Tribe, who has seen three generations of changing attitudes, said: "In the Navajo way of thinking, leadership is really a man's business. The men say that a woman's place is in the hogan, not in the council."

Once dislodged from their traditional role the women withdrew deeper into the remnants of tribal life. Commissioner of Indian Affairs Hiram Price perceived the sorrowful result when he reported, in 1882, that "The intelligent, decent Indian girl is a problem." His annual report to the Congress quoted the remarks of the principal of the Hampton Normal School for Indians, General S. C. Armstrong, who wrote: "There is absolutely no position of dignity to which an Indian girl, after three years of training, can look forward with reasonable confidence. There is nothing for her but to enjoy or suffer in the present state as best she may."

"The Kneeling Squaw" was expendable. Her life on the reservations was not only confining but crippling, for she was to be usually ignored by the dominant society. She was rarely elected to tribal leadership. She was not selected for schooling. She was burdened with her traditional role in tribal life but was denied any official voice in tribal decisions.

"It is understandable that the superficial white observer concludes that the Navajo woman is little better than a chattel of her husband," wrote one anthropologist.

The heritage of tribal women was not that easily obliterated. It had merely withdrawn into the kinship family so deeply that it was not visible to outsiders.

Symbols of the power of women are preserved in different ways by different tribes:

Among the Mescalero and White Mountain Apaches, that symbol is the ceremony of puberty rites for young girls. It is one of a few of the old religious rituals that is strictly adhered to and widely celebrated in the traditional way by these tribes.

Among the Navajos, that symbol, one of many, has been built into the very structure of the hogan; for to this day the hogan is built upon four poles—the east pole named after the Earth Woman; the south pole after the Mountain Woman; the west pole after the Water Woman; and the north pole after the Corn Woman. Literally the homes of the Navajos are supported by their women—and would collapse without them.

In everyday life the tribal women often have more than symbolic influence. Where they are heard and to the degree that they are listened to, it is by the guiles and wiles that are more traditional to white women than to Indian women. "By vigorous use of their tongues [they] frequently nullify decisions made by their men," it has been said of Navajo women. It is pathetic evidence of the external powerlessness to which tribal women in a once matriarchal society have been reduced.

Some women have been elected to tribal councils. But they have been few. Like Mrs. Wauneka of the Navajos, they have been exceptions, or exceptional.

However there has never been an Indian tribe that elected a woman as tribal chairman. Several women have made the attempt. None of them has won. One bold tribal lady, who had seemingly been elected at the polls, promptly had her election invalidated by the tribal council of men. In itself this would hardly be extraordinary were it not that in every crisis that has faced the Indians in the last generation women have been recognized as leaders.

In the Fish-Ins in Washington State one of the undaunted spokesmen for the fishermen was Janet McCloud of the Nisqually Tribe. Of the three young Indians who organized the Washington State Project, Sandy Johnson, a young college girl of the Makah Tribe, was one of the staunchest. When the Urban American Indian Protest Committee was formed in Minneapolis, one of the two organizers was a young Indian girl, Mary Thunder.

When the Dakota Sioux successfully fought the State Jurisdiction Law over their lands, several Sioux women were leaders of the campaign, though no tribal women held a top position on any Dakota Sioux reservation.

When the end of World War II brought demands for intertribal unity and the National Congress of American Indians was founded, it was a Sioux young woman, Helen Peterson, who was chosen its executive director. The "United Nations of the tribes" has had women in many of its leading positions: Georgeann Robinson, of the Osage, is first vice president, and Helen Mitchell, of the Quinault, is secretary. While of its regional vice presidents three are women: Elsie Ricklefs, of the Hoopa Valley Tribe, Agnes Savilla of the Mohave, and Alvina Grey Bear of the Standing Rock Sioux.

And when ten young Indians founded the National Indian Youth Council five were college girls. Of the three top officers of that youth movement two were young women: Shirley Witt, of the Mohawks (first vice president) and Joan Noble, of the Utes (second vice president). It is not unusual for young women to be prominent in youthful politics, but this emphasis on femininity cannot be equaled by the leadership of any non-Indian collegiate group.

None of these women who are national Indian leaders held positions of equal importance within their own tribes. Why the seemingly strange double standard? It is more than an expression of the baffling peculiarity of tribal politics.

These women have had to go outside of their tribes to be recognized as leaders. Within tribal life they were trapped by the confines of their own history. Once unburdened by the weight of obligations that no longer functioned, they were freer to reassert themselves and to draw upon their heritage as women.

Tens of thousands of Indian women have come into the cities. For the last decade they have been leaving the reservations in growing numbers, not to seek their fortunes—few have any expectation of finding any—but to find a fuller, freer life for themselves. Many have made the trek to the cities simply to find the meagerest of jobs.

More often than the tribal men, these tribal women have been able to cross the cultural divide from rural to urban life without losing their way. One survey of the Indian community of Chicago indicated that half of the Indian women in that city were not living with their husbands. The husbands had left, unnerved by the hectic momentum of urban life, the ghettos of crowded rooms, the smoggy sky, and the humiliation of unemployment lines. Or they had sought solace in the nearest bar, or had hitchhiked back to the reservation where *they* felt freer.

In the cities the power of the women has been recognized by the extratribal communities. Election of tribal women to the leadership of these urban Indian centers has been a phenomenon in modern Indian life. The San Francisco Indian Center during the winter of 1966–67, for instance, had four women on its board of directors and one man. Of the seven officers of the California group, three were women. The Indian Center of Chicago had three women on its board of directors.

Los Angeles, Minneapolis, and New York City clubs of urban Indians all have women among their leaders. So do the Indian centers in other cities, almost without exception.

"We adapt like crazy," said Mary Lou Payne of the young Indian women. The women, especially the younger women, are more resilient and flexible, more accepted and accepting, more capable of outward change and inner stability than their husbands are at times. "No one adapts like an Indian, if given half a chance. I'm schizophrenic myself," the Cherokee girl said.

The older and traditional Navajo woman, Mrs. Anne Wauneka, thought there was a more profoundly Indian way to explain the staying power of the young women. She said: "I see a lot of these educated Navajo girls typing. They went to school. As secretaries they have been taught to use shorthand, they have been taught to use typewriters. This is the way an office should run. This person is using what she has been taught. And she has been paid. And this is done for economy reasons.

"And she has been taught to live in a nice house where you just touch the walls and the lights come on. Where you touch a certain metal, turn it, and the water is running. Yet she is an Indian. Her belief is within her. Her heritage is within her. She is just an image in the office, who copied what the white man has taught her to do, for economy reasons. But she is a Navajo and will always remain an Indian.

"An Indian is an Indian," Mrs. Wauneka said. "She may have a dark complexion. She may have a light complexion. She may have blue eyes. She may not have. But she is an Indian."

Sitting in the living room of her suburban home in Window Rock, the Navajo capital, on a sofa bright with Navajo rugs as upon a throne, Mrs. Anne Wauneka talked of these changing women. In the room several men of the tribe sat about her, as her court would about a queen.

Her clothes were regal. The subtle brown velvets of the traditional Navajo woman's gown flowed to her feet. Her breast was adorned with splashes of silver and turquoise jewelry, which encircled her fingers as well.

If there were a queen in the United States, it would have to be this woman, the most honored and most powerful of Indian women leaders in modern times, the daughter of the last of the great chiefs of the Navajos. Her crown, however, was a knot of white sheep's wool that bound her black hair in the ancient way.

She talked of those who had said a woman's place was in the hogan:

"We are all human beings. To me it doesn't really matter whether it's a woman, or whether it's a man. Their structure is the same. They have a brain to think with. This is what I always base my opinion on in dealing with people. And the problems are the same. And the teaching is the same. And the house they live in is the same. And the food that is placed on the table is the same. When you serve to the people you don't say that a man eats this kind of food so they go to another place. And the language is the same. And the subject to be discussed is about the same.

"So everything points to a human being. Whether it's a man or a woman. To my way of thinking there should be woman leadership as there should be man. Because the problem remains. And the problem affects both sex. If a leader is needed, although it is a woman, I would say it should be used."

Combining the qualities of Mary Lou Payne and Anne Wauneka, resilience and inheritance, the ability to change and yet retain and draw upon the traditional sources of the power of tribal women, the image of the contemporary Indian woman is being created. She is no longer the shy Indian maid of romantic legend. She is no longer "The Kneeling Squaw." She wears a bouffant hairdo, has a diploma in her purse, and dances the Twist, but in her heart is the rediscovery of her strength as an Indian, and a pride in the unique beauty of her Indianness.

In the town of Whiteriver on the Apache Reservation of White Mountain, there is an old trading post that has been modernized into a supermarket. Hanging above the checkout counters was a display of cradleboards. And the young Apache girls who worked the office machines in the tribal office across the road came in with mini-skirts to shop; their eyes were amused as they saw the portable baby carriages in which they themselves had been carried—they had seen plastic imitations in the drugstores of Phoenix that were not half as comfortable.

On the Rosebud Sioux reservation of South Dakota, the tribal newspaper, *Eyapaha,* told of one such—a Crow Creek girl, Marlene Bearheels—who has journeyed, it said, "from the jobless reservation world to the world of the machine that seems to be replacing man." This descendant of the warriors of Spotted Tail and Red Cloud was studying data-processing machines and office automation at Rocky Mountain College.

"This is a good field to get into, especially for Sioux students," said Miss Bearheels. She cheerfully added, "I hope to get a job in Florida."

There is a newspaper column in the *Navajo Times,* "The Law and You," that offers tribesmen legal advice. One day the law columnist talked about the legality of love and the illegality of children. And for weeks and weeks after Navajo women laughed at the advice offered.

Love is not legal to the white man unless you "buy marriage licenses," the tribal newspaper informed its readers. "A little piece of paper may not make a man and his wife better people in the eyes of God, but it sure helps in keeping the 'paper work' straight."

The "white man's law" was odd. It was even said that if a wife's husband died, and she didn't have that "little piece of paper," the justices in the white man's courts "might even say the children were not of [her] husband." But that was not to be believed. No matter how powerful the white man thought a "little piece of paper" was, he could not really think that babies could be made that way.

Humor the "white man's law," the tribal newspaper concluded, by obeying it. It was even said that without that "little piece of paper," children, as well as love, were not legal. If the readers had been married in the religious ceremony of the tribe, they would be well advised to "buy marriage licenses."

"Make it easier for your children to live in the white man's world. Don't brand them as 'illegitimate' in the white man's world."

Wahleah Lujan, the demure Taos Pueblo beauty, who was Miss Indian America for 1967, was standing in the lobby of a hotel in Denver. She had left her courses in sociology at Fort Lewis College to tour the country and plead the cause of her people.

The young woman in the resplendent robes of her pueblo, pure alabaster cloth embroidered with brilliant designs, stood there in confusion. For the whirlwind public-relations tour had taken her into a strange world of urban madness, from the calm of her muted adobe.

A Denver matron murmured in the politest tones, "Tell me, what foreign country do you come from?"

"What did you say?"

"I said to her," Wahleah Lujan said smiling, "that I came from Taos."

The old Hopi grandmother told of her grandson who visited her in Oraibi for the summer, but could not sleep at night in the ancient village because "it is too quiet." Her daughter was a schoolteacher in Tucson, who lived in a suburb near an Air Force base. "Quiet is frightening, if you come from a city of jet planes," the grandmother said.

Oraibi is high on a mesa, a parched pueblo, dry as dust, in the midst of the desert where there has never been any running water. The Hopis have lived there for one thousand years. Now, the young women of Oraibi carry their clothes to a newly built self-service laundromat.

In a little café on the Navajo reservation, a young girl was reading her book. She was seated on a worn stool beside a holey screen door through which the desert sands sifted, as they have for an eternity.

"What are you reading?" she was asked.

"Russian."

"It looks like Navajo."

"Navajo?" the girl laughed. "These days, if you study science you have to read Russian."

Within the barbaric beauty of Monument Valley an Indian mother and her little son were herding sheep. The mother, Mrs. Rose Greyeyes, her son too, were suddenly thrown by the horses, frightened by an explosion in the sky where a jet plane had broken the sound barrier. The mother and son were both injured. Laconically, a tribal newspaper commented: It is "a type of accident nonexistent a few years back."

In the old Southwestern-style Hotel Adams in Phoenix, Arizona, a project of the Federal Development and Training Act was under way. The goal: "To convert shy Indian girls into scintillating waitresses" and "motel housekeepers."

At Window Rock a young mother patiently wheeled her newly bought baby carriage back and forth on the narrow strip of cement sidewalk outside the lodge. It was one of the few bits of paved sidewalk on the sixteen-million-acre reservation. And she had to show off her prized purchase. But the baby carriage was empty. The infant was in the arms of his father, who was inside the lodge, watching television.

There was a "cooking column" in the *Navajo Times*. In it Sarah Twomey asked the ladies of the tribe, "How many of you remember when your rooftops were covered with apples drying in the sun?"
Well, she said, that's "old-fashioned."
If an up-to-date Navajo housewife dries fruit nowadays, wrote Mrs. Twomey, in her recipe for dried cantaloupe Indian-style, she "pops them into an electric oven" and then stores the fruit, not on the roof of her hogan, but in plastic bags.

The Mohawks of the Caughnawaga Tribe, whose muscular men have been famed for their daring as high structural steel workers, had a most articulate and beautiful spokeswoman. She was a high-fashion model. Kahn Tineta Horn, in her twenties, educated in Montreal, New York, and Paris, had been elected to the National Council of Indians of Canada. Her voice in behalf of her people has been heard in the Parliament in Ottawa, and in the political arenas of Washington.
Before becoming an Indian leader, the young Mohawk girl had been "Princess Canada," the counterpart of "Miss America."
"My people were disturbed when I left the reservation," Kahn Tineta recalled. "They acted as if they thought I was betraying them. But I knew I would suffocate if I stayed there.
"It was a difficult thing. My mother thought I should marry and raise children the way other Mohawk girls do. My family thought I would lose my identity, or something. They had real anxieties about it. And a lot of them still look at me funny when I visit my family on weekends."

On the reservation af the Oglala Sioux, Mrs. Irving, who said she was a direct descendant of the warrior Crazy Horse, was elected mayor of the town of Pine Ridge.

Laura Peshlakai, a young Navajo girl, came home to her reservation town of Crystal, New Mexico, population 250, after visiting New York City. She had been feted at the Waldorf-Astoria and had attended youth conferences throughout the urban East.

Her thoughts on coming home?

"We feel very strongly that we do not want to be used as showpieces or our homes as tourist attractions. It is about time that people saw us as we really are, not as the colorful vanishing primitives, but as alert, responsible citizens of the United States.

"We have realized that we can have the best of our culture, the best of the White Man's culture, and apply it to our lives. In this way we will play our part in bringing sanity and unity back to the world."

In the woods of Minnesota, on the Leech Lake Reservation of the Chippewa, a young girl said: "The American Indians are a very proud people, no matter what tribe they are from. But so are most of the white people.

"Though nowadays we are told we are all a defeated nation, our parents still teach us to be proud we are Indians and never to be ashamed, no matter what some white people tell us. Some of the whites sure like to push us around, or try to, but if we fight back, they soon enough leave us alone. My folks always tell me to stick up for myself and fight back, and then when I do, they say it's the old Indian in me, always fighting.

"The American Indian today, though he is supposed to be civilized, conformed, etc., still has a lot of the old ways in him. He does things the way some of his ancestors did. So we Indians of today really aren't too much different from Indians of before. We are supposed to be more civilized and educated today. But then, weren't we, before the white man came? Maybe not in his way, but in ours, very much so."

17

WARPATH ON
THE RESERVATIONS

It's trouble, trouble, trouble,
With the damn redskins,
From the damn redskins,
From the damn redskins.
PETER LA FARGE*

Old Cinnijinni Clah was a Navajo medicine man. He was, he thought, one hundred years old. He was born, he thought, in the time of the "Long Walk" when his people had been force-marched for four hundred miles across the deserts of New Mexico to imprisonment at Fort Sumner during the Civil War. And the old man lived in the old way in Coyote Canyon where he had successfully ignored the twentieth century until his one-hundredth year.

The venerable medicine man had then registered to vote for the first time in his life and had voted in his first election.

Who did Cinnijinni Clah vote for? He voted for his grandson, Monroe Jymm, a crew-cut, dark-rim-eyeglassed, business-suited student at the University of New Mexico, who was running for the State House of Representatives from McKinley County. Jymm won. There was another young Navajo, James Atcitty, who had also attended the University of New Mexico, running that year for state representative from San Juan County. He won too.

* © Copyright, Edward B. Marks Music Corporation. Used by permission.

Since the councils of the conquistadores in the early 1600's the governments of New Mexico had been composed exclusively of white men. This was the first time in the 350 years of white governmental rule that Indians had been elected. "There has never been an Indian in the State of New Mexico Legislature, until this year," said the *Navajo Times*. Suddenly there were two. Less than enthusiastic was the wary comment of one of the McKinley County leaders of the Democratic party. "If this keeps up the Indians will take over," he said.

The Navajos and Zuñis outnumbered the whites in McKinley County by two to one; for they constituted from 60 to 70 percent of the population. Until now the Indians had never exercised any political power. There was but one Indian on the county school board; there were no Indian teachers in the municipal schools of Gallup; no local officials were Indian. If these old medicine men and their collegiate grandsons began to meddle in local politics, who knew where it might lead?

"It's true," Vine Deloria, Jr., said. "McKinley County can be easily taken over by the Indians. They could get together and set up rural Indian political machines. They could nominate an Indian slate on the ticket of either the Democratic or Republican party. It doesn't matter which. They could win control of the administrative structure of the whole county. If they do that in 1968, they would show the way. That would be real 'Red Power.'"

When the young Navajos journeyed to New Mexico's capitol in Santa Fe to take their elected seats they were welcomed with motions to unseat them. It was the story of what had happened to the Sioux who had been elected to the Shannon County school board in South Dakota all over again. That state's Legislature had hurriedly passed a special law to invalidate the Indians' election. Later, another Navajo elected in New Mexico was barred from the Legislature because he appeared in tribal dress. The Governor had to apologize.

After a long fight the Indians won their right to be elected. It whetted the somewhat skeptical Indians' curiosity about the possibility of more political representation.

Jymm and Atcitty were both Democrats. They were elected in

1964. But two years later, in the elections of 1966, both were replaced by Navajo tribesmen who were Republicans—Jake C. Chee and Wilbert C. Begay. That year the Indians sent another tribal member, Tom Lee, to the New Mexico State Senate; another first.

In the saguaro cactus State of Arizona, dry country for Indian voters, yet another young Navajo was elected to the Legislature. Lloyd House, like his fellow tribesmen, was the first Indian in the history of his state to be chosen for the state's governing body. Politically his election was a sensation. House put on his big black old-style Navajo hat, with the high crown and wide brim, and jauntily took off for the state capitol. "I expect to be the image of the Indian in the Legislature," the young man said with a grin.

New Mexico and Arizona had been the last states where Indians were legally disenfranchised. The Indians were "given" American citizenship and the "right" to vote by the Act of Congress of 1924. But in New Mexico and Arizona voting rights were denied to Indians until 1948, twenty-four years later. So the election victories of the Navajos were somewhat startling to the political pundits who had not thought they had a chance.

Yet even more startling were the numbers of tribesmen who had trekked to the polls. Just a few years before, in the mid-1950's, of an estimated twenty-five thousand Navajos of voting age less than three thousand had registered to vote. And fewer still had voted.

Out of the hogans they came. Not merely the city Indians in the towns but the Navajos in the back country voted by the thousands. Their power at the polls had grown so suddenly it left the politicians stunned. These, among the most traditionalist of Indians, who had always shunned the white man's politics, had formed a cohesive and large voting bloc. In the next election they succeeded in unseating the incumbent Congressman in northern Arizona. The Navajos, who were counted as Democrats, further confounded the experts by replacing a liberal Democrat—Congressman Senner— with a conservative Republican—Congressman Steiger.

"More than one tradition [has been shattered] indicating that the Navajo people, as well as other Indians, are going to vote for representatives in the State," said an editorial in the *Navajo Times;* "this also shows . . . that the Navajo people are emerging from leadership [of whites?], not only in Tribal elections, but on the State and National level as well."

The tribal newspaper added: "This will [be] indicate[d] in the very near future."

It was a prophecy of practical politics that was to be quickly fulfilled. Within two years the powerless and less than politically adept tribes had elected more tribesmen to the legislatures than they had in the previous history of the West.

"Fifteen Indians are now being seated in six Western state legislatures," Secretary of Interior Stewart Udall commented after the 1966 elections, "and other Indians are taking office as judges, county officials, and others of public trust. It is noteworthy that several are women."

Up in Alaska two Athapascan Indians, one member of the Tlingit Tribe, and two Eskimos had been elected to the State Legislature. They had even surpassed the success of the Navajos.

William Hensley, the young Eskimo representing the villages about Kotzebue, was one of those elected to the Legislature. He had not really campaigned, he said, for the village elders had assured him he would be elected. He was. The success of the Eskimos seemed incongruous. These genial and retiring hunters, just below the Arctic Circle, had never organized or been interested in politics and knew little about elections. How did Hensley explain it?

"Alaska is merely part of a movement. Kind of a phenomenon, in fact. The native people are waking up," Hensley said. "We have a great deal of political agitation among the native people in Alaska. The native people have finally come to the point where they realize that there is a threat to their land, a threat to their way of life. Along with this has come a political awakening. Life up there, in the villages, is pretty quiet. Most of the native people haven't any communications except by radio, once in a while. I think it's quite a phenomenon that they are interested in political action."

The phenomenon had spread to unlikely places. In Montana, the Flathead Tribe had elected a tribal member to the State Senate.

So had the Blackfoot Tribe. The Cherokees in Oklahoma, more familiar with politics, had elected three of their tribesmen to the State Senate. One was elected president pro tem of that body. While in Idaho, the chairman of the tribal council of the Coeur d'Alene Tribe, Joseph Garry, had been elected to that state's Senate.

Garry, a former president of the National Congress of American Indians, said he believed that a small Indian vote could hold the balance of power in a tight election. There were but two hundred Indian votes in his district of eighteen thousand, he said.

"There is an awakening to political power that we can have," Vine Deloria, Jr., said. "Some of the tribes are just beginning to realize that in close elections, like we have been having, the Indian vote could be decisive in a dozen Western states.

"We could have the 'swing vote' if we vote together as Indians," Deloria, Jr., said.

The Indian tribes "could be decisive" in Wisconsin, Minnesota, North Dakota, South Dakota, Montana, Idaho, Nevada, Arizona, New Mexico, Alaska, and Oklahoma—"if we could get a consensus there," Deloria, Jr., said. "But there are sixty tribes in that state." Washington would be tougher, "though in some counties the Indian could easily be the swing vote," he said. "California would be the same story. If we had a real close election, and the Indians were well registered, and the tribes got out the vote, we could swing almost any one of those states. We already have in some elections."

Senator McGovern of South Dakota had been elected by Indian votes, Deloria, Jr., thought. "In every county where there was an Indian vote, we gave him a larger margin than he won by. He won by less than five hundred votes." Deloria's election figures indicated that among others who would have lost without the Indian swing vote were Senator Metcalf, in Montana; Senator Church, in the Idaho primary; Governor Rölvaag in Minnesota, in 1962; and Senator Cannon in Nevada.

"The Indians in Nevada could put in, or take out, a Governor, a Senator, or a Congressman. It's that close there," Deloria, Jr., said. "But if you want to work a swing vote it has to be close. That's something we are learning how to do. It gives us leverage that we never had before, because our voters are so few. We are politically conscious now. We are just beginning to know what to do."

Evidently whatever the tribes are doing they are doing well. "While Democratic candidates strain for re-election in the West, the Administration is showering fresh attention on the Blackfeet, the Flathead, the Sioux, and practically every other Indian tribe across the Mississippi," the Washington *Post* reported. It quoted a spokesman for Senator Metcalf as saying that the Montana elections had been so close "even the Yugoslav vote could swing it." And then he added: "Montana has an undetermined number of Yugoslavs and about 20,000 Indians."

So sensitive and decisive had the Indian vote become in some localities that Congressman Thomas S. Foley, a Democrat in Washington State, was said to have asked that Commissioner of Indian Affairs Bennett stay away from his state before the elections. He feared a "Red Backlash," the Congressman reportedly said.

The Indians were willing to be wooed, either by the Democrats or by the Republicans. In the Southwest the Republican county chairmen of the five counties of the Navajo Reservation proclaimed "that self-rights of the Indian be encouraged and preserved." In the Northwest the Democrats said the same. Wherever they went to the polls in recognizable numbers, the tribes discovered they had old friends they had never known they had.

Barbecues for political candidates began to outnumber the church suppers of the missionaries. And the Indians enjoyed them, no doubt.

In the past, the tribal Indian had disdained the ballot box, joked about it, but rarely voted. He stayed at home and sat out the election. The gloomy statistics of Indian indifference had been glumly gathered by the House Committee on Interior and Insular Affairs in 1956. Of the 143,078 Indians of voting age on the reservations that year, less than half—57,818—had qualified to cast a ballot, and 25,582 had actually done so. Little more than 17 percent had voted.

How strong the political power of the tribes could be may be seen by a rundown of the registered voters on a few of the key reservations:

	Voting Age	Registered
Colville Tribes	2,241	85
Cheyenne-Arapaho	1,985	397
Pine Ridge Sioux	6,153	2,237
Rosebud Sioux	4,521	1,400
Yakima	1,500	200
Menominee	1,112	411
White Mountain Apaches	1,500	100

It was the Choctaw Indians who faced the double jeopardy of the Mississippi mystique—being both nonwhite and Indian—who illustrated how high the nonvote could go. The Choctaws in the 1956 elections had a voting-age population of 1,278. Of these, 27 qualified as voters, by state law. And 9 finally voted.

A few of the tribes, it was true, were even then alert to the possibilities of politics.

	Voting Age	Registered
Blackfeet	2,942	2,000
Assiniboin and		
Sioux of Fort Peck	1,440	1,200

There were still other tribes who restored the lopsidedness to to the scales:

	Voting Age	Registered
Ramah Navajos	360	0
Fort Berthold	725	0

The apathy, fear and unfamiliarity with voting of the tribal Indians were blamed for this dismal situation. But these were not the only, nor necessarily the primary, causes of the haphazard attitudes of the tribes that then prevailed.

Lack of enthusiasm of the Indians for voting, said the U.S. Commission on Civil Rights, "is no doubt due, in some measure, to lack of interest, and to mixed loyalties, the deepest of which is to the Indian way of life. Whatever the cause, it is clear that years of distress and political confusion have not bred the kind of respect for the white man's institutions that encourages the pursuit of social betterment through the medium of the ballot box."

Discrimination was not the sole cause of Indian nonvoting, the Commission on Civil Rights observed. But many states had a tedious history of officially denying the vote to Indians. As late as 1956 the State of Utah revived a statute that prohibited Indians on reservations from voting. The Supreme Court of Utah upheld the law; but the Legislature, under a barrage of pressure, retreated and repealed it.

The sensitivity to ethnic voting and civil rights laws has since made even anti-Indian politicians nervous. Blatant and obvious disfranchisement of Indians has become an anomaly. More subtle methods of de facto discrimination have been used: local prejudices, gerrymandering of Indian counties, and literacy laws.

The literacy law has been particularly noisome. Raymond Nakai, chairman of the Navajo Tribe, has estimated that "One half of the adult population [of his tribe] cannot vote for the President, or Representatives for Congress, because of State Literacy Laws." His charge was given credence by Lewis S. Meyer, director of registration for the Democratic party of Arizona, who during the 1964 elections had warned, "Means will be used to deny registration to the Indian." These "abusive actions will take place in the use of the literacy test," Meyer said, "in the name of preserving the status quo."

Many of the elder Indians neither read nor write English. The literacy laws have therefore been an effective method of disqualifying the older generation of first Americans from the democratic process. Wisdom has been measured by literacy tests. Thus, the wisest men of the tribe often cannot vote.

The gerrymandering of Indian counties has been an equally effective way of discouraging the tribal voter. In South Dakota this has taken the form of dividing the voting power of the reservation Indians by pairing Indian and non-Indian counties in single legislative districts. By this device the Indian vote has been canceled out. When in the Shannon County elections for county school board the Indians did manage to achieve a majority for their candidates, the South Dakota legislature gerrymandered its way out of that misfortune by dividing the county itself into separate Indian and non-Indian voting districts.

Where the Navajos predominate, in northern Arizona, the counties are shaped like string beans, with the county seats, without exception, located in the non-Indian towns of the lower regions. Half of the polling places are off the reservations. It means long trips to town. Where the towns are unfriendly or hostile—as many border towns on reservations have been—it means long and uncomfortable waits on line. It means insulting experiences. It means humiliation by election clerks who but a decade ago would have treated an Indian wishing to vote as a joke.

Once these obstacles are overcome the Indan has the choice of candidates who usually ignore him, who promise him nothing and who keep their promises.

Anne Wauneka wistfully said: "We vote for Congressmen in Washington, whether we know them or not. We are told they are there in our behalf, whether they are or not. Many times you hope you are being represented. I hope they know there are people here, the back-door neighbors. Let me put it that way."

Even if they vote, who listens to the Indians? In the years past their vote was too insignificant to count. Of the 61,616,638 votes cast for Eisenhower and Stevenson in the election of 1956, the combined vote of all the reservation Indians in the country amounted to a grandiloquent 4/100 of 1 percent of that total.

"Let's face the hard facts, disillusioning though they are," wrote J. Donald Adams in the *New York Times* soon thereafter, "the Negro's vote counts, the Indian's doesn't."

His lack of influence in power politics of the two-party system could not have disturbed the tribal Indian too much. It wasn't his system. He had never had any power in the processes of government that governed him. He had "powerless power," as Mel Thom said. "There was a general conclusion that Indians receive the same old 'mush' under both [Democratic and Republican] administrations. It is just that one party has stirred it faster than the other."

The serene and stern Paul Bernal, of the Taos Pueblo, has his own view of "the political game." "If a man sits here and he says he is a Democrat and a man sits there and he says he is a Republican, and then the two men get up and exchange seats, the white man calls that democracy. That is not democracy to the Indian."

Young or old, the new tribal leader is a political sophisticate. He has to be to survive in the complicated world of tribal politics. But he is not a politician in the contemporary sense. He is rarely tied, or aligned, with either of the two parties permanently. The Republican and Democratic parties neither especially attract him, nor anger him. They exist. He will therefore work with them. Either one, or both. Of course there are exceptions. But most of the new Indians have this nonchalant approach to party politics.

His politics are "Indian." The labels are incidental, and interchangeable. Some of the fieriest Red Muslims and Red Nationalists voted for Senator Goldwater in the presidential election. They were not conservative Republicans. In the very next election many of them voted for liberal Democrats.

Vine Deloria, Jr., sought to explain this: "Indians are folk people. We have folk values that are emotional and spiritual. We do not necessarily vote on dollar-and-cent-things. We are not necessarily going to vote for the party that offers us the most programs, the biggest programs. Politicians never understand that. We vote for what we sense is the man who is nearest to the Indian values. And that is something intangible," he said. "You could create an emotional issue with Indians the night before the elections, and they will all go from one party to the other party."

The nonpolitical politics of the Indian were shown in a story that Herbert Blatchford told. One day the leaders of both the Republican and Democratic parties came to him. Elections were coming. He was the leader of a "chapter house" of the Navajos, a political unit of the tribe, in the city of Gallup. And they wanted his support. The politicians outlined the programs and promises of their parties, the things they would do for the Navajos in Gallup if their candidates won.

Blatchford asked them, in turn: "What is your honesty quotient?" He laughingly recalled they both looked at him in wonder.

"I tried to tell them that the Navajos wouldn't vote for a man because of those party platforms. They would vote for what they thought about the individual man, his honesty quotient," Blatchford said. "But my visitors must have thought I was putting them on." They went away shaking their heads. He said, "I guess they thought I was a crazy Indian."

The disdain of the tribal Indians for the politics of the two-party system is inherent in tribalism. It is not that they do not vote for, join, and favor one party over another. Rather, they have an underlying unity as Indians, whatever the uproarious debates, factional fights, or election alliances they engage in from time to time.

Since the founding convention of the National Congress of American Indians held in Denver, Colorado, in November, 1944, this attitude has been clearly defined. In his keynote speech Ben Dwight, of the Choctaw Tribe of Oklahoma, who was convention president, said:

"I don't think we will have to get into Democratic or Republican or Socialist politics and rely on those different parties to carry out our program. I think in our minds ninety percent of the Indians are in accord, whether they be Democrats, Republicans, etc. I think we can write our own kind of program that all parties will have to get behind."

Dan Madrano, of the Caddo Tribe, who was elected the first secretary of the National Congress, reiterated this view: "I heard someone say a while ago that we must leave out politics. I tell you, if we [are to] get any place, we have to get into politics. *Not partisan politics.*"

The tribal chairman of the Rosebud Sioux, Antoine Roubideaux, put it personally and conclusively: "I am not a minister. I am not a Republican. I am not a Democrat. I am not a Socialist. I am nobody but a poor Indian." His politics, Roubideaux told the convention, "transpired in my heart."

Within his tribe the tribal Indian might vote his heart. The reasons of the heart did not usually prevail at the polls. If the swing vote was to become a political reality the tribes would have to attend to some of the more prosaic tactics of politics. But, "Organization was not of the Great Spirit's gifts to the tribes," said the Minneapolis Indian leader Gerald Vizenor.

"Just registering the Indians in a county and getting them to vote is enough to create a decisive swing vote at the precinct level in most Western states," Deloria, Jr. said. "Once the tribes get the idea they will go out into the villages and explain it to the people. We would then be able to determine hundreds of local elections."

The response was hesitant and uneven, Deloria, Jr., said. The skepticism of the tribal leaders was deep. It had two causes, he thought. One was their lack of experience with electoral politics; then too power politics really didn't "mean anything" to most Indians, he said.

Mostly what held the tribes back was the feeling that this was the "white man's government," he said. It was another country, a foreign force that they had to recognize and bargain with. But that was all. It wasn't "their government."

"If the tribes get to feel betrayed once more, they will withdraw once more," Deloria, Jr., said. "That's what Indians have always done in self-defense. They will withdraw." Like the warriors of old, the new political warriors of the tribes practiced an ancient tactic. When the Indians were attacked, they united and fought back. But when they were defeated or felt betrayed or had won they withdrew. In the brief history of one decade of tribal political activity they have several times repeated the old way of the warriors.

Once more the tribal leaders fear a new government campaign of termination, as during the 1950's. And once more, as in the 1950's, they are uniting politically. Voicing that fear was the San Francisco Indian Center's cry of lamentation: "The Indian has finally come to the end of the trail. The choice is being an Indian or trying to be like a non-Indian in beliefs. Everything points to the end of the Indian, his termination. It only seems sensible that the Indian must take action to remove the threats of termination and cultural oblivion."

And voicing the cry for tribal unity are the chantlike and calmer words of Anne Wauneka: "The Indians have got to get together. To strongly organize. And be heard. Let the Indians be heard. Let their voices be heard. Now it is getting to the point where we would like to be heard. The Indians would like to express themselves. Whether it would be in their favor or not, they would like to express themselves.

"Maybe the only way out for us is to elect our own people to represent us in Congress. Represent us in the state government. It remains to be seen."

Echoes of these thoughts—of political independence and tribal unity—have been heard increasingly among Indian leaders. In the Taos Pueblo, Paul Bernal was troubled by them. He seemed a man of infinite endurance. He had always, as had the other Pueblo Indians, been cautious and wary of the white man's politics, wishing not to enter them. He had trusted his friends, the white politicians, to help the Pueblo.

He was no longer sure he trusted them. He thought they had betrayed the Taos Pueblo's fight for the religious shrine, Blue Lake, and the land around it. Bernal told of a conversation he had with Senator Clinton Anderson, whom he had trusted. It reflected the changing attitudes and growing impatience of even the older, more conservative tribesmen:

"I said to Senator Anderson: 'I know little white men and medium-sized white men and big white men. I know the biggest white man of all. But that does not frighten me.'

"I said to Senator Anderson: 'Just because you are a big white man and I am a little, merely an Indian, does not mean that I will do what you say. No!' I said. 'My people will not sell our Blue Lake that is our church, for $10 million, and accept three thousand acres, when we know that fifty thousand acres is ours. We cannot sell what is sacred. It is not ours to sell.'

"I said to Senator Anderson: 'Only God can take it away from us. Washington is not God. The U.S. Senate is not God.'

"I said to Senator Anderson: 'Why do you want to steal our sacred land?'

"Senator Anderson said: 'Paul, I like you. But there is timber on that land, millions of dollars of timber.'

"I said to Senator Anderson: 'It is our sacred land. We will wait.'"

These things made him decide to think again about who was the friend of the Indian, Bernal said. Once the Indian would let these things happen; he would weep. Now the Indian knew how to fight back.

"That is why I told the All Pueblo Council: 'If the Senators and

Congressmen come to you and tell you what they will do for you, do not believe them. They are not your friends. They will give you crumbs.' That is why I told the All Pueblo Council, 'If an Indian is ugly, illiterate, and poor, and if an Indian is well-dressed, and college educated, he is your friend. The white man is not your friend; he is your friend only when he wants something from you. He will forget you. The Indian cannot forget.'

"I have been thinking: What can the Indian do to save *himself?* Now I have decided. The Indian tribes have to unite. The Indian tribes have to unite first in the state. State by state. Here in New Mexico the Navajos, the Apaches, and the Pueblos have to walk together to the Governor in Santa Fe. Then they will have strength. They will have to vote together. They will have to vote, not for this party or that party, for this man or that man, but for themselves. Then they will have strength."

"One day we are going to have political unity of all the tribes," Deloria, Jr., said: "And we are going to have it nationally."

Tribal chairman of the San Carlos Apaches, Marvin Mull, had this in mind when he called for an "Indian bloc vote." His idea was to adopt the techniques of the big-city machines to the needs of the rural and tribal Indians. The Indian bloc vote would not necessarily mean the Indians would vote *for* Indians but they would vote *as* Indians. By voting together even weak tribes would be strong.

"It is time that all the Indians in the Southwest begin to see their goals as those of neighboring tribes and similar to their own," Mull told a meeting of the tribal council of the Navajos.

To his appeal, the *Navajo Times* replied: "Let's join Marvin Mull and unite with all Indian tribes in the United States."

The San Carlos Apaches' leader thought that before this could happen each tribe would have to unite within itself and each voter would have to be registered. He would begin with his own tribe.

In the rugged, cactus-strewn hills of the reservation of the San Carlos Apaches, above the gorge of the Salt River Canyon, voter registration is not easy. The tribesmen are scattered beyond the arroyos. It is difficult enough to reach, much more so to register, the far-flung families.

Year by year this was done, until the voter registration of San

Carlos was as high as that of the rest of the country. The brother tribe of White Mountain Apaches had an even harder task. Up the dangling roads onto the grassy plateaus at ten thousand feet their herds wandered to summer pasture. Many of the tribesmen drifted like the mountain winds. Jeep trails had to be used to reach them. It was hard for voting registrars to find some families in their summer wickiups of branches and brush hidden in the tall timber. In the mountain valley riverbeds, on little farms, there were some who could not be reached at all.

Jeeps and pickup trucks were mobilized by the tribal council. The voter registrars logged eight hundred miles, not counting those up and down. Getting out this vote was no routine of doorbell ringing. It was a job for fools, or dedicated Indians. When the voter registration drive was finished the White Mountain Apaches had the highest registration in the state. The Apaches had registered from 67 to 81 percent of the eligible voters in their precincts.

Little more than a decade ago the tribe had registered but 6 percent of its voting-age members. About 100 voters. Now some 1,474 turned out to vote. The increase was almost 1,500 percent!

Once the registration was done the Apaches invited all the candidates to come and talk to the tribal council. They endorsed some. And they didn't endorse others.

"It was not on a political-party basis. It was done to build an 'Indian ticket,' " Deloria, Jr., said. "They posted that ballot sheet with their endorsement in the tribal office. They called for an Indian bloc vote. They went out and brought the tribesmen in to vote and talked to them.

"Every one of the candidates the White Mountain Apaches voted for won in the primaries. I guess they are good talkers."

Marvin Mull said: "We are better informed on political affairs on all levels. We are no longer a primitive, colorful, vanishing Indian."

Up in South Dakota the Sioux took this one step further into battle, as the Sioux would.

The legislature of the state, in the spring of 1963, had voted to take over the civil and criminal jurisdiction on the reservations. Governor Archie Gubbrud had signed the bill into law. Under Public

Law 280, passed by Congress in the Eisenhower Administration, any state had the option of enacting such legislation, without the consent of the Indian tribes involved. The law had the effect of halting federal protection and services in many fields. The Indians' ability to hold on to their resources and traditions was thereby weakened. Many tribal leaders thought that was its purpose. Its advocates said, however, it was merely aimed at giving Indians the rights "to full citizenship." The tribes had fought to have the law amended by Congress, demanding the right to vote on their fate. The "consent clause" had never been added.

On March 15 the Governor signed the law. On March 25 the Sioux tribal leaders met and formed the United Sioux Tribes to fight state jurisdiction. By launching a petition drive to place the issue before a state-wide referendum, they hoped to repeal it. And by June 5 they had collected the required 18,500 valid signatures.

And the battle was on.

The Sioux had no experience in state politics. Led by William Whirlwind Horse, of the Oglala Sioux, and later by Cato Valandra, of the Rosebud Sioux, they plunged into a year-long campaign to defeat the law. Hundreds of meetings were held throughout the state, television and radio campaigns begun, posters and brochures and "Fact Kits" were prepared, newspaper advertisements were run, tribal telephone committees were set up and the electronic war of the Sioux was heard on all media of mass communications. In the old Indian tradition they hired an advertising agency in Sioux Falls to scout the enemy terrain.

In the state capital a Keep Faith Committee was founded, long before that phrase gained national prominence, by friends of the Indians to carry the tribesmen's message to the public. South Dakota's Council of Churches declared its opposition to the jurisdiction law. The Episcopal Church declared that in "Christian conscience" it had to do the same, while on the Sioux reservations the opposition of many Catholic parishes was led by Father Joseph Karol.

The Sioux tribal leaders appealed to their tribesmen: "In this time of crisis for the Sioux Nation you all need to take part in the coming election, or you will soon have no nation."

And then the proclamation added: "The democratic process is

like a lovely Sioux maiden: abuse her and she'll turn on you with hate and anger. Cherish her, and she'll cooperate with you and give you strength."

It was the language of the Indian. Who but an Indian would turn an election leaflet into a love poem?

The fight over jurisdiction was, however, ugly. Some of the ranching interests saw it as an opportunity—by removing the legal protection of the federal government from the reservations—to get nearer to ownership of Indian grazing lands they had to lease. The John Birch Society in the prairie towns entered the fray with a fury. Racist, anti-Indian sentiments were publicly revived and played upon. "The preachers of hate and discord" were everywhere, the Sioux paper *Eyapaha* said.

"They have called us a miserable people and have set us against each other," said Dan Howard, a leader of the Standing Rock Sioux. "I have been branded as a problem because I am an Indian." But the truth was that he, and other Indians, had grown up on reservations that were refuges for "escaped white prisoners, thieves, bad women and whiskey peddlers," whom the State of South Dakota allowed to thrive there.

Howard, a prominent rancher and state official, was indignant: "No wonder we are suspicious [of the state jurisdiction], because we have seen those who make policy for us, use us for others' benefits, then discard us. We've been fools and tools used by them. New laws, new cultures, new religions were used to purposely destroy our dignity and our leadership. Society runs by give and take, but they fool us and lead us into things that we don't know.

"We are a reasonable people," Howard said, "but we like to be consulted. We like to be represented. We need to get some Indians elected to state offices—before the all-state jurisdiction." The Sioux had not been consulted.

State Senator James Ramey, who headed the legislative committee that recommended state jurisdiction, denied these accusations. "In my own mind, this jurisdiction law will make the Indians progress at a faster rate," Ramey said. "It is time for South Dakota to become progressive. These cultural enthusiasts are holding the people back."

Ramey, himself a rancher and landowner in the Sioux area, explained: "The bankers wanted to give the Indians credit, but found they couldn't foreclose [on the reservations]; since the state didn't have jurisdiction in Indian country, there was no way to collect." He wished to help the Indians get that bank credit, he said.

The Sioux were unconvinced. Legislative hearings on the law had permitted them but thirty-five minutes to present their views, they declared through their tribal lawyer, Raymond Hieb. Ramey's committee, which had prepared the law, had toured several states to gather information but had not visited a single reservation in their own state. If the legislature wished to help them, why hadn't it consulted them?

" 'One foot in the door and the rest is easy' is an old saying of the white man, since the taking of Manhattan Island for a string of beads," was the caustic comment of the Oglala Sioux Matthew High Pine, head of his tribe's Law and Order (police) Committee: "We as Indians are not about to give up our homeland without resistance to any legislation that would have this effect."

The tribal Law and Order official found his views echoed by a Sioux in the state prison, who wrote in *Eyapaha:* "Eventually, this [jurisdiction by the state] will mean a land sale for the poverty-stricken Indian, in line with the whites' long-range plan to get Indian land."

It was the first time since the Battle of the Little Big Horn that the Sioux tribes had been so united. But history had joined them on a very different sort of battlefield. The descendants of the warriors were apprehensive as election day neared. "We prayed," the Reverend Deloria said. "Then we voted."

Few of the Sioux had ever voted. At most 40 percent, and in most elections often fewer. That November 3 an estimated *90 percent* of the eligible Sioux voters went to the polls.

Enos Poorbear, tribal chairman of the Oglala Sioux, spoke of his feelings on election day: "What made me feel the best was to see some of the people come into Wamblee, where I live, driving a team and wagon. And they brought their neighbors. They wanted to do this thing by themselves."

By four to one the state jurisdiction law was defeated—with

201,389 votes opposed and 58,289 in favor. The unexpected result of the victory was the defeat of State Senator James Ramey.

The war dance of triumph of the Oglala Sioux, on the Pine Ridge Reservation, was one of many. Lower Brûlé, Cheyenne River, Standing Rock, Sisseton, Yankton and Rosebud burst forth in their own celebrations. Young and old, illiterate and university educated, the Sioux danced as they always had when a battle had been fought and won. Everyone who had a feather stuck it in his hair. Headdresses were everywhere. The relics of the great victories of the past reappeared. Loudspeakers blared the traditional war dances from modulated tapes. The pots were set to boiling behind the tribal offices on the Rosebud Reservation. Huge vats of meat, steaming over five-foot logs, were tended by Mr. and Mrs. White Horse and a feast was had.

Old Tom Boneshirt led the dancing, as he always did. It was reported thus by the tribal newspaper:

Ancient to the modern age, and in accordance with the traditional beliefs of our forefathers, the Rosebud Sioux Tribal Council sponsored a Victory Dance.

The performances were authentic and apparently the ceremony was successful. At the Pow Wow there was plenty of meat and everybody was welcome to take part in the dancing. During the festivities, beaded relics were awarded to the uncommon individuals who rendered unselfish service to our cause.

We shall survive!

18

UNCLE TOMAHAWKS AND
HIDDEN COLONIALISTS

The green doors of the Episcopal church were shut. Not locked, nor barred; but shut tight.

Inside there was a meeting of the "Colonial Offce" of the United States Government. There was no sign on the church doors saying "No Indians Allowed." Yet all but a few Indians had been barred. So had the press. When the two hundred tribal leaders who had come from sixty-two tribes throughout the country had tried to walk into the meeting they were told it was "closed" to them. And the church doors were shut in their faces. The "Colonial Office" was planning "*the* most creative period in the history of the American Indian people"—but someone had forgotten to invite the natives.

The Indians stood on the steps of the church waiting in the cool sun of the spring in Santa Fe.

Some sighed in resignation; it was an old story to them to be treated like Indians. Some were furious at the insult. One of the younger men muttered to himself: "Let's break the doors open. Let's picket. Let's do something." Those near him, who had overheard, shook their heads in sympathy. "We won't go where we're not wanted," an elder tribal leader said. In dismay, he recalled that the government officials had refused even a delegation of the tribes inside the church. Not even a silent observer was permitted to enter.

"It was a missionary conference of the 1880's to convert the heathen," was the indignant comment of Vine Deloria, Jr. He had led the tribes of the National Congress of American Indians up to the shut doors. "They were afraid to let the heathen in," he said.

"Here we were, the leaders of 400,000 Indians. Here was the government holding the most important meeting on Indians in thirty years. And they wouldn't let us in. We thought we would be welcomed with opened arms. 'Let's sit down and plan together,' we thought they would say. It never dawned on us that they would close the doors.

"Imagine if the government held a conference on Negro affairs but closed the doors to the Negro leaders! You just don't do things like that in the United States these days"—he paused—"except to Indians."

Inside the church, the Secretary of the Interior, Stewart Udall, was asking the officials cloistered behind the green doors, "How do we build a bridge of getting the Indian people involved with mainstream America?" That was the problem they faced.

"We are at a crucial turning point in terms of Indian administration and Indian affairs," the Secretary said. The "reorganization at a top level" of the government, and "the winds of change," that he had spoken of before, the Secretary said, meant that there would be "new programs," "new laws," "new opportunity," "new focus," "new solutions," and "new blood."

"When one looks at Indian resources today, one asks himself the question 'What would IBM or AT&T, or Standard Oil of New Jersey do if they owned this particular piece of land and these resources?' . . . 'How do we get Walt Disney and Standard Oil interested in developing Indian reservations?' Can we do this?" There was "not a major corporation in this country that would not take [the] resources these Indians have and increase the value ten or twenty times in the next twenty years."

The Secretary said: "One way might be to let the tribes mortgage their reservations." But that too posed a problem. "You can't mortgage Indian land. Why shouldn't Indians mortgage their land?" Of course, "Maybe the Indian people and [their] lawyers are going to back away and say they don't want this." It was simply a suggestion.

In any event the Secretary said, ". . . the big thing is to get the Indians into the money markets of the country—to the banks—into the economic mainstream. . . . Forget the past. . . . Get a smile on your faces. . . ."

These were daring departures from the traditional idea of Indian lands held in sacred trust by the government. But they were to be incorporated in the original draft of the Indian Omnibus Bill drawn up by the Interior Department a few months later.

It was to give the Secretary the power to sanction the mortgaging of Indian land that the Omnibus Bill stated:

"For the purpose of securing loans guaranteed or pursuant of this act, Indian tribes are authorized, subject to the approval of the Secretary, to execute mortgages or deeds of trust land title to which is held by the United States . . . (Sec. 416)" and "Property mortgaged or hypothecated pursuant of this section shall be subject to foreclosure and sale in accordance with the laws of the State in which the land is located . . . without the approval of the Secretary . . . (Sec. 102)."

To the hushed and churched men of the "Colonial Office" these thoughts came, as one described it, "with a thud of silence that startled us. Like a revolver shot with a silencer." He might have been reminded, as perhaps he was, of the Allotment Act of 1887, which had less grandiosely aimed at giving each Indian family land and permitted them to sell it in order to teach them to adopt "the habits of civilized life." So successful had the act been that in the next forty-five years the Indians lost 90 million of their 140 million acres.

The House Committee on Indian Affairs, at that time, had overridden a minority report that pleaded: ". . . If this were done in the name of greed, it would be bad enough; but to do it in the name of humanity, and under the cloak of an ardent desire to promote the Indian's welfare by making him like ourselves, whether he will or not, is infinitely worse."

It might, in this historical light, have been wise to shut those green church doors. The tribes were already suspicious that there were new plans being drawn up to terminate their reservations.

On the steps in the street, the Indians had given up their vigil of silence. They walked away from the church, finally. They walked to the New Mexico State Land Office building and began an impromptu meeting of their own. And for two days the two meetings went on side by side. In one the men of the government discussed the affairs of the Indians, without the Indians. In the other the Indians discussed the affairs of the government, without the government. The Theatre of the Absurd had come at last to ancient Santa Fe. But the script was not by Beckett, but by the "Colonial Office."

The absurdity was total. For among the government officials, in the closed-door meeting, were several tribal leaders who also worked for the "Colonial Office." Not much was said in one meeting that was not soon known in the other.

Little by little the government officials unobtrusively came down the street to meet with the Indians. With proper protocol the first to come was the Commissioner of Indian Affairs, Robert Bennett. And the Indians, ever the hosts, though barred from his meeting gave him a banquet. He stayed to play a little jazz piano. He tried to explain the inhospitality of his colleagues: "We don't want to wash our dirty linen in public." Later he added that, after all, "The Bureau of Old Age and Survivors' Insurance has meetings where they don't invite all the old people."

And the Secretary of the Interior himself then came to the Indians' gathering to pay his respects, and to tell them of his mortgage plan. And this time the Pueblo Indians in the nearby Rio Grande Valley gave him a feast in friendship. Everything seemed peaceful as ever.

On the last day of the "Colonial Office" meeting, when the invited guest of the National Council of Churches, the Reverend Russell Carter, had refused to enter, when the Indians were barred and the newspapers had spread the story across the country, two tribal leaders were permitted to enter the church—if they "didn't say anything."

"It was old-fashioned paternalism," Deloria, Jr., said. "They told us we would be consulted later on the decisions that they had made for us."

So ended "The Battle of Santa Fe"—without a treaty of peace this time, for it was but one more skirmish in the unending political Indian Wars.

The history of the "Colonial Office" is unending. It is the oldest bureau in the government. Established in 1824, the Bureau of Indian Affairs of the Department of the Interior of the United States Government had been rechristened by the younger Indians in Santa Fe by the name it had avoided for a century and a half.

"Colonialism" is a dirty word in the lexicon of our democracy. It has always been so, as would be expected in a country that began as a former colony in revolution against colonialism. The Declaration of Independence is the classic document of a colonial people's desire for self-determination. Understandably the country has recoiled from the thought and the sight of colonies within its own borders. It may be this that has rendered the Indians invisible to the conscience of the country. The accusation of the new Indian leaders that the government had in fact subjected the American Indians to a policy of colonialism, and that it continued to do so, came as a shock without recognition.

The government had always denied the existence of native colonialism. So sensitive had it been to the mere hint that the Commissioner of Indian Affairs, Robert Bennett, was moved to indignantly deny the charge—which appeared in a letter from South Africa in the *New York Times*—that likened the government's treatment of the Indians to that country's apartheid discrimination against its native people.

Yet a tour of the Indian reservations and a study of the methods by which they have been governed, as the new Indians have been eager and angry to point out, reveals disturbing clues of a "hidden colonialism." "Hidden colonialism" was precisely the term used by the Cherokee anthropologist Robert Thomas in his "Colonialism: Classic and Internal" (*New University Thought*, Winter 1966–67) to describe the labyrinth of legality that concealed "this kind of colonialism," that has not been "obvious structurally to the observer." Thomas wrote: "You could see the British administrators in an African colony, or the agents of the Bureau of Indian Affairs on the Indian Reservation." The "hidden colonialism" was "less observable but has to a large degree had the same kind of effect." Classic colonialism was thereby "Americanized," Thomas wrote.

In seeking to show how this "hidden colonialism" works, Thomas spoke of a familiar reservation situation. He wrote:

I'll take an Indian reservation, partly because I am more familiar with them, and partly because it's the most complete colonial system in the world that I know about. One of the things you find on Indian reservations is exploitation of natural resources. (Now, I don't want to give the impression that the U.S. government goes out with big imperialistic designs on Indian reservations. Were it that simple, were there nice clean-cut villains, you could just shoot them or something. But it isn't that simple.)

Let's say the U.S. government is in charge of the resources on an Indian reservation and cuts the timber. You have a "tribal sawmill," which is tribal only in the sense that it is located on the reservation, but the people in the government bureaucracy actually run it. They are legally told to do that and they have no choice. They aren't being 'mean' to the Indians, they're just supposed to run the sawmill. . . .

So the people who tend to get the jobs in the sawmill are the "responsible" Indians. Now you can imagine who the responsible Indians are. They are the people who are most like whites in many ways, and hence, most "cooperative," that is, they keep their mouths shut and their noses clean. This makes for bitter factionalism on many reservations and is another outcome of this classic colonial structure. . . .

When the resources are sold and the returns go into the tribal treasury, the people who have control of it—insofar as anybody on the Indian reservation has control of anything—are these marginal people. . . . The raw materials from this reservation are, of course, sold outside the reservation area. The U.S. Government deducts from the sales of these resources the costs of providing social services to the reservation. . . .

Like Gaul of Roman times the world of the reservation has been divided into three worlds by this hidden colonialism. In a "Memoranum" to the Bureau of Indian Affairs area director, marked "Confidential," the acting superintendent of the Fort Peck Agency in Montana, Harvey W. Starling, in 1964 offered a graphic description of these "three worlds":

The three worlds of the reservation—the BIA, the Indian, and the local non-Indian exist side by side, but rarely overlap. Politically, the non-Indian and Indian find it advantageous at times to form alliances with each other. Such alliances, however, do not open the door to real social intercourse, and the invisible barrier between Indian and White remains intact.

In its description of a Bureau, or "Agency Town," the National Indian Youth Council offered a similar portrait of "three separate communities in one . . . living side by side, with no intercommunication."

Elaborating on the effects of these "three worlds" upon the employees of the Bureau, the "Memorandum" said:

"Many of the non-Indian employees lack the capacity or desire to understand why the Indians' behavior and points of view differ from their own. They do not wish to communicate with Indians on a social plane. They work with Indians during the day, but on their own time they associate with the BIA fraternity, or, to a far lesser degree, with members af the local white community."

The employees of the Bureau, too often, have "no real interest in the Indian people and no new insight into the problems at hand," the Fort Peck "Memorandum" continued.

How widespread this attitude has been was evidenced in Oklahoma, where a Bureau superintendent was quoted by the Comanche teacher Roxie Plumlee as having told her: "We are just a bunch of bureaucrats sitting here passing time. Therefore we can't be of any help to you."

"Here's the tragic thing," said Deloria, Jr. "There are good men in the Bureau who want to do good. Who want to do the right thing. But the right thing for many people who want to do good is always in terms of their own value system. God help us from those who want to help us!"

Fort Peck's forthright "Memorandum" spoke of the Bureau employees who "know that their stay will be of few years' duration" and who look upon this "as a period of servitude." The local inhabitants, "who have seen government workers come and go and know that 'nothing is ever accomplished' " reinforce the feeling of "The employee himself [who] considers the situation to be futile and does not believe he can make any lasting improvements." So that "These employees never really confront the problems that surround them. . . ." The portrait of a colonial administration could not have been more succinctly sketched. Of course the word "colonialism" itself was not mentioned in the Fort Peck "Memorandum."

The "invisible barrier" has been quite visible in the physical appearance of most reservations. Like forts in hostile territory the homes and buildings of the Bureau employees have been clustered together, isolated from the Indian villages. Nowadays these government outposts look like oases of suburbia in the midst of squalor.

Lame Deer, Montana, on the Northern Cheyenne Reservation is typical. On one side of the highway, set apart, are the buildings of the Bureau town, while the Indians live on the far side. The picture is a replica of the Chippewa Reservation in Turtle Mountain, North Dakota, where the two towns are neatly dissected by the highway—with the Bureau's suburbia on one side, and the shacks of the Indians on the other.

To bridge "the invisible barrier" that divides these reservations into separate worlds—economically, politically, socially, and even physically—the Bureau has had to rely increasingly upon Indian personnel. In direct proportion to the growing influence of the tribal movements for self-determination the hiring of Indians to staff the apparatus of government has increased. And this too is reminiscent of the experience of declining colonial governments.

Robert Thomas said of these Indian government employees: "Their job is to mediate between the Indian Bureau and the Indians. They have very little power beyond that which the Bureau will give them."

"Uncle Tomahawks" has been the name given these Indians by the new Indians. It is the Indian version of the derisive "Uncle Tom." The Youth Council has broadly defined these "Uncle Tomahawks" as "Indian leaders satisfied with the status quo." But, in more explicit terms, Clyde Warrior, the president of the Youth Council, charged: "Uncle Tomahawks are those Indian leaders who are allied with the Bureau of Indian Affairs and who say what the government wants them to say."

"Many reservations are run by Indian puppets of the government," said Robert Burnette, head man of the American Indian Civil Rights Council. "They are traitors to their people. By using these puppets the government plays a game of divide and conquer."

The weary, overworked tribal officials who are castigated as "Uncle Tomahawks" by the new Indians protest, not their innocence, but their usefulness. In the dealings with the United States Government these tribal leaders act as liaison men between separated nations. As they see it, their job is "to get as much for my people as I can," as one said. He reasoned: "The difference between the younger men and the older leaders is that they are free to criticize, but we have to keep our tribes alive. We have to work with the white man."

"I will always compromise my feelings to get something for my people," said another tribal leader. "The white man doesn't know and doesn't care what I feel. He sees me smile and he thinks I agree with him. Let him think what he likes, so long as I get what my tribe needs."

The colonialism of the reservation system has reduced these tribal leaders to the role of "supplicants." It is much as Commissioner Francis Walker forecast one hundred years ago, when in establishing the Western reservations he urged the tribesmen be made "supplicants for charity." Because the tribal lands and funds are held "in trust" by the government these tribal leaders in effect work for the government.

Leaders of the tribes, faced by the forked tongues of disguised colonialism, replied with a two-faced "Uncle Tomahawkism." The result has been divisive both socially and within themselves.

Some of these ex-officio government employees nonetheless have become Red Muslims. In fact, many of the new Indians have worked for the Bureau at one time or another, and many continue to do so while agitating for self-determination of the tribes. The Bureau jobs are the most easily accessible to Indians. And as the new Indian movements developed the government hired more and more Indians to counterbalance them.

The apparatus of colonialism has been growing enormously like a political amoeba. It has grown in contradiction to its decreasing function at a time when much of the work of the Bureau is being taken over by the tribes.

One reason for the paradox may be that the Indians have little or no elective control over the governmental apparatus. Therefore its size is not weighed by their needs, or their democratic voice. But a more compelling reason is a peculiarity common to most colonial systems. The monies that are fed by the government into its bureaucracy emerge from it in proportionately diminishing returns. So much so that the colonial system has tended to become increasingly administrative and self-perpetuating. There are more and more offices that do nothing but service other offices. It has been estimated that the Bureau has one employee for every twenty Indians. Less amiable critics say that there is one employee for every sixteen Indians.

Mel Thom, in his testimony before the Senate hearings on urban poverty, offered some statistics on the discrepancy between monies spent and services supplied. Thom told the Senators: "In recent years the expenditure of the federal government for each Indian has ranged from an average of $650 to $900 per capita annually. Looked at another way, this would amount to an annual income of $4,685 for a family of five people if paid directly to the Indians. The average Indian family income, in fact, is less than $1,600."

The portrait of "hidden colonialism" was complete. Where did the monies go? It hardly mattered.

If the philosophy underlying the governing of the Indians is colonialism, whether hidden or open, then paternalism is the method by which it is enforced. Paternalism is not, as has often been said, a more democratic and charitable form of the older European colonialism, bereft of the onus and history with which classic colonialism has been afflicted. It is not of benevolent design. It is simply a tool that is peculiar to our country for historical and geographical reasons. That is, it works better. Paternalism is inherent in the nature of the relationship of the tribes with the government. With a candor that was marked, the Commissioner of Indian Affairs Robert Bennett pointed to this: "Under the circumstances, and by the relationship that exists between the federal government and the Indian people, it is very difficult to get away from complete paternalism. This is a relationship based upon a trustee and a ward. So you get into this kind of situation, and it is very easy for the paternalistic attitude to develop."

In the *Harvard Law Review* ten years before Ralph Nader had less formally observed just how complete this "complete paternalism" tended to become: "Telling the Indians when to go to bed and when to get up is not just a whimsical bit of paternalism. It has deep roots in a long tradition of Indian-Bureau policy."

Paternalism toward the Indians is indeed an old tradition. It predated the idea of the welfare state. It predated the George Orwellian nightmare vision of the Big Brother. The Bureau of Indian Affairs is, after all, the oldest, most deeply entrenched, continuous system of bureaucracy in the federal government—established in 1824. In a historical sense the paternalism toward the Indians was the political laboratory for the philosophy and methods of governmental largess that were to typify the big brother concept of the twentieth century. The Indians had been guinea pigs for methods of governing to be widely applied—albeit more subtly.

And because of its long and tenacious hold on a bureaucratic apparatus the Bureau has more government employees serving fewer citizens, proportionately, than any other.

"Like walking through molasses," was how Mary Lou Payne spoke of dealing with the Bureau. But the forms of its paternalism are not a single mass. Rather they form an intricate web, are multicolored and ingeniously changing, "with the changing times," as Commissioner Bennett said.

As there are different kinds of parents, so there have been varied kinds of paternalism. One was based on the egocentric belief of the white invaders of Indian territory that the original inhabitants were "wild beasts" who—if not wholly inhuman—were surely less than human. Paternalism based on the "wild beasts" theory of Commissioner Francis Walker (in 1872) not only made decisions for the Indians, but did so without any need for the pretense of consulting them.

It was blatant, crude, and confidently racist. Of course, it is no longer prevalent in the "Colonial Office"; and it was never overt. It does, however, continue to have a loyal if small following.

"Unspoken" was the belief of "many BIA employees," said the "Memorandum" of the acting superintendent of the Fort Peck Agency, Harvey Starling, "that the Indian is generally, and by nature, lazy, dirty, unreliable and immoral."

In Oklahoma, the Comanche tribal councilwoman Mrs. Bonnie Turner reported a principal of the Fort Sill Indian School who "referred to Indian minds as being 'fuzzy' and that all Indians have a 'smell.' "

His attitude was not untypical, Mrs. Turner said, for many of the officials of the Bureau in that part of Oklahoma expressed much stronger views.

Then there is the paternalism of benevolence. It is kindly and more fatherly. In the past century it was beautifully voiced by the benevolent view of General S. C. Armstrong, who was principal of the Hampton Institute for Indians in the 1880's. The general wrote: "The Indian cannot govern himself. He is a child and needs a father. . . ." And these views too—of the paternalism of benevolence —have been politely, if not so subtly, modified by the necessities of "modern" fatherhood. The young Indians have dubbed the latter-day guises of the paternalism of benevolence "the do-gooders" or "the friends of the Indian approach."

The *Report of the Commission on the Rights, Liberties, and Responsibilities of the American Indian* of The Fund for the Republic —known more mercifully as *The Indian: American's Unfinished Business* (University of Oklahoma Press, 1966)—compiled by two distinguished savants and friends of the Indians, William A. Brophy and Sophie D. Aberle, reflects what the new Indians call "the do-gooder" kind of paternalism. "It is not easy for the Indians to conduct their own regimes, but the very difficulty makes it worthwhile for them to try."

"The Great White Ultimate Trustee—myself," as the Secretary of the Interior, Stewart Udall, jokingly referred to his position, uses another variation of the modern father approach. In his speech at Santa Fe the Secretary said: "Let's give new leadership *to* the Indian people" and "do what is right *for* the Indian people." He added that the Commissioner had told him "that if a superintendent, or area director, did his job right, he probably would not be particularly popular *with* the Indian people. The Spirit of Santa Fe was the spirit of *asking ourselves* what *our* Indian peoples want," the Secretary said (emphasis added).

The kindly words infuriated the young Indians. In the era when tribal leaders are seeking self-determination they have no patience with fatherly benevolence, however well-intentioned. The thought that the Bureau was once more asking "ourselves" what "our" Indians wanted was met with a howl of derision and anguish.

The annoyance of the elder Indians was evident in the words of Anne Wauneka: "Whoever is the head of this particular government, they never ask the Indian people what they think. They always say, this is the best *for you*. We are going to do this *for you*. Everything is *for you*. I think the Indians are getting tired of this."

But the youth were even angrier. "Our Big Brother, our protector, the Bureau of Indian Affairs, says it is the 'helper' of the Indians. But its actual mission has been to take away [the voice] of the Indians, to control the Indians, and to keep the Indians out of the white man's hair," the Yurok Indian leader of California, Alyce Williams, said.

The fatherly tone of big brotherism was a mask for the "cultural genocide condoned by the Department of the Interior," said Bruce Wilkie, the Fish-In leader of the Makah Tribe.

Said Clyde Warrior, "The natives were always restless and so the Bureau and its Uncle Tomahawks were always trying to calm the natives down. It has been their job throughout history."

"We've been victims of a paternalistic, colonial system in which we've always had plenty of advisors to tell us what to do," Mel Thom said. "And 'If you don't do it you're an incompetent Indian.' We've gone this route. The people who are our bosses tell us what we want. And that's what we end up with. I've yet to see Indians getting in on top policymaking. That's not done. And there's not much indication it ever will be done—voluntarily."

"Our colonial bosses [in the Bureau] aren't interested in having a bunch of Indians on their necks," Thom said.

"His master and his whipping boy," the Bureau had long been in double jeopardy on the reservations, said the Fort Peck "Memorandum." The Secretary of Interior, Stewart Udall, likened it to a "scapegoat" that was "kicked around," by the critics of Indian policy. "You are damned if you do, and damned if you don't, and so why stick your neck out?" the Secretary said had become the motto of the Bureau. No matter what it did, the Indians would attack it.

In the early days when the Indians first went on the reservations the Bureau was the only white world they knew. To them it represented not only the government, but the whole of the world outside. So the Bureau had been the obvious and easy target for the vengeance and grievances of Indians. Yet the Bureau was also the buffer against the world it represented. The cumbersome bureaucracy that so inhibited, socially crippled, and demoralized the tribes was a stultifying form of protection. It was almost as impenetrable from outside the reservations as from inside. And it grew denser as the Bureau grew. It was odd, but as the power of the Bureau decreased with the rebuilding of tribal strength and with the government's dissipation of some of its functions to other agencies its stolid nature had become more and more solidified.

"If ever there was a giant earthquake in the country," Deloria, Jr., said, "I would run for the Bureau. Nothing will shake that."

Long ago the tribal leaders learned to wend their way through the labyrinth of red tape and to laugh at the tangled paradoxes. The labyrinth had a homey touch. It had grown familiar and known. It threatened them with few surprises. And whatever the frustrations of dealing with a colonial apparatus they were at least predictable frustrations.

In many of the tribes the recommendations of a Presidential Advisory Committee to reorganize the Bureau were met with unease. The transferring of some of its functions in the field of education to the Department of Health, Education, and Welfare brought mixed feelings. On the reservations the opinions were divided. Not that the tribal leaders opposed modernizing the bureaucracy. It was the bureaucracy itself, not its modernization, that they opposed.

An older tribal leader in New Mexico, himself a prominent educator, made the significant comment: "It's good to know your enemy. We know the Bureau. Anyway, it is weak now. On its last legs. If the tribes keep up the pressure to run things themselves, soon we would be able to take over the Bureau's services. But if they give it over to one of those aggressive agencies we'll never be able to win self-determination from them. We will have to begin again. At the beginning. To try to convince a whole new carload of bureaucrats that what we want is to do these things ourselves."

The Red Muslims and younger tribal leaders think the system of colonialism is more complex than any single agency, or any group of officials. Having studied its legal history they know that if the relationship of the United States Government to the Indians has been one of colonialism it has been legislatively and legally the most elaborate system of colonialism in world history.

In the very first Congress, of 1778, one of the very first pieces of legislation concerned the Indians. Ever since that time the rulings have been piling high until there are now more than five thousand federal statutes and two thousand federal court decisions relating to the status, control, and welfare of the Indians. Nowhere in history has the "complex and unique legal character" (U.S. Commission on Civil Rights) of a colonial people, living within the country of the colonialists, been so meticulously and self-consciously defined. And redefined. And redefined.

The hold of colonialism—and its godchild, paternalism—upon the Indians would not be loosened by having a more effective agency do the work of the Bureau. "Though, I think, most of the young people would like to see education removed from the Bureau," Deloria, Jr., said, "and so would I. It's not the whole solution. Sure, we need enlightened, modern administration. Especially in education. The mood is one of doubt, however. Many of the tribal leaders say it was just passing the buck to avoid our demand for self-determination."

Colonialism is too ingrained in the minds and methods of those who govern the tribes to be changed by an administrative reshuffling. It is not a matter of men, but of laws. The legislation governing Indians has always been tied in one way or another to the phrase "the Secretary of Interior may authorize, in his discretion." The Indian Reorganization Act of 1934, generally thought of as the epitome of liberalizing law toward the tribes, was replete with "the Secretary of Interior may authorize . . ." "the Secretary of Interior is hereby authorized to proclaim . . ." "the Secretary of Interior is directed to make rules and regulations." Even the tribal elections have had to be governed by "the Secretary of Interior under such rules and regulations as he may prescribe. . . ."

So it has gone, unto this day.

The original draft of the Indian Omnibus Bill—known as the Indian Resources Development Act of 1967—that was born in the minds of those at the church in Santa Fe—was monotonous with the repetitious phrase: "The Secretary is hereby authorized in his discretion . . ." "the Secretary may impose such conditions and limitations as he deems appropriate and he may revoke a certificate at any time . . ." "under agreement approved by the Secretary . . ."

John Belindo, the Kiowa-Navajo youth who was the Washington representative of the National Congress of American Indians,* thought

* As this book goes to press, fall, 1967, Belindo was made executive director of the NCAI.

the phraseology ". . . the Secretary is hereby authorized . . ." told the whole story of paternalism. "The Indian can easily see who is boss. Everything he does must first have the approval of the Secretary of the Interior, or someone under him. Granting of citizenship did not give the Indian the right of self-determination. As a matter of practice, the Indian has been, and is, almost wholly governed by directives issued by the Secretary of the Interior under the broad discretionary powers granted him by Congress."

"To the Indian the Indian Bureau is absolute dictator of Indian affairs," Belindo said. It was farcical to say, as the "Statement of Purpose" of the Omnibus Bill had, "It is the purpose of this Act . . . to permit [the Indians] to exercise greater initiative and self-determination."

There is but one thing the Indian can do without anyone's permission. He can leave his reservation. Going to the city to be integrated or assimilated requires no governmental approval. If he forgets his tribal way of life, his religion, his Indianness, there is no law that stands in his way. He may dance, if he wishes, on Sundays, in feathered headdress, at the YMCA. He may join protest marches of urban Indians nostalgic for their lost heritage. He may even sell, or mortgage, or foreclose his trust lands without the permission of "the Secretary at his discretion," according to the Omnibus Bill.

But, if he wishes to be a tribal Indian, he has to have permission. Paternalism governs only those things the Indian does as an Indian. On his reservation. In the tribal way. He is politically a child as long as he believes in tribalism—in the legal eyes of paternalism.

Where did the nursery theory of politics come from? It is as American as oratory on the Fourth of July, the Congressional elections, kindness, charity, and the "Death Song" of the Sioux. In truth, paternalism is democratically legislated colonialism. And it is uniquely American.

The legislation of paternalism has been aimed at the integration of the Indian into the melting pot so that he would be acculturated into the American way of non-Indian life. For the anomaly of the tribal communities—"this little island of culture" (Senate Judiciary Committee), "this alien culture" (U.S. Commission on Civil Rights) —has been a living reminder of the theft of a continent.

Paternalism was devised not so much as a disguise for colonialism or even as a pleasant synonym. Its purpose was to eliminate colonialism by eliminating the colonials—by legal persuasions and by democratic integration.

The Indians are no longer quiescent. In the tribes there is a growing mood of self-assertion that rejects the temptations of integration. Instead there is a restive urging for self-determination.

"It is about time these people start to think twice," said Anne Wauneka, "because they are dealing with human beings. The President of the United States is not any different from anybody. He is also a human being, built the same way any other human being is built. Maybe the peace of mind is stronger than any other. Maybe they are wiser than any other. But that does not mean they overlook the people they represent.

"Now no one can any longer control the thinking of the Indians, saying, I am your trustee, I am doing your thinking, I am educating you. Now it is too late. Let the Indians be heard. Let their voices be heard," the Navajo woman said.

The Sioux leader Cato Valandra typifies this mood. He is a man of few words—so few he rarely speaks. And no more than necessary. One of those chain smokers who hardly puffs, he holds his cigarette in tight lips. Listening to himself, before he speaks, he has an immutable quiet in his eyes that stills a word in passage. "He can witch the back off a Raleigh pack at twenty paces, with those eyes," a friend said of him. It may have come from looking out at the world through eyes that beheld his positions as tribal chairman of the Rosebud Sioux, and president of the United Sioux, and treasurer of the National Congress of American Indians. He has the demeanor of power tightly held.

Valandra hardly is the stereotype of the volatile Sioux. Whatever his humors were, they barely touched his lips. He reflects that quiet, determined, confident, unspoken mood of defiance of the tribal leader who has had enough of paternalism.

He was reminded of a story, he said, that expressed what he thought. Once there was an old Indian who went on a delegation to Washington to see his Congressman. The old Indian told his Congressman he had a bill to propose that would solve "the Indian problem."

"What's that?" the Congressman asked.

"It's called," the old Indian said, "the 'Leave Us Alone Bill.'"

Men grow in knowledge of their inner strengths slowly, or in bursts of energy that take them by surprise, the two forming a rhythmic counterpoint, back and forth, testing the process of their growth in the world against which they have pitted themselves. Thus it has been for the Indians—except that for the Indians the tests have seemed endless. For not only has the white world sought to remake them in its own image—and, failing that, imposed a false-feathered image upon them—but the Indians have rejected and withdrawn from the world of whiteness. The Fort Peck "Memorandum" of the Bureau had said: "The Indians have insulated themselves from the pain of being rejected by the white man and they have in turn rejected him, whom they despise and envy. . . . The white man has rejected the Indian as an inferior, and the Indian has rejected the white man out of hatred for this one-sided and high-handed judgment of himself."

In this Mexican standoff the process of testing was something like effecting a wedding between two moving targets. Not merely were they moving, but they were taking potshots at each other. The strongest bond between them has been their mutual distrust.

Existence of a tribal society is tenuous within the borders of a country that is the largest exporter of technological achievements. It is not that tribal society threatens the existence of the technological way of life. Its threat is moral. Like the early Christian within ancient Rome, the Indians have to be converted or devoured—but legally.

The comparisons were drawn by the new Indians. Mel Thom said of the historical parallels: "The forced assimilation and cultural genocide to which the Indian people have been subjected is a deprivation of human rights without parallel in the free world."

Legislators were appalled. The paternal concern and fatherly trusteeship of the government had only sought to offer the Indians "their rights as full American citizens." What did their new Indians want?

What they wanted was what the new Indians called Red Power. And what the tribal elders called self-determination. And they were ready to make their demands known to the country.

19

RED POWER

"Hail to the Chief" sounded on the loudspeakers. The dignified delegates of the tribes, one hundred strong, marched into the convention hall, banners aloft on tall sticks, a bit self-consciously—Fort Berthold, White Mountain Apache, Cherokee. The procession was a ritual of political conventions. And the tribal delegates at the 23rd annual convention of the National Congress of American Indians indulged in this ceremonial of sanctified hoopla with as much conviction as did anyone else. Except for the old man.

The old man marched at the end of the processional, proudly holding high his stick on which there was no banner. Just a stick.

Was he the clown dancer of the political ritual? He may have been, though his stolid face was solemn and unsmiling. The Indians in the ballroom of the Sheraton Oklahoma, in Oklahoma city, seemed to think so; for they roared with approving laughter, and applauded this mockery of the rites of the whites.

It was from a "Patriotic Dinner" held by the tribes to honor an imposing dais of young war veterans and retired generals that the processional had marched. Eskimo leader Miles Brandon had sung "The Ballad of the Green Berets" in deep-voice reverence. He had been interrupted by the war whoop of "Dode" McIntosh, the principal chief of the Oklahoma Creeks—an eerie cry of a wrathful wild turkey. There had been the usual Fourth of July oratory, and the tribal delegates were restive.

One of the war heroes who had been honored, Clarence Tallbull, of the Cheyenne-Arapaho, led the marchers. He mounted the podium, strode to the microphone, a huge young man with the build of a Marine Corps sergeant.

Tallbull boomed, "We thank you all for being sports. That's what conventions are for." He said, almost as an aside, "Let's stick together like this, and show Oklahoma that we have Red Power. Red Power!" The young war hero repeated the words as though they had taken him by surprise. He had to savor what he had said, and what it meant.

"Red Power means we want power over our own lives," said Vine Deloria, Jr., the organizer of the convention and director of the Congress. "We do not wish to threaten anyone. We do not wish power over anyone. We are only half a million Indians. We simply want the power, the political and economic power, to run our own lives in our own way.

"It frightens people, I know," Deloria, Jr., said, "to talk of Red Power, but we don't want to frighten them. We want to shock them into realizing how powerless the Indians have been. We feel that if we don't get Red Power—now—we may not be around much longer.

"Of course," he said, grinning, "if our way of life turns out to be better, more human, than yours, that would be your problem. Not ours. We would never force anyone to live as we do. We never have."

The "summit meeting of the Indian people" had begun. In the convention call to "All Chiefs, Chairmen, Governors, Presidents, Spokesmen and Headmen of the American Indian Tribes of North America," the stolid, redoubtable leader of the Mescalero Apaches, Wendell Chino, who was chairman of the Congress, had sounded an alarm: "Never have the times been so perilous. We find ourselves again threatened by unilateral action on the part of [the United States] Congress to curtail progressive programs in favor of a cessation of federal responsibilities to the Indian people. The current situation clearly calls for a unity seldom achieved in the past. . . ."

Unity and power—these were the themes. In the history of the tribal Indians neither had ever been more than the chimera of visionaries.

And so they had come, the chiefs and headmen, the university graduates and old religious men, from northmost Alaska to the Everglades of Florida, gathered at the "summit" in the ballroom of the Sheraton Hotel. Four hundred tribesmen of one hundred tribes.

"You won't find any feathers here," said the Reverend James L. Partridge of the tribal council of the Creeks, meticulous in a business suit and silk tie. He had no sooner spoken when two Indians walked by: one an old man, his long braids tucked onto *his* business suit, and the other—younger—with his gorgeous beaded tie hidden by *his* business suit, and a huge, foot-long feather stuck in his tan Stetson.

"Okay, put on your feathers and collect your per diem," intoned Vine Deloria, Jr., opening the convention.

"We don't decide things in conventions. We don't decide things in smoke-filled committee rooms," said Shirley Witt. "It's just a place to get together. To get the feel of everyone's thought. That's the Indian way of consensus. Like in the old councils. It's a silent process," she said. "It takes time."

On the ballroom floor of the Sheraton under the not-quite-crystal chandeliers began what Deloria, Jr., called "the first skirmish of the last battle. If we lose this one, there won't be another."

"You people are on the precipice of power," Commissioner Bennett told the delegates. But it was power that could "lead to destruction" if the tribes "fall into the pattern of racial agitation." There would be a "new role for tribal governments" and a "larger role" for the Indians' Congress, the Commissioner said, but tribalism would have to be homogenized and modernized. The tribes had to accept "goals of economic and social compatibility with the other peoples of the country."

Later, in an interview in the Farmington *Times* of oil town Farmington, New Mexico, the Commissioner said that the government ought to legislate the end of tribalism. "Bennett strongly believes that the profit motive must be introduced on Indian reservations, if Indian capital enterprises are to be properly managed under Indian ownership and/or actual management," the Farmington *Times* wrote. Since half of the Indians are "in a transitional stage of breaking away from their reservations, they would be encouraged to do so. They would be permitted to sell their interests in Indian lands," the Commissioner was quoted as saying. He believed all these goals would be furthered by the Omnibus Bill.

At the convention the tribal leaders ridiculed this Omnibus Bill as the "Ominous Bill," the "Anonymous Bill," and the "Ambush Bill." "We have called it everything," one tribal leader said, "but the Magnanimous Bill."

"Signs of trouble!" was the rejoinder of former Commissioner Philleo Nash, the Kennedy appointee, who had "resigned" to make way for the new policy. Now that he was no longer with the Interior Department he would speak freely, Nash said: "If there is going to be trouble I want to be with you. Not with anyone else." The Indians promptly made him an honorary member.

Wendell Chino, president of the Congress, set the battle lines. Once again the enemies of the tribes were gathering, he said, "the politicians, the bankers, and all the other parasitical forces [who] would as soon see the Indian disappear—either by acculturation or termination.

"Let us not linger in the dark halls or be satisfied in engaging in idle talk," Chino said. "We agree with Commissioner Bennett that the time of decision has arrived. The day of the march and the day of action has arrived,"

The Apache leader, slow to anger, grew angry. He spoke of the charge of "racial agitation": "The Indian human being wished to solve his own problems in his own way, without paternalistic supervision or threats." His resonant voice, deep as the murmur of a puma, rumbled out over the loudspeakers: "If we are given the opportunity to exercise self-determination we shall succeed. We say to the Congress of the United States and to the Secretary of the Interior that the puny participation extended to us is becoming unbearable. We want and desire greater participation in the formation of legislation and policies affecting our people."

"Self-determination by the Indian people in their quest for social and economic equality"—these were the first words of the first article of the first resolution passed by the convention. In the genesis of nationalism the words "self-determination" were akin to "Life, Liberty and the Pursuit of Happiness." "Self-determination? That's 'Red Power' spelled backwards," said Deloria, Jr.

"Up in Alaska we don't call it that," William Hensley, who had been elected a vice president of the Indian Congress, said. "We call it Native Power. In my legislative district in Alaska, ninety percent of the people are native people. What else is political power there but Native Power?

"And on an Indian reservation where everyone is an Indian, what else would political power mean but Red Power?" said Hensley. "If you have self-determination, and everyone, or almost everyone, belongs to one national group, then I guess you have a kind of nationalism. That's not something that somebody on the outside thought up. That's not an intellectual theory. That's the fact of practical political life among the Eskimo and Indian people," Hensley said. "So it doesn't matter what you call it. It exists."

Nationalism was nothing new to the Indians. The tribes had begun to call themselves nations as soon as they knew the English meaning of the words. The Iroquois Nation, the Cherokee Nation, the Sioux Nation, the Hopi Nation—so it had been written in the treaties and histories from the beginning. It was with "sovereign nations" that the Government of the United States had entered into these treaties with the tribes. Congress in halting any further signing of treaties in 1871 had reaffirmed that political definition: ". . . no obligation of any treaty lawfully made and ratified with any Indian nation or tribe prior to March 3, 1871, shall hereby be invalidated or impaired." That is, the tribes that had been recognized as nations before the cutoff date were still to be so recognized.

Legality of the nationhood of the Indians was equally recognized, in one degree or another, by court after court. The United States Court of Appeals of the Tenth Circuit, in 1959, had held that the tribes were, in effect, sovereign nations within the nation. Declared the court: "Indian tribes are not States. They have a higher status than that of States. They are subordinate and dependent *nations* possessed of all the powers as such only to the extent that they have been expressly required to surrender them to the superior sovereign, the United States."

Three years later, in 1962, that same United States Court of Appeals of the Tenth Circuit decided that this national sovereignty of the tribes was an "ever-changing concept of an artificial entity."

Were they or were they not, then, nations? The roaming tribes and nomadic bands, the ancient pueblos and villages on the rivers, of the past, had no word in their languages for the idea of nationhood. They spoke of themselves mostly as "The People," or "The People who did this or that."

The curious thing was that it was the Government of the United States which had first called them nations; which had so treated them, as defeated and "dependent" nations with semicolonial status; which had, by attempting to destroy the old tribalism, sufficiently weakened its rigid and narrow boundaries to help create the basis for the new tribalism—the Red Nationalism.

In fact, the "young educated Indians" who founded the National Congress of American Indians were mostly employees of the Bureau of Indian Affairs. The government in the traditional practice of colonial administration had sent them from post to post, from tribe to tribe. By this divide-and-conquer technique it had built the extra-tribal bonds that led to the new form of Indianness.

The country had recognized the Indians as nations when they hardly knew the meaning of the word. Now that they were recognizing themselves as national entities, the country denied what it had created.

"Whatever the meaning of 'nation' or 'sovereignty' may be, Indian tribes and nations 'are in no sense sovereign States,' " wrote William A. Brophy and Sophie D. Aberle, citing the court's decision in *Stephens* vs. *Cherokee Nation* (1899) in their authoritative *The Indian*.

It was the old conflict. The words were different, the weapons were words, but the battle was still whether the Indian would be permitted to remain an Indian. In his testimony at the hearing on the Constitutional Rights of the American Indians, before the Senate Judiciary Committee, Vine Deloria, Jr., had fought the battle with John L. Baker, the minority counsel:

DELORIA, JR.: "It was always assumed that if you had the best social, economic, political knowledge, and applied this to the Indian, he would assimilate. . . . Now in the 1887 Allotment Act you have the idea that if you give each Indian 160 acres, that he is going to be a farmer and pretty soon you will have no Indian problem. . . . Again in the 1950's, with the idea of termination, you have the idea if you make the American Indian a businessman that pretty soon he will assimilate, and there will be no Indian problem."

BAKER: "I would assume that the thrust of that would be the maintenance of a perpetual separateness. In other words, the integrity of the tribes would be maintained and there would be a parallel system adopting the best of our system and maintaining the best of the existing system. Is that an accurate paraphrase?"

DELORIA, JR.: "I do not think it is an either/or proposition."

BAKER: "There have to be profound philosophical problems involved there, since each one of us in this room has come from a somewhat diverse background, and the common good has dictated that we, rather than remain separate, have worked to minimize our differences to provide the best for the greatest number. . . ."

DELORIA, JR.: "That is true, but I do not see any reason for assuming the disappearance of Indian tribes according to some type of sociological doctrine."

BAKER: "You think the maintaining of this little island of culture . . . will have a better effect both for the Indian and the surrounding culture than a gradual assimilation into one melting pot society."

DELORIA, JR.: "Right . . . The thing that the Indian has always feared is that an economic and political system that he does not understand would be thrust upon him."

BAKER: "I would assume that each immigrant who came to this country had the same fears. He is coming from one culture into a completely foreign culture by and large, unless he was Anglo-Saxon."

DELORIA, JR.: "That is right, sir, but they came over as individuals. *And we were here as independent nations. . . .*

"In fact, there is a great deal of talk about Indian unity, but the tribes have independent relations with each other. The National Congress of American Indians I run is a kind of miniature United Nations, with everybody taking off his shoe and hammering on the desk. *The migrations from Europe came individually, fleeing some things and seeking opportunities in others. While the tribes for the most part are, or have been, independent nations, owning their own land, having their own traditions and religions.* [Emphasis added.]

"So you cannot really compare the two. You cannot take the Indian out of his tribal tradition and compare him to an individual immigrant coming over."

BAKER: ". . . all you are doing is perpetuating this system by maintaining a complete separateness rather than a gradual assimilation of differences."

DELORIA, JR.: "There is a gradual dissolution of the differences. . . . There can be adaptations all the way along.

"What I would like to refer to in terms of assimilation is what we find in the Old Testament. The Hebrews were down in Egypt for 400 years. I am sure there was continual pressure on these people to assimilate. But the fact that they held their culture, they continued their religion, they continued to be one people, is the reason we have the great religions stemming out of these people.

"Now I would draw this analogy to the American Indian tribes. We can contribute in a great many ways, provided we are allowed to remain Indians. . . . Much has been made of the contribution of the Iroquois League to the political understanding of the Founding Fathers of this country. We suggest that at nearly every point— social, economic, political and patriotic—American Indians can contribute their knowledge of cultural interaction and social concern that is needed today in this country. . . .

"You cannot get this contribution to this society from Indians if you try to turn the Indian into a white man."

The Hebrews "way down in Egypt Land"; the Vietnamese, who long before their present travail were conquered and ruled by the Chinese for 1,182 years; the descendants of the Incas of Peru; the obstinate Basques of Spain; the resurgent French-Canadians of Quebec; the tribes throughout Africa; the Icelanders, ruled by the Danes for 638 years; the Irish, ruled by the British Empire for 740 years; the Slovaks, who were assimilated by Hungary for 1,010 years; the Iranians, who were conquered by the Arab and Ottoman empires for 1,138 years; the Uzbeks and Yakuts and Kazakhs and Tadzhiks of the Soviet Union, who survived centuries of "Russifications" . . .

And yet one need not travel to the far corners of the world to witness the power of a culture brutally suppressed and suffering cultural amnesia to survive.

When the enslaved Pueblo Indians revolted and overthrew their Spanish conquerors in 1680, the conquistadores retreated to the south. Unable to haul their heavy equipment and armor the fleeing Spaniards impressed some thirty young men of the Pueblo of Isleta as bearers and forced them to cross the desert of White Sands.

These men of Isleta were abandoned. In the dirty border town that has become the city of El Paso the refugees settled three hundred years ago—lost, unknown, and forgotten. The city grew into a metropolis of 300,000. It ought to have swallowed the band of thirty. Yet in the urban center of booming El Paso, the descendants of the Isleta men today are a community of one thousand Indians— independent of the city where they have lived and worked for three centuries. The Tigua Indians, as they are now known, have held on to their tribal government; it functions like an urban pueblo within their suburban homes. Ceremonials and religious beliefs are still practiced. In fact, their tribal governor and priest have more strongly retained customs and ancient rituals than has the Pueblo of Isleta, where they had come from three hundred years ago.

"It is amazing," said the governor of old Isleta, Andrew Abeita, who visited his lost tribesmen in the spring of 1966. He had gone to El Paso to attend the executive board meeting of the National Congress of American Indians. He and the other tribal leaders were welcomed by a delegation of the Tiguas, whom none knew still existed.

"The Seven Stones in the Sacred Drums, they still have that. The priest on the Council, they still have that. The old ceremonials that we have forgotten they still have that," said Abeita. "In Isleta we do not have many of these things any more."

At sight, the Tiguas seem to be ordinary citizens of the city of El Paso. They work in the offices and the factories. They dress and live like their white neighbors. They speak in English or Spanish, not in Tewa. But in spite of these outward appearances they are urban Pueblo Indians in their souls and in their hearts.

"Once you are an Indian, you always are an Indian, I think," said Abeita.

"We are continually discovering surviving groups of Indians in parts of the East where they have managed to hold their group together for four hundred years," Deloria, Jr., said. "Many of the traditions have long since vanished, the native languages have all but died, there are few full-bloods left. But the important thing is that they have survived and intend to stay together."

Up the Connecticut River from Yale University in the valley of industrial smog, a band of Mohicans live—land gone, religion desecrated, way of life vanquished, beliefs in museums, woodland shrines turned into parking lots for shopping centers. The "Last of the Mohicans" had been assimilated for two hundred years and had worked in factories for generations. Still they are identified as Indians. And they have their hereditary tribal chief, who holds the ancient title in the midst of the smoggy suburbs of Eli Yale's triumph.

These "little islands" of unknown Indians are nourished culturally and politically by the tribal mainlands of the reservations. Land is the source of their tenacity. "Our very existence as a people is dependent on our lands," the National Congress of American Indians has said. If they had no land of their own the knowledge of the tribal homelands sustained their faith and persistence. It is obvious in conversation with them. Like lost wanderers they watch the reservations for signs, read the tribal newspapers and know as much, or more, about resurgence of the new tribalism as some of the poor, back-country Indians who have never left the reservations.

Many of the Red Nationalists come from such isolated or assimilated bands. The emergence of the new tribalism, or tribal nationalism, brought about the emergence into the light of hidden, forgotten bands of Indians who resided in the darkness of the cities. It was as if all these years they had been waiting, waiting for the day.

Why the rebirth of tribalism? The " 'Renaissance' surge of redirected self-realization," as Professor E. Roby Leighton of the University of Arizona termed it, seems a surprising and strange phenomenon.

Historian of modern nationalism Carlton J. H. Hayes, the past president of the American Historical Association, would perhaps not have been surprised. In his emeritus work, *Nationalism: A Religion* (Macmillan), he had written, not in advocacy but in analysis, that in spite of appearances to the contrary "tribal nationalism" had not been assimilated or destroyed as easily as was popularly imagined. It had merely been "submerged."

"Tribalism was, and wherever it survives still is, a primitive, small scale and usually intense type of nationalism," Hayes wrote, ". . . however primitive, and on however small a scale." The deep roots and long life of "tribal nationalism" had been underestimated, Hayes thought. Empire building by Western nations had merely hidden it from their own recognition. But the embryo of this nationalism was not "utterly blotted out by military empires, world religions, supranational languages and literatures, or economic developments. Not at all. It was submerged, not destroyed."

In the aftermath of World War II, the resurgence of the movements for colonial independence in Africa and Asia led to a re-emergence of "tribal nationalism" throughout the world. "Nationalism [was] no longer pre-eminently European," Hayes wrote. And the newer nations differed from the older nations. Unlike the countries of the West, they were unified by tribal "racial or religio-cultural" beliefs, and by the fervor of "emotional reaction and hostility of 'colonial' peoples to Western imperialism." These newer nations were created of a "medley of tribes" that had no single language, or unity of economy, or shared geography.

"Our American Indians issue from tribes . . . many of which still exist," Hayes wrote in a cryptic aside, while discussing "Primitive nationalism and its long submergence." He did not, unfortunately, elaborate upon this. But at the time he was writing the tribal nationalism of the Red Power advocates had not taken visible form, even in their own thinking.

The university-educated Indians were not unaware of the upheavals in the colonial nations. In the years when the birth pangs of the newly emerging nations were headline news, the Youth Council leaders were in college. Nor had the significance of the ability of small, weak, and diverse tribal groups to join together in national cohesion and to free themselves of vastly wealthier and more powerful invaders been lost upon the new Indians.

Vice President Hubert Humphrey was cognizant of these feelings and some of the common problems that had given rise to them. In discerning the coming of "A New Day for the American Indian," the Vice President had written in a publication fortuitously titled *The Optimist,* "Like some of the countries of Asia and Africa, long dominated by foreign powers, the Indian tribes are coming into a sense of self-awareness, but they haven't quite found their way to take a constructive part in affairs of the larger community."

The comparison between the newly independent nations of the colonial world and the tribes of American Indians was a significant and instructive one. It was the more so in that it had been drawn by the Vice President.

"We have more in common with the Africans and Vietnamese and all the non-Western people than we do with the Anglo-Saxon culture of the United States," Deloria, Jr., said. "We do not have an Anglo-Saxon background. We have different values. We are a tribal people with tribal sympathies. It's the same *feeling* here as there. An Indian doesn't have to know, or understand, anything about Kenya, or Burma, or Peru, or Vietnam. He *feels* the way they feel."

William Hensley agreed. "If you looked closely you would find, I think, there is not much difference between the native people up in Alaska or in Africa," he said. People in all colonial regions, Hensley said, whether on the frozen tundra or in the tropical jungles, have suffered in the same way from the attitudes "of the Caucasians." "We have the same problems. We have the same solutions," the Eskimo youth said.

"Tribalism is an international phenomenon," the Cherokee Robert Thomas said. "It has a world view most people do not recognize."

"Now we have contact with Indians in eighteen countries," said the spokesman for the Six Nations of the Iroquois, Wallace "Mad Bear" Anderson. The young leader of the Tuscarora tribe had organized a conference of tribal delegates from throughout the Western Hemisphere that met in Washington in the spring of 1966. Religious prophets came from Ecuador and Mexico. They met with chosen religious men from the tribes of North and South America to discuss the social problems and apocalyptic prophecies of their people. "We are united by a religion of love and brotherhood," one of the religious men told the newspaper. "Religion is a pre-electronic intercom to the Indians."

"There is definitely an international Indian movement," said Mad Bear. "It has brought together tribes in the United States, Canada, and Central and South America, Maybe it will spread elsewhere."

Among tribes so distant and dissimilar? The descendants of Sequoyah, Crazy Horse, and Geronimo surely had little in common with the tribes of Africa, the Watusi warriors, the peasants of Vietnam, or the tin miners of Bolivia. Wasn't this but the romantic dream of those collegiate Indians who sought to recapture some semblance of their ancestral greatness?

The upheavals on the far shores of Africa, Asia, and Latin America were remote from the reservations. Few of the reservation Indians seemed aware of these developments. Besides, the diffused Indian tribes, with their divergent histories, separate languages, and jealously guarded cultures, had no national territory as did the overseas tribes. Had not the federal courts decreed that as a sovereign nation they were an "artificial entity"? The half-million tribal Indians could hardly be expected to be taken seriously if they actually thought of building a tribal nation in the midst of a huge industrial country of two hundred million.

Yet William Hensley said, "Why not? Haven't the Africans been able to develop all sorts of modern societies?"

Many of these new nations were just as "artificial," Hayes had written. The colonial powers in Africa had brought unrelated and often hostile tribes together, arbitrarily, and had staked out artificial boundaries in order to govern them, somewhat like the Indian Territory in Oklahoma, and many of the Plains reservations. And the new nations that had arisen had been built upon these colonial artifices with very few exceptions. These nations were not built upon the historic boundaries of the lost empires that had ruled before the colonists had destroyed them.

Languages of these new nations were so diverse that the colonial tongue—English or French—was often used to govern them. The foreign, nonnative tongue was the official, if not the spoken, language of the country. For the tribes spoke in mutually incomprehensible languages or dialects—like the Sioux, Navajo, and Cherokee. Hayes commented: "So long as the masses of a country are illiterate . . . it matters little whether the vernaculars are few or many."

In these things the new Indians found familiar signs and recognizable problems. They watched the overseas developments not with an eye to imitating them, but to scrutinize what, if anything, might be applied to the neo-colonialist bind the tribes were in at home.

After journeying from nation to nation around the world, Mad Bear Anderson, came home with a message that was like a revelation. "This is the dawn of a new day," he said. "I will do all in my power to see Indians unite across the continent. There is a movement of Indian nationalism in the nation. In the future we will work closely to bring our movement and the black movement together."

It had been Mad Bear who led a delegation from the Six Nations of the Iroquois to Cuba in 1958. Fidel Castro had given them a personal invitation, and Mad Bear said of that trip, "They rolled out the red carpet for us, including police escort in Cadillacs, bands, and machete-waving campesinos." The Iroquois are, however, among the most conservative and traditionalist of tribes, with no sympathies for Caribbean controversies or Castroisms. In twentieth-century terms they are not only apolitical, but nonpolitical. Why then had the chiefs gone to Cuba? Their hope at the time had been that Cuba would sponsor the admission of the Six Nations of the Iroquois to the United Nations as a sovereign and independent state.

The village and the clan had been the horizon of a tribal people. Limited and provincial, they had a vision of the world beyond the known boundaries of their tribe which was vague and feared. Now the upsurge of tribal nationalism throughout the world—"the world-wide ebullience," Hayes had called it—had burst through those limited horizons. Among the tribal leaders there was a kind of tribal internationalism that had been growing.

It is still among the Indian tribes largely apolitical. That is, it is expressed in personal and tribal ways, with a feeling that is based on the identification with human beings rather than political ideas. And it is consciously phrased to reject the cold-war concepts of the technological powers.

Anne Wauneka expressed it when she spoke of the war in Vietnam:

"Who are these Vietnam people? What do they look like? I do not know them. I have never met them. Sometimes they tell me they look like Navajos. That is said. That may be. Sometimes I was told that the Koreans look like Navajos too; I think that is so.

"My people come to me and ask: 'Why must my son fight these Vietnam people?' I say, 'I do not know.' Have they hurt the President of the United States in some way? That may be. I do not say anything about these Vietnam people who I do not know."

Mad Bear, who has visited Vietnam seven times, said simply, "When I walk down the streets of Saigon those people look like my brothers and sisters."

It is a tribal way of talking and thinking. These new and old Indian leaders are not talking about the political nature of the war at all. What they see in their mind's eye are people, tribal people, who "look like" their own tribesmen, caught in a modern conflict that has been imposed upon their culture by outside cultures. Listening to tribal Indians talk of the political wars that rage in newspapers and on the battlefields one has to pause, and wonder, at the differing ways that tribal and technological men see the same things.

"The tribal man doesn't think in middle-class or technological terms," said Robert Thomas. "He doesn't live that kind of life. If you analyze him by those standards don't expect him to know what you are talking about or to know what he is really thinking.

"So many of my university colleagues make that mistake about Vietnam," Thomas said. "They argue about this policy interpretation or that, when any tribal Indian knows that what it's all about is a bunch of Vietnamese peasants who are goddamn mad because some machine, some war machine, is flattening their crops.

"Hell, the Indians are tribal peasants. They understand *that* about Vietnam."

And yet many of the conflicts that divide the world—from the rivers of the Congo to the deltas of Vietnam—are tribal in origin, no matter who fights them. Is it perhaps a blessing in disguise to the country to have an articulate and knowledgeable tribal people within its midst—if they are listened to?

"Until the government understands the American Indian, how he thinks, what he wants, they will not understand any other people who do not share their Anglo-Saxon heritage," said Deloria, Jr. The unique position of the Indian tribes makes government policy toward them a thermometer of our foreign policy, he thinks. "So long as they try to push Indians into the mainstream of Anglo-

Saxon culture they are going to push 'backward' people into that mainstream in world affairs. And that will always be catastrophic. So long as they are trying to force us into their mold they will be unconsciously trying to do this on the international scene. Our foreign policy will consistently be on the losing side.

"It seems to me that American foreign policy is going to be in a box, as American domestic policy toward the Indians is boxed up by the same attitudes," he continued. "If they could understand the American Indian then there might be a chance in foreign affairs."

William Hensley quietly added: "This is a problem that America has world-wide. You want everybody to react just as you react. And many people in the world just don't like this."

Like the once-colonial people elsewhere in the world the new Indians are pressing for self-determination. They are demanding political independence for their tribal way of life. Together these two—self-determination and political independence—are the source of the demand for Red Power.

"Colonial Office" was sensitive to these demands. It decided to try to meet them. It had a mandate from President Johnson, who at the swearing-in of Commissioner Bennett had called for ". . . the most comprehensive program for the advancement of the Indians that the Government of the United States has ever considered. I want it to be sound, realistic, progressive, venturesome and far-sighted."

Unhappily, the government's program had become entangled in the battle over the controversial Omnibus Bill. These "legislative remedies" that Vice President Humphrey had been confident would "loosen some of the shackles and permit faster growth in Indian areas" had been rejected by tribe after tribe.

In the face of the tribal opposition the Omnibus Bill was scheduled for submission to the new Congress in the winter of 1966–67. Even the staunchest supporters of the legislation were hesitant. The prospect of putting the fat in the legislative fires only to have the Indians converge to stomp on it was chilling. In a last-minute attempt to get a favorable consensus it was decided to invite the tribal leaders to one final confrontation in Washington, D.C.

On a snowy day in early February the leaders of thirty tribes met. They argued and were argued with for four days. While the snow fell to slush in the streets the room grew thick with smoke and the oratory grew thicker. The tribes were divided. But, in the tribal way, they were divided on the same side of the Omnibus Bill. Some wished to reject the government's proposals at once. Some wished, in politeness and in distrust of instant wisdom, to request more time "to think about it."

It came time to vote, as even in meetings of Indians it must. The tribal leaders voted for more time "to think about it"—by twenty-six to twenty-four.

"Haven't Indians got any guts any more?" erupted one of the new Indians. The young man, who is a fiery national leader, stood up. "I know, and you know, that everyone in this room knows that everyone else in this room is opposed to this Omnibus Bill. We are acting like sheep. We are voting away our lands. We can't take a message to the President of the United States that says we voted twenty-six to twenty-four 'to think about it.' We will make fools of ourselves.

"If we Indians don't have any more guts than that, let's quit," he berated the tribal leaders. "And I will quit this meeting, right now." The young man strode out the door. "I hadn't gone five feet when someone called me back," he said. "Everyone had voted together to turn down the government's bill, and submit our own. It was almost unanimous—forty-four to five. That's what I call a real Indian vote."

The "Resolution of the Thirty Tribes" called for a "Foreign Aid Program" for American Indians of half a billion dollars. It proposed that "the President, the Congress and the American people take a bold, innovative step" and recognize and deal with the tribal communities of Indians in the same way that the newly emerging, independent nations of the former colonial world were treated by the United States Government.

"Let them extend to the American Indian people the massive benefits that are now being offered to the citizens of the new nations of Asia, Africa and Latin America," the tribal leaders said. "We desire an American Indian Development Fund, of low interest, long term nature, comparable to the funds committed to our South American cousins [via the Alliance for Progress], and the native peoples of Africa and Asia. Aid to these peoples totals in excess of three billion annually—more than was spent on the American Indian between 1789 and 1960.

"Let us develop a model for the former colonial world and avoid their mistakes," the tribal leaders concluded.

The long-submerged tribal nationalism of the American Indians had come of age on the political stage. Strangely, that had been set by the government itself.

In a conference called by the government, that the Indians had attended at the invitation of the government, at the national capital of the government, the tribal leaders had not merely rejected the proposals of the government. For the first time in the history of Indian affairs the tribes had publicly likened their status to that of colonial nations. And they had openly aligned their demands with those of "the new nations of Asia, Africa and Latin America."

Red Power was no longer a catch phrase. It formally and officially had been put on the public record in a resolution to the President of the United States. The quiet dreams of a few, young Red Muslims among the university-educated Indians, who had met in obscurity a few years before, had become the stated position of the major Indian tribes in the country. So wholly united were the tribes that even the individualistic Navajos, who were not members of the National Congress of American Indians, sent delegates to Washington to vote for the anticolonialist resolution. Raymond Nakai, the young, aggressive, and determinedly modern chairman of the Navajos, led his tribal delegation. He offered to personally deliver the "Resolution of the Thirty Tribes" to the President.

"The revolution in Indian thinking" that had been noted earlier at the convention of the Indians' Congress had now demanded national recognition. Curiously the newspapers and television networks covered the Indians' resolve with a blanket of electronic silence. It was understandably a matter of embarrassment and concern in some official circles that the proud and patriotic first Americans had in effect accused the government of colonialism. The old days in Indian affairs were clearly over. As Vice President Humphrey had said: "The paternalistic approach is good no longer." Yet the unresolved question was what would replace it?

Emergence of Indian nationalism at an official conference held in the auditorium of the Interior Department posed a troublesome paradox. Commissioner Bennett had reassured the Indians the government was prepared to listen to their views: "For the first time we are consulting with Indian leaders before sending legislation to Congress. This is a novel experience for them, and some are hesitant. But the whole intent is to bring Indians more into the decision-making process."

The "hesitant" Indians turned out to be remarkably unhesitant. When they rejected the government's legislation—in the Omnibus Bill—and suggested their own "Foreign Aid Program," the government was dismayed.

Undaunted by the startled reaction, or perhaps delighted by it, the tribal leaders wrote a long open letter to the President.

"It is time that the government consistently recognize that it is our servant, not our master," the letter to President Johnson read. "Upon presentation of, and analysis by, the delegates of this legislation [the Omnibus Bill], certain major titles and provisions thereof were rigorously opposed and unanimously rejected upon the grounds that they are inimical and incongruous with the present needs, capabilities and conditions of the American Indian. . . . The proposed legislation affecting mortgage hypothecation, and sale of Indian lands would render the Indian people immediately vulnerable to subversive economic forces; leading inevitably and inalterably to the prompt erosion and demise of the social and economic culture of the American Indian.

"We are again astonished," the Indians wrote to the President.

In a meeting with the tribal leaders the day after the epochal conference had ended Commissioner Bennett rejected the Indians' resolutions. He reportedly told him that he intended to back the Omnibus Bill to "the hilt." Later that day Vice President Humphrey reiterated to the tribal leaders that the administration was "solidly" behind the Commissioner. He advised the Indians to back him also.

Decision making by the Indians was going to be a more complex process than anyone had envisioned. It seemed to be a "novel experience" for the government, as well as for the Indians.

Such was the anger of the tribal leaders after the rejection of

their resolutions that Wallace "Mad Bear" Anderson spoke of re-
nouncing his citizenship. "If an Indian denounces his so-called citizenship in the United States and pledges his allegiance to his own
respective Indian nation," Mad Bear said, "is he deported? And, if
so, where to?"

The old Seneca Chief Sundown said: "The Indian has always kept
his word. Has the white man ever kept his word? Not a bit. I can't
understand the difference between the government of the United
States and the government of a state. One is the Mafia and the other
is an Apalachin meeting. Both are crooked."

Listening to the men talk, with a deepening frown on her face,
Marjorie Wilson, a Tuscarora woman, said softly: "We believe in
a peaceful movement, never to be bold. We believe our Creator is
turning his face back to us once more. God gave us this land. The
government cannot take it away by pretending to help us. They do
not fool us. They do not fool God. Land was never meant to get
rich on. That is not God's way. He will not allow the Indian to be
without a home. It is time for the white man to recognize the way
of God again. It is time for the white man to recognize the way
of the Indian again."

And before the year was out the government had rewritten the
Omnibus Bill so often it was no longer recognizable. The new Indians had won the biggest battle since the Little Big Horn with
their newly learned legislative weapons.

There was peace. Yet there was unease.

"It's just a matter of time before someone in Washington decides
he's omnipotent and gives us the Omnibus business once more,"
mused a tribal leader, returning home from the conference of the
thirty tribes. "But we wouldn't retreat any more. We have nowhere
to retreat to. And besides, now we know we can win and we know
how to win."

"You can't fool Indians any more," said John Wooden Leg,
tribal chairman of the Northern Cheyenne. "This is the year of the
thinking people."

In the mind of the Indian there was time. There was the earth.
There were the harmonies. There was his soul. There was no beginning and ending to these things. Like the blood of his body, un-

endingly, they flowed in and out of his heart; unless a piece of paper, a law by Congress, could sever these "many connections," as Anne Wauneka called them, unless his life and land could be hidden under a blanket of cement, the Indian knew the strength of these things. He did not tremble now.

He had rediscovered himself. He had rediscovered his tribal brothers. With all that had been done to him before, even then if they were done again it was doubtful if he would be legislated out of existence now.

There were all these things. There was also the government. But unlike the Indians governments came and went. He had been here before they came, he would be here after they went.

A young Indian girl came to the tribal leaders on the last day of the conference in Washington. The Taos Pueblo college girl, Wahleah Lujan, was "Miss Indian America." A soft-spoken, gentle child of a woman, who had lived all her life in the ways of her grandparents, she was a sociology student at Fort Lewis College in Durango, Colorado. Wahleah had been voted the most beautiful Indian girl in the country and had been brought to Washington to represent the new Indians.

If a symbol of the new Indian were to be sought, it was in this girl. She said: "I am a typical Taos Pueblo girl. . . . Our way of life is completely different from any modern man's ideas—it seems. The way we think, the way we live. In the pueblo everything is sacred. Life is sacred. This is the beautiful way of life that is almost unheard of in the fast world of today."

She said: "In the last twenty years we've been pushed around a lot. Our land is being taken away. Our life is being taken away. Our sacred Blue Lake, the church of our Indian religion, is being taken away. Land that has never been used by anyone else. Land that has belonged to no one but us. Land that my people have been on for six hundred and fifty years. And all of a sudden these strange people come in and tell us: You can't use this land any more! It's not yours!

"So we needed somebody. We need somebody who would go out and learn to compete with the white man on his level. We have to fight back. So I went out. I did not want to go to college. To go away. But I had to go."

She said: "If I were living in a dream world what would I want? I would want my people to be able to hold on to our beautiful way of life. I would want my people to hold on to their ways, somehow, and yet be able to be on the same shelf, or level, as the white man. I would want my people to be able to compete with this white man, and yet be able to come back to the pueblo, to live in our way. If I were living in a dream world that is what I would want. But why is that almost impossible?"

She said: "Let us be walking images of our beautiful way of life. Hold fast to your lands, to your sacred ways, to your Indian way of life.

"I hope most of all, by venturing out, to show my people one can be modern, and yet be very much part of the old way. In fact, it is becoming necessary to be modern in order to preserve the old way."

Long ago the Sioux had sung:

> *Coming is the whole world!*
> *The Nation is coming!*
> *The Nation is coming!*
> *The Eagle has brought the message*
> *to the tribe—*
> *Says the Father—*
> *Says the Father—*
> *Ate heye lo! Ate heye lo!*

APPENDICES

A. *Sources*

I have always been a wanderer.

Riding the old roads and the dirt roads by thumb, by luck, with curiosity, with ignorance, on farm wagons, on rumbling potato trucks, on rampaging motorcycles, in huge cross-country diesels, with itinerant preachers in revival tents on wheels, with migrant fieldhands in open trucks, with rodeo cowboys in English sports cars, in my earlier youth I came by chance upon the tribesmen.

It was the hot and apprehensive summer of 1946, when war had once more just ended. Everyone was beginning to breathe naturally and easily, in peaceful relief.

I was a youth trying to escape the urban gutters of New York, awed by the richness of the ancient earth. "Go west, young man," Horace Greeley had said. You will disturb no living being. He forgot to mention the self. In wonderment and bewilderment I had a love affair with the American West. That there were living beings amid the scenery did not occur to me, as it did not occur to Horace Greeley. That these living beings were Indians was coincidental. I was not seeking them out. Rather I was seeking after the source of my country and of myself. It was by accident that I found that these Indians knew sources of America that I had never dreamed of.

That was twenty years ago. That was two hundred thousand miles ago. So often since, in the summers and in the winter, I have wandered and wondered, I have listened and learned, I have exulted and cursed that scenery, until, like the Indian, I have become a part of it.

When the university experts and ordinary readers ask, as they do, How do you know these things to be true that you have written? I can only say, I do not. I know these people. I have seen them, as I have seen my own life, grow. These things they told me and I tell you may be true. Or they may be dreams, which also may be true. But how did you study the Indians, what methods did you use? the questioners persist. I say, I did not study them. I used no methods. But you must have some technique of gaining the confidence of your "informants," they say with doubting brows. I say, I had no "informants." Just some friends, some enemies. The friends were truthful, I believe; the enemies may have lied to make a fool of me. What I have written is not a study, but a book of people full of the truths and lies people tell.

Men study people they wish to know, but who are unknown. The new Indians were not unknown to me: I knew them as well as I knew myself —no more, no less. Thus this book is not written from the outside looking in, seeking clues, discovering questions. If anything, it is an attempt to translate the thoughts of the Indians into the words of the white man.

The truth of the matter is that I did not wish to write this book. As the new Indians became more and more vital and involved in their new tribalism I sought to convince my Indian friends to write their own book. They would not. Some were editors of tribal newspapers, some were experienced writers, but they kept their best manuscripts in their desk drawers. They wanted the country to listen to them. They knew how to write. But they would not. Unwillingly, I came to believe that their ingrained distrust of the words of the white man, of communicating with him in his "foreign language," was so deep that they froze at the thought of writing what was in their hearts. Speeches at conferences, editorials in the newspapers, resolutions in tribal councils—these were simple. Writing what was closest to them was more difficult.

"Being an Indian is a mystical feeling Indians have in the gut of their stomachs," said an Oklahoma Indian boy who was a pre-law student. "White men are not mystical. You can't explain it to them."

"I always talk to the university people. I never tell them anything important," said an old religious man in Minnesota.

And yet I knew the new Indians wanted the story to be told. It was time to tell it. "Let us not linger in dark halls, or be satisfied in engaging in idle talk," the Apache leader Wendell Chino had said. "The day of the march and the day of action has arrived." Red Power could not be silently won.

"Who is to tell it?" asked the Navajo woman Anne Wauneka.

So it was suggested: Let this writer say what we feel. Let him be the human tape recorder for whatever we want to tell, and whatever we want to keep to ourselves he will respect. Let us write a book together . . . . I am not selfless, or without thoughts. But neither my ideas nor my publisher's editing would interfere with what the Indians had to say. The book would be theirs, to whatever extent they wished to make it so.

We talked about it for a few years. We agreed, at last, that I would try to write such a book.

One summer the National Congress of American Indians sent a letter to the reservations throughout the country. It began:

To All Tribal Chairmen:

For many years he [the writer] has supported the right of American Indian people to speak for themselves. He can write a book on what is currently happening on Indian reservations, what Indians think about American society, about their own cultures, about the future. . . . There are too many things happening in the modern world for us to remain silent about what we want and think. Stan will be a *faithful recorder* of what we as Indian people actually want and think should be done, or not done, in the future. We urge all tribes to give Stan the fullest cooperation in getting his book ready for publication. We are fortunate that Stan will help us put in words what we all feel in our hearts. We urge all Indian people to work with Stan in bringing the message you feel is most important to the attention of the reading public.

Many doors were opened by the letter. Hearts opened more cautiously, if at all. For what man, even in the closest friendship, enters truly into the heart of another? Why should an Indian, in any event, who read that letter but did not know me, trust this white man above any other because of a piece of paper? There were many I talked to who could not read. There were many who pretended they did not know of me or the letter, keeping it in their pocket until they were convinced I wanted nothing from them, whereupon they laughingly would take the letter from their pockets, and say, "We do not believe words. We believe in people."

I wanted nothing from them. Perhaps that was the method used in writing this book; it recommends itself to the thoughtful and humbler conscience.

Anyone seeking human knowledge, or doing scholarly research, on Indian life—not necessarily the same thing—faces two high barriers. The first is the United States Government. Not merely have the nearly two hundred years of federal policies toward the Indians been purposefully destructive of tribalism, but the paternalistic and authoritarian nature of these governmental policies has alienated the tribesmen, made them suspicious, and subtly pervaded the atmosphere of any relations whites have with Indians.

Coming to the Indians one does not come alone: the history of two centuries of betrayal and deception are at the elbow of every visitor. He talks, but the Indian hears other voices. He acts, but the Indian remembers previous promises. Whichever way the visitor seeks to declare his honesty, no matter how nakedly he attempts to strip himself of the past, he comes with the burden of that past on his back, like a curse he cannot easily exorcise.

Were this history to be nonexistent there would still be the second barrier, that of the cultural gap. It is more like an abyss. The Navajo teacher Kathyrn Polacca simply said, "We talk different languages." She was not talking of words, but of what they mean. For the tribal man has so many vastly different values, ideas of time and earth, beliefs about human life and religion, that he may use the words of the white man but still be speaking a wholly different language.

Men have attempted to bridge this cultural gap in many ways. None of these were relied upon in the writing of this book, and yet in describing how this book was written, from whom and how the thoughts in it were gathered, it may be of interest to the reader, and the researcher, to explore the ways in which it was *not* written. And could *not* have been.

One way, by far the most favored, is reportage. It seeks to isolate and thereby study "the human objects of history," as Michael Harrington has said of Oscar Lewis's method in compiling *La Vida*. Wisely recognizing that the people to be studied are likely to consider the stranger in their midst to be an "outsider" and "middle class," both of which he is indeed likely to be, the hope is that the distortions in communication that this might cause can be overcome by objectifying the people—as "human objects." The individuals are singled out and tape-recorded in infinitesimal detail. It is a long and laborious process that is rescued from being boring only by the excitement inherent in the stark and precise revelation of any life.

It is akin to the naturalistic school of acting. The human beings are portrayed nakedly. But the in-depth interviews are too often oddly scardeep. Moreover, the intense individuality of the portraits have their own built-in distortion of the communities of people they hopefully represent. For typicality has many faces, as journalists well know. It is a vague quality that can be made to materialize in many guises.

The second method is mechanical. Like specimens in a sociology laboratory, the people to be studied are measured by a series of technological devices—multiple interviews, statistical medians, computerized data. Every word is mathematically totted, every pause is timed, every thought is weighed against previous data.

It is akin to a sociological Gallup Poll. The techniques of social scientism are utilized to reduce the human beings to abstractions, and to control the unknown not by the "manageable malice" that Malinowski spoke of, but by manageable statistics. Using the exact and expert devices of technology these methods manufacture volumes of data, fill the academic journals, and reward the bookkeepers of culture with Ph.D.s' and consultant's fees.

But, rather than bridging the cultural gap, these approaches have widened it. They conceal a perverse principle, which is this: the more technologically expert, efficient, and impersonal the method the less useful and truthful it will be in reflecting the thoughts and feelings of a nontechnological people. Their suspicion of it, their resistance to it, increase with its expertise.

And the reason is inherent in what separates the two worlds. These methods are a microcosm of the finest, most thoughtful achievements of a technological society and of scientific logic. But this very thing that makes them so precise makes them sterile when applied to a people whose way of living, whose way of thinking, whose humanism are the antithesis of the technological and scientific. There is an inverse ratio in this: the more proficient the methods, the less effective they are!

The tribal man and his tribal society are intensely human. He is personal and direct. He trusts what he sees and feels and senses. He is also deeply religious.

"Science and technology have become pervasive and have caused the world of 'nature' to be removed from our direct senses," said Charles R. DeCarlos, the director of automation research at IBM. "The rhythms of the world beat to the cycle of machines rather than the circling of the sun. We feel the distance between old rituals grounded in myth and nature and the new and man-created reality of the city. The steady accumulation of technical accomplishment changes the environment of our value systems."

DeCarlos, who is a poet as well as a computer scientist, fears that "a technological society takes on aspects of dehumanization." He quoted T. S. Eliot:

> Where is the life we have lost in living?
> Where is the wisdom we have lost in knowledge?
> Where is the knowledge we have lost in information?*

Can we then know a people who are "grounded in myth and nature"? Who have not been alienated from the knowledge of their "direct senses"? Not by hiding behind mechanical methods that translate human beings into the equations of technology, and thus further separate the worlds of nonmachined men and manned machines. These methods tend to confirm the easy conceits of the white technologists and to confuse information with knowledge.

To know a human being you have to feel with him, to be with him, to love him. From the inside out. Not from the outside in. I believe that strongly. There is to me no such thing as instant knowledge that can be learned with empty hearts and without dirty hands. Any such knowledge is hollow; it is an artifice. Without the joy and pain of participating in the life one wishes to know one learns "nothing important."

The words in this book were written man to man, face to face. Where a tribal leader was at ease in both worlds a tape recorder might be used. But these formal interviews were made specifically to be broadcast over WBAI-FM, in New York, as part of an all-Indian series, "Who Speaks for the Indian?" In most instances the thoughts of the Indians were

* Chorus from "The Rock," *Collected Poems 1909–1962*, New York, Harcourt, Brace & World, 1963.

recorded by memory, in conversation, as friends talk. In other words, the book was written by word of mouth. In fields, by mountain streams, in homes and on porches, in trading posts and on ranches—wherever Indians gathered to talk.

Is it then necessary for someone who wishes to know the Indian to travel for twenty years, for two hundred thousand miles, as I did? No, but it would help. What is necessary is that whoever wishes to know the Indian must go to the Indian. Not to visit, but to live. Not to judge, but to learn. Length of time and acquisition of information are less important than a full heart and open mind.

And so, in writing of the sources of this book, I must begin and end with the Indian tribes, tribal organizations, and tribal newspapers, that is, the Indians themselves. Of these tribal sources some that I might suggest are these:

The National Congress of American Indians
1346 Connecticut Avenue, N.W.
Washington, D.C. 20036
Executive Director, John Belindo (Kiowa-Navajo)

Founded in November, 1944, so that "Indians themselves could freely express their views and wishes on national legislation and policy." The "United Nations of the tribes," representing, at various times, from forty to more than one hundred different tribes and bands. Has non-Indian, nonvoting members.

The National Indian Youth Council
Post Office Box 118
Schurz, Nevada 89427
Chairman, Mel Thom (Paiute)
President, Clyde Warrior (Ponca)

Founded in August, 1961: "We, the younger generation, at this time in the history of the American Indian . . . band together on a national scale in meeting the challenges facing the Indian people [to] recognize the inherent strength of the American Indian heritage," and "believing in a greater Indian America." Represents not tribes but individual young Indian students. Has non-Indian, nonvoting members.

The United Sioux Tribes
Rosebud, South Dakota
Chairman, Cato Valandra

Founded in 1963, "to present the correct image of the Sioux, promote Indian unity, and representation wherever possible." Representing nine Sioux tribes and bands in North and South Dakota.

The All-Pueblo Council
Santo Domingo Pueblo

Santo Domingo, New Mexico
Secretary, Benny Atencio

Founded, it is believed, in 1680. Uniting the seventeen pueblos in New Mexico, originally to direct the Pueblo revolt against the Spanish conquistadores. Did not meet for 242 years, until 1922, when legislative action threatened Pueblo land. Now meets regularly.

There are many other tribal federations and tribal groups. But the above suffice to indicate the character and breadth of intertribal and extratribal organizations that evolve and direct policies and programs of, by, and for the Indians.

There are also tribal newspapers that articulate the wishes and voices of the Indians. A few of the many score of these publications to which non-Indians may subscribe to learn of Indian opinion are:

The Navajo Times
Post Office Box 428, Window Rock, Arizona 86515
Weekly. Subscription, $4.

Fort Apache Scout
Post Office Box 898, Whiteriver, Arizona 85941
Monthly. Subscription, $1 in Arizona; $1.50 out of state.

Tundra Times
Post Office Box 1287, Fairbanks, Alaska 99701
Weekly. Subscription, $8.

ABC (American Before Columbus)
National Indian Youth Council
Post Office Box 118, Schurz, Nevada 89427
From time to time. Subscription, with membership, $5.

The Sentinel
National Congress of American Indians
1346 Connecticut Avenue, N.W., Washington, D.C. 20036
From time to time. Subscription, with membership, $10.

Indian Voices
University of Chicago
1126 East 59th Street, Chicago, Illinois.

The Indian Historian
American Indian Historical Society
1451 Masonic Avenue, San Francisco, California 94117
Quarterly. $3.50.

Many of the tribal newspapers are written solely for the members of the tribes. Editors of some of these requested that I not list them for they neither cared about, nor wanted, non-Indian, nontribal readers. And this was true as well of some of the tribal groups—especially the religious groups—who, as one young Indian leader said, "Just don't want to be bothered by intellectual tourists who have lost their religion and want to borrow ours. Please do not list these things. We do not wish to lose them."

There are many things that the Indians did not wish told in this book. Either they did not repeat these to me or asked me not to tell them. Once again I have respected their wishes, much to the sorrow and dismay of my understanding editor at Harper & Row, Jeannette Hopkins. But it was what we had agreed, and these things are not for me to tell.

Religion is one of these. There is a chapter on religion, "The Christ Who Never Came," but it is only the religion of the white man, the way Christianity has affected the Indians and what they think of it, that the religious men wished to talk about. It is not Indian religion. To the Indian his religious beliefs are integrated into everything he thinks, says, and does; and conversely into everything he will not say and will not do. He willingly talks of certain rituals, and invites the outsider he trusts to observe them. He no longer has to hide them from governmental prohibitions. But the essence of his religion, the soul of its mysticism, he will say nothing about. And neither does this book.

And so, in the end, to know the Indian words are not enough. Words are like faces. The soul is not always revealed by them. To know the Indian one has to go to him. To be with him. To feel with him.

That is how this book was written.

B. *"Let Us Develop a Model for the Former Colonial World. . . .": Resolution adopted 44 to 5 by leaders of thirty tribes, at the conference called by the United States Government, Department of the Interior, Washington, D.C., February, 1967.*

We, the representatives of 30 Indian Tribes from 10 states, having met for four (4) days in Washington, D.C., at the invitation of the Commissioner of Indian Affairs to consider the first general legislation in Indian Affairs since the Indian Re-organization Act of 1934, do present this as our recommendation for legislation.

We appreciate the hospitality of the Commissioner of Indian Affairs and his willingness to listen to our views. However, we are unable to regard the proposed legislation under discussion as major legislation or as designed to solve the many pressing problems of poverty on our reservations.

We, therefore, propose to the President, the Congress, and the American people that they take a bold and innovative step. Let them extend to the American Indian people the massive benefits that are now being offered to citizens of the new Nations of Asia, Africa, and Latin America. We need technical assistance and development loan funds. We sold our ancestral lands to the United States in return for perpetual protection through federal trusteeship. We do not expect to pay twice.

Instead of the Omnibus Bill, we propose as an alternative that the Federal Government should honor its obligations to the First Americans developing legislation along the following lines:

EDUCATION: The American People are committed to education and American Indian citizens have long been fully committed to education. We desire improved facilities, expanded programs on all levels, and more college and graduate scholarships.

ECONOMIC DEVELOPMENT: We desire an American Indian Development Fund, of low interest, long term nature, comparable to the funds committed to our South American cousins (via the Alliance for Progress) and the native peoples of Africa and Asia. Aid to these peoples totals in excess of $3 billion annually—more than was spent on the American Indian between 1789 and 1960.

To provide prompt rapid economic growth in the underdeveloped areas of our own country, the Indian reservations, we should immediately provide $500 million in loan funds in this proposed fund for economic development of the reservations.

To do less is to deny our own First Americans assistance in social and economic development that we are now already providing others world-wide.

We American Indians are tired of proposals which offer limited assistance and exact as the price the risk of losing our traditional protections afforded by federal trusteeship. We have increasingly good relations with the Bureau of Indian Affairs and are not hampered by present laws and statutes in our community development. However, like any undeveloped area, we need the capital to develop. Trusteeship by the Federal government was the price the United States government paid for this continent and we do not agree to give it up now, nor in the future.

Human and economic development is the essence of trusteeship. Poverty should no longer be its mark or result. The economic development of American Indian Tribes and Reservations is a special instance of the War on Poverty. We are combatants in that war and we are beginning to win. We are not willing to surrender our role and become passive beneficiaries. We like our relationship with the Bureau of Indian Affairs and see our future in an important relationship. Let us develop a model for the former colonial world and avoid their mistakes.

A Great Society will not willingly or knowingly waste the human and economic resources of its people. Let us continue to develop for the benefit of our Indian people and our country.

C. *"Tribalism and the Modern Society": Unsigned editorial in the* NCAI Sentinel, *National Congress of American Indians, XI, No. 2. Spring, 1966.*

Recent events seem to us to be preparing the ground for a new understanding and appreciation of Indian Tribes in modern society. It will take wisdom, brains and maturity by Indians and non-Indians to realize to the fullest extent all the implications that can be possible for our society in the future if current movements are fully understood. But especially among the non-Indians some cherished ideas concerning Indians must be reluctantly left behind no matter how reasonable they appear at present.

One must acknowledge that a major portion of the globe is experiencing unrest and that revolutions and social unrest stem from two factors that appear quite unrelated but in fact are intimately related. They are nationalism and technology. Senator Harris in a speech on the Senate floor in April accurately stated that Indians are feeling an increasing pull to make an Indian adaptation to the modern world and we have all seen clippings from California and Washington state where Indians are standing up for their rights in the same manner as people all over the globe. There seems to be an intellectual acceptance of technological society and a real desire by American Indians to learn what American society is and how one finds economic security in it. At the same time there is an ever increasing rejection of the social values of the "mainstream" and a return to Indian values.

In much the same way as Chinese, South Americans, and other people, traditional social values are being brought into play by Indians more and more. A recent news story told how in China there is now an institution for the teaching and furtherance of ancient Chinese medicine complete with the spiritual world of ancient China and that this type of medicine has gained a great deal of respect in spite of the highly materialistic nature of present Chinese philosophy which appears to be a radical Marxism. In the Congo also, tribalism and folk values have all but destroyed any possibility of stable government formed along the traditional western lines.

There can be little doubt that technology has contributed the major impetus to this yearning for old ways. Technology has as a basis the creation of the inhuman human. The cog who fits into a certain gear mechanism and performs a certain "function" as part of a machine. Men are called not to a vocation as in the old ways, or many times, even to the skill of a trade, rather they are asked to sell a certain portion of their time to inhuman labor. This labor is not inhuman in the sense of working conditions or wages as in the old days of the Industrial Revolution.

Rather it is inhuman in the sense that men now get little if any personal fulfillment from their toil and to counter this feeling they are then told to "recreate," that is, to make more and better use of their time in "recreation." Technology makes people feel an obligation to live but does not give a reason for acting or the feeling of having done something that is important to the person himself.

It would seem to us that cities and urban areas ought to be reconsidered as smaller and more compact communities with an extended tribal system and that a city should be seen more as a confederation of neighborhoods with different values and social patterns than as a uniform mass of people with the same problems and outlooks and values. The so-called "mainstream" is composed mainly of people for whom technology has created a desire to conform and not as a personal society where enduring values and ideas have free reign. Values cannot be mass values or else they become truisms that have no application to people or to real situations. Values must be oriented toward the individual person and real for that person within a group that accepts responsibility to live according to its values. We cannot help but feel that within tribal societies values are created and endure which will eventually conquer mass truisms that have no real connection with people and their problems.

The foolishness of the present situation in Indian Affairs is that too many people are trying to re-state old mass truisms such as "assimilation" without taking into account that in the present society for anyone of any race, creed, color or religion to "assimilate" into the values of the mass of people whose lives are directed by technological considerations is to forfeit the chance to live constructively, beautifully, and meaningfully. We would like the policy makers in Indian Affairs to go beyond legal considerations and fancy formulas and ask themselves if it is better to gain the whole world and lose one's life or to accept oneself as a person with certain principles and work to make real values more real to more people. The tribe, we feel, must always receive primary consideration as it is the group within which people are allowed to express themselves and realize that they truly are people with definite values, ideas, hopes and goals and unless a society is allowed to express its goals, it cannot long endure.

D.

1. "On the 'Wise All-Knowing' White Friend"
   Excerpt from an editorial in *NCAI Sentinel,*
   National Congress of American Indians. Vol.
   XI, No. 2. Spring, 1960.

To wistfully look to the Oliver La Farges for counsel is sheer folly today as events are moving too fast in American history to have Indians take a back seat in decision-making in favor of a "wise all-knowing" white friend. Yet let us not kid ourselves, the Oliver La Farges are still around and increasing everyday. They appear whenever and wherever there are problems, programs, and activity. They still seek to influence and counsel and end up creating confusion. Many are found among the anthropologists and sociologists who inhabit the reservations each summer while the Indians are off to powwows and migrant labor. They appear in various guises of wise "evaluators" who evaluate tribal programs and projects. They appear as helpful Indian Interest groups who mix in tribal politics under the disguise of technical assistance.

Perhaps no other group in America is so plagued with people wanting to do right and good and ending up in a state of total confusion. The Santa Fe meeting had 62 tribes coming together as a single voice to say to the country, "It is time we had a say in our own future." There is still a great need to communicate this unity and sense of responsibility to the country at large. To much of the general public the odd idea still remains, the only way to help Indians is to give funds and support to other non-Indians to go and work among the Indians. It is time to break this attitude and move on to other things. Instead of giving support to non-Indians to do good it is time to support Indians to do better.

We have seen the Indian Interest groups recognize this principle at Santa Fe. It is now time to go on from there and change the old paternalistic attitudes straight across the Board and this can only be done by Indian people and tribes taking a firm stand and not wavering. It is the least we can do if we really want to claim descent from such men as Joseph, Geronimo, Crazy Horse and Sequoyah.

2. "Watts and Little Big Horn"
Editorial from *NCAI Sentinel,* National Congress of American Indians. Vol. XI, No. 2. Special Issue, 1966.

There seems to be a sudden preoccupation with Indian Affairs in the newspapers, in Congress, and in the movies this month. We can't help feeling that a great deal of misunderstanding is being spread by people who are interested in Indians but who don't have the facts and aren't aware of the issues involved.

Basic to misunderstanding is the assumption that has silently been acknowledged as an eternal truth for most of American History: that somehow, in some way, perhaps tomorrow, the American Indian will ASSIMILATE and disappear. He will vanish!!!

This theory, the "ten little, nine little, eight little Indians" theory, celebrated in song and story by millions of non-Indian children for hundreds of years, should be laid to rest once and for all. It should not form the basis of Indian policy and groups working with Indians should not base programs and program projections on the natural course of events working toward assimilation.

In El Paso, Texas, in March during the Executive Committee session of the NCAI we were greeted by a group of Tigua Indians, descendants of a group marched south from Isleta Pueblo by the Spanish in the middle 1600's. Somehow they had survived 300 years right inside El Paso, keeping their ceremonies, their form of government, their culture. Rather than assimilating or vanishing, the group has grown. Should we form a new rhyme? 10 little, 11 little, 12 little Indians?

In addition we are continually discovering surviving groups of Indians in parts of the east where they have managed to hold their group together for 400 years. Admittedly many of the traditions have long since vanished, the native languages have all but died, there are few full bloods left. But the important thing to remember is that they have survived and intend to remain together as long as possible.

In 1887 the Dawes Allotment Act was passed. It was highly advocated by the Churches whose battle cry had become "Send a red-blooded Christian after a Redskinned Heathen." The purpose of this Act? To assist in the eventual assimilation of Indians by giving them that most precious gift possible—160 acres and farm equipment!!! Today we have a fantastically complicated problem of fractional interests owning small pieces of land as a result of the great experiment in assimilation.

A recent study, *Beyond the Melting Pot,* points out that in New York City over a period of 3 generations the ethnic groups have remained characteristically themselves in spite of all sociological theories and programs devised to "melt them." Such efforts have by and large proved fruitless and the book frankly admits that all forms of social and political organization have been forced to adapt to the different groups rather than being able to force conformity from them.

Granted that assimilation has not and will not work, we still have a serious problem of making sufficient progress with, for and by Indians so that they are not made obsolete by the onrushing technology of today. We would suggest that new Indian policy be formed to take into account the differences in culture and outlook that Indians have with the rest of American society. And we would not suggest that we begin with a group of anthropologists talking about beads and braids and dances. When we advocate recognition of cultural differences we are thinking primarily of the ways that people act and react to situations, the way they view the world, and the values that they consider most important. For example, profit, while dearly worshipped by the rest of the society, is not particularly dear to tribal hearts. Tribal enterprises are operated more to provide employment and opportunity than to create dividends. The rest of society has a mania for "giving" to every noble cause. This is climaxed of course by the "One Great Hour of Sharing" initiated by the churches. Indians would rather share daily than give weekly, monthly, at income tax time, or by fund raising appeals. Indians truly believe that the gift without the giver is bare and with the giver it is sharing, not giving.

We would advocate, therefore, a program of acculturation rather than a temporary patchwork of assimilationist programs. Acculturation is, we feel, a program by which tribes can be encouraged to change behavior patterns by giving them the opportunity to develop programs incorporating their present values with new opportunities for human resource advancement. Teach HOW credit works by allowing tribal credit unions to be developed, teach HOW to manage land by allowing tribes more freedom in leasing and range management and land consolidation. Let them find programs which will work rather than being forced to submit to programs which do not work.

There is continual emphasis on bringing the poor into the "mainstream" of American society. Quite often this means the ridiculous assumption that poor, and especially rural, people must assume a value system that will always be foreign to them. There is not that much stability in the "mainstream" that a certain set of values will prove to be universally valid. And the "mainstream" itself must inevitably give way to innovations demanded by the poor to fit their needs.

We believe that the solution to Indian problems lies with development of human and natural resources of the people where they are—on reservations. Watts, California should be warning enough that it is too late to solve problems of rural folk people when they are penned up in an urban area without any hope for the future. We would not like to see Watts re-enacted in Billings, Albuquerque, Boise, Rapid City, Minneapolis, Spokane, Phoenix, Reno, Portland, Omaha, but it will unless problems are solved where they exist.

E. *Preamble to the Constitution of the National Indian Youth Council, Founding Resolution, and Statement of Purpose. August 10, 1960, Gallup, New Mexico.*

Preamble to the Constitution

We, the younger generation, at this time in the history of the American Indian, find it expedient to band together on a national scale in meeting the challenges facing the Indian people. In such banding for mutual assistance, we recognize the future of the Indian people will ultimately rest in the hands of the younger people, and Indian youth need be concerned with the position of the American Indian. We further recognize the inherent strength of the American Indian heritage that will be enhanced by a National Indian Youth Council. We, the undersigned, believing in a greater Indian America, in order to form a non-profit corporation for the purposes hereinafter enumerated, do hereby certify as follows:

Founding Resolution

WHEREAS, the National Indian Youth Council holds it to be in the best interest of Indian people for better understanding of conditions for all Indians to carry forward our policies to make clear the inherent sovereign rights of all Indians;

WHEREAS, in order to gain this end the National Indian Youth Council strongly opposes the termination of federal trusteeship over Indians, and;

WHEREAS, the National Indian Youth Council holds that it is morally and legally right that Indians have a voice in matters of jurisdiction directly or indirectly affecting Indians, and;

WHEREAS, the National Indian Youth Council recognizes the inherent rights guaranteed all people in statutes of the United States and holds Indians must exercise their rights:

Now therefore be it resolved, that the National Indian Youth Council endeavors to carry forward the policy of making their inherent sovereign rights known to all people, opposing termination of federal responsibilities at all levels, seeking full participation and consent on jurisdiction matters involving Indians, and staunchly supporting the exercise of those basic rights guaranteed American Indians by the statutes of the United States of America.

Statement of Purpose
By Melvin D. Thom, Chairman

The history of the American Indian records the suppression of a proud people and meager redresses by the federal government. Today, the suppressed are still a proud people who have made many concessions to a changing world. Through the years, individuals, agencies and organizations have acted on behalf of the Indian people. These individuals and organizations have enjoyed a considerable extent of success; yet there remains an important role which can only be occupied by the Indian people themselves.

This role is one of understanding and assumption of leadership responsibilities for the values and beliefs which make our Indian people worthy of honor and pride. This role has been and is being filled by dedicated Indians. However, if we are to maintain and strengthen our position as America's original inhabitants, the younger generation of Indian people must participate in fostering of our values and beliefs.

A group of young Indians who first met at the American Indian Chicago Conference and later at Gallup, New Mexico on August 10-13, 1960, have formed the National Indian Youth Council which considered the above stated position. This group decided after considerable preliminary correspondence and deliberations that the NIYC shall be organized to develop greater leadership responsibilities, especially when our basic values and beliefs are jeopardized.

WITH THE BELIEF THAT WE CAN SERVE A REALISTIC NEED, THE NATIONAL

INDIAN YOUTH COUNCIL DEDICATED ITS ACTIVITIES AND PROJECTS TO AT-
TAINING A GREATER FUTURE FOR OUR INDIAN PEOPLE. WE BELIEVE IN A
FUTURE WITH HIGH PRINCIPLES DERIVED FROM THE VALUES AND BELIEFS
OF OUR ANCESTORS. WE FURTHER BELIEVE IN A STRONG PLACE IN AMER-
ICAN SOCIETY BEING HELD BY INDIAN BLOOD, AND THE DEVELOPMENT OF
GREATER LEADERSHIP WITH INDIAN YOUTH.

The Indian people are going to remain Indians for a long time to come.
However, every ethnic group of people who are to live within a changing
world of good and bad influences must possess a sense of security within
their own group. Being of Indian origin should always be held in high
regard but never as a disadvantage. American Indians rightfully hold an
esteemed and influential position based on their past and present record.
Generosity, understanding of feelings, and values based on fairness is
well-known to the Indian people and their friends. The adaptability of
natural talents of our people are to be revered. Notwithstanding our
present and potential achievements, there is and always will be need for
the Indian people themselves to protect our birthright. We should never
abuse the integrity of our people.

There are many particular problems and needs facing our people,
which we acknowledge. A great amount of lip service has been given to
"Indian problems and solutions"; so much that we are sometimes labeled
as a problem people. Of course, this is not fair! The ultimate realization of
man lies in being content with his livelihood and beliefs. This goal can
only be realized with individuals and leaders of strong character. It is the
aim of the NIYC that we promote activities and projects for the development of upstanding leaders.

Our Council does not intend to draw lines with elaborate rules nor do
we intend to propose any radical movements. WE CONSIDER RULES BASED
ON INDIAN THINKING AS BEING SUFFICIENT. It is hoped that the overall
purposes and goals will guide the organization to its success. We sincerely
hope that all Indians will join us in establishing and maintaining a greater
Indian America.

F. *"Which One Are You?: Five Types of Young
Indians." Clyde Warrior, President, National Indian
Youth Council, ABC: Americans Before Columbus,
II, No. 4. December, 1964.*

Among American Indian youth today there exists a rather pathetic
scene, in fact, a very sick, sad, sorry scene. This scene consists of the
various types of Indian students found in various institutions of learning
throughout American society. It is very sad that these institutions, and
whatever conditioning takes place, creates these types. For these types
are just what they are, types, and not full, real human beings, or people.
Many of you probably already know these types. Many of you prob-

ably know the reasons why these types exist. This writer does not pretend to know why. This writer can only offer an opinion as to names and types, define their characteristics, and offer a possible alternative; notice alternative—not a definite solution. All this writer is merely saying is he does not like Indian youth being turned into something that is not real, and that somebody needs to offer a better alternative:

Type A—SLOB or HOOD. This is the individual who receives his definition of self from the dominant society, and unfortunately, sees this kind in his daily relationships and associations with his own kind. Thus, he becomes this type by dropping out of school, becomes a wino, steals, eventually becomes a court case, and is usually sent off. If lucky, he marries, mistreats his family, and becomes a real pain to his tribal community as he attempts to cram that definition [of himself] down the society's throat. In doing this, he becomes a Super-Slob. Another Indian hits the dust through no fault of his own.

Type B—JOKER. This type has defined himself that to be an Indian is a joke. An Indian does stupid, funny things. After defining himself, from cues society gave him, he proceeds to act as such. Sometimes he accidentally goofs-up, sometimes unconsciously on purpose, after which he laughs, and usually says, "Well, that's Indian." And he goes through life a bungling clown.

Type C—REDSKIN "WHITE-NOSER" or THE SELL-OUT. This type has accepted and sold out to the dominant society. He has accepted that definition that anything Indian is dumb, usually filthy, and immoral, and to avoid this is to become a "LITTLE BROWN AMERICAN" by associating with everything that is white. He may mingle with Indians, but only when it is to his advantage, and not a second longer than is necessary. Thus, society has created the fink of finks.

Type D—ULTRA-PSEUDO-INDIAN. This type is proud that he is Indian, but for some reason does not know how one acts. Therefore he takes his cues from non-Indian sources, books, shows, etc., and proceeds to act "Indian." With each action, which is phony, we have a person becoming unconsciously phonier and phonier. Hence, we have a proud, phony Indian.

Type E—ANGRY NATIONALIST. Although abstract and ideological, this type is generally closer to true Indianness than the other types, and he resents the others for being ashamed of their own kind. Also, this type tends to dislike the older generation for being "Uncle Tomahawks" and "yes men" to the Bureau of Indian Affairs and whites in general. The "Angry Nationalist" wants to stop the current trend toward personality disappearance, and institute changes that will bring Indians into contemporary society as real human beings; but he views this, and other problems, with bitter abstract and ideological thinking. For thinking this [he] is termed radical, and [he] tends to alienate himself from the general masses of Indians, for speaking what appears, to him, to be truths.

None of these types is the ideal Indian. . . .

It appears that what is needed is genuine contemporary creative thinking, democratic leadership to set guidelines, cues and goals for the average Indian. The guidelines and cues have to be *based on true Indian philosophy geared to modern times.* This will not come about without nationalistic pride in one's self and one's own kind.

This group can evolve only from today's college youth. Not from those who are ashamed, or those who have sold out, or those who do not understand true Indianism. Only from those with pride and love and understanding of the People and the People's ways from which they come can this evolve. And this appears to be the major task of the National Indian Youth Council—for without a people, how can one have a cause?

This writer says this because he is fed up with religious workers and educationalists incapable of understanding, and pseudo-social scientists who are consciously creating social and cultural genocide among American Indian youth.

I am fed up with bureaucrats who try to pass off "rules and regulations" for organizational programs that will bring progress.

I am sick and tired of seeing my elders stripped of dignity and lowrated in the eyes of their young.

I am disturbed to the point of screaming when I see American Indian youth accepting the horror of "American conformity," as being the only way for Indian progress. While those who do not join the great American mainstream of personalityless neurotics are regarded as "incompetents and problems."

The National Indian Youth Council must introduce to this sick room of stench and anonymity some fresh air of new Indianness. A fresh air of new honesty, and integrity, a fresh air of new Indian idealism, a fresh air of a new Greater Indian America.

How about it? Let's raise some hell!

G.   *"So You Want to Be a Leader":* Unsigned editorial in American Aborigine, *National Indian Youth Council, IV, No. 1, 1965.*

Is the word "Leadership" a misnomer? What does it mean to be a leader? The general connotation about leadership seems to rest within the idea that people cannot help themselves unless they are led to some conclusion. Since we are speaking in the English language, we are presuming that the word has its roots in the European concept of human relations. So many of us have just accepted this presumption without question, but let us examine it as closely as we can to make sure that we are not confusing two general concepts on how people should help one another through human relationships.

If all of the History of Europe could be put in a nutshell, it could be said that the central thought around government, and bodies politic follows the idea that people are much like animals who need to be led to pasture and water. Put in these terms the whole concept of leadership seems ridiculous. But, observe well the history of Europe where most of the governments have followed the thought of anarchy, monarchy or dictatorships. From the time of Caesar even to your present day communist organizations or even the United States economic giant, we find that there is the thought of dominance by a central figure. It is the presumption of European Americans that the President of the United States is the leader who goes about to lead a hundred and eighty million people to the so called "promised land." It is an American Indian concept that makes America different from Europe. In spite of the fact that the President of the United States is considered the leader we have also divided the powers of government between several different levels of human affairs. This is uniquely an American form of political arrangements. Whether the European Americans want to recognize it or not, history will bear out the fact that the American form of government is not a European concept.

So if you want to be leader on the American European terms, you must go about with the idea that you are a superior being who must lead your inferiors into the paths that are supposed to be good for them. It is your job to make decisions and presumptions without consent or consultation of the people for whom you are making decisions. You are to go about and advertise every four years the qualifications which you think your constituents will follow, then forget about them for the rest of the four years until you approach them again. You are to presume that they have relinquished all their rights of decisions and ambitions to depend on your thinking alone. You are not supposed to level yourself to the lower rungs of the ladder because you are supposed to be above reproach. The common idea to follow is for a leader to decipher the actions and behavior of people at a glance of the crowd and assume that your evaluation is superior to all. It matters very little if you have the ability to listen to the long drawn out meetings of tribal affairs, for it is only necessary for you to shake their hands. If this be your concept of leadership, then *divorce* yourself from tribal affairs and *enter the ring* with all of the *other* Americans who relinquished their rights and privileges to someone who they *think will do a job* for them because they *neither have the time nor the interest to work* for the group with whom they live.

On the other hand if you are of a mind to be of service to Indian people, your concept will have to be in line with the customs and traditions of those people who have long suffered through the results of the fore-going kind of leadership. You will have to leave behind all the grand concepts of being popular and being an outstanding personality. The requirements for being a tribal leader have need of this quality but it is far more than the simple surface abilities that make enduring Indian leaders.

The requirements for Indian leadership is not so clearly defined so that any person can adopt the idea that he can lead and be placed in the forefront of the group he represents. Simply because the different tribal groups do not have written constitutions does it make it inferior for them to exist as a sovereign entity? There are no magic words to define tribal groups as a nation who can satisfy their needs and wants. It has never been the belief of the Indian people to set down in detail, the needs of the tribes as a whole. It has been their expression to follow the symbols, customs, and traditions of the wisdom of past generations. Even the most complicated leadership qualities were expressed in the different kinds of stories to illustrate the way in which things are best accomplished. They have symbolized the many things that they feel are of the greatest value in terms of different figures and color codes to pass on from generation to generation. It is the Indian concept of leadership to generalize as clearly as possible all the things that are needed by a tribal group. These generalities are supplemented by details at the moment of their undertaking by people who are more capable of living with detailed information and detailed necessities. These are the reasons why there are so many clans and societies, which are complimentary to tribal leadership. In this way, the Indian solves the problem of getting stale-mated by petty details so that the work of tribal affairs may continue in some kind of a balance. It is this balance that has made the American somewhat different from the European governments. It is this balance that has made the Indian form of government all inclusive of all its members. It was presumed that every member of the tribe must carry its weight and responsibility toward the existence of the entire tribe. It seems that the kind of person that is chosen out of this group is not always aware of his abilities to serve the people.

This brings up a special point. Because Indian leadership is based on the entire group, it becomes necessary to find a person who has the respect of all of the different segments of the tribe. In a nutshell, this means that the person who is selected is chosen on the basis of what he has been doing to serve the group. This is the concept of a *public servant*. An Indian may go about his daily task with such friendliness and level-headedness to serve anyone he meets, and this is the kind of person who gains the trust of many people. That person is not above stopping whatever he is doing to listen and discuss the most menial problems of his neighbors. He may sit quietly in the background at the tribal meetings and say very little, but in time someone is going to ask him to speak and share his opinions as he has in the smaller things. As time goes on, that person may put together many of the smaller things and if in his actions he shows that he can handle bigger problems and contributes towards the guidance of the group, he will sooner or later be asked to represent or serve the group. Most of the time he is not aware that the people would like him to serve. When the group voices its opinion that this person should be in charge of this or that task, it is usually an indication of the accumulation of trust in his behavior. It takes many years for this trust to build up with a certain person so it is also necessary for a person to be patient in his daily affairs.

So now we have the problem of patience. Patience is a virtue among nearly all Indian peoples; including Asiatics. Why is it so high on the list of Indian requirements? Why is it that persons who have shown that they are physically alert and agile have never been endowed with the group's desire for him to be a public servant. Physical ability is often admired by Indian peoples and a great deal of emphasis is placed on it in public ritual and demonstration of tradition. Perhaps, this is a form of recreation. It may be a form of competition to build up stamina. It may even be a desire on the part of parents to exhibit their training through the young people. However, as time goes by in the lives of young people, physical abilities become less and less important. The older a person gets and the better he can contain his temper and gripes toward the inconveniences of living, the more he seems to be noticed and given attention. The belief in patience is sometimes so highly admired that it may be the turning point of a decision in favor of one of two leaders of equal capabilities. But as the Indian does not think so much in terms of individual details, for there is always a counter balance, the world-view will be the base for decision. As patience counter-acts reactionary behavior: so does tolerance counter impulsiveness.

There seems to be a very fine thread of difference between the English usage of tolerance and patience. Those of you who speak an Indian tongue will readily know that there is a difference and this difference is contained in the interpretations of behavior. Patience seems to be a word which is attributed to the physical behavior of people. It is a term that has to do with the timing of physical or mental acts, while the term "tolerance" has to deal with the emotional disciplines and the expressions of belief. Tolerance seems to precede the development of Patience. For a person to tolerate a great many inconveniences in the behavior of his relatives, family and neighbor is usually considered a special attribute of Indian head man or public servants. This is not an easy quality to obtain, but we find it amongst the expression of many of the older leaders. It is, perhaps best represented by the statement that we have all heard at one time or another which is: "I can think of no one that I hate."

So you want to be Indian leader—then rise up and start practicing what the customs and traditions of a noble people present to you. First, find the willingness to listen to what your group desires. Second, be willing to humble yourself to be a servant of the group you wish to represent. Third, learn to wait and be patient for the real issues to come to the surface before drawing your conclusions. Fourth, cultivate within yourself a desire to meet anyone and everyone without the belief that there are superiors and inferiors and be able to say along with the rest of them that there is no product of the great spirit that you can hate.

The decision of what concept of leadership you want to develop within yourself is totally up to what the individual wants to receive. The opportunity to rise up and accumulate experiences for your goals are at your finger tips. The European concept of leadership contains the belief of dividing people against themselves so they can be easily controlled. If this be your desire, mainly, to control, you have a ready made situation to build upon. But if you choose the Indian concept of unity and solidarity for the benefit of all and you believe in the public servant idea, then you have a long and lingering preparation ahead of you. The Indian form of leadership may not have the pomp and personality satisfactions that the European version of leadership seems to thrive on, but it must be remembered the form of government under which the general public lives was originally an Indian form of government. Just because it has been warped out of shape by the anxieties and paranoia that spewed out of the poor-houses and debtors prisons of Europe all over the Good Mother Earth does it make a bad form of government? Out of all the parts of the world that could be chosen to absorb these self-inflicted illnesses, the Great Spirit chose the American Indian to be the "goat." After being downed for 573 years, the Indian Tribes have not lost faith that they can rise again. This is your heritage in leadership abilities. . . . And the foundation on which to build—"A Greater Indian America."

H. *"Historical Survey of American Indians." Herbert Blatchford, formerly Executive Director, National Indian Youth Council, American Aborigine, II, No. 1.*

It is normally understood that the history of the American Indian began with the discovery of the American continent in 1492. We tend to forget that a certain amount of restlessness was needed on the part of the Europeans to cause them to move from home base. The best reason for this anxiousness can be found in the writings of Marco Polo. As the son of a Venetian merchant, Marco Polo went along on adventures to the Orient with one purpose in mind. This purpose was popular with many people in Europe, and it was the want for physical comfort and luxury. To this day, it is what many European descendants strive for. That comfort is gained through the ownership of physical wealth. The easiest way to gain wealth is by exchanging wealthy things which are thought to be useful to other people. When these people are far apart and the exchange has to take place through a person in the middle, this action is known as commerce. Trade and commerce becomes the life blood of wealth, luxury, and comfort. After a person has gained enough wealth to assure him continued comfort for a long time, that person is often referred to as having attained prestige. Since a wealthy person does not have to compete for wealth, he has to defend his wealth. And since wealth and prestige go hand in hand, the final result is that they have to defend what they call "Sacred Honor." Our understanding of this term is that it means to defend the pride a person has in his being able to do something better than anyone else. When honor is envied by a group of people, those people need to exert more and more energy to keep up with the wealthy members of their group. This continual rush for getting wealth pushes people to find new ways to become wealthy with less effort. It was for this reason, it seems, that Marco Polo inspired Columbus and the Italian people to look for more trade with Asia. In this way, commerce became the common denominator for all European anxiety to become wealthy.

Columbus was a man who was moved to ride the wide seas in search for a new trade route. This new route was to take him to Japan—to where Europeans believed there was a great source of comfort and wealth. Columbus was so moved to find this new trade route that he left behind his loyalty to his native Italy and asked for help from a foreign country. Spain felt the need to compete for wealth in her own defense because Portugal was already skilled in the art of trade with the Orient. This would seem to be the reason Spain was willing to help Columbus in his anxiousness to search for a new trade route to Asia. While Columbus was on his way to the Orient, it appears that he was so engrossed with a solution to solve his worldly problems that the discovery of some islands which made him stop his journey caught him by complete surprise. In this unexpected surprise, his first reaction must have been one of fear. We can guess that this is what might have happened from his failure to explore the mainland beyond the islands which he must have calculated as China—surely, he could have gotten supplies to continue his voyage. Instead of exploring the land, he planted a sterile staff of wood bearing a flag in the name of the Queen of Spain, then high-tailed it for home to tell "Mother!" of his great discovery. As all good mothers do, Queen Isabella listened intently to her hypocrite child, and started to make plans to make the most of this threat. She had to give a good reason to continue exploring this discovery, for the Spanish treasury was almost empty. And in those days, the most reasonable people were found in the universities and monasteries. For all intents and purposes, the universities and the church were the same thing, so she must have done the right act by allowing the church and universities to help answer the questions of her subject children—or else the church had a pipeline to the treasury because the only other way to pay for the exploration of the new world was from the Queen's personal wealth. There must have been a good reason for the Church coming to the aid in outlining the policy for occupying the new land, but those reasons are not quite clear for us to say for sure. In any event, the job of explaining how to deal with this new found obstacle to wealth was accepted by a theologian—Francisco de Vitoria of the University of Salamanca sometime between 1492 and 1539. We don't know why this answer took such a long time, but we can only guess that the Spanish needed time to get adjusted to having the blanket jerked from them in their sleep—after all, they thought the earth was flat. Because Columbus did not sail off the table, so to speak, it took almost two generations of thinking for them to believe there was a new world. Padre Vitoria gave his lectures in 1539 by saying that, first of all, Indians were free men. Being free men, he advised, they should not be taken into slavery—Columbus had already claimed his share. Because they were free men, he said, the Indians had their own customs and laws by which they lived. Vitoria presumed that any dispute could be settled on the basis of native law. He told his audiences that native properties should not be disturbed and that their property could be obtained by "Fair Trade." This fair trade was thought to be best administered by the Queen and/or her representatives—in Central and South America this bureaucracy still lives on, for Spain left behind those first impressions. The final advice was that the administration should work for the welfare of the inhabitants, and that this administration should have the intent of being temporary; as temporary as bureaucratic cancer. This all sounds very flattering, but a person must remember that there are differences between theory and practice especially where motives are disguised—by religion. Since the discovery of America was a surprise, Vitoria had the job of encouraging the Spanish people to explore, but with caution and respect. Respect was necessary lest the trade route was closed; so it was almost a dire need to delay as much as possible until more was known about the inhabitants. The Portuguese and the Dutch opened new trade routes and ports on basis of friendship treaties in Asia; so because of uncertainty, the Spanish traders must have thought that diplomacy would be better than war. They might have presumed that diplomacy would pacify unexpected trouble until the administration had enough time for trade to become established and successful before making explorations. One fact appears to remain consistent in European diplomacy and that is after treaties are made there remains an unrestrained urge to continue to try to dominate the way of life and reason—even in disregard of treaty provisions. Reasons as to why this is true does not come to us very easy—on the surface this doesn't look healthy.

The English people did not enter the history of Indian peoples directly until late in the sixteenth century or early in the seventeenth century. They seemed to have made a different approach than the Spanish in facing foreign countries and their laws. Their law courts provide a better measure by which to find how Englishmen faced changing events. In English Common Law, the first case about foreign policy toward foreign rights of inhabitants was known as Calvin's Case in 1609. The question before the court was this: Does a person from a foreign land have a right to sue for property in an English court? This question came up when a Scotchman sued the English for the return of his property in an English court. In the final result, the court replied that the Scotchman was not really a foreigner to England since he was born after Scotland was conquered by England. At the surface, this case says very little about the Indian, but for the English colonies, this case was repeated over and over as a source of jurisdiction. In essence, the court settled the question that two national customs or constitutions can exist under one common jurisdiction by rights of diplomatic treaty arrangements—even where one nation was conquered by war. What happened was that Scotland kept its customs, but shared its sovereign jurisdiction with England. This became English law, and it was this law that was later used in dealing with the Indians in America. From this information, we can understand the feelings of the English people that point in the direction which says that treaties are highly respected documents. Because the English Common Law follows the reasoning which comes from its peoples talking among themselves, we will need to let time pass in order to find out how this rule of law was stretched to cover the inhabitants of the Americas.

The Dutch people entered American Indian history early in the seventeenth century. Their entry into history was based on the fact that the Netherlands were one of the great naval powers during this period. On June 3, 1621, the Dutch West Indies Company was formed. This company was modeled after the Dutch East Indies Company which was chartered on March 20, 1602. Both of these companies were designed to be trade monopolies under charters issued by the Netherlands States-General. These trade companies were in competition with Portuguese naval companies over the development of trade routes to the Orient. Since it was naval custom to open trade routes by treaties, it follows that trade routes build trade stations. These trade stations were agreed upon by treaties and this process brought colonization to the trade countries. As colonization expands in this country, there is nearly always a tendency for the people to enter into disputes over land. By the time the Dutch West Indies Company was formed, there was keen competition between the Spanish, Portuguese and the Dutch. The Dutch settled in what is now known as the State of New York, and the Dutch-Indian land disputes over colonization did not become hostile until between the years of 1640 and 1643. Since the Dutch East Indies Company was authorized to enter into treaties with Asiatic countries, this practice was brought to America by the Dutch West Indies Company. The earliest treaty with the American Indian that we are aware of was signed around 1643. This first treaty was made between the Mohawks and the Dutch in or around Albany, New York. Because the Dutch dealt with foreign countries on the basis of treaties, we can assume that the Dutch were familiar with Vitoria's Lectures of 1539. We can assume this because we read accounts which reveal that the Laws of the Indies which were made in 1542 were considered customary law of trade, and that these laws were based on the lectures of Vitoria. Because treaty making was the law of the seas then, we can presume that it was only natural for treaties to be signed with the American Indian. Treaty making presumes two thoughts which are very basic to trade relations. By European standards, treaties could only exist between two equal but separate parties. Accordingly, the second presumption is that Indian Sovereignty was equal to Dutch Sovereignty. This is our first concrete evidence of Indian-European treaty relations.

Since foreign relations with England did not develop as rapidly as with other nations of Europe and took the path through English Common Law, we find our next English exchange of foreign affairs being resolved in the case of Blankard V. Galdy, 341 (Trin., J. W. & M.) 1694. The question before the English court was whether a sovereign nation can change the laws of a conquered nation above and beyond the treaty agreements? The English courts decided this could not be done and that the English law could not be imposed on a conquered nation unless this was done by treaty agreement. From this decision, we can presume the English held it to be true that the common and customary laws of the inhabitants should be changed only by mutual consent and agreement, however, this was not an exclusive rule of law because the English reserved the right to cancel harmful customary law by declaration.

In our present search for history of the American Indians, we find that the French did not enter into Indian history until about 1663. This French entry was made by René Robert Cavalier, Sieur de la Salle, by his exploration of the area which was known as the "Northwest Territory." It appears that the French entered the new world only because of the weakening naval strength of the Dutch navy which held a monopoly on trade on the high seas, and which kept the French from doing extensive exploration. The Dutch control on the high seas was broken on or about 1661 when the Dutch were defeated in Brazil by the Portuguese. In this defeat, the Dutch and the Portuguese treatied that the Dutch would withdraw from further colonization of the New World, thus, the Dutch were supplanted by the English in New York after the Dutch-Portuguese treaty was signed. Under European custom, it appears that the English were abiding by the customs of the seas at the time of their entry into North American Trade Zones. By these actual developments the American Indians were assured that the treaty making method of 'Fair Trade' would continue to remain in force. It also appears that the French resented the trade relations between the Indian and the English about as badly as they resented trade relations between the Indian and the Dutch. From 1663 on, French trappers did everything within their power to get the English or the Indians to break the terms and conditions of their treaties. This chicanery on the part of the French kept the relationship between the English and the Indian unstable for nearly a hundred years. The animosity that was caused by this instability smouldered between the French, the English and the Indian until it was resolved by the fire of the French and Indian War between 1753 and 1763. Those ten years of turmoil were brought to a close by the defeat of the French. This defeat, in turn, brought about the Royal Proclamation of October 7, 1763 by the English Crown. The provisions of this proclamation were two-fold: First, it prohibited the issuing of patents to deprive the Indians of their aboriginal land titles; and Secondly, it provided that Indian Land Title could *only be changed or altered* through the purchase of land from the Indian by signing a treaty based on 'Fair Trade' agreements. From these developments, we can presume that the English felt that it was only fitting and proper to retain the Dutch Maritime Trade Law practices. This would also show their intent to embody the English Common Law with the Spanish, Portuguese, and the Dutch developments. The only feelings we are aware of from the French is that they cared little about being statesmen and diplomats, but they preferred to be great lovers—of fur trapping and causing unstable conditions to get what they wanted at any cost to other people. With these facts, we can presume that the doctrine of sovereign equality and diplomatic influence was restated by the English after the defeat of the French.

We have now come to the document known as the Articles of Confederation of the United States of America dated November 15, 1777. We refer to this document of the United States because the Indians were not mentioned in the Declaration of Independence. The Declaration of Independence was an instrument voicing a misunderstanding between England as the mother country and the American colonies as her children. The Articles of Confederation was the first expression of these colonies for themselves after they declared themselves independent from England. There was only one mention made about the Indian in these articles. In Article VI, the Continental Congress took as its job the regulation of commerce between foreign countries, the several states and Indian tribes. Ten years later, this provision was made to cover more area by an ordinance issued to influence the adoption of the new constitution. This ordinance is known as the "Northwest Territory Ordinance of July 13, 1787." This is the document which is often quoted as the United States' first impression in Indian Relations. It provided: "The utmost good faith shall always be observed towards the Indians, their lands and property shall never be taken from them without their consent; and in their property, rights and liberty, they shall never be invaded or disturbed, unless in just and lawful wars authorized by congress; that laws found in justice and humanity shall from time to time be made, for preventing wrongs being done to them, and for preserving peace and friendship with them." In spite of the fact that people have ridiculed this and other documents as "dirty scraps of paper," they were then documents of the highest order and they were regarded as the law of the land. The feelings behind these "dirty scraps of paper" appear to be quite clear. The, then, new government of the United States wanted to make its position crystal clear that they wanted nothing but friendship with the Indian. In order to assure this friendship the Continental Congress was willing to adopt a doctrine of equal but separate nations. They evidently felt that the doctrine of diplomatic procedure and practice must continue. They also continued the doctrine of 'Fair Trade' practices to assure the friendship of the Indian in their search for independence from their mother country. We can be relatively sure that the Indian held the balance of power at that time between the United States and the British Commonwealth.

Forty-one days before the adoption of the Constitution of the United States of America by the Continental Congress on September 17, 1789, the provisions of the Northwest Territory Ordinance were enacted into statute on August 7, 1789. It is difficult to understand why this action was taken before the passage of the constitution and we can only guess that this was done to assure the passage of the Constitution of the United States. In the constitution itself, the Indian was mentioned only two times. The first time they were mentioned is in Article I—Section 8. That section provided that the United States government "Shall regulate commerce with foreign nations, among the several states, and with Indian tribes." This provision was brought forward from the wording in the Articles of Confederation word for word. We can presume from these expressions on paper that the United States government wanted, without much doubt, to hold on to their first impressions. In addition to retaining their original provisions, Congress held that they should constitute as the law of the land the doctrines of equal but separate nations, diplomatic practices of negotiating treaties, fair practices, procedures on 'Fair Trade,' and to incorporate into law the doctrine of sovereign immunity from representation in foreign nations. These acts of Congress almost assured the Indian that the United States wanted to continue to apply the practice of free and independent nations.

These good intentions were destined to change in the future, but as far as we can determine in accompanying congressional acts and deeds, the Congress intended to hold on to the friendship of the Indian as late as January 17, 1800 when another act of Congress stated that there shall be a fine and a period of imprisonment for anyone within the sovereign boundaries to attempt to alienate the loyalty of the Indian from the government of the United States. We could assume that the Indian was in the favor of the United States, but we should also be aware that this is just an inkling of a change in attitude—an attitude which seemed to say that now was the time to dominate Indian Relations. It was becoming more and more apparent that the congress wanted to create a monopoly of Indian Relations without the consent of the Indian. Evidently they felt that the fear of the Indian balance of power was diminishing at this point or that they felt they could control this power in some way.

As you may have noticed by this time, we have been following a path of history which is outlined by different documents we have read about the development of history with regard to the American Indian. We are following some guide-posts that were settled by lectures, law cases, treaties, and proclamations.

This point ends the first phase of our search for a realistic appraisal of what most realistically took place in the history of European-Indian relations. From this point on historical events are highly seasoned with contradictions and half truths which tend to discolor and disguise the real motives behind what was done in Indian Relations. When Will Rogers was honored as a humorist by the Congress of the United States, he commented that he was happy to join the company of elite jokesters "When they pass a law it's a joke, and when they joke it's a law," and we just might find the better truth to what he said.

I. *Chronology of Indian History: 1492-1955*, American Aborigine. *National Indian Youth Council. Vol. IV, No. 1. 1965.*

Year

1492 Discovery of the American Continent which was mistaken as the Asiatic Coast.

1539 Lectures of Francisco de Vitoria at the University of Salamanca, Spain, advocating that Indians were free men and were exempt from slavery. They were to be dealt with through treaties and fair trade.

1542 "Laws of the Indies" was published by Vitoria.

1609 Sovereign rights were reaffirmed by the English courts in the judgement of "Calvin's Case."

1619 Virginia Company started the first Mission schools which were abandoned in 1622.

1621 The Dutch West India Company was formed on the principles of opening trade routes by means of treaties.

1643 First known Indian treaty signed between the Mohawks and Dutch, in the State of New York.

1663 The French occupied the "Northwest Territory."

1694 The English court held that sovereign nations cannot change the customs and laws beyond their treaty agreements.

1753 The French and Indian War started as the result of sovereign interferences between the English, French and Iroquois Confederacy.

1763 The French and Indian War ended making it illegal to issue patents on Indian land, and establishing the principle that Indian land title cannot be altered without a treaty. This was the first appearance of the provision "The utmost good faith shall always be observed towards the Indian, their lands and property shall never be taken from them without their consent, and in their property, rights and liberty shall never be invaded or disturbed."

1777 The Articles of Confederation assumed the job of "regulating commerce between . . . the several . . . Indian tribes."

1783 Congress issued a proclamation warning against purchasing of or squatting on Indian land.

1787 The "Northwest Territory Ordinance" of July 13, 1787 adopted the provisions of the English Royal Proclamation of 1763 as the policy of the United States of America.

1788 Indian Affairs was administered under the Secretary of War.

1789 The "Northwest Territory Ordinance" was enacted into United States Statutes on August 7.

1789 The U.S. Constitution adopted the provision "THE CONGRESS . . . Shall regulate Commerce between . . . the several . . . Indian Tribes."

1793 Congress appropriated $20,000 to treaty with Indians.

1794 The Pickering Treaty between the U.S. and the Senecas was signed.

1796 U.S. started "factory" stores which sold American supplies to Indians on credit.

1800 Congress enacted a statute to provide a fine and a period of imprisonment for anyone . . . to attempt to alienate the loyalty of the Indian from the government of the United States.

1803 $3,000 was appropriated to civilize and educate the heathens.

1804 Cherokee removal clause was attached to the Louisiana Purchase provisions. Some Cherokees moved to Arkansas by 1811 without ceding their lands.

1812 Andrew Jackson was "saved" from being captured by a Creek Regiment during the Creek War.

1814 In the Treaty of Fort Jackson, Andrew Jackson stripped the Creeks of their land and left them to be removed to "Indian Country." He then recruited Creek and Choctaw warriors to fight the Seminoles.

1816 Congress enacted a statute to restrict Indian trade licenses to American citizens as opposed to Canadian traders.

1819 Another appropriation was made to civilize and educate the Indians. A $10,000 annual appropriation was known as the "civilization fund."

1822 The government "Factory" stores were discontinued. These stores appeared to be used to buy American factory products to sway the trade away from English traders.

1824 A Bureau of Indian Affairs was established within the War Department. A white girl was burned in effigy in Connecticut for marrying an Indian-mixed blood.

1828   The case of Worcester vs. The State of Georgia entered in the Courts of the United States for a decision that Indians were sovereign nations and are not subject to state laws.

1830   The Removal Bill was enacted into statute by which tribes were later moved into the Oklahoma "Indian Territory." $500,000 was appropriated.

1832   Abraham Lincoln joined the army to fight Indians in the Black Hawk War.

1834   The Indian Trade and Intercourse Act was passed which gave the Army the opportunity to quarantine Indians so that they could assimilate enough civilization to take their place "in the mainstream of American life." This was supposed to take 30 years to accomplish. This was also known as the Reorganization Act of 1834.

1835   A Cherokee faction signed the Treaty of Echota providing for Cherokee removal to Oklahoma. The Seminole War started, which cost the U.S. 1,500 men and $50,000,000.

1836   The Creeks were removed to Indian Territory and on the way 311 Creeks were drowned when a steamboat sank out of negligence. About half of the Creek Nation arrived at Fort Gibson (1,000).

1838   The Cherokee Removal or the "Trail of Tears" took place. Four thousand Cherokees lost their lives in this trek.

1840   The Winnebagos were removed to "Indian Country" because the lead miners wanted them out—it cost about 50% of the tribal members, and most of these returned to the Wisconsin River by 1845.

1843   The Bureau of Indian Affairs issued a solution to Indian Affairs by promoting "less pay for less population"—(reduce the population and the land will be cheaper to buy).

1846   The Winnebagos were again removed to Blue Earth River, Minnesota, but they migrated back to Wisconsin and Iowa. In 1862 they were removed again, to Crow Creek in South Dakota. During these removals they were fed a meal of "entrails and heads" stewed in a vat every other day. From Crow Creek most of them left for Nebraska and Wisconsin. The Southwest was occupied by the U.S.

1848   The Treaty of Guadalupe Hidalgo was signed between the U.S. and Mexico ceding the Southwest areas to the U.S.

1849   Gold was discovered in California and all Indians had to live with wagon trains and prospectors. California Indians were relieved of almost all possessions. All this brought the spread of infectious diseases and wiped out large portions of Indian groups. The Mandans came out with a hundred members. The Mission Indians in California survived with 1/10th of their former members. The Bureau of Indian Affairs was transferred to the Department of the Interior.

1854   Congress provided for Indian lands to be taken in trust for Indians after the tribes ceded other lands to the government.

1860   Most Indians became neutral in the Civil War. "Indian Country" became the "no-man's land" between two battle lines. The election campaign of 1860 proposed to remove the Five Civilized Tribes again.

1864   The Navajos and Apaches took "The Long Walk" to the Pecos Country to be "quarantined for civilization." The Cheyennes and Arapahoes were burned out at Sand Creek, Arkansas.

1867   A "Peace Commission" was established and it made a survey of Indian Affairs. They recommended that the "treaty process" be abandoned. A Board of Indian Commissioners were appointed; a period of "graft" ensued.

1871   Congress passed a statute to stop all treaty making with Indian tribes. The "white" hunters began wholesale killing of buffaloes. Indian burial grounds were invaded for bones for button manufacturers.

1876   George Armstrong Custer surprised a wintering camp on the Little Big Horn River, but was "wiped out." He was killed on the first assault in the middle of the Little Big Horn River. It was published that each Indian killed cost the government $1,000,-000. The Indian population was down to 44,000 souls. Geronimo and his 36 men kept 5,000 troops busy.

1877   The Nez Percé were removed to Oklahoma but returned to Idaho that year.

1878   Congress makes an appropriation to provide for Indian Police which brought about the establishment of the Courts of Indian Offences in 1883.

1887   The Dawes Severalty Act, or the "Allotment Act," was passed in Congress to divide up Indian lands to Individuals.

1910   A Division of Medical Assistance was established after communicable diseases had reduced the population under 250,000 people.

1924   Congress enacts a statute to provide for Citizenship to all Indians.

1934   The Wheeler-Howard Act was passed (Indian Reorganization Act II) to allow tribes to incorporate with the government.

1940   Congress provides for naturalization procedures for Indians to become citizens.

1946   Congress establishes the Indian Claims Commission to compensate Indian tribes for the loss of land.

1949   Hoover Commission recommends that certain tribes be terminated from federal trusteeship.

1953   Congress agrees, concurrently, to adopt a policy for termination of Indian tribes. Revision in liquor laws stops Indian prohibition. Jurisdiction over Indian lands allowed to be taken over by the States.

1955 Medical Assistance transferred to the Department of Health Education and Welfare.

J. Statistics on Indian Tribes: Population and Land

1. GENERAL OBSERVATIONS AND QUESTIONS

Legally there is no definition of an Indian. There are hundreds. In its official bulletin "Orienting New Employees" of the Bureau of Indian Affairs, the United States Department of Interior declares, "The determination of who is an Indian, legally speaking, depends on some treaty, law or rule that is involved. A person may be legally an Indian for some purposes, but not for others."

And the United States Commission on Civil Rights has commented: "In the course of time there have accumulated 389 treaties, more than 5,000 statutes, some 2,000 Federal court decisions, a raft of Attorney General opinions, numerous administrative rulings, 141 tribal constitutions, 112 tribal charters, a gigantic set of regulations, and an encyclopedic manual—all especially applicable to Indians."

Who then is an Indian? He wears several "masks" of definition, wrote the Commission.

"Because of differences in definitions," laconically commented the former United States Commissioner Philleo Nash, in his cautious introduction to "United States Indian Population and Land" statistics, ". . . there has been a wide variation in statements about Indian population which has sometimes led to misunderstanding." That understatement is here emphasized.

2. POPULATION STATISTICS

It is not the Indian who is illusive. Rather it is the manner in which he has been defined.

The Bureau of the Census defines an Indian as someone whose "Indian blood is one-fourth or more, or if the person is regarded as an Indian in the community in which he lives." But for practical purposes the census takers do not go by either of these vague rules.

Census takers, in 1940 and 1950, were told "not [to] ask questions about race and use their own judgement." These polite guesses about a person "one-fourth or more" Indian blood "resulted in many undercounts." How do you "judge" blood content? Then in 1960 the census takers were told to ask about race: "Persons were asked if they were Indian." And the population statistics rose sharply. Yet in these years— 1940, 1950, 1960—the census takers had to subjectively decide either to "judge" for themselves or to ask the person interviewed. And the

Indian who had gone to the city to escape the discrimination and poverty of his reservations, perhaps by "passing" as white, had to subjectively decide to answer honestly.

Needless to say, these statistics tended to fluctuate rather arbitrarily. One illustration was the Indian population figures for the State of Texas:

1900	470
1910	702
1920	2,109
1930	1,001
1940	1,003
1950	2,736
1960	5,750

The more questions asked about race, and the more freely Indians answered them, the larger the population. When in 1930 and 1940 no such questions were asked, the population accordingly declined.

Population statistics therefore reflected the methods and attitudes of the census takers, as much as the numbers of Indians. Nowhere was this more obvious than in the counts of the city Indians, who were an increasingly large proportion of the total Indian population.

And there is an additional problem that faces the census taker on the rural reservation. The isolated and scattered back-country settlements, where family relations do not fit the census forms, and people are frequently moving within the extended kinship family, make an educated guess difficult. Estimates by the various tribes, in such cases, invariably are greater than the seemingly precise statistics of the Census Bureau.

For instance: the Navajo tribe's population was listed as 84,302 in the 1960 Census. Yet the tribal estimates ranged from 105,000 to 115-000. On the more than sixteen-million-acre reservation an accurate count of the constantly shifting, nomadic population is quite impossible. Tribal officials have said the *only* accurate count ever made of Navajos occurred during World War II when sugar rations were issued, and every Navajo voluntarily registered to receive his ration.

These problems have led to some widely varied estimates of the Indian population. As can be seen by the following:

Bureau of Indian Affairs, 1962	367,179
U.S. Census Bureau, 1960	552,220
Robert Thomas and Samuel Stanley, University of Chicago, 1950	571,824
Vine Deloria, Jr., director, National Congress of American Indians	1,000,000 [at least]
Mel Thom, chairman, National Indian Youth Council	1,500,000

3. ESTIMATES OF INDIAN POPULATION SINCE 1492

1492	800,000[a]
1600-1845	1,153,450[b]
1860	44,021[c]
1870	25,731
1880	66,407
1890	248,253
1900	237,196
1910	265,683
1920	244,437
1930	332,397
1940	333,969
1950	343,410
1960	523,591[d]

[a]U.S. Commission on Civil Rights Reports, 1961, Vol. 5. p. 116. The generally accepted estimate today, though previous estimates have been much higher—up to 12,000,000 [Catlin].

[b]James Mooney, "The Aboriginal Population of North America North of Mexico," *Smithsonian Miscellaneous Collection*, Vol. 80. No. 7, 1928. Also *Encyclopaedia Britannica*, Vol. 12. p. 203. Includes "British America" and "Greenland."

[c]U.S. Census Reports

[d]U.S. Census Report: The addition of 28,078 Eskimos and Aleuts raises the estimate to 551,669.

4. STATE INDIAN POPULATIONS—1960 DECENNIAL CENSUS

States WITH Federal Reservations		States with NO Federal Reservations	
Alaska	14,444	Alabama	1,276
Arizona	83,387	Arkansas	580
California	39,014	Connecticut	923
Colorado	4,288	Delaware	597
Florida	2,504	Georgia	749
Idaho	5,231	Hawaii	472
Iowa	1,708	Illinois	4,704
Kansas	5,069	Indiana	948
Louisiana	3,587	Kentucky	391
Michigan	9,701	Maine	1,879
Minnesota	15,496	Maryland	1,538
Mississippi	3,119	Massachusetts	2,118
Montana	21,181	Missouri	1,723
Nebraska	5,545	New Hampshire	135
Nevada	6,681	New Jersey	1,699
New Mexico	56,255	New York	16,491

North Carolina	38,129	Ohio	1,910
North Dakota	11,736	Pennsylvania	2,122
Oklahoma	64,689	Rhode Island	932
Oregon	8,026	South Carolina	1,098
South Dakota	25,794	Tennessee	638
Utah	6,961	Texas	5,750
Washington	21,076	Vermont	57
Wisconsin	14,297	Virginia	2,155
Wyoming	4,020	West Virginia	181
		District of Columbia	587

	51,653
471,938	471,938

Indians, Total	523,591
Eskimos and Aleuts (Alaska)	28,078

TOTAL	551,669

5. INDIAN LAND

The geographic estimates of Indian land are not as inadequate and indefinite as the population statistics. But they are as fluctuating. And as subject to legal definition.

One cause is the vast number of treaties that divided these lands, and then subdivided them, so that ownership is tangled in generations of litigation. Then, too, Indian land comes under a host of legal definitions: tribal land, trust land, allotment land, and so on.

But the primary reason is the irony of history. The Indian Claims Commission has before it hundreds of claims to lands that tribes claim as theirs by right of treaty. Each year, as these claims are reviewed by the Indian Claims Commission and the federal courts, millions of acres are legally awarded to the tribes. In most cases the federal government settles these claims, with the tribes' consent, with a cash settlement. However, where the tribes, and individual Indians, have voted not to accept the federal government's settlement terms the land is legally theirs.

California Indians have thus claimed, been awarded, and legally hold title to some 80 percent of the State of California. Yet official statistics (below) list a mere 467,169 tribally held acres in that state.

In the State of Florida the Seminole tribe has similarly claimed, been awarded, and holds title to some 80 percent of that state. Official figure: 78,974 acres.

There is, too, the matter of cultural conflict over the meaning of land ownership. Recently one of the leaders of the Iroquois League of Six Nations, Wallace "Mad Bear" Anderson, declared, "The United States

Government has violated its treaties with our Nation. Since the white man occupies our land, in New York State, only by virtue of those treaties, if he breaks the treaties then they are null and void. That's all right with us! For then the land will revert to our ownership in his legal terms."

6. STATISTICS ON INDIAN LAND

Land Area (Acres)

STATE & AREA	Tribal Land	Allotted Land	Government Owned
Alaska	87,636	9,311	4,064,714
Arizona	19,389,073	260,395	90,506
California	467,168	86,175	119
Colorado	746,420	5,131	573
Florida	78,974	0	0
Idaho	400,448	390,601	41,859
Iowa	4,105	0	0
Kansas	1,784	26,420	321
Louisiana	262	(.16)	0
Michigan	7,816	9,427	4,016
Minnesota	670,525	55,194	28,698
Mississippi	16,270	209	214
Missouri	0	373	0
Montana	1,613,201	3,640,283	128,286
Nebraska	14,235	52,818	322
Nevada	1,062,316	80,260	7,811
New Mexico	5,886,887	649,138	77,837
North Carolina	56,414	0	159
North Dakota	130,075	736,176	6,703
Oklahoma	58,627	1,638,609	35,469
Oregon	496,062	195,615	1,252
South Dakota	1,933,166	2,920,546	138,920
Texas	0	11	0
Utah	2,045,157	70,292	439
Washington	1,827,842	722,465	83
Wisconsin	60,015	86,048	39,447
Wyoming	1,759,596	127,663	1,499
TOTAL	38,814,074	11,763,160	4,669,274

SELECTED BIBLIOGRAPHY

It sometimes seems as though there are limitless numbers of studies of the Indians. Even more studies than Indians. The Selected Bibliography herewith offered will make no attempt to survey this vast array. Many excellent general and specific bibliographies may be found in the works listed in the section titled "Historical and Background Studies."

Since this book has attempted to afford the new Indians the typographic means to speak for themselves this bibliography will emphasize that aspect of the literature.

The Selected Bibliography is divided into nine sections to accomplish this purpose: I. The New Indians, II. Studies of the New Indians, III. Hunting and Fishing Rights, IV. Education, V. Religion, VI. Art and Literature, VII. The Old Indians, VIII. Government Reports and Documents, and IX. Historical and Background Studies.

Works are arranged alphabetically, by title. The unusual method has been used because many of the authors are unknown to non-Indian readers.

ABBREVIATIONS USED IN THE SELECTED BIBLIOGRAPHY:

AA—*American Anthropologist*

AAIA—American Association on Indian Affairs, New York

AAPSS—American Association of Political and Social Sciences, Philadelphia

ACPA—American Catholic Philosophical Association, Washington, D.C.

ABC—*Americans Before Columbus,* National Indian Youth Council

ASU—Arizona State University, Phoenix

BIA—Bureau of Indian Affairs, Washington, D.C.

GPO—Government Printing Office, Washington, D.C.

JOAIE--*Journal of American Indian Education*

NCAI—National Congress of American Indians, Washington, D.C.

UA—University of Arizona, Tucson
UOCalP—University of California Press, Berkeley
UOCP—University of Chicago Press, Chicago
UONP—University of Nebraska Press, Lincoln
UOOP—University of Oklahoma Press, Oklahoma City
YUP—Yale University Press, New Haven, Connecticut

I. THE NEW INDIANS

American Indian Resources Study, 1967: Programs of the NCAI and
Executive Director's Report. 1. Automation and Indian Education, 2.
Government as Employer of Last Resort, 3. Rural America and
Regional Development, *et al.* 42 pp. Mimeographed. NCAI, Wash-
ington, D.C., November, 1966.

Challenge of Changing Winds. Wendell Chino. Keynote address NCAI
Convention. Mimeographed. NCAI, Washington, D.C., November,
1966.

Cherokee Stories: "Relocation," "Indian Names and Whitemen Numbers," "The Origin of Medicine," *et al.* In English and Cherokee. Carnegie Project. Tahlequah, Oklahoma. June, 1966.

Chicago American Indian Center: Service Report. William Red Cloud,
Chairman of Board. Chicago, 1966.

"Colonialism: Classic and Internal." Robert Thomas. *New University
Thought,* Vol. 4, No. 4. Winter, 1966-1967.

"Crisis in Communications." *NCAI Sentinel,* Special Issue. Vol. XI,
No. 2. Spring, 1966.

"Custer Myth Revised, The." *NCAI Sentinel,* Convention Issue. Vol. XI,
No. 1. Fall, 1966.

"Declaration of Indian Purpose." American Indian Chicago Conference.
June, 1961.

Development of Indian Resources, The. Henry W. Hough. National
Congress of American Indians Fund. Denver, Colorado. 1968.

"Earth Around You Is Your Storehouse." Interview with Sun Bear, editor of *The Native Nevadan.* Richard Ogar. *The Berkeley Barb.* Spring,
1967.

"Efficiency of the Bow and Arrow as a Fighting Weapon, The." *NCAI
Sentinel.* Vol X, No. 5. December, 1965.

First Convention of the NCAI: Proceedings. Mimeographed. 55 pp.
NCAI. November 15, 1944.

"For a Greater Indian America." Mel Thom. *The American Indian.* San
Francisco. March, 1964; *ABC.* Vol. VI, No. 4. Dec., 1964; *ABC.* Vol.
II. No. 5. June, 1965.

"Historical Outline: 1492-1955." *American Aborigine.* Vol. IV, No. 1.
1961.

Hopi Way of Life Is the Way of Peace. As told by Andrew Hermequaftewa, Bluebird Chief. Shungopavi, Second Mesa Post Office, Arizona. No date, most likely early 1960's.

"How Should an Indian Act?" Clyde Warrior. *ABC*. Vol. II, No. 5. June, 1965.

"Indians as Human Beings." Earl Old Person, Chairman, Blackfoot Tribe. *Indian Voices*. Chicago. December, 1966-January, 1967.

Indians in Minnesota, The. Gerald R. Vizenor. 1. What Is an Indian?, 2. The Ojibways, 3. I Wonder What We Look Like, 4. Pow Wow, and 5. Acculturation. *Twin Citian*, Minneapolis. May, 1966.

"Indian Tests the Mainstream, The." D'Arcy McNickles. *The Nation*. New York. September 26, 1966.

"Indian War 1963-1964." Mel Thom. *American Aborigine*. Vol. II. No. I. Gallup, New Mexico.

"I Remain to Some, a Savage, But a Proud Indian: Faith, Hope and Abandonment." Chief Norris, Klamath River Tribe. *The American Indian*, San Francisco. June, 1964.

Land Grab Attempt [of] Tuscarora Indian Reserve. League of North American Indians. 15 pp. 1961.

"Left Flank and Right Flank." Herbert Blatchford. *American Aborigine*. Vol. VII. No. 1. Gallup, New Mexico. 1961.

Miracle Hill. Emerson Blackhorse and T. D. Allen. UOOP. 1967.

Navajo Yearbook, The. Ed. Robert Young. Navajo Agency, Window Rock, Arizona. 1961.

New Trail, The. Phoenix Indian School. Phoenix, Arizona. 1953.

"Our Land Speaks (Dena Nena Henash): A Statement of Policy of Conference of Athabascan Chiefs." Tanana, Alaska. *Indian Affairs*, AAIA. August, 1962.

"Participation of Indians in Public Life." *Navajo Times*. Window Rock, Arizona. February 2, 1967.

Passamaquoddy Indian Conditions. Andrea Bear. Mimeographed. 12 pp. 1964.

Policy Resolutions of NCAI: 1954-1966. 131 pp. NCAI, Washington, D.C.

"Powerless Politics." Robert Thomas. *New University Thought*. Vol. 4. No. 4. Winter, 1966-1967.

"Right Flank and Left Flank: The City Indian and The Reservation Indian." Shirley Hill Witt. *American Aborigine*. Vol. II, No. 1. Gallup, New Mexico. 1961.

"So You Want to Be a Leader?" *American Aborigine*. Vol. VI. Gallup, New Mexico. 1965.

Termination Policy, A Study of the. Gary Orfield. Mimeographed. 127 pp. NCAI, Washington, D.C.

Tribal Council, the Place of the. J. C. Morgan, Chairman, Navajo Tribal Council. Radio Speech, March 7, 1939. Navajo Tribe, Window Rock, Arizona.

"Tribal Indian Land Rights Association, Explained." A. A. Hopkins-Duke. *Navajo Times.* Window Rock, Arizona. February 27, 1964.

Tribal Government: The Origin of the Navajo Tribal Government. 39 pp. 1966. Navajo Tribe, Window Rock, Arizona.

"Tribalism and Modern Society." *NCAI Sentinel.* Vol. XI, No. 2. Washington, D.C. Spring, 1966.

"Voice of the American Indian, The." Nancy Lurie. Report on the American Indian Chicago Conference. *Current Anthropology.* 2. 478-500.

"Which One Are You? Five Types of Young Indians." Clyde Warrior. *ABC.* Vol. 2, No. 4. December, 1964.

"Will the Relocation Officer Relocate Himself?" Wamblee Wastee. *The American Indian,* San Francisco. May, 1964. Other articles by same author: "An Open Letter to the Commissioner," June, 1964; "The Trouble with Capitalists Is—the Only Thing They See Is Money," July, 1964.

White Mountain Apache Tribe, The. White Mountain Apache Tribal Council, White River, Arizona. 33 pp. No date, most likely early 1960's.

Who Are the Native Americans? Native American Movement. 1963.

Writer's Reader, The. Students of the Institute of American Indian Arts, Santa Fe, New Mexico. Issued annually. Opinions, legends, autobiographic sketches, poetry. Mimeographed.

II. Studies of the New Indians

"American Indians and American Life." *Annals.* AAPSS. May, 1957.

American Indians Dispossessed. Walter Hart Blumenthal. George S. MacManus Co. Philadelphia, 1955.

American Indians in Transition, The: Report of Werner-Gren Conference. Ed. John Povinse. *AA.* Vol. 56. No. 3. 1954.

Apologies to the Iroquois. Edmund Wilson. Random House. Vintage Books. New York. 1966.

Backwash of the Frontier, The: The Impact of the Indian on American Culture. A. Irving Hallowell. Smithsonian Institution, Washington. 1958.

Cherokee People Today, The. Albert Wahrhaftig. Translated by Calvin Nackedhead. English and Cherokee. 45 pp. Carnegie Project. Tahlequah, Oklahoma. 1966.

"Community and the Caretakers," Albert Wahrhaftig. *New University Thought.* Vol. 4, No. 4. Winter, 1966-1967.

"Culture Change and the Personality of Ojibwa Children." Stephen T. Boggs. *AA.* Vol. 60, pp. 47-58.

Indian, The: America's Unfinished Business. Report of the Commission on the Rights, Liberties and Responsibilities of the American Indian.

The Fund for The Republic. Compiled by William A. Brophy and Sophie D. Aberle. UOOP. 1966.

"Indian Self-Government." Felix S. Cohen. *ABC.* Vol. II, No. 5. June, 1965.

"Indians Want a New Frontier, The." Oliver LaFarge. *New York Times Magazine.* June 11, 1961.

"Language and Passive Resistance Among the Eastern Cherokee." John Gulick. *Ethnology.* Vol. V, No. 1. Winter, 1958.

"Narragansett Survival: A Study of Group Persistence Through Adopted Traits." Ethel Boissevan. *Ethnohistory.* Vol. VI, No. 4. Fall, 1959.

Native Americans, The. Robert F. Spencer and Jesse D. Jennings. Chap. XII. "American Indian Heritage: Retrospect and Prospect." Harper & Row. 1965.

"Navajo and Zuñi Veterans: A Study in Contrasting Modes of Cultural Change." John Adair and Evon Vogt. *AA.* Vol. 51. October-December, 1949.

"Note on Cherokee-Delaware Pan-Indianism, A." W. W. Newcomb, Jr. *AA.* Vol. 57. 1955.

"Persistence in Chippewa Culture and Personality." Ernestine Friedl. *AA.* Vol. 58. 1956.

Redbird Smith Movement, The. Robert Thomas. Smithsonian Institution. Bureau of American Ethnology Bulletin, 180. Washington, D.C. 1961.

"Revitalization Movements." Anthony F. C. Wallace. *AA.* Vol. 58. 1956.

"Tuscarora Tribalism and National Identity." David Landy. *Ethnohistory.* Vol. V, No. 3. Summer, 1958.

III. Hunting and Fishing Rights

"Fisher Indians in Fight for Treaty." Janet McCloud. *The Indian Historian.* American Indian Historical Society. San Francisco. Vol. 4, Nos. 1 & 2. Winter, 1966. Spring, 1967.

"Fish-Ins: Their Whys and Wherefores." *NCAI Sentinel.* Washington, D.C. Vol. X. No. 5. December, 1965.

Indian Hunting and Fishing Rights: A Legal Survey. Prepared for NCAI by Wilkinson, Cragun and Barker, attorneys. Washington, D.C. May, 1967.

"Indian Uprising for Civil Rights." Hamilton Bims. *Ebony.* February, 1967.

"Notions of Nature, Man and Time of a Hunting People, The." Murray Wax. *Southern Folklore Quarterly.* September, 1962.

IV. Education

"American Indian Education for What?" Murray and Rosalie Wax. *Midcontinent American Studies Journal.* Vol. VI, No. 2. Fall, 1965.

"Cultural Deprivation as an Educational Ideology." Murray and Rosalie Wax. *JOAIE*. Vol. III. January, 1964.

Dormitory Life: Is It Living? In-Service Training Pamphlet. BIA, Branch of Education. 1959.

Dropout of American Indians at the Secondary Level. Murray and Rosalie Wax. Mimeographed. 63 pp. Emory University, Atlanta, Georgia. 1964.

Education for Cultural Change. Ed., Willard Beatty. BIA. 1953.

"Indian Education." Clarence Wesley, Chairman of San Carlos Apache Tribe. *JOAIE*. Vol. I. No. 1. June, 1961.

Indian Education Conference, Proceedings. College of Education, ASU. March, 1960.

Indian Education in Arizona, Annual Reports of. Arizona State Department of Public Instruction, Division of Indian Education. Phoenix, Arizona.

Indians in School. James Officer, Bureau of Ethnic Research. UA. 1956.

Journal of American Indian Education. ASU. Tempe, Arizona.

New Mexico, Division of Indian Education, State Department of Public Instruction, Annual Reports. Santa Fe, New Mexico.

Report of Indian Education. Herbert Blatchford. Mimeographed. 11 pp. McKinley County Schools, Gallup, New Mexico. Undated.

Research in Indian Education: Reports of Annual Conference of Coordinating Council. Arizona State Department of Public Instruction, Division of Indian Education. Phoenix, Arizona.

"Warrior Dropouts, The." Rosalie Wax. *Trans-Action.* May, 1967.

V. RELIGION

NOTE: Religion is a germinal and integral force in the movements of the new Indians. However, because of the nature of the religious beliefs it is the subject about which the new, as the old, Indians are most reticent. Where the leaders and participants in religious groups, such as the Native American Church—Peyote Cult—offered little or no written works the secondary works are omitted. Instead, a few of the general and classic works are listed.

Blue Lake Area, The: An Appeal from Taos Pueblo [for] Religious Freedom. Taos Pueblo, New Mexico. No date.

Book of the Hopi. Frank Water. Source material recorded by Oswald White Bear Fredericks. Viking. New York. 1963.

Ghost Dance Religion and the Sioux Outbreak of 1890, The. James Mooney. Ed., Anthony F. C. Wallace. UOCP. 1965.

Hopi Way of Life Is the Way of Peace. As told by Andrew Hermequaftewa, Bluebird Chief. Shungopavi, Second Mesa Post Office, Arizona. No date.

Iroquois Book of Rites, The. Ed., Horatio E. Hare. 2 Vol. D. G. Brinton. Philadelphia. 1883.

Missionary in a Cultural Trap, The. Vine Deloria, Jr. Mimeographed. Unpublished paper.

"Navaho Chantways and Ceremonials." Father Berard Haile. *AA.* Vol. 40. 1938.

Religions of the Oppressed, The: A Study of Modern Messianic Cults. Vittorio Lanternari. II. The Peyote Cult. III. Other Prophetic Movements in North America. Knopf. New York. 1963.

Religious Concepts of the Navajo Indians. ACPA, Proceedings, 10th Annual Meeting. Father Berard Haile. 1935.

Sacred Formulas of the Cherokee. James Mooney. 7th Annual Report of the Bureau of American Ethnology. Washington, D.C. 1891.

Sacred Pipe, The: Black Elk's Account of the Seven Rites of the Oglala Sioux. Ed., Joseph Broun. UOOP. 1953.

Wakinyan: Contemporary Teton Dakota Religion. Stephen Ferara. Museum of the Plains Indians. Browning, Montana. No date.

Warriors of the Rainbow: Strange and Prophetic Indian Dreams. William Willoya and Vinson Brown. Naturegraph Co. Healdburg, California. 1962.

World's Rim, The: Great Mysteries of the North American Indians. Hartley Burr Alexander, UONP. 1953.

VI. ART AND LITERATURE

Aboriginal American Authors. Daniel G. Brinton. Philadelphia. 1883.

American Indians and Their Music. Frances Densmore. Women's Press. New York. 1926.

American Indian Prose and Poetry: An Anthology. Margot Astrov. Original title—*The Winged Serpent.* Capricorn Books. New York. 1962.

American Rhythm, The: Studies and Reexpressions of AmerIndian Songs. Houghton Mifflin. Boston. 1930.

Assays, Kenneth Rexroth. V. *American Indian Songs.* New Directions. New York. 1961.

"Contemporary Indian Art: A Portfolio of Indian Drawings." Clara Lee Turner. *Arizona Highways.* Phoenix. Vol. XXVI. No. 2. February, 1950.

"Heritage of Indian Art." Daniel McPike and David C. Hunt. *American Scene Magazine.* Gilgrease Institute of American History and Art. Tulsa, Oklahoma. 1965.

Indian Art of the United States. Douglas F. and René d'Harnoncourt. Museum of Modern Art. New York. 1941.

Indian Art in America, Frederick Dockstader. New York Graphic Society. 1962.

Indians' Book, The: Indian Lore, Musical and Narrative. Natalie Curtis Burlin. Harper & Brothers. 1907.

"Indian Independence Through Tribal Arts." Lucy Bacon. *New Mexico Magazine.* January, 1932.

Institute of American Indian Arts, The: Basic Statement of Purpose. The Staff. Santa Fe, New Mexico. February, 1965.

Library of American Aboriginal Literature. 8 Vol. Philadelphia. 1882-1890.

Rhythm of the Red Man, The. Julia Buttree. A. S. Barnes. New York. 1930.

Roots of American Culture, The. Constance Rourke. II. *The Rise of Theatrical: The Indian Background.* Harcourt, Brace. New York. 1942. Harvest Books. 1967.

Sky Clears, The: Poetry of the American Indian. A. Grove Day. UONP. 1951.

Smoke Signals. Publication of Indian Arts and Crafts Board of U.S. Department of Interior. Frederick Dockstader, Chairman. Washington, D.C.

Songs of the Indians. Mary R. Van Stone. El Palacio. No. 48. 1941.

Studies in Classic American Literature. D. H. Lawrence. IV. "Fenimore Cooper's White Novels." Doubleday. New York. 1953.

VII. THE OLD INDIANS

NOTE: There are many chronicles of the lives and thoughts of outstanding figures in Indian history. It is the aim of this brief list to highlight some of those whose ideas and examples have influenced the thinking of the new Indians and the new tribal nationalism.

Aboriginal American Oratory: The Tradition of Eloquence Among the Indians of the United States. Louis Thomas Jones. Southwestern Museum. Los Angeles. 1965.

Autobiography of Black Hawk, The. Ed., J. B. Patterson. 1882.

Black Elk Speaks: The Life Story of an Oglala Sioux. Ed., John G. Neihardt. UONP. 1962.

Blackfoot Lodge .Tales. George Bird Grinnell. Scribner's. New York. 1903. UONP. 1962.

Chief Standing Bear: An Autobiography. Houghton Mifflin. Boston. 1926.

Civilization. Thomas Wildcat Alford. Ed., Florence Drake. UOOP. 1936

Crashing Thunder: The Autobiography of an American Indian. Ed., Paul Radin. Appleton. New York. 1926.

Indian Legends of the Pacific Northwest. Ed., Ella E. Clark. UOCa1P. 1966.

Indian Tales. Jaime de Angulo. Hill and Wang. New York. 1953.

Legends and Tales of She-She-Pe-Ko-Naw. Stories of the Wisconsin Indians. Ed., Beauford and Kathleen Marceil. Libman Press. Green Bay, Wisconsin. 1965.

Plenty Coups: Chief of the Crows. Frank B. Linderman. UONP. 1962.

Smoke from Their Fires. Charles James Nowell. YUP. 1940.

Soul of an Indian, The. Charles A. Eastman (Ohiyesa). Houghton Mifflin. Boston. 1911.

Sun Chief: Autobiography of a Hopi. Don C. Talayseva. Ed., Chellan Ford. YUP. 1942.

Wooden Leg: A Warrior Who Fought Custer. Interpreted by Thomas B. Marquis. UONP. 1962.

VIII. GOVERNMENT REPORTS AND DOCUMENTS

Attorney General Robert F. Kennedy, Remarks: Speech before Convention of NCAI, Bismarck, North Dakota. Department of Justice. Washington, D.C. September, 1963.

"Building Indian Economies with Land Settlement Fund." Robert L. Bennett. *Human Organization*. Vol. XX, No. 4. Winter, 1962-1963.

Constitutional Rights of the American Indian. Hearings, Subcommitee on Constitutional Rights, Committee of the Judiciary, U.S. Senate. 89th Congress. GPO. June 22, 23, 24 and 29, 1965.

Indian Health Program, A Review. Hearings, Subcommittee on Indian Affairs, House Interior and Insular Affairs Committee. 88th Congress. GPO. May 23, 1963.

Indian Land and Its Care. Edgar L. Wight, David P. Weston, and Clyde W. Hobbs. BIA. 1953.

Indian Unemployment Survey. Part I: Questionaire Returns. House Interior and Insular Affairs Committee. 88th Congress. GPO. 1963.

List of Indian Treaties. House Interior and Insular Affairs Committee. GPO. September, 1964.

Orienting New Employees. Selected papers, including: Benjamin Franklin's "Remarks Concerning the Savages of North America." BIA. Branch of Education. 1959.

Present Relations of the Federal Government to the American Indian. 1. Employees and Expenditures of BIA, 2. Indian Claims, 3. State Expenditures for Indian Welfare, 4. Indian Voting, and 5. Organizations. 85th Congress. GPO. December, 1958.

United States Civil Rights Commission, Report of. The American Indian, 1. Introduction, 2. Legal Status, 3. Status as a Minority, and 4. Conclusions. Vol. 5, pp. 115-160. 1961.

United States Indian Service, The: A Sketch of the Development of the BIA and Indian Policy. BIA. 1962.

IX. HISTORICAL AND BACKGROUND STUDIES

A Century of Dishonor. Helen Hunt Jackson. Ed., Andrew F. Rolfe. Harper & Row (Torchbook). New York. 1965.

As Long as the Grass Shall Grow. Oliver La Farge. Alliance Book Corp. 1940.

Changing Indian, The. Oliver La Farge. UOOP. 1942.

History of the American Indian, The. James Adair. Edwin and Charles Dilly. London. 1775.

Indian and the White Man, The. Ed., Wilcomb. E. Washburn. Excerpts of historical documents. Doubleday (Anchor Books). New York. 1964.

Indian in America's Past, The. Ed., Jack D. Forbes. Excerpts of historical documents. Prentice Hall. New York. 1964.

Indians and Other Americans. Harold E. Fey. and D'Arcy McNickles. Harper & Brothers. New York. 1959.

Indians of the Americas. John Collier. North American Library. Mentor Books. New York. 1961.

Indians Today: The Past and the Future of the First American. Charles A. Eastman (Ohiyesa). Doubleday, Page and Co. New York. 1915.

Indian Tribes of the United States, The: Ethnic and Cultural Survival. D'Arcy McNickles. Oxford University Press. New York. 1964.

Native Races, The. Hubert H. Bancroft. Bancroft and Co. San Francisco, California. 1886.

On the Gleaming Way: Navajos, Eastern Pueblos, Zuñis, Hopis, Apaches and Their Land and Their Meanings to the World. John Collier. Allan Swallow (Sage Books). Denver, Colorado. 1962.

Red Man in America, The. Henry R. Schoolcraft. Lippincott, Grambo Co. Philadelphia. 1847.

Savages of America, The. Roy Harvey Pearce. John Hopkins University Press. Baltimore. 1953. Reissued as: *Savagism and Civilization*, paper. 1967.

Warriors Without Weapons. G. MacGregor. UOCP. 1946.

INDEX